T0304737

ENTERPRISE SUSTAINABILITY

Enhancing the Military's Ability to Perform its Mission

ENTERPRISE SUSTAINABILITY

Enhancing the Military's Ability to Perform its Mission

DENNIS F.X. MATHAISEL
JOEL M. MANARY
CLARE L. COMM

CRC Press
Taylor & Francis Group
Boca Raton London New York

CRC Press is an imprint of the
Taylor & Francis Group, an **informa** business

CRC Press
Taylor & Francis Group
6000 Broken Sound Parkway NW, Suite 300
Boca Raton, FL 33487-2742

First issued in paperback 2017

© 2009 by Taylor and Francis Group, LLC
CRC Press is an imprint of Taylor & Francis Group, an Informa business

No claim to original U.S. Government works

ISBN 13: 978-1-138-11527-9 (pbk)
ISBN 13: 978-1-4200-7858-9 (hbk)

Library of Congress Cataloging-in-Publication Data

Mathaisel, Dennis F. X.
    Enterprise sustainability : enhancing the military's ability to perform its mission / authors, Dennis F.X. Mathaisel, Joel M. Manary, and Clare L. Comm.
        p. cm.
    Includes bibliographical references and index.
    ISBN 978-1-4200-7858-9
    1. United States--Armed Forces--Operational readiness. 2. United States--Armed Forces--Weapons systems. 3. United States--Armed Forces--Equipment. 4. United States. Dept. of Defense--Management. I. Manary, Joel. II. Comm, Clare L. III. Title.

UA23.M3223 2010
355.6'21--dc22   2009011790

Visit the Taylor & Francis Web site at
http://www.taylorandfrancis.com

and the CRC Press Web site at
http://www.crcpress.com

Dedication

The authors dedicate this book to all the women and men who serve our country in the war on terrorism.

Contents

Preface xix

Acknowledgments xxiii

About the Authors xxv

Chapter 1
Availability: The Current Military Supply Chain 1
    Preface 1
    1.1   Availability of Materials and Parts to the Warfighter 1
    1.2   The Military Supply Chain and Logistics System 3
          1.2.1   The Defense Logistics Agency 8
          1.2.2   Differences between Military and Commercial Supply Chains 10
    1.3   Managing the Inventory 12
          1.3.1   Push vs. Pull Supply Chains..14
          1.3.2   The Bullwhip Effect 16
          1.3.3   Push-Pull Supply Chains 17
          1.3.4   Kanban as a Pull Trigger..18
          1.3.5   Risk Pooling...19
          1.3.6   Echelon Networks...19
    References..21

Chapter 2
Availability: Enhancing the Military Supply Chain 23
    2.1   Three Principles for an Effective Military Supply Chain 23
          2.1.1   Integration 23
          2.1.2   Collaboration 24
          2.1.3   Trust 25
    2.2   Six Steps for Enhancing the Military Supply Chain 27
          2.2.1   Step 1: Establish an IPT.. 27
          2.2.2   Step 2: Develop an Implementation Plan 28
          2.2.3   Step 3: Measure Performance.. 29
          2.2.4   Step 4: Design Your Supply Chain 29
          2.2.5   Step 5: Select and Apply Best Practice Technologies 30

       2.2.6   Step 6: Manage the Supply Chain Implementation...................................30
  2.3   Redesigning the Military Logistics Network 31
  2.4   Information Technology Enhancements...35
       2.4.1   The Goal..35
       2.4.2   The Infrastructure...36
               2.4.2.1   Interface Devices 36
               2.4.2.2   Communications.. 36
               2.4.2.3   Databases 36
               2.4.2.4   Systems Architecture 37
       2.4.3   Standardization...38
  2.5   Software Enhancements 39
       2.5.1   Comprehensive Software Packages..39
       2.5.2   Strategic Planning Software 39
       2.5.3   Collaboration Software Standards and Packages...............................39
               2.5.3.1   Order Management Systems (OMS)....................... 39
               2.5.3.2   Customer Relationship Management (CRM)........... 39
               2.5.3.3   Manufacturing Execution Systems (MES)............... 40
               2.5.3.4   Warehouse Management Systems (WMS)............... 40
               2.5.3.5   Transportation Management Systems (TMS)......... 40
  2.6   Case Study: The SCOR Model 40
  2.7   Case Study: The PRISM Model..45
       2.7.1   Current Requirements Forecasting in the Military:
               The U.S. Air Force Process... 46
       2.7.2   The Disadvantage of Current Military RDF Methods 47
       2.7.3   Commercial Reliability-Based Requirements Forecasting 48
       2.7.4   PRISM... 49
  2.8   Conclusion: Successful vs. Unsuccessful Supply Chain Initiatives....................51
References..53

Chapter 3

Operational Availability...55

Preface 55
  3.1   Introduction to Operational Availability 56
       3.1.1   Definition of Ao.. 58
       3.1.2   Historical Perspective... 58
       3.1.3   Why Is Ao Important? 59
  3.2   The Mathematics of Ao 60
       3.2.1   Uptime/Downtime Equations... 60
       3.2.2   Mean Time between Failures Equations 62
       3.2.3   Specific Systems Equations.. 64
               3.2.3.1   Continuous-Use Systems 65
               3.2.3.2   Intermittent-Use Systems.......................................65
               3.2.3.3   Impulse Systems 65
  3.3   Models for Ao.. 66
       3.3.1   Level of Repair Analysis (LORA) Model 66

3.3.2 Sparing to Availability (STA) Model...............................67
3.4 Mission Profile...68
  3.4.1 Operational Profile...70
  3.4.2 Logistic Mission Profile..71
  3.4.3 Environmental Profile...72
3.5 A Guide to Ao Analysis...72
  3.5.1 Preproject Research and Development Phase........................73
    3.5.1.1 Objectives..85
    3.5.1.2 Data and Models...85
    3.5.1.3 Ao Analysis...86
    3.5.1.4 Documentation...91
  3.5.2 Concept and Technology Development Phase.........................91
    3.5.2.1 Objectives..92
    3.5.2.2 Data and Models...92
    3.5.2.3 Ao Analysis...94
    3.5.2.4 Documentation...97
  3.5.3 System Development and Demonstration Phase.......................99
    3.5.3.1 Objectives...100
    3.5.3.2 Data and Models..100
    3.5.3.3 Ao Analysis..101
    3.5.3.4 Documentation..106
  3.5.4 Production and Deployment Phase................................108
    3.5.4.1 Objectives...108
    3.5.4.2 Data and Models..109
    3.5.4.3 Ao Analysis..110
    3.5.4.4 Documentation..118
  3.5.5 Sustainment Phase..118
    3.5.5.1 Objectives...119
    3.5.5.2 Data and Models..119
    3.5.5.3 Ao Analysis..119
    3.5.5.4 Documentation..123
3.6 Conclusion..124
Suggested Reading...125

Chapter 4

Reliability...127
Preface...127
4.1 Introduction to Reliability.......................................128
  4.1.1 The Mathematics of Reliability.................................128
  4.1.2 Reliability Modeling...130
  4.1.3 Application of the Reliability Model...........................131
4.2 Reliability by Design...131
  4.2.1 Reliability Allocation...133
    4.2.1.1 Objective of the Allocation................................133

    4.2.1.2 Practical Considerations in Reliability Allocation..................134
    4.2.1.3 Reliability Allocation Methods.......................................134
  4.2.2 Reliability Prediction...137
    4.2.2.1 Objective of Prediction..137
    4.2.2.2 Reliability Prediction Procedures................................137
  4.2.3 Failure Mode, Effects, and Criticality Analysis
    (FMECA)..139
    4.2.3.1 FMECA Objectives..139
    4.2.3.2 Application of the FMECA...139
    4.2.3.3 FMECA Procedures..141
 4.3 Reliability Design Approaches..142
  4.3.1 High Reliability Configuration and Component Design.......142
  4.3.2 System Graceful Degradation..142
  4.3.3 Redundancy..143
    4.3.3.1 Redundancy Techniques...144
    4.3.3.2 Redundancy Disadvantages.......................................146
 4.4 Reliability-Centered Maintenance...148
 Suggested Reading..154

Chapter 5
Maintainability 155
 Preface 155
 5.1 Overview..155
  5.1.1 Preventive Maintenance vs. Corrective
    Maintenance..156
  5.1.2 Inherent Availability...157
 5.2 Preventive Maintenance...157
  5.2.1 Objective of Preventive Maintenance...............................157
  5.2.2 The RCM Analysis Process...158
    5.2.2.1 Types of Preventive Maintenance 159
    5.2.2.2 Scheduled On-Condition Tasks.................................162
    5.2.2.3 Scheduled Rework Tasks..162
    5.2.2.4 Scheduled Discard Tasks...165
    5.2.2.5 Safe Life Limits 165
    5.2.2.6 Economic Life Limits...165
    5.2.2.7 Scheduled Failure Finding Tasks................................165
  5.2.3 Age Exploration Program...166
 5.3 Corrective Maintenance...166
  5.3.1 Objective of Corrective Maintenance...............................166
  5.3.2 Techniques for Corrective Maintenance...........................167
  5.3.3 Repair Maintainability Procedures..................................167
 5.4 Testability and Diagnostics...169
 5.5 Maintainability and Logistics Requirements.............................170
 5.6 Maintainability and the Acquisition Process.............................170
 5.7 Maintainability and the Manufacturing Process........................172

5.8   Maintainability and Safety 173
References 176

Chapter 6
Supportability 177
Preface 177
6.1   Supportability Metrics..177
    6.1.1   Mean Downtime for Outside Assistance (MOADT)............178
    6.1.2   Mean Downtime for Documentation (MDTD) 178
    6.1.3   Mean Downtime for Training (MDTT) 179
    6.1.4   Mean Supply Response Time (MSRT)...................................179
    6.1.5   Mean Requisition Response Time (MRRT) 179
    6.1.6   Mean Downtime for Other Reasons (MDTOR) 179
6.2   Determining Mean Logistics Downtime 179
    6.2.1   MLDT Calculation Using a Decision Tree............................180
    6.2.2   Probabilities Used in Estimating MLDT 181
    6.2.3   Replacement Rates..182
    6.2.4   Alternatives When the MLDT is Insufficient 183
6.3   Designing for Supportability 184
6.4   Trade-Off Analyses...185
    6.4.1   Level of Repair Analysis (LORA) 185
    6.4.2   The Logistics Management Information (LMI) Database........186
References 187

Chapter 7
Capability: Performance-Based Logistics 189
Preface 189
7.1   Introduction 190
    7.1.1   Purpose and Scope..190
    7.1.2   Definitions 191
        7.1.2.1   Metrics and Measures...191
        7.1.2.2   Performance-Based Management 191
        7.1.2.3   Performance-Based Measurement and Performance-Based Management..191
        7.1.2.4   Performance-Based Logistics 191
    7.1.3   The Third Wave..192
    7.1.4   The Foundations of PBL 193
7.2   PBL Program Activities 195
    7.2.1   Define Program Requirements 196
    7.2.2   Define Stakeholder Objectives..196
    7.2.3   Establish the PBL Team and Define Roles...............................197
        7.2.3.1   Integrating across Traditional Stovepipe Organizational Boundaries 198
        7.2.3.2   Establishing the Public/Private Support Strategy IPT 198

7.2.4 Perform Strategic Planning...198
    7.2.4.1 Setting Strategic Directions 199
    7.2.4.2 Setting Strategic Objectives, Goals, Targets, and Initiatives 199
    7.2.4.3 PBL Strategic Planning.......................................199
    7.2.4.4 PBL Tactical Planning..200
    7.2.4.5 Beyond the Strategic Plan 200
7.2.5 Identify the PBL Candidates and Opportunities 201
    7.2.5.1 Coding to Identify Candidates for the Application of PBL......201
    7.2.5.2 Identifying PBL Opportunities..............................201
7.2.6 Define the Performance Baseline 201
    7.2.6.1 Current Baseline Support Concept 201
    7.2.6.2 Maintenance Concept 202
    7.2.6.3 Baseline Performance and Cost 202
7.2.7 Formalize a Performance-Based Agreement 203
7.2.8 Identify Product Support Providers and Allocate Workload 203
7.2.9 Perform a Business Case Analysis (BCA) 204
7.2.10 Define the Roles 205
7.2.11 Establish the Product Support Integrator...........................205
7.2.12 Identify the Performance Metrics Architecture.....................206
7.2.13 Integrate Key Processes...214
7.2.14 Define a Performance Data and Reporting Schema.................215
    7.2.14.1 Metric Linking in the Reporting Scorecard Structure 217
    7.2.14.2 Non-Automated Graphic Presentations 217
    7.2.14.3 Automated Measurement Data Sharing................217
    7.2.14.4 Selecting a Reporting Schema.........................218
7.2.15 Define Win-Win Performance-Based Incentives.................... 225
7.2.16 Define a Dispute Resolution Process................................ 225
7.2.17 Define the Performance Contracting and Tasking with Providers 227
7.2.18 Monitor Performance and Identify Actions 230
7.2.19 Conduct Formal Performance Reviews..............................230
7.2.20 Identify Opportunities for Improvement 232
    7.2.20.1 Measurement of the Results.............................236
7.3 PBL Case Study: The V-22 Osprey 236
7.3.1 Maintenance Support Plan 238
    7.3.1.1 Phased Maintenance......................................238
    7.3.1.2 Interim Support..238
    7.3.1.3 Interim Contractor Support..............................239
    7.3.1.4 Contractor Logistics Support (CLS) 239
7.3.2 Baseline Performance Metrics....................................... 239
7.3.3 PBL for the V-22...240
7.3.4 PBL Strategic Planning...241
7.3.5 Performance-Based Incentives 244
7.3.6 PBL Implementation 244
7.3.7 Regular Performance Monitoring and Feedback.....................245

      7.3.8   Formal Technical Performance Reviews 245
      7.3.9   Lessons Learned 245
  References...247

Chapter 8
Capability: Performance Measures 249
  Preface 249
  8.1   Introduction 250
      8.1.1   The Selection of Performance Measures..250
      8.1.2   Metric Frameworks..251
            8.1.2.1   Rome Laboratory Software Quality Framework 252
      8.1.3   Collection of Measurement Data..252
      8.1.4   Analysis of Measurement Data 253
      8.1.5   Reporting of Measurement Information...253
  8.2   General Performance Measures 253
  8.3   Lean Measures...256
      8.3.1   Lean Enterprise Measures...257
      8.3.2   Enterprise Flow-Related Measures...257
      8.3.3   Information Flow-Related Measures...257
      8.3.4   Lean Leadership-Related Measures...258
      8.3.5   Other Lean-Related Measures 258
  8.4   Process Improvement Measures 258
      8.4.1   Common Process Improvement Measures 258
      8.4.2   Organizational Design Measures...259
      8.4.3   Process Development-Related Measures 259
      8.4.4   Process Capability Maturity-Related Measures...259
      8.4.5   Relationship Development-Related Measures 259
      8.4.6   Customer Focus-Related Measures...259
      8.4.7   Enterprise Stability-Related Measures..260
      8.4.8   Workforce Capability- and Utilization-Related Measures......................260
      8.4.9   Learning Environment-Related Measures...260
  8.5   Sustainability and Supportability Performance Measures 260
      8.5.1   Readiness and Flying Hour Measures...261
      8.5.2   Maintenance Measures 262
      8.5.3   Supply Chain Measures...268
      8.5.4   Support Equipment Measures...273
      8.5.5   Manpower and Personnel Measures..275
      8.5.6   Training Measures...276
      8.5.7   Technical Data Measures...277
      8.5.8   Facilities Measures..278
      8.5.9   Computer Resources Support Measures 278
      8.5.10 Packaging, Handling, Storage, and Transportation Measures.................279
      8.5.11 Design Interface Measures..281
      8.5.12 Logistics Footprint Measures...284
  8.6   Case Study: Rockwell Collins San Jose (RCSJ), California 285

8.6.1 The RCSJ Performance-Based Logistics Concept................................... 285
8.6.2 Organization of the PBL Program.. 286
8.6.3 Program Phases 287
8.6.4 Maintenance Support.. 287
8.6.5 Service Parts Provisioning... 288
8.6.6 Reliability.. 288
8.6.7 Navy Depot Site Support.. 289
8.6.8 Navy/Marine Corp Base... 290
8.6.9 Engineering Design Activities... 290
8.6.10 Configuration Management.. 290
8.6.11 PBL Program Metrics 291
References.. 292

Chapter 9
Affordability...295
Preface 295
9.1 The Life Cycle... 297
    9.1.1 Presystem Identification Phase.. 297
    9.1.2 System Acquisition Phase 298
    9.1.3 Sustainment Phase.. 299
    9.1.4 Final Disposal... 300
9.2 Life Cycle Cost (LCC)... 300
    9.2.1 DoD Policy on LCC.. 302
    9.2.2 LCC Patterns.. 303
    9.2.3 LCC Categories 303
        9.2.3.1 Funding Appropriation.. 304
        9.2.3.2 Work Breakdown Structure (WBS)... 305
        9.2.3.3 Life Cycle Cost Elements.. 305
    9.2.4 LCC Data Sources 307
        9.2.4.1 Maintenance Data 309
        9.2.4.2 Technical Data 310
        9.2.4.3 Supply Support Data 310
        9.2.4.4 Support Equipment Data...311
        9.2.4.5 Computer Support Data 311
        9.2.4.6 Facility Data..311
        9.2.4.7 Training and Training Support Data...311
        9.2.4.8 Management Data..312
        9.2.4.9 Related Programs Data...312
    9.2.5 LCC Drivers..312
    9.2.6 Uses of LCC 312
9.3 The Life Cycle Costing Process..312
    9.3.1 Identify the Purpose of the Analysis 313
    9.3.2 Identify the Baseline (Reference System) and Alternatives.......................313
    9.3.3 Develop the Ground Rules and Assumptions 314
    9.3.4 Select the Relevant Cost Structure and Elements.....................................314
    9.3.5 Determine the Cost Estimating Technique 314

	9.3.6	Select or Construct a Cost Model	315
	9.3.7	Identify the Input Data Sources and Obtain the Data	317
	9.3.8	Estimate and Evaluate the Relevant Costs: Run the Model	317
	9.3.9	Assess the Risk and Uncertainty: Rerun the Model	317
	9.3.10	Perform Sensitivity Analysis: Rerun the Model	318
	9.3.11	Develop the Recommendations and Document the Results	320
9.4	LCC Trade-Off Analysis Tools		321
	9.4.1	System Effectiveness vs. LCC Analysis	321
	9.4.2	Independent Cost Estimate (ICE)	322
	9.4.3	Business Case Analysis (BCA)	323
	9.4.4	Analysis of Alternatives (AoA)	324
9.5	Currency Discounting		326
	9.5.1	Analysis Period	326
	9.5.2	Discount Rate	326
	9.5.3	Constant Currency vs. Current Currency	327
	9.5.4	Differential Cost Changes	327
	9.5.5	Present Value of Money	328
9.6	Case Study: Precision Approach Radar Modernization Project		328
	9.6.1	Purpose and Scope	329
	9.6.2	Alternatives	330
	9.6.3	Methodology	330
		9.6.3.1 Define the Purpose of the Analysis	330
		9.6.3.2 Identify the Baseline and Alternatives	330
		9.6.3.3 Develop Ground Rules and Assumptions	330
		9.6.3.4 Select Relevant Cost Elements and Structure	331
		9.6.3.5 Determine Cost Estimating Technique	331
		9.6.3.6 Select or Construct a Cost Model	331
		9.6.3.7 Identify Input Data, Sources, and Collect the Data	331
		9.6.3.8 Estimate and Evaluate Relevant Costs	332
		9.6.3.9 Perform Sensitivity Analysis and Identify/Verify Major Cost Drivers	332
		9.6.3.10 Perform Risk and Uncertainty Analysis	332
		9.6.3.11 Develop Recommendations	332
	9.6.4	Summary of the LCC Analysis	332
References			336

Chapter 10
Marketability 337

	Preface		337
10.1	The Role of Marketing		337
	10.1.1	Product	338
	10.1.2	Price	338
	10.1.3	Place	338
	10.1.4	Promotion	339

10.1.5 People...339
10.1.6 Process..339
10.1.7 Physical Evidence 340
10.2 The Target Market..340
    10.2.1 Stakeholders 342
    10.2.2 Management..342
        10.2.2.1 Tier 1: Executive Council....................................343
        10.2.2.2 Tier 2: Division Steering Group 343
        10.2.2.3 Tier 3: Program Review Council 343
        10.2.2.4 Tier 4: Program Requirements Teams 344
10.3 Communication Vehicles...344
    10.3.1 Project Team Meetings 344
    10.3.2 Staff Meetings 344
    10.3.3 Transformation Area Team Meetings...................................344
    10.3.4 Town Hall Meeting...345
    10.3.5 Story Boards 346
    10.3.6 Email..346
    10.3.7 Web Site 346
    10.3.8 Newsletter 346
    10.3.9 Gap Workshops 347
10.4 Communication Information Protocol 347
10.5 Communication Schedule..347
10.6 Managing the Change 347
10.7 Key Action Steps...351
    10.7.1 Establish the Motivation for Change and a Sense of Urgency...............351
    10.7.2 Build a Guiding Coalition 352
    10.7.3 Develop a Vision and Strategy for Change 352
    10.7.4 Communicate the Vision...353
    10.7.5 Empower Broad-Based Action 354
    10.7.6 Generate Short-Term Wins 354
    10.7.7 Sustain the Momentum: Consolidate Gains and Produce More Change...355
    10.7.8 Anchor New Approaches in the Culture...............................355
10.8 Gap Analysis...355
    10.8.1 Stage 1: Establish the Motivation for Change and a Sense of Urgency...356
    10.8.2 Stage 2: Build a Guiding Coalition......................................357
    10.8.3 Stage 3: Develop a Vision and Strategy for Change 358
    10.8.4 Stage 4: Communicate the Vision 358
    10.8.5 Stage 5: Empower Broad-Based Action................................359
    10.8.6 Stage 6: Generate Short-Term Wins.....................................360
    10.8.7 Stage 7: Sustain the Momentum: Consolidate Gains and Produce More Change 360
    10.8.8 Stage 8: Anchor New Approaches in the Culture.................361
10.9 Best Practice Case Study: Tobyhanna Army Depot 361
    10.9.1 Best Practice: Communications Strategy Plan 362

Appendix A: Example Meeting Agenda 363
Appendix B: Example Meeting Minutes and Action Item Update 364
Appendix C: Communications Information Protocol 365
References.. 366
Index **367**

Preface

An increased military operational tempo, aging weapon systems, an aging workforce, limited financial resources, and new technologies are some of the reasons why the military needs an aggressive transformation plan for its sustainability. *Sustainment* is the maintenance, repair, and overhaul (MRO) practices that keep the systems (the products of the military enterprise) operating and up to date (via new technology upgrades) throughout their entire life cycle. The goal is to achieve a quantum leap in sustainment throughput and efficiency by transforming military depot workload and processes into those of best-in-class commercial-type facilities. In order to produce a successful transformation, military depots require an integrated set of activities and support methods that execute their strategic vision, program concepts, acquisition strategy, schedule, communications plan, and implementation strategy. To accomplish this objective, this volume is the second in a series of books under the title *Sustaining the Military Enterprise*. The series is an analysis of, and prescription for, the strategies, principles, and technologies that are necessary to sustain the military and the weapon systems it develops and utilizes.

The first volume in the series, *An Architecture for a Lean Transformation*, described process improvement initiatives that can help sustain the military enterprise in the most effective manner. It then presented a high-level system-wide architecture to accomplish that objective, and it provided the reader with the tools needed for the transformation. This second volume prescribes a treatment of concepts and tools for enhancing the ability of the military to perform the mission of maintaining, repairing, and overhauling its weapon systems. The treatment focuses on five abilities:

Availability: Improving the availability of required parts, facilities, tools, and manpower/operators. The discussion in this ability analyzes the military supply chain and then recommends a corrective course of action. Military MRO processes require large numbers and types of parts that have become obsolete. When a part is not available and a backorder is placed in the supply system for the required asset, an awaiting parts (AWP) condition occurs in which the maintenance shop may be forced to postpone the current repair operation and work on something else, or stop repair action completely. Among the adverse consequences resulting from AWP conditions and subassembly support is failure to meet depot overhaul schedules and to provide a timely supply of weapon systems to the warfighter. AWP also increases the cost of depot-level maintenance because of disruptions to production (i.e., work stoppages and rescheduling), the introduction of workarounds, such as cannibalization, and increased facility requirements. The objective of the discussion is to develop an improved understanding of current materials and parts support processes, inventory management practices, and supply chain integration strategies being used in both government

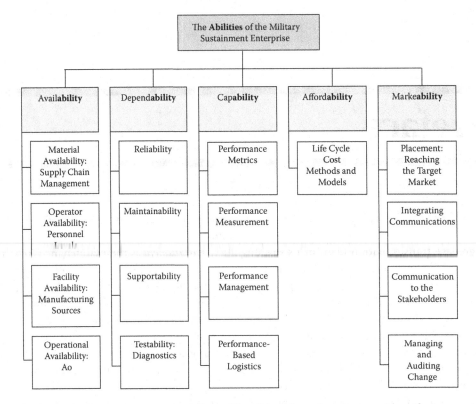

and commercial sustainment enterprises. The discussion also aims to identify innovative solutions for improving the performance of depot-based MRO operations. Included in this availability discussion is what has been called operational availability (Ao). Ao is defined as the probability that the system will be ready to perform its specified function in its intended operational environment when called for at a random point in time.

Dependability: Enhancing the dependability of the weapon systems being used by the warfighter to perform the mission. This discussion includes reliability, maintainability, supportability, and testability practices and technologies. Reliability is the science behind a system performing a mission consistently without failure, degradation, or placing high demands on the support infrastructure. Maintainability is the measure of the ability of a system to be retained in or restored to operable condition. Supportability is a measure of the ability to support the warfighter by satisfying the requirements associated with restoring a failed system to full mission operation. Testability is a characteristic that allows the status (operable, inoperable, or degraded) of a system to be determined and faults within the system to be isolated in a timely and efficient manner. The ability to detect and isolate faults within a system, and to do so efficiently, prior to release of the system for use by the warfighter is the least the MRO enterprise can do to ensure safety.

Capability: Enhancing the capability of the enterprise to perform the mission. This aspect of ability deals with identifying a framework of performance metrics, performance measurement, and performance management for assessing the effectiveness of the military sustainment enterprise. Performance metrics are the units or standards of measure for the overall quantitative or qualitative characterization of performance. Performance measurement is the process of collecting, analyzing, and the proper reporting of performance data to identify opportunities for system and process improvements. Performance management is the translation of the data to useful information and the techniques that will be used to drive continuous performance improvement. Performance-based logistics (PBL) will also be addressed in this topic. PBL is a widely recognized and recommended management approach within the military for improved performance, improved system readiness, and reduced cost through the implementation of government-industry partnerships. The essence of PBL is to provide incentives, not barriers, for the achievement of objectives and to measure performance by collecting, analyzing, and reporting performance data and using the resulting information to drive improved quality.

Affordability: Methods and models for analyzing and improving the life cycle cost (LCC) of a system or a project. LCC models calculate estimates for the operating and support costs for a weapon system or a major project initiative by adding the present worth of the initial investment to the operating, maintenance, and overhaul costs over the life of the system or project. LCC models range from simple high-level cash flow and payback analyses to detailed business case analyses (BCAs) that include net present value and rate of return on the investment.

Marketability: Identifying the target areas (market) for improvement and enhancing the methods and models to serve that market. To the military, marketing is essentially communication, which enhances the promotion and placement of performance improvement initiatives to the stakeholders. Specifically, how do you motivate decision makers within the military to adopt change? How do you sell performance improvement concepts to those who are culturally resistant to change and believe that a performance improvement technique, like Lean production, is just another total quality management scheme? How do you communicate changes and their consequences to all stakeholders (Congress, public, other forces in the military, media, and personnel not directly involved with the project)? Lastly, how do you manage and audit the changes brought on by the new initiatives?

Sustainment aims to maintain the readiness and operational capability of deployed systems through the execution of a support program that meets the system performance requirements in the most cost-effective manner over the system's life cycle. The scope of support varies among programs, but it generally includes supply, maintenance, transportation, sustaining engineering, data management, configuration management, manpower, personnel, training, habitability, survivability, safety, occupational health, information technology supportability and interoperability, and environmental management functions. Sustainment strategies must evolve and be refined throughout the system's life cycle, particularly during the development of subsequent blocks of an evolutionary strategy, modifications, upgrades, and reprocurement.

Acknowledgments

The authors thank Babson College, the University of Massachusetts–Lowell, the Massachusetts Institute of Technology, the U.S. Air Force, the U.S. Army, and the U.S. Navy. The Babson College Faculty Research Fund provided funding in support of the benchmarking research in this book. The Lean Sustainment Initiative at MIT provided the incentive and knowledge that led to the production of this book.

About the Authors

Dennis F. X. Mathaisel is professor of management science in the Department of Mathematics and Science at Babson College, and holds a doctor of philosophy degree from the Massachusetts Institute of Technology. For 20 years he was a research engineer at MIT. He was also cofounder and president of Scheduling Systems Inc., a computer software firm, and in the early 1970s he was a branch manager at the McDonnell Douglas Corporation.

Dr. Mathaisel's interests focus on the sustainability of complex and aging systems. He is an expert in Lean sustainment, and was an MIT co-lead for the Lean Sustainment Initiative for the U.S. Air Force. Dr. Mathaisel has written a book and several papers on Lean sustainment and enterprise transformation. Through his experience working with several government and commercial organizations he has learned how an effectively designed and executed enterprise transformation plan can promote the vision, commitment, sense of urgency, senior leadership buy-in, and shared goals and objectives that are necessary for a successful adaptation of enterprisewide Lean sustainment.

Dr. Mathaisel has consulted for the Federal Aviation Administration, the National Aeronautics and Space Administration, the U.S. Air Force, and the U.S. Department of Transportation (Office of the Secretary); Pratt & Whitney; FedEx, and the Flying Tiger Line; and Continental Airlines, Garuda Indonesia Airline, Hughes Airwest, Iberia Airlines, Northwest Airlines, Olympic Airlines, Pan American World Airways, Trans World Airlines, USAirways; among many other institutions. These assignments have focused on enterprise sustainment, the application of Lean manufacturing to sustainability, decision support systems, maintenance and logistics, scheduling, fleet and route planning, and transport systems analysis and engineering.

Dr. Mathaisel is a private pilot and an owner of a Cessna 182 aircraft based at Hanscom Air Force Base, near Lexington, Massachusetts.

Joel M. Manary holds a master's of science degree in logistics and systems acquisition management at the Air Force Institute of Technology. He is an MIT research fellow, and has participated in several studies as part of the MIT Advanced Studies Program. He is a senior systems engineer for Ocean Systems Engineering Corporation (OSEC) and is home based in Oceanside, California. He is the lead systems engineering subject matter expert in the Systems Engineering Process Office (SEPO), a staff agency supporting SPAWAR Systems Center Pacific in San Diego. He has over 20 years of experience in acquisition program management and systems engineering management. He was a program manager of an automated tool improvement project. He was a senior systems analyst, staff consultant, and advisor to senior managers in the Office of the Secretary of Defense, Department of Defense, and Naval Air Systems Command (NAVAIRSYSCOM), where

xxvi ■ *About the Authors*

he provided and supervised direct support to project managers, senior systems analysts, senior systems engineers, scientists, and technical personnel. He also has over 20 years of experience in operational systems support, as an active duty Air Force maintenance officer. He performed as a senior systems analyst and maintenance officer at the organizational level, intermediate level, and military depot level. Joel is an avid classic car buff and has restored six Mustangs for his six children, as well as a 450 SL Mercedes for his wife and a Rolls Royce Silver Cloud for himself.

Clare L. Comm received a PhD in marketing from the University of Cincinnati, where she taught marketing courses. She is professor of marketing in the College of Management at the University of Massachusetts–Lowell, where she specializes in services marketing and buyer behavior. She has also taught at Babson College, Radcliffe Seminars Program, and the University of Indonesia for MIT's Flight Transportation Laboratory. She has written numerous articles in the area of the marketing of services and sustainability (higher education and the airline industry). Her recent publications appear in *Benchmarking: An International Journal, International Journal of Sustainability in Higher Education, Journal of Business & Economics Research*, and *International Journal of Business Excellence*. Dr. Comm is a member of the editorial board of the *International Journal of Business Excellence* and a frequent textbook reviewer for the McGraw Hill Publishing Co. She is also an Alfred P. Sloan Foundation affiliate. Affiliates are scholars and researchers who have a shared commitment to a research approach that places great value on direct contact with industry for insights, data, and observations. This information is shared by affiliates at conferences and forums around the world.

Chapter 1

Availability: The Current Military Supply Chain

Preface

Depot maintenance production requires all types of parts that are requisitioned from depot supply. When a part is required, is not available, and a back order is placed in the supply system for the required asset, an awaiting parts (AWP) condition exists. In AWP situations the maintenance shop may be forced to postpone the current repair operation and work on something else, or stop repair action completely. Among the adverse impacts resulting from the lack of adequate and timely piece-part and subassembly support is failure to meet depot overhaul schedules and to provide a timely supply of serviceable reparable items. AWP also increases the cost of depot level maintenance because of disruptions to production (i.e., work stoppages and rescheduling), the introduction of workarounds, such as cannibalization and rob-backs, and increased facility requirements (AFMC 2000). Having spare parts available when needed to perform required maintenance is critical to the Department of Defense's accomplishment of its missions. Shortages of spare parts are a key indicator of supply chain system problems that can result in the unavailability of weapon systems to meet mission requirements. Despite additional funding provided by the U.S. Congress to address this issue, the military sustainment system is still reporting concerns about spare parts shortages (GAO 2001a, 2001b).

The objective of this chapter is to develop an improved understanding of current materials and parts availability, support processes, inventory management practices, and supplier integration strategies being used in both government and commercial sustainment enterprises in order to identify innovative solutions for improving the performance of depot-based maintenance, repair, and overhaul (MRO) operations.

1.1 Availability of Materials and Parts to the Warfighter

The lack of availability of materials and parts has been cited by the U.S. General Accounting Office (GAO 2001a, 2001b) as a critical problem in achieving the targeted mission capability rates for Air Force, Army, and Navy weapon systems. In both government and industry sustainment enterprises, the right types and quantities of materials and parts must be available when and where needed in order for them to provide the required services efficiently, flexibly, and responsively under varying demand conditions. This requires a comprehensive supply chain management (SCM) system encompassing the entire sustainment enterprise. More broadly, there exists a critical need to build seamlessly integrated supplier networks supporting the sustainment system to address a spectrum of serious problems, such as the pervasive AWP problem, which in fact reflects many deep-seated and interrelated issues, including spares policy, parts obsolescence, and diminishing sources. They also include practical issues related to lead times, purchasing, parts funding, leveraged buy, buy frequency, batch sizes, and transportation and storage. They further encompass technical issues, such as technical data availability and parts standardization.

The Department of Defense (DoD) operates the world's largest supply chain, spends more than $80 billion annually on logistics, and employs more than 1 million logistics personnel. DoD supply chain managers manage approximately 5 million consumable and reparable items that are procured from more than 100,000 suppliers and distributed to more than 30,000 customers. Similar to most enterprises, DoD is being challenged to reduce supply chain costs and improve customer satisfaction. As the department transitions from traditional methods of support to industry-proven best practices, senior DoD logisticians need to monitor the supply chain's overall performance continuously to ensure that policy and process changes achieve the desired results (LMI 1999).

The right types of materials and parts must be available in the right quantities at the right place and at the right time, at an affordable cost, in order for the sustainment system to provide the required services efficiently, flexibly, and responsively under varying demand conditions. This requires the building of a sensible inventory of parts and seamless supply chains supporting the sustainment system. The building of integrated supply chains is essential for addressing the critical awaiting parts problem, encompassing issues related to lead times, batch sizes, buy frequency, obsolescence, diminishing suppliers, parts proliferation and standardization, cannibalization practices, and technical data availability.

The author's previous research in the area of materials and parts shortages, concentrating on organic[*] repair operations as well as benchmarking commercial component repair processes,[†] has highlighted a number of salient findings. One key finding is that the current organic system is designed to operate in a static environment, while it actually faces a highly variable repair demand environment, where a series of intertwined problems—long supplier lead times, awaiting parts (AWP), extensive cannibalization, and chronic back order queues—vie for attention. In this respect, the lack of an adequate and reliable inventory management system is strongly indicated. It is also clear that many built-in institutional rigidities block the system's transition toward a more flexible, responsive, and agile sustainment enterprise, where the required materials and parts are delivered just in time, upon demand, when and where they are needed. In the same vein, a larger question concerns what types of demand forecasting models would be best under different sets of conditions (e.g., demand variability, frequency of repair, cost of repair, etc.).

---

[*] Organic repair refers to the MRO services performed internally by the military depots, as opposed to using outside commercial contractors to perform the services.

[†] The Lean Sustainment Initiative (LSI) at the Massachusetts Institute of Technology (MIT) was a joint project between Headquarters Air Force Materiel Command (HQ AFMC) and the Air Force Manufacturing Technology (ManTech) program in support of the Air Force Lean Logistics (LL) program. The LSI project operated from May 1997 to December 2001. The author, Dennis Mathaisel, was a team leader in the project.

An additional key finding relates to the lack of proactive integration of repair and technology upgrade functions, which assumes great importance in light of the increasing parts obsolescence and diminishing manufacturing sources problems. Finally, previous research underscores the absence of a concerted strategic approach to the difficult challenge of designing and building integrated supplier networks.

These findings are consistent with other research findings by the U.S. General Accounting Office and the various military materiel commands (i.e., Air Force Materiel Command) indicating that there exists a serious and pervasive materials and parts availability problem facing the sustainment system. These findings also suggest that commercial providers of component repair services, as well, must overcome similar problems, particularly in addressing acute AWP problems. Together with the results of the benchmarking efforts examining commercial repair operations, these findings define the context for this chapter's study of supply chain and logistics management.

1.2 The Military Supply Chain and Logistics System

Supply chain management (SCM) is a set of approaches utilized to efficiently integrate the logistic network so that the right quantities are produced and distributed to the right locations at the right time in order to minimize system-wide cost while satisfying service level requirements. The DoD defines SCM as "a cross-functional approach to procuring, producing, and delivering products and services to customers. The broad management scope includes sub-suppliers, suppliers, internal information, and funds flow."* What is the distinction between supply chain and logistics? The supply chain is the linkage of every player and action necessary to get the raw materials processed into the finished goods and then distributed to the customer. Logistics, according to the DoD, is "in its most comprehensive sense, those aspects of military operations which deal with: (a) design and development, acquisition, storage, movement, distribution, maintenance, evacuation, and disposal of materiel; (b) movement, evacuation, and hospitalization of personnel; (c) acquisition or construction, maintenance, operation, and disposition of facilities; and (c) acquisition or furnishing of services."† So, there is not a lot of difference between the terms *supply chain* and *logistics*. Some people use the terms interchangeably. In the military sustainment community, *supply* is often associated with material management and distribution. *Logistics* has three primary subfunctions: supply, maintenance, and transportation. Therefore, SCM is really logistics chain management. What everyone does agree on is that the supply chain is a complex network of facilities and organizations. Figure 1.1 is a simple characterization of this network.

Basically, there are five players in the supply chain network:

1. The suppliers, which includes the raw material suppliers, the manufacturers of the individual components of the system/part, and the original equipment manufacturer (OEM) who assembles or manufacturers the components into the system
2. The procurement or purchasing personnel who order the system or part
3. Production, which is the military MRO depot
4. Distribution, which is the military logistics network of transports and trucks
5. Customers—the warfighter

---

* U.S. Department of Defense, Dictionary of Military and Associated Terms, April 2001 (as amended through August 2002).
† Ibid.

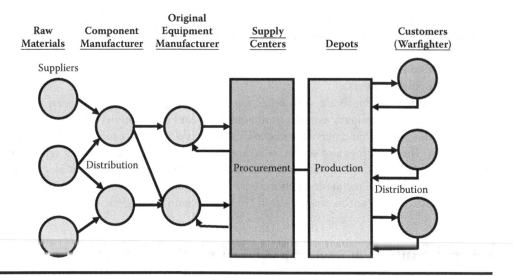

Figure 1.1 The military MRO supply chain.

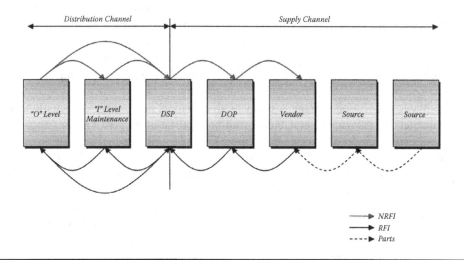

Figure 1.2 Military sustainment supply chain.

As illustrated in Figure 1.2, the distribution channel includes the processes necessary to provide a ready-for-issue (RFI) spare part to the warfighter, including the technical maintenance services provided by the maintenance sustainment organizations. The supply channel on the right in the figure includes the processes necessary to replenish the RFI stock inventory required to support the distribution channel. This process includes replenishing the consumables, the maintenance, repair, and overhaul of RFI spares, and the associated lower-level supply chain activities. Note that there are seven levels for the distribution and supply chain. Another perspective of this complexity is provided in Figure 1.3, which places the item manager in the center of the complicated supply channel and distribution channel activity.

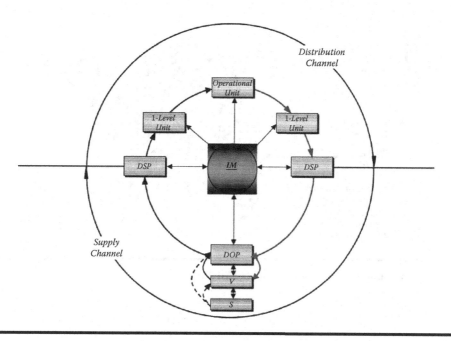

Figure 1.3 Military sustainment distribution and supply channels.

According to the DoD:

> To supply materiel and logistics services to DoD units throughout the world, the DoD Components maintain a supply chain consisting of weapon system support contractors, retail supply activities, distribution depots, transportation networks including contracted carriers, Military Service and Defense Logistics Agency (DLA) integrated materiel managers (IMMs), weapon system program offices, commercial distributors and suppliers including manufacturers, commercial and organic maintenance facilities, and other logistics activities (e.g., engineering support activities (ESAs), testing facilities, cataloging services, reutilization and marketing offices).*

There are more than a hundred thousand active suppliers in these supply channels. Figure 1.4 gives an idea of the extent of this network of suppliers (as of 1999).

The supply chain thread also consists of a number of inventory control points (ICPs), MRO depots, and DLA-managed distribution depots (Figures 1.5 to 1.7). Items stocked in the wholesale system are procured from vendors (or repaired in maintenance depots) and stored in the distribution depots. The items are shipped to retail supply activities to replenish their inventory or directly to customers. The wholesale system also manages and arranges for nonstocked items to be shipped directly from the vendors to retail supply activities or customers.

The DoD retail supply chain is made up of hundreds of retail supply and intermediate-level maintenance activities that stock, repair, and store assets. They replenish their inventory from the

---

* U.S. DoD, "Supply Chain Materiel Management Regulation" (DoD 4140.1-R), May 23, 2003, para. C1.2.1, p. 16.

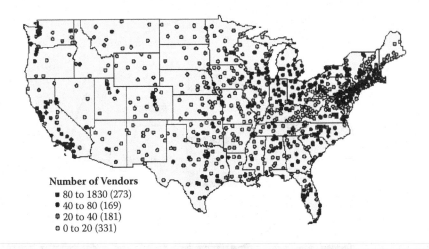

Figure 1.4 DoD supplier locations. (Source: LMI 1999.)

AMCOM	U.S. Army Aviation Missile Command
CECOM	U.S. Army Communications-Electronics Command
DESC	Defense Energy Support Center
DSCC	Defense Supply Center, Columbus
DSCP	Defense Supply Center, Philadelphia
DSCR	Defense Supply Center, Richmond
MCLB	Marine Corps Logistics Base
NAVICP	Naval Inventory Control Point
OC-ALC	Oklahoma City Air Logistics Center
OO-ALC	Ogden Air Logistics Center
SA-ALC	San Antonio Air Logistics Center
SM-ALC	Sacramento Air Logistics Center
TACOM	U.S. Army Tank-automotive and Armaments Command
WR-ALC	Warner-Robins Air Logistics Center

Note: AF = Air Force; USMC = United Stated Marine Corps.

Figure 1.5 Inventory control points. (Source: LMI 1999.)

Note: ALC = Air Logistics Center; AMARC = Aerospace Maintenance and Regeneration Center; NADEP = Naval Aviation Depot; NSY = Naval Shipyard; NUWC = Naval Undersea Warfare Center.

Figure 1.6 MRO depots. (Source: LMI 1999.)

Note: AFB = Air Force Base.

Figure 1.7 Distribution depots. (Source: LMI 1999.)

wholesale supply system or directly from suppliers. At the end of the supply chain are the customers. Their orders are filled from organizational supplies, designated retail supply activities, the wholesale supply system, or directly from vendors. The DoD Activity Address Directory, maintained by the Defense Automatic Addressing System Center, contains the DoD Activity Address Codes (DoDAACs), which identify every unit, activity, and organization that has the authority

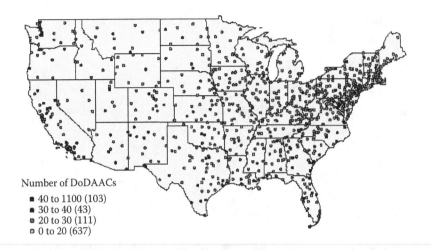

Number of DoDAACs

■ 40 to 1100 (103)
■ 30 to 40 (43)
◙ 20 to 30 (111)
▫ 0 to 20 (637)

Figure 1.8   DoD CONUS customers. (Source: LMI 1999.)

to requisition or receive materiel. More than thirty thousand DoD customers (i.e., requisitioners) place materiel orders.

Figure 1.8 shows the distribution of continental United States (CONUS) DoDAACs.

Such a supply chain model is good for the support of large, slowly changing platforms and systems, but it is not adequate for today's agile and responsive military since it possesses these negative characteristics:

■ It is a seven-tier sustainment system (Figure 1.2).
■ It contains uncoupled processes.
■ It has fragmented organizational structures.
■ It possesses uncoordinated supplier and distribution channels.
■ It is a push-, not pull-, oriented system, which violates one of the fundamental principles of Lean.
■ The model is not responsive in today's maintenance, repair, and overhaul environment.

1.2.1 The Defense Logistics Agency

The Defense Logistics Agency (DLA) is a U.S. Department of Defense (DoD) agency. The DLA director reports to the undersecretary of defense for acquisition, technology, and logistics through the deputy undersecretary of defense (logistics and material readiness). DLA is the DoD's largest combat support agency, providing worldwide logistics support in both peacetime and wartime to the military services as well as several civilian agencies and foreign countries. It also provides logistics support to other DoD components and certain federal agencies, foreign governments, international organizations, and others as authorized.

To accomplish this mission, DLA, which is headquartered at Fort Belvoir in Northern Virginia, utilizes the support of three defense supply centers (DSCs), a defense distribution center (DDC), DLA central, and service centers (SCs) (Figure 1.9).

The Defense Supply Center Columbus (DSCC) is one of the largest suppliers of weapons systems spare parts (Table 1.1). DSCC manages more than 1.6 million different items and accounts for

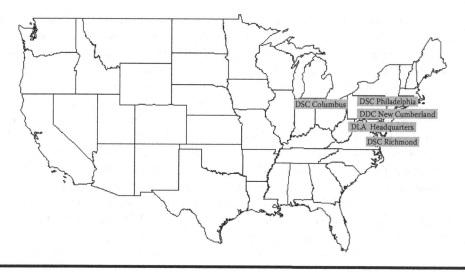

Figure 1.9   DLA's defense supply centers (DSCs) and distribution center (DDC).

more than $2.3 billion in annual sales. DSCC was the first inventory control point (ICP) in DLA to develop a weapons system approach toward materiel management. Weapons system management is now standard procedure in DLA, and DSCC is the lead ICP for land, maritime, and missile weapons systems.

The Defense Supply Center Richmond (DSCR) serves as the aviation supply chain manager for the Defense Logistics Agency and serves within the DoD as the primary source of supply for more than 1.25 million repair parts and operating supply items. DSCR's mission is to provide best-value aviation weapon systems and environmental logistics support to America's armed forces—on land, at sea, and in the air.

DSCR's core mission is to supply products with a direct application to aviation. These items include a mix of military-unique items supporting over thirteen hundred major weapons systems and other items readily available in the commercial market. They range from critical, safety-of-flight air frame structural components, bearings, and aircraft engine parts, to electric cable and electrical power products, lubricating oils, batteries, industrial gases, precision instruments, environmental products, metalworking machinery, and consumable items. DSCR also operates an industrial plant equipment repair facility in Mechanicsburg, Pennsylvania. DSCR's primary customers are the Army, Air Force, Navy, and Marines. The center also supports other government agencies, such as the U.S. Postal Service, National Aeronautics and Space Administration, U.S. Forestry Service, and Department of Transportation. The value of the products and services DSCR provides as the aviation supply chain manager exceeds $3.1 billion annually. DSCR handles 5.3 million requisitions and supports 24,500 customers per year. Approximately twenty-three hundred dedicated military and civilian employees work at DSCR. The center continues to transform to meet the needs of the nation's warfighters by adopting commercial business practices, such as electronic commerce, the quality vendor program, customer value contracts, and direct vendor delivery to improve service.

The Defense Supply Center Philadelphia (DSCP) supplies and manages over $7.66 billion worth of food, clothing and textiles, pharmaceuticals, medical supplies, and general and industrial items in support of America's warfighters worldwide and their eligible dependents. Other customers include America's schoolchildren participating in federal school lunch programs, and other non-Defense Department customers. Whether it's in the United States, Europe, or the Pacific Rim, this peacetime revenue stream affords DSCP leverage in enhancing and ensuring wartime readiness. As a global logistic supply chain integrator, DSCP provides a seamless supply system that can be utilized in both peace- and wartime operations. DSCP's success also can be attributed to the partnerships and alliances we have established with stakeholders and customers. The defense distribution center (DDC) in New Cumberland, Pennsylvania, was established in 1997 through the consolidation of the former Defense Distribution Region East and the former Defense Distribution Region West. The DDC is the lead center for distribution for DLA. Responsibilities include receipt, storage, issue, packing, preservation, worldwide transportation, in-transit visibility, and redirecting en route, when required, of all items placed under its accountability by the Defense Logistics Agency and the military services. The DDC's twenty-six distribution depots located throughout the United States and around the world store 4.0 million stock numbers in 327 million square feet of storage space and process more than 26 million transactions annually. Clothing and textiles, electronics, industrial, general, and construction supplies, subsistence, medical material, and the military services' principle end items are among the commodities for which the DDC is responsible.

In addition to these supply centers, DLA provides other services. The defense distribution center in Pennsylvania operates a worldwide network of twenty-five distribution centers that receive, store, and issue supplies. Defense National Stockpile Center is an international commodity broker of strategic and critical materials that sells and maintains these materials to reduce U.S. dependence on foreign supply sources. Defense Reutilization and Marketing Service provides the DoD with worldwide reuse, recycling, and disposal solutions that focus on efficiency, cost avoidance, and compliance. Defense Logistics Information Service is involved in the creation, management, and dissemination of logistics information to military and government customers using the latest technology. Document Automation and Production Service is the single manager for all DoD printing and duplicating, and provides automated information products and services to DoD and designated federal activities.

DLA Europe serves as a DLA world presence and focal point for DLA matters in Europe and for common European support serving customers in the United States and in the European Command. DLA Pacific is a focal point within the Pacific, and directly services DLA by providing customer assistance, liaison, services, war planning interfaces, and logistics support to the U.S. Pacific Command.

DLA Central, in Florida, serves as the focal point for logistics in Southwest Asia and oversees three DLA contingency support teams in Kuwait, Afghanistan, and Iraq, with its customer support representatives working to bridge communications between DLA and the warfighter.

1.2.2 Differences between Military and Commercial Supply Chains

In many ways, the DoD supply chain is similar to the supply chains of commercial suppliers because many of the products and supplies contained within the DoD supply chain are also available commercially. However, differences in optimization criteria lead to a number of characteristics that set the DoD supply chain apart from the commercial supply chain. Some of the most important of these differentiating characteristics are (Engles et al. 2004):

■ *Readiness.* The primary purpose of optimizing the military supply chain is to enhance readiness for war. Knowing the location and status of all materials needed to support operations is an essential component of readiness.

■ *Long supply lines.* War is an international activity, which means that lines of supply to support operations are long. Without auto-ID technology that provides real-time visibility of items moving from the suppliers to the front-line troops, it is extremely difficult to maintain accurate knowledge of supply-chain-wide inventories.

■ *Variety of items.* Military operations require a large number of items, ranging from everyday supplies to food and clothing to specialized equipment. Different categories of items have different standards for inventory accuracy and visibility.

■ *Unstable demand.* Military demand is often variable and unpredictable because conflicts can happen anywhere in the world at any time. When a conflict occurs, demand for supplies increases dramatically and existing stockpiles of material are depleted quickly. Accurate inventories are critical to maintaining readiness in the presence of variable demand.

■ *Moving endpoints.* The end, or destination, points of the military supply chain generally move forward with advancing troops and are either terminated or transformed, creating additional difficulties for transportation and inventory management.

■ *Priority.* The military supply chain operates on priorities set by unit commanders based on urgency of need.

■ *Equipment reliability and maintenance.* Military operations take place in all types of environments and on all kinds of terrain. Under battle conditions, it is important that all identification technologies work effectively and that system maintenance is minimal.

■ *Detection.* In a theater of operations, the military must always be careful not to divulge information about its position that would be advantageous to the enemy.

Table 1.1   Fact Sheet for the Defense Logistics Agency (DLA)

Items managed	5.2 million
Requisitions per day	54,000
Contracts awarded per day	8,200
FY02 sales and services	$21.5 billion
FY03 sales and services	$25 billion
FY04 sales and services	$28 billion
FY05 sales and services	$31+ billion
Comparable Fortune 500 company (by budget)	#54
Number of weapons systems supported	1,312
Value of inventory (defense distribution center)	$89.2 billion
Number of employees	21,429 (down from 65,000 in 1992)
Number of military personnel	528 active duty (Army, Navy, Air Force, Marine), 615 reservists

Source: DLA. Retrieved from the website www.dla.mil/facts.aspx on July 26, 2006.

Table 1.2 Conflicting Functional Objectives

	Impact of Objectives on Inventory	Impact of Objectives on Customer Service	Impact of Objectives on Total Costs
High customer service	⇧	⬆	⇧
Low transportation costs	⇧	⇩	⬇
Low warehousing costs	⬇	⇩	⬇
Reduced inventories	⬇	⇩	⬇
Fast deliveries	⇧	⬆	⇧
Reduced labor costs	⇧	⇩	⬇
Desired results	⬇	⬆	⬇

The complexity of the military supply channels indicates there is an opportunity to integrate many of the system functional elements to effectively meet MRO supply system and customer requirements concurrently. But this opportunity does not come easy. In fact, supply chain problems are very difficult to solve, which is why so many researchers have spent considerable time and effort on the problems. Why? The answer is because of the conflicting functional objectives of supply chain management (Table 1.2). The desired results are to reduce inventory, increase customer service, and reduce costs. However, the functional objectives of achieving high customer service, low transportation costs, low warehousing costs, reduced inventories, fast deliveries, and reduced labor costs conflict with the desired results. This is what makes the problem so difficult.

1.3 Managing the Inventory

Gone is the push manufacturing day when a sizable amount of stock was pushed out the production system and inventory was held by the customer just in case it was needed (Figure 1.10). Today, Lean supply chain management and Lean logistics imply that one should optimally position inventory and related information to match the pull demand from the customer. Some researchers advocate this pull just-in-time strategy, where inventory arrives when it is needed. But, there are at least three reasons why some buffer stock must be held in inventory:

1. To protect from unexpected variations in demand for the materials or parts
2. To account for the significant uncertainty in supplier availability (i.e., variations in the lead time to obtain the materials or parts)
3. To make use of the economies of scale associated with ordering, producing, and shipping bulk quantities

Obviously, the words *uncertainty* and *variation* dominate any discussion on inventory management. Supply chain uncertainty can be classified into four general types: process, supply, demand, and control (Geary et al. 2002):

Figure 1.10 Inventory example. (Source: Zeng 2005.)

- *Process uncertainty* affects an organization's internal ability to meet a production delivery target. The amount of process uncertainty can be established by understanding each work process's yield ratios and lead time estimates for operations. Also, if the particular product delivery process is competing against other value streams for resources, then the interaction between these must be studied and codified.
- *Supply uncertainty* results from poorly performing suppliers not meeting an organization's requirements and thereby handicapping value-added processes. It can be evaluated by looking at supplier delivery performance, time series of orders placed or call-offs and deliveries from customers, actual lead times, supplier quality reports, and raw material stock time series.
- *Demand uncertainty* can be thought of as the difference between the actual end-marketplace demand and the orders placed with an organization by its customers. Demand uncertainty can also be quantified by measuring how well companies meet customer demand. For example, poor on-time delivery or fill rates are often a result of demand uncertainty, though this is not always the case. If a customer suddenly places a weekly order that is twice the typical order size, it may be the result of a shift in underlying demand, or it may just be that the customer has modified safety stocks or ordering rules.
- *Control uncertainty* is associated with information flow and the way an organization transforms customer orders into production targets and supplier raw material requests. The level of control uncertainty can be determined by comparing customer requirements, supplier requests to deliver, and production targets over the same time periods. Control uncertainty is driven by the algorithms and control systems that are used to transfer the customer orders into production targets and supplier raw material requests. In a pure demand-pull environment, the linkage between supply and demand is clear and control uncertainty is eliminated. However, companies typically use order batching and lot sizing, which obscures the linkage between demands placed and true requirements.

Each of these uncertainties creates a drag on operational performance. However, supply chain professionals often are so busy dealing with the fallout from uncertainty (such as stock-outs, missed shipments, and oversupply) that they do not have time to attack the root cause of the problem. The issue has been complicated even further over the course of the last decade by the movement away from the vertically integrated supply chain. Now, rather than confronting the uncertainty generated just by activities within the operational domain of a single organization, we must manage uncertainty across a host of supply chain participants. Outsourcing, the virtual organization, and modular manufacturing all contribute to supply chain uncertainty issues. All of this makes it more important now than ever before to understand the relationship between supply chain performance and uncertainty (Geary et al. 2002).

According to the Performance Measurement Group (PMG), a supply chain benchmarking subsidiary of the management consultancy PRTM* a well-organized company can generally execute successfully at a 90% or higher level. While this means that any one of a set of ten scheduled events is highly likely to have a favorable outcome, simple probability calculations also indicate that there is only a 35% chance that all ten will successfully happen. Simple mathematics demonstrates a disturbing likelihood: an organization facing a very simple scenario that requires the coordination of only ten independent events will most likely fail to deliver two times out of three. Because no one can predict which of the ten scheduled events will fail to be executed, a supply chain professional must be prepared for any of the ten to fail. Uncertainty prevails (Zonnenberg and Geary 2000).

The appropriate metric to measure variability is the standard deviation. But it is the coefficient of variation (COV) that is a better metric for the uncertainty or risk:

$$\text{Uncertainty or risk} = \text{Coefficient of variation} = \frac{\text{Variance}}{\text{Average}}$$

A coefficient of variation greater than 1.0 means that the variation is greater than the average. The greater the variation, the greater the risk or uncertainty. To offset the risk, buffer stock is used to protect against inventory stock-outs and back orders. The problem is balancing the amount of safety stock against the costs associated with holding the inventory. So, inventory managers need to understand the difference between push and pull supply chain systems.

1.3.1 Push vs. Pull Supply Chains

Traditional supply chains follow a push system, holding inventory at the point of consumption. In a push supply chain system, inventory is stored in anticipation of a need or sale. The amount of inventory that is stored is based on a forecast of the future demand. Figure 1.11 illustrates this process. The customer sends a forecast of the demand to planning. The forecast is frequently reconciled against the actual customer orders. Upon receipt of the forecast, planning initiates the production process with the raw material suppliers and its production shops. The finished goods are distributed to the supply centers and held in inventory. The inventory is used as primary hedge against uncertainty and variability in both the demand and lead time to production and distribution. Thus, a push system is a planning-based approach. The control mechanism is usually a material resource planning (MRP) computer system or an enterprise resource planning (ERP) computer system.

---

* PRTM (Pilliglio Rabin Todd & McGrath) Inc. is an operational strategy consulting firm that codeveloped the Supply Chain Operations Reference (SCOR) model with the Supply Chain Council.

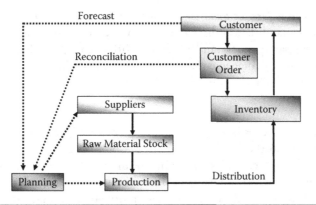

Figure 1.11   The push supply chain concept. (Source: Zeng 2005.)

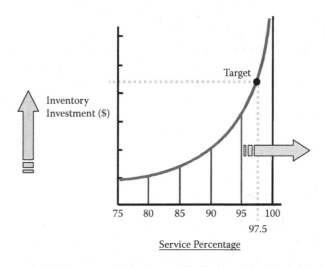

Figure 1.12   Customer service–inventory dilemma. (Source: Zeng 2005.)

Unpredictable variation is the nemesis of plan-based push systems. The variation is due to inaccurate demand forecasts, unpredictable lead times in production, and unpredictable lead times in distribution/transportation. Safety stock is held as a buffer against such uncertainties to improve target customer service levels, but this increase in safety inventory comes at a price (Figure 1.12).

Obviously, it takes some time for a push-based supply chain to react to a changing marketplace. Long-range forecasts are essential to a push system. There are some basic principles of all forecasts. These include:

- *The forecast is always wrong.* It is impossible to forecast any supply and demand exactly. You can come close, but you will never be completely accurate.
- *The longer the forecast horizon, the worse the forecast.* It is difficult to match supply and demand, and it is even more difficult if one needs to predict customer demand for a long period of time, such as the next 12 to 18 months.

■ *Data updates lead to forecast updates, and aggregate forecasts are more accurate.* As the firm receives more demand data, it uses the data to update its forecast, and therefore update inventory levels, safety stock, and order quantities. However, these data updates cause traditional inventory management to experience the bullwhip effect, a phenomenon common in push supply chains (see Section 1.3.2 on the bullwhip effect) (Simchi-Levi and Simchi-Levi 2005).

Because a push system relies heavily on long-range forecasts and can cause a bullwhip effect, some enterprises shifted to the other extreme, a pure pull system, holding no inventory at all (Figure 1.13). In a pull supply chain system, no upstream supplier or manufacturer should produce a good or service until a downstream demand from the customer triggers a requirement. In a perfect world, pull synchronizes production processes, information, and facilities to actual customer demand requirements, and the good or service is delivered just in time (JIT).

In a pull supply chain, production and distribution are demand driven and based on actual customer demand rather than forecast. In a pure pull system, the enterprise does not hold any inventory and only produces to order. These systems are very attractive since they allow the enterprise to eliminate inventory, reduce the bullwhip effect, increase service levels, and generally react nimbly to a changing market. Unfortunately, there are many industries in which it is very difficult to implement a pull supply chain strategy. For example, production lead times of aircraft engines or avionics are too long, making it impractical to react to demand information. Furthermore, in a pull strategy, it is frequently more difficult to take advantage of economies of scale, since production and distribution decisions are in response to specific customer demand. Batch production or efficient transportation modes, such as truckloads, are hard to achieve (Simchi-Levi and Simchi-Levi 2005).

1.3.2 The Bullwhip Effect

Suppliers have observed that while customer demand for some specific products does not vary much, inventory and back order levels fluctuate considerably across their supply chain. In fact, they noticed that variability increased as one travels up the supply chain from the customer through the supply centers to the supplier. This is called the bullwhip effect (Figure 1.14). There are a number of reasons for the bullwhip effect:

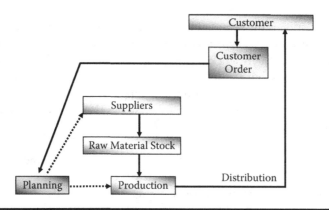

Figure 1.13   The pull supply chain concept. (Source: Zeng 2005.)

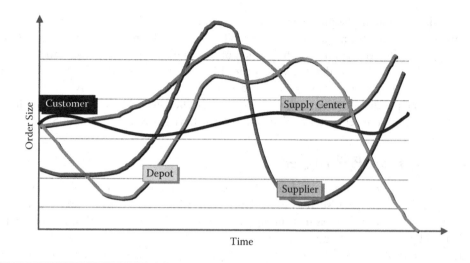

Figure 1.14   The bullwhip effect. (Adapted from Lee et al. 1997.)

- Traditional inventory management techniques practiced at each level in the supply chain lead to the bullwhip effect.
- Increase in lead time will also increase the bullwhip effect.
- The increased number of network levels/echelons (without the demand information insight) will also increase the bullwhip effect.

Centralizing the demand information can significantly reduce the bullwhip effect, because in a centralized world every player in the supply chain network has the same knowledge about demand levels and lead times. The key is to reduce uncertainty, variability, and lead times, and develop strategic partnerships so that everyone is on the same page.

1.3.3 Push-Pull Supply Chains

The advantages and disadvantages of push and pull supply chains have led some enterprises to look for a new supply chain strategy that takes advantage of the best of both worlds—enter a hybrid of the two systems: push-pull supply chain systems. In a push-pull strategy, some stages of the supply chain are operated in a push-based manner, while others are operated in a pull-based strategy. The push system is typically in the initial stages, and the pull system occurs in the later stages. The interface between the push-based stages and the pull-based stages becomes the push-pull boundary (Simchi-Levi and Simchi-Levi 2005).

For example, component inventory for a large system, like an engine, is built to stock and managed based on a forecast (push based). Final assembly of the engine is built to order in response to a specific customer request (pull based). Push is the part of the manufacturer's supply chain prior to assembly, while pull is the part of the supply chain that starts with assembly and is performed based on actual customer demand. In this case, the manufacturer takes advantage of the last principle of all forecasts: aggregate forecasts are more accurate. Demand for a component is actually the sum total of all finished products that use that component, and finished goods demand is easier to predict than component demand. This, of course, leads to safety stock reduction. Dell Computers is an excellent example of the impact the push-pull system has on supply chain performance. Dell keeps an inventory of components and assembles only when there is an actual order (Simchi-Levi and Simchi-Levi 2005).

In a push-pull system, the push part is applied to the portion of the supply chain where long-term forecasts have small uncertainty and variability and can be reasonably predicted. On the other hand, the pull part is applied to the portion of the supply chain where uncertainty and variability are high, and therefore, decisions are made only in response to realized demand. Inventory is a necessary evil. A push-pull supply chain is designed on the premise that inventory is essential in an effective supply chain strategy, but careful long- and short-term planning can reduce it to the minimum necessary to meet customer demand (Simchi-Levi and Simchi-Levi 2005).

1.3.4 Kanban as a Pull Trigger

Kanban, a Japanese term, means "signal." A kanban is a physical card or other signal, which contains specific information, such as part name, description, and quantity, that triggers a pull withdrawal or production process in a supply chain. The quantity that is withdrawn or produced is predefined by the kanban (Figure 1.15).

Kanban is one of the primary tools of just-in-time systems. It signals a cycle of replenishment for production and materials, and it attempts to maintain an orderly and efficient flow of materials throughout the entire supply chain. With kanban, lead times and stock levels are reduced drastically. Figure 1.16 illustrates the difference between a kanban system and an MRP system.

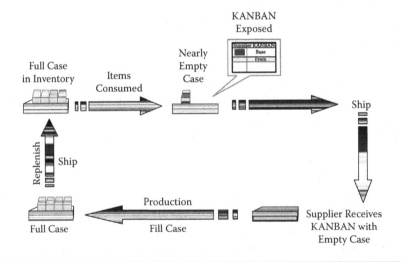

Figure 1.15   The kanban cycle.

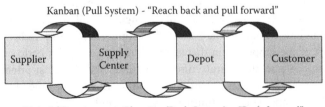

Figure 1.16   Kanban vs. MRP—pull vs. push.

1.3.5 Risk Pooling

Demand variation can be reduced if one aggregates the demand across locations. This is called risk pooling. The reduction in variability by pooling the resources and inventory allows planners to reduce safety stock levels, and therefore reduce the average inventory across the enterprise. This is, in concept, the purpose behind DLA. DSCC supplies weapon systems spare parts and manages construction and electronic spare parts. DSCR is the lead center for aviation weapon systems, environmental logistics support, and the primary supply source for nearly 930,000 repair parts and operating items. DSCP supplies and services U.S. service members with food, clothing, textiles, medicines, medical equipment, and general and industrial supplies. While no one in the military is required to buy from the DLA, DLA does aim to capitalize on economies of scale it garners to provide the best prices and delivery system to the warfighter.

1.3.6 Echelon Networks

Managing the buffer stock inventory can be a daunting task for an enterprise with thousands of parts and materiel that are stored in various locations. The challenge is even greater when the locations are situated in different tiers or echelons of the enterprise's distribution network. In single-echelon networks (Figure 1.17), new product shipments are stored at a supply center, which is then distributed to the depots or warfighter. In a single-echelon situation, the lead times are between the external supplier, the supply center (SC), and its customers (depots and warfighter). The enterprise's order supply strategy depends on cost, ordering constraints, bracket discounts, and inventory policies and procedures. For this reason, the replenishment quantities depend on a combination of internal and external factors. Table 1.3 provides the drivers for parts or materials by National Stock Number (NSN) or Stock Keeping Unit (SKU) number located at a supply center (Lee 2003).

Now consider the same product in a multiechelon network that includes a regional supply center (RSC). In multiechelon networks, new product shipments are first stored at the central supply center (SC), and then distributed to a local or regional supply center. The same inventory drivers described in the single-echelon network apply for the NSN, but some other issues emerge:

■ What is the proper measure of demand to the SC and RSC, and how should this demand be forecasted?
■ How do you measure the demand variation into both supply centers?

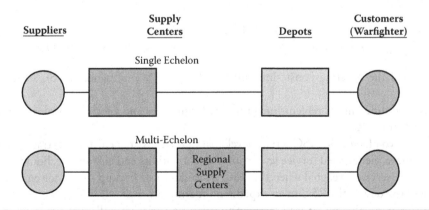

Figure 1.17   Single- vs. multiechelon systems.

Table 1.3 Inventory Drivers for a Part Located at a Supply Center (SC)

Inventory	*Description*
Demand	Rate of National Stock Number (NSN) flow out of the SC
Demand variation	Fluctuation of the NSN outflow from period to period
Lead time	Expected time delay between ordering and having the NSN available to fulfill demand
Lead time variation	Fluctuation of the lead time from order to order
Replenishment review frequency	Frequency with which the SC checks its inventory position to see if a new order is needed
Order supply strategy	The SC's supply objective, which depends on the economic trade-offs between carrying inventory, handling, transportation, and purchase cost
Service level goal	The SC's service commitment to the customers
Inventory position	The SC's available stock, taking into account the on-hand inventory, on-order quantities, back orders, and committed stock
Cost	Ordering cost, handling cost, holding cost, and capital outflow

Source: Adapted from Lee 2003.

- How do larger orders to the SC affect the order supply strategy for the RSC?
- What is the optimal service level goal between the SC and RSC and their customers?
- How do you factor the individual SCs' inventory positions into the RSC replenishment decisions?
- How do the inventory drivers at the RSC, such as the replenishment review frequency and the service level goal, affect inventory and service levels at the SC level?
- When faced with a limited supply situation at the SC, how should one allocate product down to the RSCs?

Because the RSC also stocks inventory for the NSN/SKU, the replenishment decision at each SC also must address some new questions because of its relationship with a supplier:

- How will the ordering constraints imposed by the RSC influence the SC's order supply strategy?
- How will different SC replenishment review frequencies and alternative order supply strategies affect the RSC?
- How do you factor the RSC service level goal into the SC replenishment strategy?
- To achieve the targeted service level commitment with its end customers, should the SC use the same service level goal when the RSC is available as a backup source for end customers?
- How can you use the RSC in an expedited ordering process?
- Do the external supplier lead time and lead time variation still play a role in the RSC's replenishment strategy?

An echelon distribution network, whether single or multiple, presents many opportunities for inventory optimization that the enterprise must pursue to offset potential increases in transportation, warehouse, and occupancy costs. The key to achieving those savings is to use an echelon strategy to manage inventory. Total inventory visibility and control is required, lead time and ordering decisions must be coordinated across the whole chain, and centralized control with total asset visibility is a critical attribute for echelon inventory policy implementation. It is not a simple task to pursue such a strategy because of the multiplicities of inventory drivers and the complexities in modeling the interactions of the drivers between echelons. Nevertheless, the benefits are worth the effort. Taking the right approach can yield rewards on both sides of the inventory equation: better customer service with less inventory. Using a true echelon approach is the ultimate win-win strategy for inventory management (Lee 2003).

So, the optimal deployment of inventory is a vital function for an enterprise. The well-documented benefits of running an operation with leaner inventory range from a permanent reduction in working capital to increased turn times for the end product and higher customer satisfaction. As Forrester Research pointed out in a recent report, the ability to increase inventory turns is a key differentiator between highly successful and more poorly performing companies (e.g., Wal-Mart vs. Kmart; Dell vs. Compaq). These are commercial examples, but Wal-Mart and Dell have best-practice distribution and inventory systems that are applicable to military supply chains (Lee 2003).

References

Engels, Daniel W., Koh, Robin, Lai, Elaine M., and Schuster, Edmund W. 2004, May-June. Improving Visibility in the DOD Supply Chain. *Army Logistician*. U.S. Army Logistics. PB 700-04-3. 36: 20–23.

Geary, Steve, Paul Childerhouse, and Denis Towill. 2002, July. Uncertainty and the seamless supply chain. *Supply Chain Management Review* 6:52–61.

Klapper, L.S., Hamblin, N., Hutchison, L. Novak, L., and Vivar, J. 1999, June. Supply Chain Management: A Recommended Performance Measurement Scorecard, Logistics Management Institute, Report. LG803R1.

Lee, H. L., Padmanabhan, V., and Whang, S. 1997, Spring. The bullwhip effect in supply chains. *Sloan Management* Rev.38: 93–102.

Simchi-Levi, David, and Edith Simchi-Levi. 2005. Inventory positioning: Exploring push and pull supply chains [Editorial article]. *Parcel Shipping & Distribution*.

U.S. Air Force Materiel Command (AFMC). 2000, February. *Awaiting parts (AWP)/backorder integrated product team (IPT) study.* Wright-Patterson Air Force Base, OH.

U.S. General Accounting Office (GAO). 2001a, July. *Navy inventory: Parts shortages are impacting operations and maintenance effectiveness.* Report to Congressional Committees, GAO-01-771.

U.S. General Accounting Office (GAO). 2001b, July. *Army inventory: Parts shortages are impacting operations and maintenance effectiveness.* Report to Congressional Committees, GAO-01-772.

Zeng, Amy Z. 2005. Supply chain analysis and design. Department of Management, Worcester Polytechnic Institute, Course Material OIE 544.

Zonnenberg, J. P., and S. Geary. 2000, July/August. What it means to be best in class. *Supply Chain Management Review*, p. 47.

Chapter 2

Availability: Enhancing the Military Supply Chain

2.1 Three Principles for an Effective Military Supply Chain

The complexity of the military supply chain presents an opportunity to improve many of the system functional processes to effectively meet the maintenance, repair, and overhaul (MRO) supply system and customer requirements concurrently. This chapter identifies innovative solutions for the availability of materials and parts and for improving the performance of depot-based MRO operations. We begin by adhering to three words: *integration*, *collaboration*, and *trust*. They are fundamental and intuitive principles, but making them work will go a long way toward enhancing a Lean and effective supply chain.

2.1.1 Integration

Improvements to the supply chain can be obtained by better integration among the players in the network. As indicated in Chapter 1, the five players are the suppliers, procurement, production, distribution, and the customers (Figure 2.1). In the current situation (top of Figure 2.1), not all of the players share data (e.g., demand variations or performance metrics) or information (e.g., new theater operations or Lean initiatives). Thus, the first phase toward better integration would be to assimilate the internal players in the military MRO community so that data and information are shared. Phase 2 is true integration among all players, where data and information are shared among all partners.

Cooper et al. (1997) identify four possible means of better management of the integration of a supply chain: dyadic, channel integrator, analytic optimization, and keiretsu or vertical integration. A dyadic approach concentrates on one level up or one level down in the chain and is often a starting place for developing an integrated supply chain. Examples are Honda of America Manufacturing and the Xerox Corporation, both of which form close working relationships with their immediate channel partners and encourage these players to do the same. The other three means of better management go further up or down the supply chain. The channel integrator

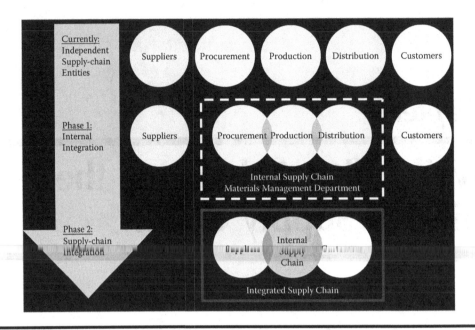

Figure 2.1   Supply chain integration. (Source: Zeng 2005.)

approach is where one party, a channel leader, plays the key role in setting the overall strategy for the channel and in getting channel members involved in and committed to the channel strategy. An example quoted by Cooper et al. is Chrysler. In the analytic optimization approach, an organization, the channel leader, uses computerized modeling to determine the best supply chain configuration for its operations. The example quoted here is Hewlett-Packard. The keiretsu/vertical integration approach has a clear, centralized channel leader. Mitsubishi and Toyota are quoted examples of the keiretsu approach. The method of management differs, depending on the relative strength of the supply chain members and use of technology, such as computerized models for optimization of the supply system (e.g., optimal inventory management).

2.1.2 Collaboration

Effectively managing the increasing warfighter demands and product offerings in complex global supply chains requires good collaboration between all partners in the chain (Table 2.1).

Information collaboration refers to the sharing of information and knowledge among members of the supply chain. They should share demand information, inventory status, capacity plans, production schedules, promotion plans, demand forecasts, and shipment schedules. The members also coordinate forecasting and replenishment.

Resource collaboration refers to the redeployment of decision rights, work, and resources to the best-positioned supply chain member. Shared warehouses, inventory pooling, and supplier hubs are examples of this.

Organizational collaboration is where supply chain partners need to define and maintain their channels of communication, whether those channels involve electronic data interfaces (EDIs), Internet exchange, account teams, or executive briefings. The performance measures for the supply chain members also need to specified, integrated across the chain, and monitored.

Table 2.1 Dimensions of Collaboration

Dimension	Exchanges	How
Information	Data, knowledge	Information sharing, collaborative planning, forecasting, and replenishment
Resource	Decisions, work	Decision delegation, realignment, outsourcing
Organizational	Accountability, risks/costs/gain	Extended communication and performance measurement, realignment

Regardless of the form of the collaboration, relationships between parties may differ, so these factors must be considered and negotiated when developing the partnerships:

- Duration of the relationship (short vs. long term)
- Obligations (the responsibilities, both internal and external to the collaboration, of each partner)
- Expectations (planning goals, performance analysis, and benefits and burdens)
- Interaction and communication (cooperation)

An effective partnership demands commitment from top management. Data and information must be made available to all parties, so some barriers (e.g., confidential practices or sensitive data) must come down. In addition, power and responsibility within an organization might change. For example, contact with customers may switch from sales and marketing to logistics.

2.1.3 Trust

Trust is not something that can be easily measured or identified. The elements of trust will typically vary considerably depending on the situation (Figure 2.2).

It has been said that trust without some kind of vulnerability simply cannot exist, and that trust involves adhering to commitments to others or a stated course of action even if the probability of failure is greater than that of success. Trust is rarely all encompassing. One may trust the partner on some issues but not on others. Mutual trust is based on sharing information, sharing the management of the entire supply chain, and sharing gains or losses (Table 2.2).

Here are some issues that one should avoid:

- *Adverse selection*: Inability to evaluate accurately the quality of the assets the other partner brings to the relationship. It may be difficult to assess whether a supplier's production system is truly capable of meeting your cycle time requirements.
- *Moral hazard*: Inability to evaluate the assets committed when a relationship exists. If a supplier promises to increase the capacity of its system to meet your future requirements, and you have no way of auditing it to ensure that it is actually investing in this capacity, then a moral hazard exists.
- *Asymmetric investment*: Occurs when one partner commits more to the relationship than the other.

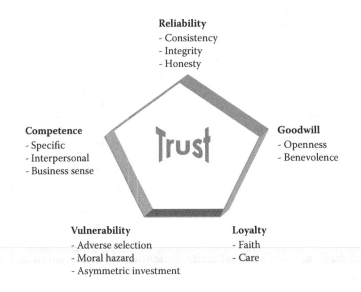

Reliability
- Consistency
- Integrity
- Honesty

Competence
- Specific
- Interpersonal
- Business sense

Goodwill
- Openness
- Benevolence

Vulnerability
- Adverse selection
- Moral hazard
- Asymmetric investment

Loyalty
- Faith
- Care

Figure 2.2   The nature of trust. (Source: Zeng 2005.)

Table 2.2   Power vs. Trust

	The Power Game	*The Trust Game*
Modus operandi	Create fear	Create trust
Guiding principle	Pursue self-interest	Pursue what's fair
Negotiating strategy	Avoid dependence by playing multiple partners against each other. Retain flexibility for self, but lock in partners by raising their switching cost.	Create interdependence by limiting the number of partnerships. Both parties signal commitment through specialized investments.
Communication	Primarily unilateral	Bilateral
Influence	Through coercion	Through expertise
Contracts	Closed, or formal, detailed and short term. Use competitive bidding.	Open, or informal, and long term. Check market prices occasionally.
Conflict management	Through detailed contracts Through legal system	By selecting partners with similar values and increasing mutual understanding Through procedures such as mediation or arbitration

Finally, there are five general rules of thumb for building a trusting relationship:

1. Follow through on commitments, and act in a predictable manner.
2. Choose a partner with a record of experience in the technology. Ensure that the partner is assigning competent, knowledgeable, and experienced people to managing the relationship.
3. Choose an individual who has a high level of knowledge in the technology or function, good people skills, and good commonsense knowledge.
4. Vulnerability needs to be carefully managed by supply partners through information sharing, which ensures the other partner that its interests will be protected.
5. Show genuine responsiveness to your partner's needs, and demand the same of your partner if necessary. Be willing to go out on a limb if the situation requires it.

2.2 Six Steps for Enhancing the Military Supply Chain

The technology-driven supply chain of today is transforming military MRO depots, their suppliers, distributors, manufacturers, and resellers. They are now working together more closely and effectively than ever. Thanks to networked supply chain management (SCM), all of the entities in the supply chain can operate as a unified entity, sharing tasks once isolated. Integrated processes within the supply chain cut down on redundancy and improve efficiency, and this allows you to share timely information about demand, minimize inventories, enhance quality, and improve performance. In addition, a networked supply chain helps you speed turn times through collaboration with suppliers and the warfighter. While the technologies and tools are available, their implementation requires commitment and perseverance. To assist, this section offers an implementation approach (Table 2.3) that builds on the experiences of successful private sector companies and takes into account the special characteristics of the military sustainment environment.

2.2.1 Step 1: Establish an IPT

SCM success and failure are directly related to the degree of top management support and an integrated product team (IPT). Team membership is critical. Key groups of high-level executives with the decision authority and resources must be selected. An executive sponsor is essential, and a key executive leadership role is required. Cross-functional team selection is required for the integration of the principles across functional process barriers. Functional integration must occur within the organization before integrating the extended enterprise. Full-time team membership is highly recommended.

Table 2.3 Six Steps for Enhancing the Military Supply Chain

Step 1	Establish your implementation team.
Step 2	Develop your own supply chain implementation strategy.
Step 3	Measure performance.
Step 4	Design your supply chain.
Step 5	Select and apply best practices and technologies.
Step 6	Manage supply chain implementation.

To obtain cooperation from others outside of the implementation team, present a persuasive argument that shows the benefit to each department. Build a rapport with all participating organizations to become a part of the team. Link rewards and measures to the overall supply chain goals, rather than focusing narrowly on individual functional departments. Include substantive team members from partner organizations. Fragmented organization structures need to be reviewed for possible barriers to progress.

2.2.2 Step 2: Develop an Implementation Plan

The supply chain implementation plan must be a formal document that is credible to management and all stakeholders. An outline of the plan might include:

■ Mission statement
■ Goals and objectives
■ Tasks and processes to achieve goals and objectives
■ Performance goals
■ Risk management
■ Assessment and metrics
■ Plan of action and milestones (POA&M), which should use a phased approach

The Rockford Consulting Group,* as an example, developed an SCM implementation strategy with a closed-loop development effort that includes four stages:

■ Diagnostics and concept development
■ Detailed action planning
■ Capability building
■ Results measurement

Cisco Systems, Inc.,† proposes six stages:

■ *Business assessment and requirements*: Evaluate current supply chain processes, identify a strategic SCM vision, obtain senior management sponsorship, and select specific performance measurements and metrics.
■ *Evaluate and select technology*: Determine the best technology software and hardware to support SCM business needs and strategic vision.
■ *Build model and test*: Connect business process to technology features, referred to as mapping, customizing configurations, and test.
■ *Pilot*: Test technology in a controlled deployment relevant to selected areas of the supply chain.
■ *Training*: Familiarize users with new technology, business tools, processes, and operating activities.
■ *Full deployment*: Implement the full solution to the entire organization.

---

* www.rockfordconsulting.com.
† www.cisco.com.

In both of these cases, the initial strategy-planning step was completed before proceeding with further SCM development.

2.2.3 Step 3: Measure Performance

Performance metrics are important for monitoring the progress of supply chain improvement initiatives. Some in the military sustainment community are not using metrics that reflect twenty-first-century conditions. For example, depots and warehouses are assessed by value and inventory. But, in reality, depots and warehouses move products that are really replenishments. What you measure is what you will achieve! There are ten dimensions to service quality:

1. Tangibles
2. Reliability
3. Responsiveness
4. Competence
5. Courtesy
6. Credibility
7. Security
8. Access
9. Communication
10. Understanding of the customer

Optimal supply chain metrics are required for optimal supply chain design. Significant work has been already accomplished in this area from both government and industry. For example, see the Logistics Management Institute (LMI) report "Supply Chain Management: A Recommended Performance Measurement Scorecard" (LMI 1999).

2.2.4 Step 4: Design Your Supply Chain

This step focuses on describing the supply chain through a graphical representation of the end-to-end process. Computer-aided tools are commercially available to help with the graphics. They range from simple flowchart programs to more complex computer-aided design/computer-aided manufacturing (CAD/CAM) modeling or integrated definition (IDEF) modeling.* The graphical representation would be high level and similar to the one presented in the Supply Chain Council's SCOR model, discussed below. It starts concurrently with step 3. Current metrics are compared to a desired end state, and then a gap assessment is conducted using standardized criteria, such as in the SCOR model.

Unlike a traditional development approach, where an "as is" state is transformed into a "to be" state, begin by establishing an initial baseline structure. Baseline structures are compared to the characteristics and related metrics of a future supply chain design, and then proceed to apply specific business practice changes and metrics in developing the "to be" baseline. More specifically, Table 2.4 presents some recommended actions.

---

* IDEF is a group of modeling methods that can be used to describe operations in an enterprise. IDEF was created by the U.S. Air Force and is now being developed by knowledge-based systems. Originally developed for the manufacturing environment, IDEF methods have been adapted for wider use and for software development in general.

Table 2.4   Recommended Actions for Designing a Supply Chain

Action	Subaction	Description
A-1		Document the future supply chain requirements.
A-2		Create a high-level operational concept document.
A-3		Create an initial "to be" (future) supply chain design.
	A-3-1	Analyze and map the proposed supply chain process elements.
A-4		Validate the "to be" model against the objectives and business practice changes.
	A-4-1	Modify the "to be" diagram and documentation.
	A-4-2	Develop the proposed performance metrics.
A-5		Overlay the future metrics on the "to be" process diagram.
A-6		Create an end-state process description.

2.2.5 Step 5: Select and Apply Best Practice Technologies

Technology is a key enabler, but it has turned out to be more of a fad than reality to some organizations. The application of new technologies has sometimes done more harm than good. Information technology (IT) also doesn't work when it is implemented over an ineffective process. A system-wide technology strategy is required to address many of these issues. IT should support multiple levels of decision making, and it should have a comprehensive view of material flows, information flows, and service flows through the supply pipeline. Seek out and study the best practices in IT from other best-in-class organizations to obtain some lessons learned.

In searching for supply chain technologies, look for these three essential capabilities:

1. Technology that supports day-to-day operations across the entire pipeline
2. Technology that facilitates the logistics planning process, decision making, production support, and shipment processes
3. Technology that supports strategic "what if" analysis, including supply chain network design, configuration, and simulation

One recommendation: The integration and implementation team(s) must prevent a "technologies in search of applications" developmental approach. In other words, don't employ a technology just because it has great features and hope that it will find some application to supply chain management.

2.2.6 Step 6: Manage the Supply Chain Implementation

Obtain senior management's commitment and support to address any existing barriers and their underlying support structures. Assign leaders, goals, milestones, measures, and rewards to processes rather than functions. Deemphasize the functions and instead focus on core processes. Combine the processes into an effective supply chain with linked objectives. Align milestones, measures, and rewards to achieve process and supply chain goals. Use the linked objectives and

Table 2.5 Organizing the SCM Implementation Effort

Process Area	Purpose
Integration team	To ensure compliance with the team's strategy and plan of action and milestones (POA&M)
Supplier development and management	To develop and oversee the collaborative management of suppliers
Organizational development and training	To develop organizational changes to facilities and SCM implementation, and to identify training requirements
Information access and exchange	To identify and coordinate overall SCM information sources and exchange requirements
Customer requirements and interaction	To identify customers and their information, supply chain performance, materials, and service requirements

aligned measures to inspire supply chain participants. Finally, provide the stakeholders with the proper training and resources needed to prosper in the new environment.

The goal is to optimize the entire supply chain. This requires systems thinking, which is a business discipline derived from general systems theory. Optimizing the functional subelements of the chain does not optimize the overall system—these are lessons learned from a decade of business process reengineering. The categorization outline shown in Table 2.5 presents an approach to subdividing the SCM team into focus working level groups and to organizing the SCM implementation effort into logical elements. This approach supports the use of analytical tools, such as the SCOR model.

Does your management structure support supply chain cost reductions? Despite the expense of SCM services and software tools, the vendors promise a synchronized supply chain with the use of their services and products. It would be easy to blame these "masters of supply chain optimization" if the cost reductions are not achieved. But, the reality is that our own policies, management actions or inactions, and organizational structures hold the root causes for unsuccessful SCM initiatives.

2.3 Redesigning the Military Logistics Network

To support the warfighter and the MRO depots, the military must create and maintain the most efficient supply chain logistics network that is possible. The design of this network is strategically important. The number and location of the distribution centers, the transportation strategies, and the information technologies are major determinants of supply chain performance. Strategic supply chain design and analysis must consider a wide range of alternatives, including site locations, product mix, transportation, inventory deployment, suppliers, cost service levels, constraints, and supply chain operations.*

For years, researchers and practitioners in supply chain management have primarily investigated the various processes within manufacturing supply chains individually. Recently, however, there has been increasing attention placed on the performance, design, and analysis of the logistic network as an enterprise. This attention is largely a result of the rising costs of manufacturing and MRO, diminishing manufacturing sources and resources, shortened product life cycles, and the globalization of

---

* The Supply Chain Results Company (www.i2.com).

the supply chain. The current interest has sought to extend the traditional supply chain to include reverse logistics, to include product recovery for the purposes of recycling, remanufacturing, and reuse. Within manufacturing research, the supply chain concept grew largely out of two-stage multi-echelon inventory models, and it is important to note that considerable progress has been made in the design and analysis of two-echelon systems. Generally, multistage models for logistics network design and analysis can be divided into four categories, by the modeling approach. The modeling approach is driven by the nature of the inputs and the objective of the study. The four categories are:

1. Deterministic analytical models, in which the variables are known and specified
2. Stochastic analytical models, where at least one of the variables is unknown, and is assumed to follow a particular probability distribution
3. Economic models
4. Simulation models

The interested reader is referred to Beamon (1998) for reviews of models of this type.

An important component in logistics network modeling and analysis is the establishment of appropriate performance measures/metrics. A performance metric, or a set of performance metrics, is used to determine the efficiency and effectiveness of an existing system, or to compare competing alternative systems. Performance metrics are also used to design proposed systems, by determining the values of the decision variables that yield the most desirable level(s) of performance. Available literature identifies a number of performance metrics as important in the evaluation of supply chain effectiveness and efficiency. These measures can be categorized as either qualitative or quantitative and are listed in Table 2.6 (Beamon 1998).

Table 2.6 Performance Measures Used in Logistics Network Design Models

Category	Performance Metric	Description
Qualitative performance metrics (Qualitative performance measures are those measures for which there is no single direct numerical measurement, although some aspects of them may be quantified.)	Customer satisfaction	The degree to which customers are satisfied with the product or service received; may apply to internal customers or external customers.
	Flexibility	The degree to which the supply chain can respond to random fluctuations in the demand pattern.
	Information and material flow integration	The extent to which all functions within the supply chain communicate information and transport materials.
	Effective risk management	All of the relationships within the supply chain contain inherent risk. Effective risk management describes the degree to which the effects of these risks are minimized.
	Supplier performance	With what consistency suppliers deliver raw materials to production facilities on time and in good condition.

Table 2.6 (Continued)

Category	Performance Metric	Description
Quantitative performance metrics (Quantitative performance measures are those measures that may be directly described numerically.)	Cost minimization	The most widely used objective. Cost is typically minimized for an entire supply chain (total cost), or is minimized for particular business units or stages.
	Sales maximization	Maximize the amount of sales dollars or units sold.
	Profit maximization	Maximize revenues less costs.
	Inventory levels	Minimize average inventory levels.
	Inventory investment minimization	Minimize the amount of inventory costs (including product costs and holding costs).
	Fill rate maximization	Maximize the fraction of customer orders filled on time.
	Stock-out	Minimize stock-out probability.
	Product lateness minimization	Minimize the amount of time between the promised product delivery date and the actual product delivery date.
	Customer response time minimization	Minimize the amount of time required from the time an order is placed until the time the order is received by the customer; usually refers to external customers only.
	Lead time minimization	Minimize the amount of time required from the time a product has begun its manufacture until the time it is completely processed.
	Demand variation	Minimize product demand variance or demand amplification.
	Function duplication minimization	Minimize the number of business functions that are provided by more than one business entity.
	Buyer-supplier benefit	Maximize buyer-supplier benefit (e.g., Shared Savings).
	Supply chain capacity	Maximize available system capacity.

Source: Adapted from Beamon 1998.

In modeling the logistic network design, the performance metrics are expressed as functions of one or more decision variables. These decision variables are then chosen in such a way as to optimize one or more of these performance measures. Some of the decision variables used are (Beamon 1998):

- Distribution center (DC)–customer assignment: Determining which DC(s) will serve which customer(s).
- Plant-product assignment: Determining which plant(s) will manufacture which product(s).
- Buyer-supplier relationships: Determining and developing critical aspects of the buyer-supplier relationship.
- Product differentiation step specification: Determining the step within the process of product manufacturing at which the product should be differentiated (or specialized).
- Number of product types held in inventory: Determining the number of different product types that will be held in finished goods inventory.
- Production/distribution scheduling: Scheduling the manufacturing and distribution.
- Inventory levels: Determining the amount and location of every raw material, subassembly, and final assembly storage
- Number of stages (echelons): Determining the number of stages (or echelons) that will comprise the supply chain. This involves either increasing or decreasing the chain's level of vertical integration by combining or eliminating stages or separating or adding stages, respectively.

Each military MRO depot can be conceived of as a decentralized center that is connected to a centralized hub or a major distribution center that, in turn, distributes supplies. If end items are in need of repair parts, the technology is available to signal low stock (i.e., kanban) for that particular repair part, so it can be reordered instead of waiting for carcasses. Having a centralized materials and parts distribution system does reduce both safety stock and average inventory, and overhead costs are lower. However, lead times in getting the stock to the customer can be higher in centralized systems if the distribution channels are not fast. MRO depots are used to having some amount of stock on hand when they repair a system. Imagine opening up a system that needs to be repaired and discovering that a part is needed and not on the shelf. If it takes 1 or 2 days at best for the part to arrive from a centralized warehouse, the system has to be put aside until the part arrives. This is the lead time that contributes to the awaiting parts (AWP) problems that the depots have been experiencing. Increasing the number of distribution centers does improve customer service levels due to the reduction in average travel time. However, inventory cost is increased in a decentralized system due to increased safety stock requirements to protect against uncertainties in demands, and total network overhead and setup costs are also increased. Transportation cost is, of course, dependent on the configuration of the network. Thus, the question is: How does one determine the optimal logistic network design for military sustainability? A solution adopted by the Defense Logistics Agency (DLA) is to use good modeling, that is, decision support systems (DSS) as well as IT modernization. DSS are used to address various problems, from strategic problems such as logistics network design to tactical problems such as assignment of products to distribution centers. DSS are also used to analyze the day-to-day operational problems like production scheduling, product delivery, and shipment planning.

Over the past several years, DLA has been using DSS models and IT to overhaul the processes and technology used to ensure timely delivery of supplies to the military. The effort is a 6-year, $751 million IT modernization project that rivals the largest ever undertaken in the business world, and is punctuated by the urgency of an ongoing global conflict. Among the challenges are the replacement of customized legacy systems with off-the-shelf software, finding ways to use technology to evolve business processes aimed at making government more responsive, and gaining the high-level management support needed to achieve long-term goals. DLA has been unrolling pieces of this DSS and IT modernization project for years. By the time the project wraps up, DLA hopes to have changed its entire logistics network design and overall strategy from warehousing to real-time delivery. It will use data culled from radio frequency identification (RFID) tags. The new system is intended to provide a big-picture view of military demands, as well as the ability to work more efficiently with suppliers to meet those demands. It can track what's in the supply chain on an item-by-item basis and get a close-up view of what's being consumed, the rate of consumption, and the cost of certain types of procurements. In the end, the six thousand or so staffers at DLA will have access to new software and IT to help them forecast demand and procure the 5 million items the DLA supplies as well as manage fifty-four thousand orders a day.*

2.4 Information Technology Enhancements

Supply chain management principles span the entire enterprise, from suppliers to the customers. The internal and external information requirements are different for each entity within this enterprise-wide value chain (interagency). The information requirements for the functional departments within each organization (intra-agency) are also different. The timeliness and availability of this information are critical. Most IT systems in the military MRO community are diverse and disconnected across the enterprise. They are, in essence, islands of information. But the information flow across the entire supply chain enterprise is critical. Rapid advances in information technology are changing SCM practices and business rules. This section will introduce the latest IT solutions for SCM, but their implementation will require cultural and structural changes in the military supply chain community.

2.4.1 The Goal

The primary goal for SCM information technology is to link point of purchase or production seamlessly with the point of delivery. Specific goals are to:

1. Collect information on each part, material, and end item from production or purchase point to delivery, and to provide its complete visibility in the supply network
2. Access any data in the system from a single point of contact
3. Analyze, plan activities, and make trade-offs based on information from the entire supply chain
4. Have the information trail follow the product's physical trail

The flow of information and the flow of products in the chain currently are in reverse of each other (Figure 2.3). The goal is to have the information trail *follow* the product's physical trail. Real-time data are required for effective supply chain planning and management. For the most part, military MRO information systems tend to be islands. Different information systems were established for different purposes (e.g., item management, demand forecasting, resource scheduling), and they are not coordinated or integrated outside their functional areas. In an ideal supply chain world, the goal would be to have real-time data available to everyone in the network through any interface device, whether it is a workstation, laptop computer, or handheld device, like a personal digital assistant (e.g., PalmPilot). The information technology infrastructure is critical in the success or failure of any system implementation, and IT forms the base for SCM data collection, transactions, system access, and communication.

---

* Larry Greenemeier, "Supply-Chain Management: Real-Time Readiness Gets a New Look," TechWeb, June 2, 2005. http://www.techweb.com/news/showArticle.jhtml?articleID=163700159. Retrieved September 10, 2008.

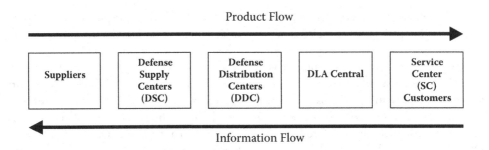

Figure 2.3 Flow of information and products in the chain. (Source: Adapted from Simchi-Levi et al. 2000, p. 223.)

2.4.2 The Infrastructure

The components of a supply chain IT infrastructure are the interface/presentation devices, communications, databases, and the systems architecture.

2.4.2.1 Interface Devices

Some commonly used data interface devices include personal computers, voice mail, Internet devices, bar code scanners, and personal digital assistants. To automatically capture data, bar code readers and radio frequency identification (RFID) tags are becoming increasingly popular. Product tracking is accomplished through the bar codes, RFID tags, and Global Positioning Systems (GPS).

There are two competing standards for all of these devices:

1. Wintel standard: Window interface on Intel-based computers
2. Java and Web browser standard: Internet application interface standard

In addition, enhanced graphics interfaces that include geographic information technology and three-dimensional graphics displays are operationally integrated with the GPS receivers.

2.4.2.2 Communications

For communications between the supply chain network agencies, the interface devices mentioned above are connected through an internal system (e.g., local area network, mainframe, or Internet). There are two trends emerging in communications:

1. Wireless technology is replacing many landline/hardwired communication links.
2. Advanced SCM enterprises are establishing one single point of contact for all global access communications.

2.4.2.3 Databases

Database management systems (DBMS) organize software information into data structures. The types of information include:

■ Transaction information
■ Status information

Table 2.7   Types of Supply Chain Management Databases

Legacy database	Hierarchical or network database. Stores large amounts of data and performs extensive processing. Online and batch components, cumbersome to use.
Relational database	Data stored in related structures that allow standardized reporting and querying; example is Structure Query Language (SQL).
Object database	Allows objects to store different types of data, such as graphs or numeric information. Allows unlimited database processing and operations. Expensive. Requires high-end processing hardware and software management and maintenance capability.
Data warehouses	These databases combine data from other systems to allow query by sophisticated analysis tools.
Data mart database	Same as data warehouse, except smaller and more localized.
Groupware database	Specialized for group activities and may be extended with many new application software, such as CAD/CAM and configuration management.

- General information
- Forms and templates
- Group collaboration information

There are six types of databases (Table 2.7).

2.4.2.4 Systems Architecture

Systems architecture is the configuration structure of the IT components for the supply chain network, such as the databases, interface devices, and communications. The interfaces define the relationships between the components for information processing and flow. The design is based upon how the components are integrated to form the IT infrastructure. Supply chain network architectures include the hardware, the software, and the middleware, and local area networks and wide area networks (LANs and WANs).

In legacy SCM systems, mainframes or minicomputers are used and the data are accessed either through dumb terminals that just allow input and output or personal computers (Figure 2.4).

Advanced SCM network designs have switched from their legacy system architecture to client/server computing (Figure 2.5). Client/server architectures are distributed processing in which the client is the PC and the main processor is the server. Local applications reside with the client, and central applications reside with the server.

Internet architectures are another form of advanced SCM network design. It is a type of client/server architecture with the PC providing client (local browser) applications in retrieving server (World Wide Web) applications. The middleware is the application that resides between the client and server and facilitates communication between different system architectures, communication protocols, and hardware architectures. Internet architectures are best used to collect data and format them in a way that can be used globally. The advantage is that the Internet allows greater interoperability across applications and hardware platforms, and the enterprise does not

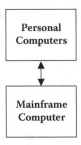

Figure 2.4 Legacy system architecture. (Source: Adapted from Simchi-Levi et al. 2000, p. 232.)

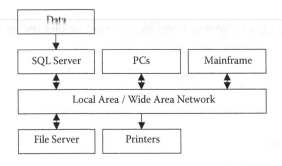

Figure 2.5 Client/server system architecture. (Source: Adapted from Simchi-Levi et al. 2000, p. 232.)

need a LAN or WAN for middleware. The disadvantage of the Internet architecture for a military SCM application is that it is not a secure system in terms of distributing classified data. But better encryption schemes are quickly eliminating this concern.

2.4.3 Standardization

The big push in SCM network design is toward the use of open system standards. There are good reasons for standardization:

- Economies of scale: Standardization means a reduced price for SCM software applications, whether these applications are commercial off the shelf (COTS) or designed specifically for military specifications (MILSPEC).
- Interconnectivity: Standardization means the use of available plug-and-play SCM software models and applications.

Open system architectures and open interface standards have been developed for supply chain management to enable different modules and systems to interact at a higher level than just file exchanges that are found in legacy systems. The best example of open system architecture is enterprise resource planning (ERP) systems, which create an enterprise backbone that integrates the forecasting, operations, scheduling, and financial systems. ERP developers are also using open interface standards so that third-party application software, such as transportation and distribution optimization models, can be integrated into the ERP platform.

2.5 Software Enhancements

The three emerging trends in software are:

1. Comprehensive software packages with a wide range of functionality
2. Strategic planning software
3. Collaboration software standards and packages that allow the entities in the chain to share information in real time

2.5.1 Comprehensive Software Packages

Enterprise resource planning (ERP) packages have now become the backbone systems for supply chain planning and scheduling. Standard modules include operations, scheduling, financial, purchasing, payroll, human resources, and other administrative functions. Central common databases are used to allow communications across functional modules, and the latest systems are adding warehouse management and other functionality.

2.5.2 Strategic Planning Software

Originally used for planning and scheduling manufacturing operations, supply chain planning (SCP) has recently moved into the distribution and warehousing world. This strategic planning tool is used to deploy inventory at the right price and right time to the right place. Modules range from demand and inventory planning to supply chain network design.

2.5.3 Collaboration Software Standards and Packages

There are five types of software in this category.

2.5.3.1 Order Management Systems (OMS)

Order management systems manage the relationship between the organization and the customer. They receive, validate, process, price, prioritize, expedite, and invoice customer orders. They also act as a bridge between planning and execution: the last step in the former and the first step in the latter.

2.5.3.2 Customer Relationship Management (CRM)

Customer relationship management packages automate the customer service functions. Some of the functions include the management of customer inquiries, technical support calls, Web inquiries, and requests for service, information, or services, such as order status, asset visibility, or account inquiries.

2.5.3.3 Manufacturing Execution Systems (MES)

Manufacturing execution systems integrate the flow of materials and work in process (WIP) with the production process. They uses dynamic real-time processing, compensating for shifts in production machine availability, inventory levels, order priorities, and labor. MES accept forecasts, cost, and planning information from the enterprise resource planning and supply chain planning systems. MES balance these data with what is really happening on the shop floor, making decisions "on the fly."

2.5.3.4 Warehouse Management Systems (WMS)

Warehouse and distribution center applications manage the inventory, order fulfillments, materials handling equipment (MHE), and labor. These systems dynamically direct and control all activities in the warehouse and distribution centers from receiving to shipping. The data that are collected automatically update the central databases, initiate billing (bill of materials), and initiate electronic data interchange status messages for customers.

2.5.3.5 Transportation Management Systems (TMS)

The goal of transportation management systems is to manage the transportation network and minimize shipping cost. Their primary functions include labor management in the shipping department, load planning and building, and shipping scheduling. They also manage inbound, outbound, and intracompany shipments with an eye on the lowest possible cost without sacrificing customer service or trading partner requirements (e.g., just-in-time inventory contracts).

2.6 Case Study: The SCOR Model

One way to better enhance the military supply chain is to use a process reference model. What is a process reference model? Process reference models integrate the well-known concepts of business process reengineering, benchmarking, and best practices into a cross-functional framework (Figure 2.6). The Supply Chain Council* (Supply Chain Council 2008) created a process reference model called SCOR (Supply Chain Operations Reference). SCOR is a framework for examining a supply chain in detail, defining and categorizing the processes that make up the supply chain, assigning metrics to the processes, and reviewing comparable benchmarks. As a process reference model, SCOR combines the well-known concepts of business process reengineering with benchmarking, best practices, and process measurement into a framework for executing a supply chain project. The most important aspect is its ability to measure strategy. The SCOR model is presented here because it is the only model that links metrics to individual supply chain functional processes, and it has been recognized[†] as an effective tool for translating strategy into supply chain

---

* The Supply Chain Council was organized in 1996 by Pittiglio Rabin Todd & McGrath (PRTM) and AMR Research as an organization for those interested in applying and advancing state-of-the-art supply chain management systems and practices. The council now has about a thousand corporate members worldwide, consisting primarily of practitioners representing a broad cross section of industries, including manufacturers, services, distributors, and retailers.
† The Logistics Management Institute (LMI) identified, evaluated, and adopted the SCOR model in 1999 to propose a set of balanced measures that senior decision makers in the DoD can use to monitor supply chain effectiveness.

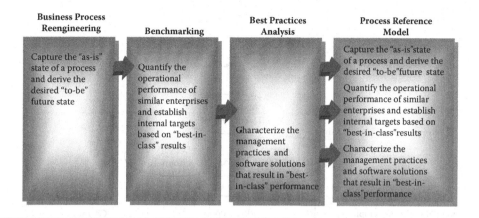

Business Process Reengineering	Benchmarking	Best Practices Analysis	Process Reference Model
Capture the "as-is" state of a process and derive the desired "to-be" future state	Quantify the operational performance of similar enterprises and establish internal targets based on "best-in-class" results	Characterize the management practices and software solutions that result in "best-in-class" performance	Capture the "as-is" state of a process and derive the desired "to-be" future state Quantify the operational performance of similar enterprises and establish internal targets based on "best-in-class" results Characterize the management practices and software solutions that result in "best-in-class" performance

Figure 2.6 A process reference model. (Source: Supply Chain Council 2008.)

Table 2.8 SCOR Model Processes

Plan	Processes that balance aggregate demand and supply for developing the best course of action that meets established business rules. These processes include the demand/supply planning elements, resource planning, demand requirements, inventory planning, distribution requirements, production/MRO scheduling, and capacity planning for all systems, subsystems, and supply channels.
Source	Processes that procure goods and services for meeting planned or actual demand. These processes include material and parts procurement.
Make	Processes that transform goods to a finished state for meeting planned or actual demand. These production and execution processes are the maintenance, repair, and overhaul functions in the depots and in the field.
Deliver	Processes that provide finished goods and services, including order management, transportation management, and warehouse management, for meeting planned or actual demand.
Return	Processes that return defective or incorrect components or systems.

Source: Supply Chain Council 2008.

performance goals. Hundreds of enterprises use the SCOR model to understand and improve their supply chains. They include aerospace and defense manufacturers, large consumer product manufacturers, and third-party logistics providers. Thus, the SCOR model is widely accepted and applied in industry and may be adopted by the American National Standards Institute as a standard supply chain process model. SCOR defines a supply chain as the integrated processes* of Plan, Source, Make, Deliver, and Return. Table 2.8 defines these processes. They span the entire chain and are aligned with operational strategy, material, work, and information flows.

Figure 2.7 depicts the five processes (plan, source, make, deliver, and return) of the SCOR model at the top level of the supply chain thread. This figure has been modified from the original design for military MRO activities.

---

* The Supply Chain Council defines processes as a grouping of activities (functions) that, taken together, result in a fully completed action in support of a customer.

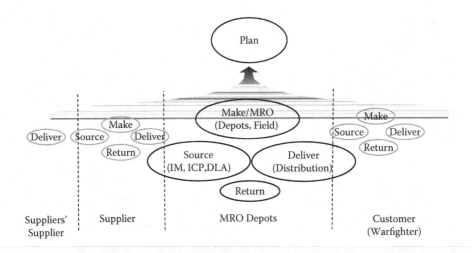

Figure 2.7 SCOR is structured around five distinct processes. (Source: Supply Chain Council 2008.)

Table 2.9 The Three Levels in the SCOR Model and an Implementation Level

Level	Description	Comments
1	Top Level: Process Types	Level 1 describes the scope and content for the SCOR model. This is the level where performance targets are set.
2	Configuration Level: Process Categories	At Level 2, a supply chain can be "configured to order" from approximately 24 core "process categories." This is the level where the operations strategy is configured and implemented.
3	Process Element Level: Decompose Processes	Level 3 consists of: • Process element definitions • Process element information input and output • Process performance metrics • Best practices • System capabilities required to support the best practices
4	Implementation Level: Decompose Process Elements	Level 4 defines the specific supply chain management practices.

Source: Supply Chain Council (2008).

From this top level, the model continues two more levels of processes and subprocesses: the configuration level and the process element level. Table 2.9 shows all three levels; it gives a small schematic to show how they relate to each other, and defines what each level means. At the bottom of Table 2.9 is the implementation level, where the specific supply chain practices are implemented.

Table 2.10 Performance Attributes and Metrics for Level 1

Performance Attribute	Definition	Metrics
Supply Chain Delivery Reliability	The performance of the supply chain in delivering the correct product, to the correct place, at the correct time, in the correct condition and packaging, in the correct quantity, with the correct documentation, to the correct customer.	Deliver Performance Fill Rates Perfect Order Fulfillment
Supply Chain Responsiveness	The velocity at which a supply chain provides products to a customer.	Order Fulfillment Lead Times
Supply Chain Flexibility	The agility of a supply change in responding to change.	Supply Chain Response Time Production Flexibility
Supply Chain Costs	The costs associated with operating the supply chain.	Costs of Goods Sold Total Management Costs Value-Added Productivity Warranty / Returns processing Costs
Supply Chain Asset Management Efficiency	The effectiveness of an enterprise in managing assets to support demand. This includes fixed and working capital.	Cash-to-Cash Cycle Time Inventory Days of Supply Asset Turns

Source: Supply Chain Council (2008).

For each level in the SCOR model, the Supply Chain Council recommends performance measures be established for each process. As an example, Table 2.10 provides the metrics for level 1.

A good reference for additional performance measures is the Logistics Management Institute (LMI) report "Supply Chain Management: A Recommended Performance Measurement Scorecard" (LMI 1999). The reason that LMI's report talks about a scorecard is that the Supply Chain Council recommends that a balanced SCORCard and gap analysis be done on the supply chain processes. Table 2.11 presents an example.

To implement SCOR, the council provides a project road map. The road map is divided into four segments:

1. Analyze your basis of competition, which focuses on operations strategy and defines the performance.
2. Configure your supply chain material flow, which maps out the high-level material flow.
3. Align performance levels, practices, and systems of your information workflow, which maps the general transaction flow.
4. Implement the supply chain changes based on the design and organize the list of projects to improve SC performance.

The road map is illustrated in Figure 2.8.

By following the SCOR project road map, the enterprise will identify disconnects in its supply chain planning process that must be resolved through supply chain optimization methods.

Table 2.11   Example Balanced SCORCard and Gap Analysis

	Overview Metrics	SCOR Level 1 Metrics	Performance vs. Competitive Population			Actual Performance
			Parity	Advantage	Superior	
External	Supply chain reliability	Fill rates	+10%	+15%	+20%	
		Awaiting parts	−10%	−15%	−20%	
	Responsiveness	Order fulfillment	35 days	25 days	15 days	
		Lead times	20 days	15 days	10 days	
	Flexibility	Response to change	30 days	25 days	20 days	
Internal	Cost	Total cost				
		Inventory cost				
	Productivity	Fill rate	+10%	+15%	+20%	
	Customer satisfaction	Stock-out	−10%	−15%	−20%	

Why use the SCOR model? The Supply Chain Council provides these reasons:

■ Communicate with current and potential vendors using common terminology and standard descriptions.
■ Use the model as a planning and forecasting tool.
■ Leverage metrics and benchmarking to determine performance goals, set priorities, and quantify the benefits of a process change.
■ Link functional and process metrics to enterprise performance in a structured way.
■ Understand the best practices to obtain the best performance.
■ Understand supply chain management and evaluate performance.
■ Identify the software tools best suited for Department of Defense (DoD) processes.

What is the value of the SCOR model? Bauhof (2004) reports these costs and benefits:

■ Two to six times return on investment within 12 months
■ Full leverage of capital investment in systems
■ Creation of an investment road map
■ Alignment of business requirements with central functions
■ Self-funding of technology investments

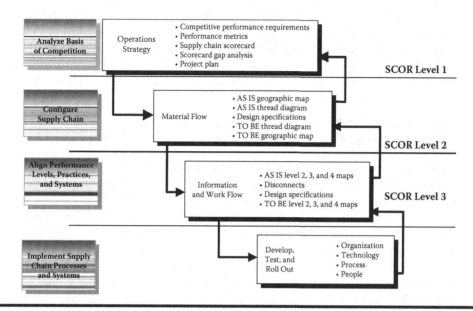

Figure 2.8   SCOR project road map. (Source: Supply Chain Council 2008.)

The most important aspect is its ability to measure the supply chain strategy. Some enterprises are good at creating strategy, but very few are good at measuring the success or failure of strategy. Measuring strategy, of course, implies that the enterprise develops a strategy and follows it. However, rarely is it measured. That is one of the primary values of the SCOR model—it's an effective tool for translating strategy into supply chain performance goals. It helps prioritize supply chain needs, drives implementation, and links performance metrics to operating and financial metrics (Bauhof 2004).

2.7 Case Study: The PRISM Model

The U.S military uses requirements definition and forecasting (RDF) models to forecast depot maintenance requirements, to forecast serviceable replacement unit (SRU) and consumable parts requirements, and to plan, schedule, and implement depot workloads and budgets. However, the military is experiencing problems due to the inaccuracy of these forecasts (GAO 2000). First, there are substantial budget problems due to unanticipated increases in maintenance and material requirements. For example, millions of dollars of assets are backlogged in awaiting parts (AWP) status (GAO 1999). Second, 35% of the parts and materials backlogs are classified as first time failures (GAO 2001a). Third, the Defense Logistics Agency (DLA) does not normally maintain safety stock levels for most high-cost, low-volume consumable components that are not designated safety stock items. Finally, DLA does not maintain supplier contracts or inventory for components that do not have a significant historical usage.

The RDF process is critical to military sustainability, maintenance, repair, and overhaul (MRO) operations on critical weapon systems (aircraft, ships, motor vehicles, weapons, and their subsystems). Improving RDF accuracies will greatly enhance MRO operations by minimizing material and parts shortages. Increased accuracy would also help improve warfighter operations by correctly predicting maintenance and logistics requirements necessary to meeting specified readiness levels. Very little research has been conducted on military requirements forecasting. Thus, this case study investigates a reliability-based approach model for RDF called PRISM. More research should be conducted in several areas to effectively improve military RDF. Thus, this case study investigates a reliability-based approach model for RDF called PRISM that integrates empirical field data into physics of failure models to predict end-of-life failure modes and rates.

2.7.1 Current Requirements Forecasting in the Military: The U.S. Air Force Process

Military depot repair requirements have traditionally been determined based on planning forecasts using worldwide reparable generation averages and asset positions that are months old. By example, for the U.S. Air Force prior to a recent Lean Logistics initiative, work that was done in the depot shops was managed in quarterly batches. For each item, the manager started with an estimate of the number of serviceable assets that needed to be repaired during the next quarter. The item manager then had to negotiate this requirement with the production management specialist and scheduler to determine how much of the work could be done by the production shop in that quarter. The negotiation attempted to reflect available carcasses plus anticipated reparable generations, and then it was typically adjusted, using expert judgment, to reflect skills and parts availability, shop capacity, and workload objectives. The scheduler's problem was that there were many batches for many different items sharing the same production resources. There is an imperative to schedule work to meet local efficiency targets, such as labor hour utilization. Once an item was made serviceable, distribution was usually made by responding to the oldest requisition first within priority groups, a practice that may or may not have reflected the most urgent current operational need (Dynamics Research Corporation 1977).

Even in peacetime, there is an inherent element of uncertainty in Air Force operations that impacts logistics support requirements. Weather disrupts training schedules and flying hours, and demand rates for spares vary from unit to unit, and even within the same unit at different times. Wartime operations introduce far more uncertainty. Threats can change rapidly, as can the availability of aircraft, aircrews, ground support personnel, facilities, munitions, fuel, and spares. It was perceived that the current methods did not provide responsive depot support to current and near-term operational requirements in peacetime. Furthermore, it was perceived that the current methods would not be responsive to future changing operational requirements or uncertain events in wartime.

The Air Force Lean Logistics initiative and logistics reengineering efforts focused on key depot processes for the purpose of improving and streamlining operations while increasing the level of support and responsiveness to customer needs. Depot repair was one of the primary processes involved in these activities. Thus, the Execution and Prioritization of Repair Support System (EXPRESS) was designed and developed to automate the depot repair program and identify repair requirements, prioritize repairs, perform supportability analysis of repair resources, and deliver front-line repair recommendations. The system takes a daily view of the customer needs and repair requirements using inputs on current global assets and the operational flying program (via the MAJCOM scenario subsystem) and identifies what should be repaired (prioritization), what can be repaired (supportability), and the distribution recommendations (Figure 2.9).

The Air Force uses the EXPRESS forecasting system to perform the majority of the requirements definition forecasting (RDF) processes for organic depot maintenance activities (Mathaisel

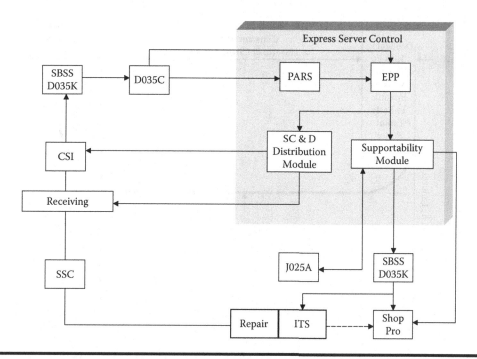

Figure 2.9 The EXPRESS system. (Source: U.S. Air Force 2000.)

1998). The process incorporates manual inputs from equipment specialists to improve the EXPRESS forecast accuracy (U.S. Air Force 2000). As a result, line repairable unit (LRU) predictions from EXPRESS are approximately 75% accurate (Mathaisel 1999). The component-level predictions, however, are approximately 25% accurate. The decrease in the percentage of prediction accuracy is due to the smaller sample rate, associated with the larger number of components contained in the LRUs. Component-level prediction methods are developed from MRO procurement history and equipment failure analysis data.

2.7.2 The Disadvantage of Current Military RDF Methods

Current military RDF methods use historical trends to forecast future repair requirements. This approach puts the forecasts at a disadvantage because equipment failure rates are different for each life cycle phase (Figure 2.10).

Traditional forecasting methodologies that are based on historical trends are only appropriate for steady-state operations observed during the useful life phase of the life cycle. The failure rate during that useful life cycle phase is constant, and equipment reliability design objectives are based upon the expected life. However, as equipment ages beyond the design life, the failure rate increases exponentially (RAC 1999a). The wear-out life cycle phase will vary depending on the type of system and operational profile (Blanchard and Fabrycky 1998). End-of-life equipment failure modes are different than those experienced during normal equipment life. Current RDF processes do not capture or predict changing failures due to end-of-life failure modes early enough to forecast change (equipment is being kept in service due to an increase of operational schedule). A greater number of AF systems are being extended beyond design life, and the forecasting accuracy is expected to decrease while equipment failure rates dramatically increase (RAND 1999).

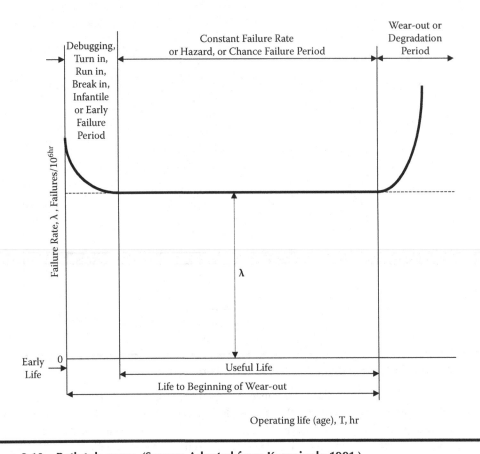

Figure 2.10   Bath tub curve. (Source: Adapted from Kececioglu 1991.)

The U.S. Air Force and the Defense Logistics Agency have since established "aging aircraft" programs to help manage these problems.

2.7.3 Commercial Reliability-Based Requirements Forecasting

Reliability-based RDF methods are not uncommon in the commercial sector. Aerospace, telecommunications, medical devices, information technology, automotive, and nuclear power are commercial industries that use reliability-based methods to support logistics operations, remanufacturing, and warranty programs to design and sustain fielded systems (Bothwell et al. 1996; Hecht 1998; Kelly 1999). For example, Honeywell Electronics in Phoenix, Arizona, developed a new methodology for in-service reliability assessment that has greatly increased RDF accuracy (Gullo 1999, 2000; Mathaisel 2001a). The Honeywell in-service reliability assessment program utilizes depot failure analysis conducted during routine depot overhauls to update reliability models. As the reliability models are updated, the new predictions are used to develop engineering design changes and to change logistics and maintenance support strategies to optimize total ownership cost and operational readiness.

Many of the industries using reliability-based RDF have developed their own reliability-based standards and methods. All these standards use prediction refinement methods by integrating empirical field data into the original reliability models (RAC 1999a).

2.7.4 PRISM

Traditional methods of reliability predictions state that the failure rate of a system is determined by the components within the system. However, the Reliability Analysis Center (RAC) of Rome, New York, determined that approximately 80% of system failures are the result of noncomponent causes, namely, design deficiencies, manufacturing defects, poor system management (system engineering), wear-out, and software-induced and no-defects-found failures. In light of this finding, a need for a new methodology to properly address these contributing factors had to be developed. The U.S. Air Force contracted with RAC to develop this new methodology to address these shortcomings in reliability predictions. In response to this request, RAC developed a new tool called PRISM (Denson et al. 1998; Denson and Keene 1998; RAC 1999b).

PRISM utilizes available data to form the best estimate of reliability. It can be tailored to the problem, has confidence bounds that can be verifiable, and is sensitive enough to address the primary reliable drivers. It adopts a broader scope in predicting reliability (RAC 2001; Dylis and Proire 2001). It factors in all available reliability data as they become available from field, test, and analysis data from the current system. The goals of PRISM are to (Denson et al. 1998):

- Estimate system failure rates and their variance
- Explicitly recognize and account for special (assignable) cause problems
- Model reliability from the user (or total system level) perspective
- Provide an intuitive reliability model structure
- Promote cross-organization commitment to reliability, availability, and maintainability (RAM)
- Qualitatively grade developer efforts to affect improved reliability
- Maintain continuing organizational focus on RAM throughout the development cycle
- Integrate all RAM data that are available at the point in time when the estimate is performed (analogous to the statistical process called meta-analysis)
- Provide flexibility for the user to customize the reliability model with historical data
- Impact (positively) the product development process and the resulting developed product

A functional block diagram (Figure 2.11) of PRISM has been developed to assess the potential applications for its use in military RDF processes. The figure characterizes the necessary inputs, processes, and outputs expected from the model.

PRISM is used to determine the feasibility in achieving a reliability goal or requirement. It aids in achieving a reliable design (i.e., derating component selection, environmental precautions, and input to fault trees). It also predicts warranty costs and maintenance support requirements. PRISM also has a grading process and factors, which are identified in Table 2.12 for each separate category.

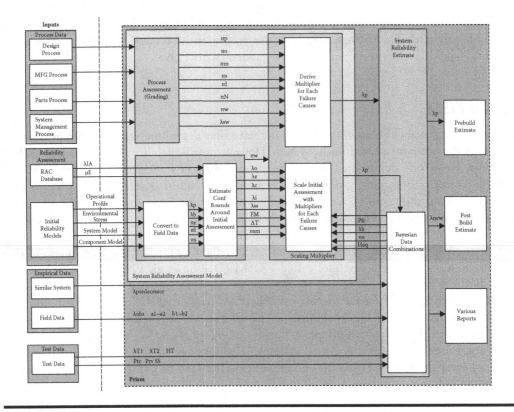

Figure 2.11   PRISM functional block diagram.

Table 2.12   Process Grading Categories (Adapted from Denson et al. 1998a)

• Design	• Engineering skill
	• Technology maturity
	• Design margin and optimization
	• Design for manufacturability
	• Development process
	• Development process matrix
	• Development documentation
	• System complexity
	• Product testing
	• Engineering design automation
	• Tools
• Manufacturing	• Design for manufacturing
	• Personnel characteristics

Table 2.12 (Continued)

	• Data and analysis
	• Manufacturing leadership
	• Manufacturing process
	• Testability
	• Technology
	• Solder joint spacing
• Parts management	• Part selection criteria
	• Parts supplier criteria
	• Custom part support
	• Critical part support
• System management consideration	• Requirements management
	• Requirements extensibility
	• Product vision
	• Requirements traceability and verification
	• Interface management
	• Operational management
	• Change management
	• Risk management
• Could not duplicate or no defect found	• Design considerations
	• Analysis and process considerations

2.8 Conclusion: Successful vs. Unsuccessful Supply Chain Initiatives

Successful supply chain management initiatives combine both strategic and tactical changes. Successful initiatives also view the supply chain from end to end, and orchestrate the implementation effort so that the whole improvement—in revenue, cost, and asset utilization—is greater than the sum of its parts enterprise-wide.

Unsuccessful initiatives tend to be functionally defined, narrowly focused, and lacking in a sustaining infrastructure. Uncoordinated change activity erupts in every department and function, and this uncoordinated activity puts the enterprise in great danger of "dying the death of a thousand initiatives." The source of failure is seldom in identifying what needs fixing. The issue is determining how to develop and execute a supply chain transformation plan.

For a successful deployment of an SCM initiative, Cisco Systems* offers a sound recommendation. Consider these five areas before your deployment:

Strategy: You need a clear understanding of your supply chain and how it contributes to your overall objectives, such as improved product quality and customer satisfaction.
- Which SCM components are applicable to your organization?
- What are your objectives, short term and long term, for deploying an SCM solution?
- Does senior management support this strategy?

Process: Your business must define the policies and procedures of your supply chain. This process includes an end-to-end understanding of vendors, customers, channels, operations, and integration capabilities.
- What part of your supply chain is on the most critical path? Which part is the most inefficient?
- What are the strengths and weakness of your supply chain?
- Do you use DLA, local supply, or other resources?
- Are you willing to extend the supply network?

People: Training, organizational culture, and organizational structure must support changes in your supply chain processes. Management and department buy-in are crucial to success. As your supply chain evolves and activities become more integrated, the importance of cross-departmental teams becomes a necessity.
- Can you train and staff a team to support the solution on a continuous basis?
- Will your employees commit to the deployment of an SCM solution?
- How can your culture and organizational structure evolve to support cross-functional teams that are affected by changes in your supply chain?

Technology: Reliable, scalable, and secure SCM applications and tools are essential for creating a successful supply chain. SCM solutions should enable effective supply chain business processes, but they are not quick fixes for any supply chain problems.
- How well equipped is your technological network to support supply chain automation applications?
- How scalable, reliable, and secure is your computer network?

Service and support: In addition to people and technology, you may want to consider outside services for rapid deployment (planning, design, and implementation) and operation of your SCM solution.
- Can I reduce my turn time or my costs if I hire a services organization with expertise and experience deploying SCM solutions, rather than training my staff to perform this task?
- How can I proactively identify and resolve problems?
- How will I migrate my system to higher levels of performance?

Because of the multiple facets of a complete SCM solution, a phased approach is recommended. Deployment timing varies depending on the needs and size of your initiative, and the size of your partner network (Cisco 2008).

---

* www.cisco.com. Note: The author revised the Cisco recommendations for military sustainment operations.

References

Bauhof, Ned. 2004, August. SCOR model: supply chain operations reference model. *Beverage Industry* 95(8).

Beamon, Benita M. 1998. Supply chain design and analysis: Models and methods. *International Journal of Production Economics* 55:281–94.

Blanchard, Benjamin S., and Wolter J. Fabrycky. 1998. *Systems engineering and analysis*. 3rd ed. Englewood Cliffs, NJ: Prentice Hall.

Bothwell, Rod, Rao Donthamsetty, Zygmunt Kania, and Ronald Wesoloski. 1996, January. Reliability evaluation: A field experience from Motorola's cellular base transceiver systems. In *Proceedings of the Annual Reliability and Maintainability Symposium*, pp. 348–59.

Cisco Systems, Inc. 2008. www.cisco.com. Retrieved September 15, 2008.

Cooper, Martha C., Lisa M. Ellram, John T. Gardner, and Albert M. Hanks. 1997. Meshing multiple alliances. *Journal of Business Logistics* 18:67–89.

Denson, William K., and Dr. Samuel Keene. 1998a, January. A new reliability prediction tool. In *Proceedings of the Annual Reliability and Maintainability Symposium*, pp. 15–22.

Denson, William K., Dr. Samuel Keene, and Joseph Caroli. 1998b, January. A new system reliability assessment methodology. In *Proceedings of the Annual Reliability and Maintainability Symposium*, pp. 413–20.

Dylis, D. David, and Mary Gossin Proire. 2001. PRISM: New models and methodologies for electronic system reliability assessment. Presentation of the Reliability Analysis Center, Rome, NY.

Dynamics Research Corporation (DRC). 1977, November. *Execution and prioritization of repair support system: Operational concept document.*

Gullo, Lou. 1999, January. In-service reliability assessment and top-down approach provides alternative reliability prediction method. In *Proceedings of the Annual Reliability and Maintainability Symposium*, pp. 365–77.

Gullo, Lou. 2000, October. In-service reliability assessment using similarity analysis and failure cause model provides accurate MTBF predictions. *Reliability, Maintainability, & Supportability* 4(3).

Hecht, Myron. 1998, January. The need for measurement based reliability evaluation. In *Proceedings of the Annual Reliability and Maintainability Symposium*, pp. 216–17.

Kececioglu, Dimitri. 1991. *Reliability engineering handbook*. Vol. 1. Englewood Cliffs, NJ: Prentice Hall.

Kelly, Jeffrey B. 1999, January. Medical diagnostic device reliability improvements and prediction tools— Lessons learned. In *Proceedings of the Annual Reliability and Maintainability Symposium*, pp. 29–31.

Klapper, L.S., Hamblin, N., Hutchison, L. Novak, L., and Vivar, J. 1999, June. *Supply Chain Management: A Recommended Performance Measurement Scorecard*, Logistics Management Institute, Report. LG803R1.

Mathaisel, Dennis F. X. 1998, May. *EXPRESS: Execution and prioritization of repair support system*. White Paper. Lean Sustainment Initiative, Sustainment Operations Team, Center for Technology, Policy, and Industrial Development, Massachusetts Institute of Technology, Cambridge, MA.

Mathaisel, Dennis F. X. 1999. *On the relationship between EXPRESS and Air Force objectives and metrics: A case study*. Lean Sustainment Initiative, Sustainment Operations Team, Center for Technology, Policy, and Industrial Development, Massachusetts Institute of Technology, Cambridge, MA.

Mathaisel, Dennis F. X. 2001, June. *Defense Logistic Agency trip report*. Lean Sustainment Initiative, Sustainment Operations Team, Center for Technology, Policy, and Industrial Development, Massachusetts Institute of Technology, Cambridge, MA.

Pyles, Raymond A. 1999, February 24. Aging aircraft: Implications for programmed depot maintenance and engine-supported costs. Testimony presented to the Procurement Subcommittee of the House Armed Services Committee, RAND. CT-149, 10.

RAND. 1999. *Aging aircraft: Implications for program depot maintenance and engine support cost*. Santa Monica, CA.

Reliability Analysis Center (RAC). 1999a. Reliability predictions methods and overview. *Journal of the Reliability Analysis Center*, 7(3): 8–11.

Reliability Analysis Center (RAC). 1999b. A tutorial on PRISM. *Journal of the Reliability Analysis Center.*

Reliability Analysis Center (RAC). 2001, July. PRISM project overview. Presentation of the Reliability Analysis Center, Rome, NY.

Simchi-Levi, David, Philip Kaminsky, and Edith Simchi-Levi. 2000. *Designing and managing the supply chain: Concepts, strategies, and case studies*. New York: McGraw-Hill.

Supply Chain Council. 2008. http://www.supply-chain.org. Retrieved September 14, 2008.

U.S. Air Force. 2000. *EXPRESS (D087X) V3.5 and Shop Pro (D087S) V4.0 operational concept description (OCD)*. Wright-Patterson AFB, OH.

U.S. General Accounting Office (GAO). 1999, April. *Air Force supply management actions create spares parts shortages and operational problems. GAO/NSIAD/AIMD-99-77*. Report to the Chairman, Subcommittee on Military Readiness, Committee on Armed Services, House of Representatives. Washington, DC.

U.S. General Accounting Office (GAO). 2000, August. *Air Force depot maintenance: Budgeting difficulties and operational inefficiencies*. GAO/AIMD/NSIAD-00-185. Report to the Chairman, Subcommittee on Military Readiness, Committee on Armed Services, House of Representatives. Washington, DC.

U.S. General Accounting Office (GAO). 2001a, June. *Air Force inventory: Part shortages are impacting operations and maintenance effectiveness*. GAO-01-587. Report to Congressional Committees. Washington, DC.

Zeng, Amy Z. 2005. Supply chain analysis and design. Department of Management, Worcester Polytechnic Institute, Course Material OIE 544.

Chapter 3

Operational Availability

Preface

The operational availability (Ao) of warfighting materials and systems is key to the U.S. Department of Defense's (DoD) ability to prevail on the fields of battle. History has shown that the military that can launch the most weapons (or sorties) wins the battles. Consider the following theoretical scenario:

> The Navy has 148 of a certain type of weapon for performing a mission that is considered essential to national defense. The Navy needs all 148 of these weapons to be mission-ready to satisfy mission requirements. Originally, over 200 of these weapons were procured, because it was generally believed that some ±50 would be down for scheduled and corrective maintenance. Currently, only 75 to 80 are available. Why? Because repair parts are in short supply for this aging weapon system, which causes a 50% operational availability (Ao) condition. Failure rates have increased over time and many needed parts are no longer manufactured unless special ordered. The cost of parts is high, and lead times are long. These weapons still perform the mission well at a cost of $10 million each per year to maintain and operate. System and parts obsolescence, along with diminishing manufacturing sources or resources, is expected to become worse each year.
>
> The fleet user has let the sponsor know that they are drafting a mission needs statement (ICD) stating a need for a replacement weapon system, since their demands for improved Ao have not yet yielded the required results. The sponsor and fleet representative have been discussing some new technology that industry is now offering. They are considering how many of the newer, more reliable systems it would take to replace the existing system.
>
> The reader has been asked for an opinion considering the following information. Alternative system A (S_A) costs $30 million per copy, and the vendor says it can achieve 85% availability based on the current design plans. Alternative system B (S_B) costs

55

$28 million per copy, and the vendor promises 80% readiness. Both of these modern systems offer much better operational availability than the current system is experiencing. The vendor for S_A reports that it is estimated that the system will require $5.5 million per system per year to operate and maintain (he will offer a warranty for this price). The vendor for S_B says a similar warranty will cost $7 million per system per year.

Which system, S_A or S_B, should be procured? How many systems should be bought? To answer these questions, the sponsor needs to define three parameters in a set of response documents: number of systems to procure, the operational availability (Ao) requirement, and the expected life cycle cost (LCC) for the weapon system. Then the sponsor needs to ensure that the selected system will fulfill its promise of both Ao and LCC when it is delivered to the user (assume an operational life of 40 years).

This chapter was prepared to help program sponsors, sustainment program managers, and other stakeholders deal with such challenging scenarios. The chapter discusses the process of developing and evaluating operational availability (Ao) thresholds; discusses the requirements, capabilities, methods, and tools that program sponsors and program managers need in order to guide the actions of the Ao analysis teams; contains guidelines on what these teams and technical support agencies need; and contains Ao objectives, models, and documentation for each phase of the sustainment of a system. Chapter 9 in this book provides the economic foundation for the life cycle cost (LCC) estimates that are required to answer the economic questions that are raised during the operational availability evaluation process.

3.1 Introduction to Operational Availability

Weapon systems are described in terms of a number of important performance parameters in today's performance-based business environment. Examples of many of these parameters are listed in Figure 3.1. Some will be identified as key performance parameters (KPPs) for specific programs, and all are important to a systems engineering design. This chapter concentrates on three of these parameters: reliability, maintainability (R&M), and certain aspects of logistics. These three are the drivers of operational availability (Ao), which is used during the systems engineering phase of a system's design, and which influences the design for readiness, supportability, and life cycle affordability.

These points are provided as a preview of the major issues that will be addressed in this chapter:

- The project sponsor (e.g., the Navy), with assistance from the system developer (e.g., the defense contractor), needs to establish tentative Ao thresholds during early project studies and must document these and other KPPs in requirements documents to form the basis for decision support analysis reported to project decision authorities.
- Ao has relevance only when linked with KPPs, such as those shown in Figure 3.1.
- Systems effectiveness (SE), which is the direct link to warfighter requirements, provides the basic foundation on which the entire system acquisition decision support process is based.
- Ao, as defined and used in this chapter, is a relatively simple concept. Underlying the Ao index, however, are a large number of supporting assumptions, data relationships, and linkages. These linkages are not only far more specific but also far more complex than the basic Ao index seems to imply.

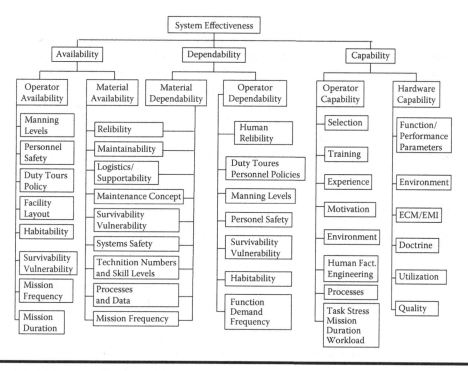

Figure 3.1 System performance parameters.

- To understand and effectively evaluate Ao during the systems acquisition process, the resource sponsor and others must become familiar with the separate components of the Ao index. These are reliability, in terms of mean time between failures (MTBF); maintainability, in terms of mean time to repair (MTTR); and supportability, in terms of mean logistics delay time (MLDT).

- Every effort should be made to explicitly consider each element of the Ao index in early threshold development and throughout the system life cycle.

- In the preproject study period (i.e., concept exploration), the resource sponsor and others should concentrate on the integrity and soundness of the warfighter's mission or systems effectiveness requirements established for the system.

- In the early project phases (concept and technology development phases), the resource sponsor and others should focus the greatest effort on refining the MTBF estimate at the system level. Because MTBF has the greatest impact on Ao, early improvement of this metric will pay high dividends later.

- By the middle project phases (system development and demonstration), specific Ao thresholds must be proposed by the program manager, included in the related program documentation, and approved by the resource sponsor. These Ao thresholds should be based on specific and, as required, system-unique consideration of supportability concepts and MLDT.

- Prior to the later project phases (system production and deployment), the resource sponsor must confirm (through system tests and related documentation) that the Ao threshold (and other KPPs) for the system is achievable in the actual fleet environment in which the system is expected to operate.

■ During the sustainment and maintenance phase, the resource sponsor must continue to monitor Ao to ensure that the demonstrated system Ao continues to meet the user's requirements. Where deficiencies exist, the support organization must put in place plans and programs to remedy the deficiencies and to bring the system Ao to meet the user's needs.

■ Throughout the systems acquisition and life cycle process, the resource sponsor should understand the data supporting Ao estimates, the methods used to analyze the data, the assumptions, and potential deficiencies. Sensitivity analysis and risk analysis should be integral parts of the resource sponsor's evaluation procedures. The questions and processes discussed in this chapter will assist the resource sponsor and others in guiding the required activities.

3.1.1 Definition of Ao

The *availability* of an item or system is a measure of the degree to which the item is in an operable state at the start of a mission when the mission is called for at an unknown (random) point in time. *Operational availability* (Ao) is defined as the probability that the system will be ready to perform its specified function in its specified and intended operational environment when called for at a random point in time. It is a percentage value: the percent of the total time that a system is expected to be operational.

$$\text{Ao} = \frac{\text{Hours that the Product is in Customer's Possession and Works}}{\text{Total Hours that the Customer Owns the Product}} \tag{3.1}$$

Ao also refers to the percent of a total fleet of systems that is expected to be operational during a reporting time period. In practical terms, availability has been defined as the ability of a product (or service) to be ready for use when the customer wants to use it. It is available if it is in the customer's possession and it works whenever it is turned on or used. If the product is in maintenance, repair, or overhaul, or the product is in the customer's possession, but it doesn't work, then it is also not available. The above definition is the classic simplified description of availability. To be useful, the concept needs quantification in order to either measure and analyze Ao requirements or demonstrate a system's performance. There are specific equations that are commonly used in its analysis. They are presented in Section 3.2 as it applies to a variety of system types. It is also important to understand that Ao only becomes useful in designing systems for readiness when the Ao value is allocated to each subassembly and component in the system.

3.1.2 Historical Perspective

The material in this chapter was initially developed to address a critical consideration in the design, development, and deployment of a combat system. The material in this chapter originally appeared as a practical guide for the acquisition of military systems under acquisition reform (Manary 2001). That consideration was and is the combined consideration of Ao and life cycle costing at all levels of systems acquisition and design-related decision making. This updated version of the material incorporates the tenets of acquisition reform, and provides additional clarity.

Common use of terms is essential. The military has defined *material readiness* as one of two prime figures of merit (FOMs) to be used for acquisition program decision support. The first FOM is Ao, which is the equivalent of material readiness or hardware availability as it is shown in Figure 3.1. The second FOM is total ownership cost (TOC) of the system or equipment under consideration. TOC is equivalent to system life cycle cost (LCC), the subject of the affordability chapter (Chapter 10) in this volume.

Material readiness overtook LCC as the prime DoD metric in the 1970s. The DoD issued a policy statement that defined material readiness as equivalent to Ao. During this period, under existing DoD integrated logistics support (ILS) concepts, major weapon systems were entered into the fleet and encountered severe readiness and supportability problems. ILS appeared to exist in policy only. In many cases, the fleet did not receive required logistics support resources. This is still often the case today. "Get well" efforts for newly deployed systems were becoming a standard practice and were consuming funds intended for more advanced systems. To determine why the military had an ILS policy but did not have ILS products in the fleet, a logistic review group (LRG) was created.

In their earliest ILS audits, the LRG found that there was no common approach to setting and evaluating material readiness requirements. The LRG further found that programs generally lacked any substantive link between their readiness requirements, the reliability levels specified by contract, and their logistic resources and planning necessary to achieve the required readiness in the fleet. Principally as a result of the early findings of the LRG, Ao was adopted as the primary measure of material readiness in the military, and it continues as such to this time. Supportability factors, including Ao, are to be integral elements of program performance requirements that relate to a system's operational effectiveness, operational suitability, and life cycle cost reduction.

3.1.3 Why Is Ao Important?

Ao requirements drive sustainability requirements and, therefore, life cycle support costs. Ao is determined by the level of reliability inherent in the design of a specific system and the supportability resources needed to achieve a desired level of operational readiness. When only inherent reliability and maintainability (R&M) are considered, the result is inherent availability (Ai). Because inherent R&M create downtime in operational use, logistic resources must be applied in increasing levels to limit additional downtime due to real-world logistic delays. When logistic delays are considered together with inherent R&M, the result is Ao. These concepts are touched upon repeatedly throughout this chapter. This repetition is a good thing, because the topic itself and its analysis are parts of iterative and repetitive processes rather than a single event, and each instance of coverage is intended to be from a different perspective in terms of levels of detail, level of the system work breakdown structure (WBS) being considered, and phase-related goals of the analysis.

Ao satisfies the classic definition for a good measure of effectiveness (MOE) and figures of merit (FOMs). Why? Because:

■ Ao represents the viewpoint of the stakeholders, i.e., those who have the right and responsibility for imposing the requirements on the solution.
■ Ao assists in making the right choice by indicating how well a solution meets the stakeholders' need.
■ Ao is quantifiable.

Blanchard (1998) states that an effectiveness FOM is appropriate in the evaluation of alternatives when decisions involving design and logistics support are necessary. Ao meets Blanchard's criteria for an effectiveness FOM.

There are many candidate trade-off parameters in the capability, dependability, and availability areas, as illustrated in Figure 3.1. The customer (the user/operator) and the sponsor will evaluate measures of performance (MOPs) or a system on many of these parameters to narrow the space to useful and acceptable alternatives. Then, systems engineers and analysts will model the alternatives considering the elements of material availability to support a decision to select the solution that best meets the customer's requirements. Figure 3.1 also shows how the performance parameters are related. Operational capability (Co) refers to the system's operating characteristics (range, payload, accuracy, and the resultant ability to counter the threat); it is the ability to counter the threat, in terms such as system performance, probability of kill, etc. Operational availability (Ao) refers to the probability that the system will be ready to perform its specified function, in its specified/intended operational environment, when called for at a random point in time. Operational dependability (Do) refers to the probability that the system, if up at the initiation of the mission, will remain up throughout the mission. Operational capability, operational availability, and operational dependability must be defined relative to the specific warfare environment and operating scenario envisioned for a given system. Combined, they determine system effectiveness (SE). The system effectiveness of a specific system in part determines the effectiveness of the ship or aircraft platform on which it is installed.

3.2 The Mathematics of Ao

There are specific equations that are commonly used in the analysis of Ao and its individual elements. These equations provide analysts and decision makers with the necessary tools and common logic for determining if Ao estimates are accurate and how each of the controllable components of Ao contribute to, or limit, a system's Ao.

3.2.1 Uptime/Downtime Equations

Generally, Ao is interpreted as the percentage of time that the system will be ready to perform satisfactorily in its intended operational environment. Uptime is defined as the element of active time during which an item is in condition to perform its required functions. Downtime is the element of active time during which an item is not in condition to perform its required functions. If it is not capable of functioning, it must be down either for maintenance or for logistics-related delays. The sum of a system's uptime and downtime, referred to as total time, is a period of time specified for potential system use. Using a system's uptime and downtime, an alternative definition to Ao that is frequently used is

$$\text{Ao} = \frac{\text{Uptime}}{\text{Total time} = \text{Uptime} + \text{Downtime}} \tag{3.2}$$

Although the above equation provides a more accurate expression for Ao, it has two major deficiencies:

1. Uptime and downtime can only be measured for a system in an operational inventory and are not measurable for a system in development.

2. If the Ao measured using this equation is less than the threshold required, the equation does not assist an analyst in determining what to do to increase the Ao.

To determine the causes and potential solutions of inadequate Ao, the components of uptime and downtime must also be defined and quantified. In particular, the effects on uptime and downtime on these controllable factors must be determined:

■ Reliability: The probability that an item can perform its specified function for a specified time interval under stated conditions. Reliability is controllable primarily by design and secondarily by ensuring that a system is used in the manner for which it was designed.
■ Maintainability: The measure of the ability of an item to be retained in, or restored to, operable condition when maintenance is performed by personnel having skill levels, using prescribed procedures and resources, at each prescribed level of maintenance and repair.
■ Supportability: The ability to satisfy material and administrative requirements associated with restoring the operation of a failed system/equipment to an operable condition.

To illustrate this definition of Ao, Figure 3.2 represents the operation of a theoretical system in terms of its uptime and downtime. The total uptime would be 10 hours, and the downtime would be 6 hours:

$$\text{Uptime} = U(1) + U(2) + U(3) + U(4) \tag{3.3}$$

$$= 2 \text{ hrs} + 2 \text{ hrs} + 3 \text{ hrs} + 3 \text{ hrs} = 10 \text{ hrs}$$

$$\text{Downtime} = D(1) + D(2) + D(3) + D(4) \tag{3.4}$$

$$= 2 \text{ hrs} + 2 \text{ hrs} + 1 \text{ hr} + 1 \text{ hr} = 6 \text{ hrs}$$

The average uptime and downtime would be

$$\text{Average Uptime} = \frac{10 \text{ hours}}{4 \text{ failures}} = 2.5 \text{ hours}$$

$$\text{Uptime/Failure} = \text{Mean Time Between Failures (MTBF)} \tag{3.5}$$

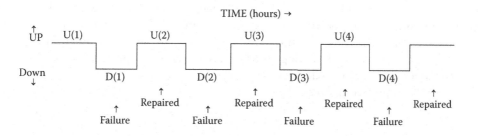

Figure 3.2   A theoretical system's uptime and downtime.

$$\text{Average Downtime } = \frac{6 \text{ hours}}{4 \text{ failures}} = 1.5 \text{ hours } \quad \text{Downtime / Failure} = \text{Mean Downtime (MDT)} \qquad (3.6)$$

Thus, using uptime and downtime, the measured Ao for this system is derived as

$$Ao = \frac{\text{Uptime}}{\text{Total Time}} = \frac{\text{Uptime}}{\text{Uptime} + \text{Downtime}} = \frac{10}{10+6} = .625 \qquad (3.7)$$

3.2.2 Mean Time between Failures Equations

Table 3.1 describes common variations on the uptime and downtime basic formula for Ao. The most common variations use mean time between failures (MTBF). One variation for the measured Ao would be

$$Ao = \frac{\text{MTBF}}{\text{MTBF} + \text{MDT}} \qquad (3.8)$$

where MTBF is the mean operating time between (successive) failures and MDT is the mean downtime per failure. MTBF is the quantitative measure of system reliability (i.e., the duration of failure-free performance under stated conditions). MDT is the quantitative measure of system downtime. MDT is broken down into two separate increments of time: (1) the time necessary to repair a failed system at the organizational level when all the resources (manpower and spare parts, for example) are available, and (2) the additional delay caused by the logistics support for the system (for example, the time required to obtain a replacement part from the supply room, the time awaiting trained personnel, or the time necessary to repair failed systems at the intermediate or depot level). The average time required to repair a system in its operating environment (when necessary resources are available) is called mean time to repair (MTTR). The average time delay caused by the logistics support system is called mean logistic delay time (MLDT).

MTTR is a quantification of inherent "designed in" system maintainability, and MLDT is a quantification of supportability that is defined to include personnel, repair at other levels, supply support, transportation, and other logistics delays not attributable to actual hands-on maintenance time (i.e., MTTR). These quantifications can be made by various methods during various phases of development (and with varying degrees of accuracy). These quantifications allow prediction of the Ao for a system in development.

The formula for predicting Ao can be written as

$$Ao = \frac{\text{MTBF}}{\text{MTBF} + \text{MTTR} + \text{MLDT}} \qquad (3.9)$$

Table 3.1   Variations on the Uptime/Downtime Formula for Ao

Inherent availability, A_i	$A_i = \dfrac{MTBF}{MTBF + MTTR}$	Ensures operation under stated conditions in an ideal customer service environment (no delays experienced while maintenance is being performed). It excludes: • Preventive or scheduled maintenance (i.e., battery replacement, oil change, etc.) • Logistics delay times (i.e., filling out paperwork) A_i is usually not specified as a field-measured requirement, since the customer service environment is rarely ideal. • Insufficient number of spare parts • Long delays to obtain repair parts • Inadequate training of repair personnel • Excessive administrative requirements
Achieved availability, A_a	$A_a = \dfrac{MTBM}{MTBM + MTTR \text{ active}}$	• Similar to A_i, except that preventive and scheduled maintenance actions are factored into the uptime variable (MTBM). The corresponding preventive and scheduled maintenance times are included in the $MTTR_{active}$ parameter. • A_a is usually not specified as a field-measured requirement, since the downtime factor does not consider the routine logistics and administrative delays that occur during normal field conditions.
Operational availability, A_o	$Ao = \dfrac{MTBM}{MTBM + MDT}$	• Extends the definition of A_i to include delays due to waiting for parts or processing paperwork in the downtime parameter (MDT). • Ao reflects the real-world operating environment, thereby making it the preferred and most readily available metric for assessing quantitative performance. • Ao is usually not specified as a manufacturer-controllable requirement without being accompanied by estimates of the logistics resources and administrative delays, induced failures, etc., which are government driven and beyond the manufacturer's control.

MTBF = Mean time between failures.
MTTR = Mean time to repair.
MTBM = Mean time between maintenance.
MTTR active = Mean time to repair for corrective and preventive maintenance.
MDT = mean downtime, which includes mean logistics delay time (MLDT), mean admin delay time (MadmDT), and other delays.

This general formula can be used to relate to the determining elements: reliability (MTBF), maintainability (MTTR), and supportability (MLDT). The result of Equation 3.9 is not as accurate as the result of Equation 3.8 for measuring Ao. Measurements usually do foil predictions. However, this does have advantages:

■ The use of MTBF to approximate uptime and the use of MTTR and MLDT to approximate downtime provide both the analyst and decision makers with discrete variables that can be individually managed and modified, regardless of the developmental stage of the system.
■ Using MTBF, MTTR, and MLDT provides a sufficiently accurate approximation of Ao to use for certain quick estimate purposes throughout the system's life cycle.

The truest measure of Ao is expressed in this formula:

$$\text{Ao} = \frac{\text{MTBF}}{\text{MTBF} + \text{MTTR} + \text{MLDT} + \text{MAdmDT} + \text{MOADT}} \tag{3.10}$$

where MAdmDT is the mean administrative delay time and MOADT is the mean awaiting outside assist delay time. Both are an index of system supportability. This expression of Ao is the truest measure because it includes the MAdmDT and MOADT metrics. It is useful throughout the life cycle of the system from concept development through disposal. In this process, the factors affecting each variable are categorized and quantified. The analyst has established a mathematical relationship for Ao that is dependent upon MTBF, MTTR, MLDT, MAdmDT, and MOADT, and a process for evaluating the effects of changes to a specific variable on the Ao.

3.2.3 Specific Systems Equations

Because systems are used in different ways, the measurement and interpretation of Ao vary from system to system. For purposes of Ao measurement and analysis, systems are divided into three classes (defined in terms of the way a system is used):

1. *Continuous-use systems*: Systems that are (nearly) always in use during operations of their host platforms. Examples are radars, radio receivers, cockpit displays, and propulsion gas turbines.
2. *Intermittent-use (noncontinuous or on-demand) systems*: Systems that have relatively long periods of standby or inactivity between uses. Examples are landing gear assemblies and auxiliary power units (APUs).
3. *Impulse (single-shot) systems*: Expendables that are generally used once, not repairable, or not returned to an operable condition. Missile systems are an example.

It may be difficult to classify systems according to continuous, intermittent, or impulse use, but this classification is required if Ao is to be computed consistently.

3.2.3.1 Continuous-Use Systems

For continuous-use systems, mean calendar time between failures is identical to mean operating time between failures, and use of MTBF in the Ao formula is consistent with the notion of measuring uptime in terms of calendar time. This notion is critical since all downtime is measured in calendar time. Therefore, the following equation provides an acceptable approximation of Ao in terms of reliability, maintainability (R&M), and supportability:

$$\text{Ao} = \frac{\text{MTBF}}{\text{MTBF} + \text{MTTR} + \text{MLDT}} \qquad (3.11)$$

3.2.3.2 Intermittent-Use Systems

For intermittent-use systems, mean operating time between failures is not equivalent to mean calendar time between failures. Thus, MTBF must be adjusted. Two ways of displaying the Ao equation with this adjustment are now being used. For aircraft systems, it is common to use

$$\text{Ao} = 1 - \frac{\text{MTTR} + \text{MLDT}}{\text{K'(MTBF)}} \qquad (3.12)$$

where K' is defined as total calendar time over total operating time. It is the inverse of the proposed utilization rate. For ship systems, an equation similar to Equation 3.12 has been constructed where K' is redefined to exclude downtime from calendar time. This term, defined as K", is

$$\text{K"} = \text{K'} - \frac{\text{MTTR} + \text{MLDT}}{\text{(MTBF)}} \qquad (3.13)$$

Equation 3.12 can now be written for intermittent-use systems as

$$\text{Ao} = \frac{\text{K"(MTBF)}}{\text{K"(MTBF)} + \text{MTTR} + \text{MLDT}} \qquad (3.14)$$

Both K' and K" have been termed K-factors, and this has led to confusion. The user should check this factor before using the equations to make sure that the correct K-factor is used. K' is only valid in Equation 3.12; K" is only valid in Equation 3.14.

3.2.3.3 Impulse Systems

The above formulas are not appropriate for impulse systems. Since these systems are generally not recoverable once they are used, the concept of downtime has little significance. As a result, the

Ao of impulse systems is quantified as the fraction of attempts at usage (firings, turn-ons, and actuations) that succeed. The formula is

$$Ao = \frac{\text{Number of Successes}}{\text{Number of attempts}} \qquad (3.15)$$

While there is some parallel between impulse cases and those associated with continuous-use and intermittent-use systems, the distinction is that an impulse system spends most of its time in standby, alert, or secured mode, is called upon to function for a relatively short time, and is generally not restored to operable condition once it is used.

3.3 Models for Ao

The equations for Ao have been translated into computer models. For decades, effective logistics managers have used three of these models as part of the supportability analysis process: the level of repair analysis (LORA) model, the sparing to availability (STA) model, and the life cycle cost (LCC) model. Each military service has developed its own instantiation of these models and has published guidance on their use. For example, COMPASS (Computerized Optimization Model for Predicting and Analyzing Support and Structures) is the U.S. Army's version of the LORA model. LORA is the U.S. Navy Naval Air Systems Command (NAVAIR) version. The reader is encouraged to search the publicly available literature for these models. This section is meant to introduce the reader to the basics of the LORA and STA models. Chapter 10 on affordability discusses the LCC model.

3.3.1 Level of Repair Analysis (LORA) Model

The purpose of the LORA model is to solve for the lowest life cycle cost repair level for each of the repairable candidates in a subsystem work breakdown structure (WBS). LORA is normally run at the subsystem level, such as a radar set or propulsion system. Inputs to the model include the system hardware information in terms of reliability, maintainability, weight, cube, volume, etc. Also, input is data concerning logistics element resources needed to repair each of the candidates at each of the three levels of maintenance: operational (O), intermediate (I), and depot (D). The model performs this sequence of calculations:

1. LORA assumes that all candidates are nonrepairable and are discarded upon failure at the O-level. Considering failure rates and the time to obtain a replacement spare from the source, the model calculates how much of an assembly must be kept at each O-level site to satisfy requisitions. The model stores all costs for each repairable candidate.
2. The model assumes all repairable candidates are sent to the depot for D-level repair. The model calculates all logistics elements required to repair each candidate. The model again stores all of these costs by repairable and integrated logistics support (ILS) element. This includes the reduced number of spares now needed at the O-level.

3. Next, the model assumes all repairable candidates are repaired at the I-level with subassemblies and repair parts going to the depot for repair. All of these costs are stored by repairable and ILS element.

4. The model then optimizes the repair level by comparing the relative costs for each repairable candidate for each of the options—discard at O, repair at D, and repair at I—and selecting the least cost option for each repairable candidate.

5. The model selects the least cost option for each candidate and prints out a comprehensive report for consideration by the analyst and lead logistician. The report shows the cost of each logistics element for each of the alternate maintenance schemes, such as the categories shown in Table 3.2.

The model assists the logistician in assigning a source, maintenance, and recoverability (SM&R) code, which defines where an item is removed and replaced (R&R) and where it is repaired. This key information is published in planning documents to guide logistics planners, and it also becomes the input data for the Ao models.

3.3.2 Sparing to Availability (STA) Model

Ao is essentially an O-level issue. It concerns keeping the operational end item or system up and ready for use at any random point in time. When a system experiences a component failure, how quickly can the right spare part be identified and obtained, the failed part removed and replaced, and the system retested? The rest of the logistics infrastructure (I- and D-levels of maintenance) exists to ensure that the right number of organizational spares is always available when needed. The exceptions are scheduled maintenance, such as a depot overhaul, and supply of operational consumables, such as fuel, ammunition, and food.

An STA model needs essentially the same input data as the LORA models, except that the operational tempo, logistics infrastructure, and hardware information at the O-level are fed into the model. STA calculates the number of each type of spare part to be kept at each O-level site in order to satisfy an Ao target value. The model essentially divides the spares budget target by the failure rate for each spare part candidate. This creates an index representing readiness per dollar spent for each part. The part with the highest index is selected. The calculations and selections are repeated until the Ao target is reached.

Some LORA models, such as COMPASS, contain an embedded STA model. Some LCC models, such as the Cost Analysis and Strategy Assessment (CASA) model, also include an STA

Table 3.2 Alternate Maintenance Schemes

	Main-tenance Man-hours	Spares	Support Equipment	Technical Publications	Training	Transpor-tation	Other	Total
All discard								
All depot								
All I-level								
Optimized								

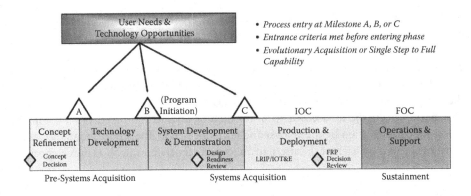

Figure 3.3   The DoD 5000 model.

component. These features allow the analyst to use the models for their primary functions plus produce a spares budget to Ao curves.

An example of an STA model is the Aircraft Sustainability Model (ASM) by Logistics Management Institute Government Consulting. The ASM sparing model, a system-oriented approach to spares management, bases spares requirements explicitly on each item's effect on overall system performance, as well as the item's unit cost. The ASM sparing model measures system performance in terms of Ao, the probability that the system is not inoperative for lack of a spare. Potential spares buys can be ranked in terms of benefit divided by cost as a measure of the desirability of adding them to the inventory.

3.4 Mission Profile

Mission profile is a chronological description of the significant events in a system's life cycle. The profile has an important bearing on the system's Ao. Thus, its definition is addressed here to highlight its importance to the project team's system design concept, selection, and specification efforts. Sometimes, the terms *mission profile* and *environment profile* have tended to be used interchangeably or synonymously, while at other times an actual or implied distinction is made between the two. Here, mission profile and environmental profile are considered as two separate steps in the generation of a single integrated mission and environmental profile. This separation aids in an orderly and methodical profile derivation. A mission profile addresses the events that are expected to occur and to have a bearing on the equipment's useful life. The environmental profile addresses the natural and induced environments associated with the mission profile events. A mission profile includes:

- System mode
- Function
- Related equipment
- Success criteria
- Function time
- Environment
- Environment time
- Maintenance constraints

Another confusing aspect of mission profile is the tendency to only consider the active mission phase of a system's life profile. For example, in the case of a missile, the mission profile is usually just the flight portions of the system's life cycle. However, the nonflight periods of a missile's life are just as meaningful as the flight periods in terms of degradation stresses impacting reliability and readiness. Consequently, there is a need to consider the mission of a system from the time of factory acceptance to the end of its useful life. As an example, Figure 3.4 illustrates the phases of the life cycle profile for a missile system.

In order to limit confusion with mission connotations, mission profile is divided into two components: an operational mission profile to address the operational phases of equipment utilization, and a logistics mission profile to address the nonoperational (storage, handling, maintenance, and transportation) phases of a system's life cycle. The relationship of these components is illustrated in Figure 3.5.

With this background, these definitions can now be provided:

■ *Mission profile*: A chronological description of the significant operations, events, functions, situations, and nonenvironmental parameters expected to occur in an item's useful life having a bearing on the item's life and performance capabilities. A complete mission profile consists of an operational profile and a logistics profile covering nominal, contingency, and emergency modes of utilization from factory acceptance through the end of the useful life.

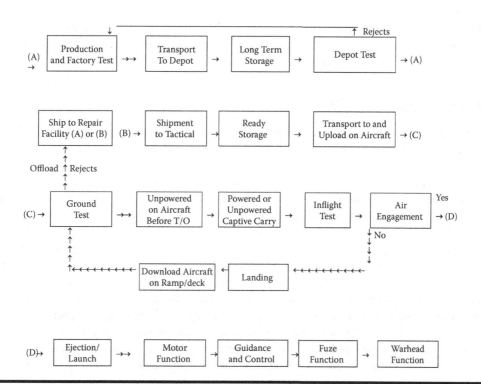

Figure 3.4   Life cycle profile for a missile.

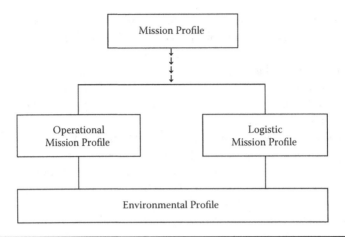

Figure 3.5 Mission profile components.

- *Operational profile*: A delineation of the conditions, circumstances, and influences that affect an item during the period of time from issue to a user organization until expenditure or disposal.
- *Logistic profile*: A delineation of the conditions, circumstances, and influences that affect an item from factory acceptance until issue to a user organization, and the return by the user organization for storage, repair, or overhaul until reissue to another user organization.
- *Environmental profile*: A description of the specific natural and induced nominal and worst-case environments associated with the operations, events, functions, situations, and parameters defined by the mission profile.

3.4.1 Operational Profile

The multimission capability of complex weapon systems often results in a number of profiles to describe the complete range of mission capabilities and requirements. A mission profile begins with the operational profile. When a range of alternative profiles is possible, it is recommended that each alternative is examined as a distinct event sequence separated by tactical phases. An example is shown in Figure 3.6. Here, in the absence of a demand for offensive action by the weapon system (i.e., patrol without launch), the patrol without launch period is of nominal duration, T. For such a mission, the entire patrol is the availability phase. There is no launch phase or flight phase. The weapon system remains on alert status, requiring a designated reaction time to commence firing (operational readiness). Should a demand be made on the weapon system (i.e., patrol with launch), the demand terminates the availability phase (t_{d1}) and initiates the ensuing launch phase (t_{d2}) and flight phase (t_p). During the launch phase the weapon system assumes a preparatory status, holds that status for a period of time up to a designated maximum, then initiates firing. The missile flight phase extends from launch to warhead fusing for detonation over the target. The availability and launch phases constitute the mission of the missile subsystem. Principal variables influencing mission length are the demand time and hold time associated with each phase.

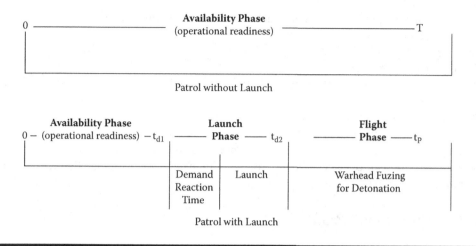

Figure 3.6 Tactical mission phases.

When the tactical phases have been defined, the subsystem operation modes in each phase and the performance functions in each mode are listed and related to the relevant mission requirements. It may be desirable to omit from the Ao analysis any modes, such as the training mode, that are not significant with respect to primary mission objectives. Each mode is tabulated against the mission phase(s) to which it applies. Performance functions required of the subsystem in each mode and phase are then listed and associated with the constituent equipment necessary for their accomplishment. A form having the general information content illustrated in Table 3.4 is helpful in organizing this portion of the mission analysis. In general, not all of the subsystem's functions will be equally essential to the mission. It is necessary to define the minimum limits of successful performance, the up status, for purposes of an Ao analysis. This is accomplished by listing the performance functions that are deemed essential to the primary mission.

3.4.2 Logistic Mission Profile

The logistic mission profile unitizes the operational mission description to identify and document the pertinent supportability factors related to the intended use of the new system/equipment. Factors to be considered include mobility requirements, deployment scenarios, mission frequency and duration, basing concepts, anticipated service life, interactions with other systems or end items, operational environment, and human capabilities and limitations. Both peacetime and wartime employment are considered in identifying the supportability factor. The results of the logistic mission profile include, as a minimum:

- Detailed maintenance concept
- Number of systems supported
- Transportation factors (e.g., mode, type, quantity to be transported, destinations, transport time, and schedule)
- Allowable maintenance periods
- Resources required for all scheduled and unscheduled maintenance

A logistic mission profile for a system, such as the missile system described in Figure 3.4, would define such factors as:

■ Proposed logistic cycle
■ Means of transportation (such as truck, railroad, or dolly) of the missile from one location to the next
■ Range of time spent at each location and the environment encountered there
■ Anticipated locations in or on the carrying or launching vehicle, where the missile will be carried or launched from, and the mix of stores carried by that vehicle
■ Required life span of the candidate missile component (such as storage life, service life, or number of flights)

3.4.3 Environmental Profile

Military systems and subsystems must be designed to survive and function in the operating or combat environment, and specifications governing the design must reflect this need. The specifications must also provide for system survivability in the worst-case transportation and storage environments that are likely to be encountered during the system's life. The formulation of detailed specifications cannot be undertaken until the specific environment conditions for the systems and subsystems have been developed in detail.

During the concept exploration phase of a system's life cycle, the project team will be able to define environmental conditions only in general terms related to similar systems. Environmental parameters must be defined to the level required to assess feasibility of a design concept, such as the effects of humidity or vibration on a specific technology. Eventually, the environmental profile must be defined in both quantitative and qualitative terms to establish specification requirements that affect the Ao components. Environmental conditions and their induced stresses have a significant impact on equipment reliability.

The definition of an environmental profile is often a difficult task during concept exploration. The program manager should be aware that the environmental conditions likely to be encountered by a new system might be considerably different from those encountered by similar systems or the system it replaces. The altitude, speed, and acceleration forces for aircraft systems and associated weapons have changed with each new generation of aircraft. Similarly, a subsystem's location on an aircraft or ship will greatly influence its environment, as will new materials used for construction, the increased density and diversity of electromagnetic fluxes' renewed emphasis on arctic warfare, and many other factors.

Although difficult, the environmental profile definition is an essential element during concept exploration, and establishes much needed criteria that affect all other acquisition phases. Unfortunately, environmental specifications for ships and aircraft systems have traditionally been covered by general specifications. These are often out of date and lack the detailed information required by the systems designers, logisticians, and others involved in the system acquisition process. Outmoded or insufficiently detailed specifications have resulted in both over- and underdesign of systems and substantial delays in development programs.

3.5 A Guide to Ao Analysis

This section provides a set of guidelines to performing an Ao analysis of the mission profile of a system. The guidelines are presented for each phase in a system's acquisition and life cycle support:

1. Preproject research and development
2. Concept and technology development
3. System development and demonstration
4. Production and deployment
5. Sustainment

These are the same phases that are recommended by the Department of Defense 5000 (DoD 2003) series policy documents that govern the Defense Acquisition System (Figure 3.3).

This phased approach to an Ao analysis is recommended because the goals of the 5000 model are the same goals for this book:

■ To deliver advanced technology to the warfighter faster
■ To reduce total ownership cost and improve affordability
■ To deploy interoperable and supportable systems

In advance of performing the Ao analysis, the project team that is conducting the analysis is encouraged to develop a set of preliminary questions. Often, simply asking the correct questions causes the right analysis to get done. When stakeholders know in advance that certain questions will be asked, they attempt to find the right answers. Thus, Table 3.3 was developed to provide a good starting point. The questions in the table deal with the system's requirements, capabilities, methods and tools, ground rules and assumptions, data sources, and documentation. In developing your own set of questions, try to align them to each phase of the system life cycle, as shown in the table and in the 5000 model. Table 3.4 provides an additional checklist of questions concerning Ao analysis.

3.5.1 Preproject Research and Development Phase

In the early phases of an acquisition, attention of the program team is directed primarily to the specification of the tentative Ao threshold range that is consistent with mission requirements. To facilitate an initial evaluation of Ao, the program team should begin as early as possible to understand and assess the assumptions and factors that are used by the milestone decision authority (MDA)* to formulate preliminary system alternatives in response to the mission needs statement (ICD). In this early period, the team should ensure that the underlying components of Ao—reliability (MTBF), maintainability (MTTR), and supportability (MDT)—are reasonable relative to the current and projected level of technology, to the current fleet operating experience for similar systems, and to the current maintenance and logistics support procedures and delay times.

To help determine tentative Ao thresholds in this preproject phase, the team is encouraged to focus on what is being demonstrated by comparable systems in the fleet or the use of the system as a part of the larger system, such as a weapons platform (ship, submarine, or aircraft) operating in a specified warfare environment. Consideration of Ao here focuses largely on its consistency with

---

* The milestone decision authority is responsible for the phases and activities of a system's life cycle structure and tasks. According to DoD Instruction (DODI) 5000, three milestones occur during the phases of a system acquisition:

Milestone A—Concept demonstration approval
Milestone B—Development approval
Milestone C—Production approval

DODI 5000.2 also lists a fourth milestone. However, a subsequent memorandum from the undersecretary of defense (acquisition and technology) deleted the fourth milestone.

Table 3.3 Guiding Questions for an Ao Analysis

DoD 5000 Phases:				
Phase A = Concept and Technology Development				
Phase B = System Development and Demonstration				
Phase C = Production and Deployment				
Later Phases = Operations and Support (O&S), Operations and Maintenance (O&M), and Sustainment				

Questions that Users, Program Sponsors, Program Managers, and Staff Should Ask	DoD 5000 Phases			
	Phase A	Phase B	Phase C	Later Phases
1 Analysis Requirements				
1-1 What are the primary requirements and objectives for Ao and LCC analysis for this project?				
1-2 How has the customer (user) of this system documented their requirements in terms of Ao and LCC? Are these requirements clear to the program?				
1-3 Has the user defined an existing fleet system that forms the baseline reference for the new capability needed?				
1-4 Has the user identified any LCC- or Ao-related Constraints? How do these relate to the existing (baseline) system? How do these relate to ground rules and assumptions for the new system? How will all analysis agencies be informed of these constraints?				
1-5 Have the objectives and thresholds for this program been defined for: Ao? LCC? Are these objectives and thresholds documented as CAIV parameters? Where? Have Ao and LCC goals been allocated to major subsystems and significant WBS items appropriate for this phase of the program?				
2 Analysis Capability				
2-1 What cost-estimating capability has the program established:				

Table 3.3 (Continued)

Questions that Users, Program Sponsors, Program Managers, and Staff Should Ask	DoD 5000 Phases			
	Phase A	Phase B	Phase C	Later Phases
(a) To directly support the government program office? (b) To support the contractor capability?				
2-2 Has the program established liaison with the Center for Cost Analysis (CCA)? Has a CCA point of contact (POC) been assigned to prepare or assist in preparation of LCC estimates? Who is it?				
2-3 Has the program team established liaison with MAC? Has a MAC POC been assigned to prepare or assist in preparation of manpower LCC estimates? Who is it?				
2-4 Has the program team established consolidated or separate analysis capabilities for supporting the three levels of program decision support: (a) Military enterprise-level decisions? (b) Military program (weapon system)-level decisions? (c) Detailed engineering trade study decisions?				
2-5 Have adequate resources for conducting Ao- and LCC-related analysis been planned and programmed in program planning documents and in the POM? Are they fully funded?				
3 Analysis Methods and Tools				
3-1 Has the program identified and documented a standard methodology for conducting Ao and LCC analysis? Is the methodology consistent with CIAG guidelines? Is the methodology consistent with NCCA guidelines? Is the methodology consistent with best commercial practices?				

(Continued)

Table 3.3 (Continued)

Questions that Users, Program Sponsors, Program Managers, and Staff Should Ask	DoD 5000 Phases			
	Phase A	Phase B	Phase C	Later Phases
3-2 What are the definitive references for the program methodology for Ao and LCC analysis? (Where is method described?)				
3-3 Has the program team identified a single or family of models for conducting Ao and LCC Analysis? What parametric (top-down) models have been selected (LCC)? What engineering estimate (bottom-up) models have been selected (LCC)? What tools or models have been selected for evaluating Ao? Where is this information documented?				
3-4 Are the same methods and models used by all (contractor and government) agencies who perform/conduct decision support analysis (for Ao and LCC) for this program?				
3-5 If no on 3-4, how has the program ensured that consistent results are being achieved and that analysis can be replicated?				
3-6 Have analysis methods and tools selected for use in this program been evaluated by NCCA or CAIG? Where is this documented?				
4 Analysis Ground Rules and Assumptions				
4-1 Has the program identified standard ground rules and assumptions for use by all agencies supporting program analysis? Are man-hour rates for operators and maintainers defined? Are operating hours per system per year defined? Are production and deployment schedules defined? Are site stand-up schedules defined?				

Table 3.3   (Continued)

Questions that Users, Program Sponsors, Program Managers, and Staff Should Ask	DoD 5000 Phases			
	Phase A	Phase B	Phase C	Later Phases
Are the phase-in and phase-out for (new/old) systems defined? Are technology refreshment schedules defined? Has the economic life (for analysis purposes) been defined? Has the design reference mission profile (DRMF) been defined? Where are the ground rules and assumptions documented and how do all analysis agencies obtain this information?				
4-2 Have all initial production and recurring support costs been included in the analysis capability? Are *all* future costs covered, to include customer costs, contractor costs, supplier costs, third-party provider costs, direct/indirect costs, variable/fixed costs, design and development costs, production/construction costs, operation and support costs, retirement and material recycling/disposal costs? Have any costs or logistics elements been identified for elimination from any specific LCC analysis? Has the rationale been documented?				
4-3 Has the baseline comparison system (BCS) been documented to the work breakdown structure (WBS) level adequately enough for establishing the point of reference for the alternatives being considered?				
4-4 What rate of cannibalization will be allowed in analyzing Ao and LCC for this program? Has the effect of cannibalization on equipment reliability (accelerated wear-out), maintenance-induced failures, and manpower turnover been included in the analysis?				

(Continued)

Table 3.3 (Continued)

Questions that Users, Program Sponsors, Program Managers, and Staff Should Ask	DoD 5000 Phases			
	Phase A	Phase B	Phase C	Later Phases
Has the rate of cannibalization vs. spares costs been documented? Has the user been briefed and agreed to this aspect of analysis?				
4-5 Has the full set of ground rules, assumptions, and analysis planning factors been reviewed and approved by applicable agencies, such as DoD CAIG, NCCA, NAVMAC, and others?				
4-6 Has the full set of ground rules, assumptions, and related analysis factors been provided to all analysis agencies (including the contractor)?				
5 Analysis Data and Data Sources				
5-1 Has the program made sure that all program analysis agencies have data access, accounts, and passwords registered with the military VAMOSC program office?				
5-2 Has the program obtained all standard military planning factors from the appropriate agencies, i.e., NCCA, NAVMAC, ISEA, and SYSCOM financial planning offices? Where is this documented?				
5-3 How has activity-based costing (ABC) been used in the development of program analysis and data?				
5-4 Have all three specific categories of analysis data been obtained and shared with all program analysis agencies: (a) Program/project data: procurement, deployment, operations tempo (b) Hardware data: all hardware-specific data and parameters (c) User operations scenario data: Factors from user's operations (labor rates, turnaround times (TATs), pipeline times, attrition/discard rates, etc.)				

Table 3.3 (Continued)

Questions that Users, Program Sponsors, Program Managers, and Staff Should Ask	DoD 5000 Phases			
	Phase A	Phase B	Phase C	Later Phases
5-5 Does the program/project plan to obtain and/or publish "default data guides" for use by analysis agencies? Where will analysis planning factors be published and referenced in program planning documents, such as logistics plans, test plans, acquisition program plans, etc.?				
5-6 How will DT and OT test data be used in modeling Ao and LCC? What program plans and contracts discuss this aspect of analysis?				
5-7 How will fleet data (3M, VAMOCS, ISEA feedback) be incorporated into Ao and LCC analysis activities? How will access to these data by all analysis agencies be accomplished?				
6 Phase-Related Ao and LCC Analysis				
6-1 Has the BCS been fully defined, modeled, and had both LCC and Ao estimates documented appropriately for this phase of the program?				
6-2 Have program-level design alternatives been identified and modeled, and Ao and LCC analysis performed at a WBS level appropriate for this phase of the program?				
6-3 Have support concepts been defined for each design alternative, and have all initial and recurring logistics resources been included in the analysis of alternatives for this phase? Is there any need to rebaseline the objectives and thresholds using CAIV guidelines?				
6-4 Have the Ao- and LCC-related objectives and thresholds been defined? Has analysis been updated for this phase of the program? Is there any need to rebaseline the program objectives and thresholds using CAIV guidelines?				

(Continued)

Table 3.3   (Continued)

Questions that Users, Program Sponsors, Program Managers, and Staff Should Ask	DoD 5000 Phases			
	Phase A	Phase B	Phase C	Later Phases
6-5 Are detailed design-related Ao and LCC drivers being identified at the appropriate level of the WBS for this phase?				
6-6 Are DT and OT test data being modeled to identify and track issues with respect to				
6-7 Are design-influencing recommendations being provided to design engineers concerning Ao and LCC "bad actors" that most affect achievement of AO and LCC objectives?				
6-8 How has sensitivity analysis been performed in the LCC analysis? Have sensitivity curves been developed for reliability, maintainability, and other factors? Which parameters were studied? What are the drivers and what are the subsystems parts most sensitive to these? Where is the sensitivity analysis documented? What actions have been taken to reduce the effect of Ao and LCC drivers?				
6-9 Is there a record of LCC and Ao analysis used as design-related decision (trade study) support? Where is the record maintained?				
6-10 Has sparing to availability curves been developed for the program? Have organizational-level spares been identified based on readiness-based sparing (RBS) models?				
6-11 Are all spares required to support the user's readiness requirement budgeted for? What is the percent funded? What Ao will the budget support?				
6-12 How has risk analysis been incorporated into AO and LCC analysis?				

Table 3.3   (Continued)

Questions that Users, Program Sponsors, Program Managers, and Staff Should Ask	DoD 5000 Phases			
	Phase A	Phase B	Phase C	Later Phases
How were risks in terms of equipment-level reliability, maintainability, and unit cost handled? How was a range of Ao and LCC targets developed?				
6-13 Is documentation in place describing plans for follow-on tracking, monitoring analysis, and reporting for Ao and the components of Ao in the operational environment? Do plans describe decision support analysis concerning system modernization, technology insertion, block upgrades, etc.?				
6-14 Is there any way to make Ao and LCC analysis more accurate for this program at this time?				
6-15 Are all traditional logistics elements for both initial logistics (procurement dollars) and recurring logistics (O&M dollars) estimated in LCC analysis?				
6-16 Are there any missing data or cost elements that can improve the confidence in the completeness of the LCC or Ao analysis?				
7 Analysis Documentation				
7-1 Have Ao or LCC requirements or constraints been documented in the mission needs statement (ICD)?				
7-2 Have AoAs been prepared at the appropriate level of detail for this phase of the program?				
7-3 Have the Ao- and LCC-related portions of the ORD been defined or updated for this phase of the program?				
7-4 Have the Ao and LCC portions of test plans been defined or updated for this phase of the program?				

(Continued)

Table 3.3 (Continued)

Questions that Users, Program Sponsors, Program Managers, and Staff Should Ask	DoD 5000 Phases			
	Phase A	Phase B	Phase C	Later Phases
7-5 Have the Ao and LCC portions of the acquisition program baseline (APB) been defined or updated for this phase of the program?				
7-6 Have Ao- and LCC-related portions of exit criteria (in terms of CAIV objectives) for the next phase been documented?				
7-7 Have other program planning documents been updated to include Ao- and LCC-related information appropriate for this phase? What are they? Logistics support plans? Systems engineering plans? Supportability analysis plans? Acquisition strategy? Master acquisition program plan? Others?				
7-8 How is documentation of design-related trade studies maintained in contractor databases? Does the government have documented plans to review these data?				
7-9 Has the project set up an integrated digital environment (IDE) to allow every activity involved with the program to cost-effectively create, store, access, manipulate, or exchange Ao, LCC, systems engineering, and supportability analysis data?				

mission-related assumptions and analysis of mission requirements. The team must integrate data and analysis from a number of sources to develop and specify an ICD and an associated analysis of alternatives (AoA) for the system.

The team also should consider addressing system effectiveness (SE) at this time. The focus will first be on the system's technical operating characteristics (e.g., range, accuracy, tolerance, speed, and definition), and how these characteristics relate to its mission and the expected operational availability.

Table 3.4   Checklist for the Ao Analysis

Purpose	Analysis objective is clear?
	Critical items have been defined?
	Analysis problem has had bounds and scope identified?
Effectiveness Parameters	Effectiveness parameters identified?
	Metrics appropriate to production function?
	Operation and maintenance requirements adequately defined?
	Any objectives ignored while others are overemphasized?
	Performance measures mistaken for effectiveness measures?
	Effectiveness of the future system accounted for?
	Correct use of expected and average values to measure effectiveness?
	Proper weighting of multiple effectiveness measures?
	Plans to analyze sensitivity to changes in assumptions?
Alternatives	Current capabilities considered as baseline?
	Mixtures of system components considered?
	Feasible/significant alternatives omitted or postponed?
Assumptions	Defined and documented adequately?
	Quantitative uncertainties addressed and factual position taken?
	Qualitative uncertainties addressed and position stated as fact?
	Assumptions pass reasonableness check?
Cost Elements	All relevant cost elements have been identified?
	Major cost categories have been identified?
	Cost element structure breaks costs down to appropriate level?
Techniques	Parametric, engineering estimate, projection form actual, and analogous system comparison have all been considered?
	Technique fits problem and program phase?
Model	Adequately addresses the problem?
	Provides logical link between cost and effectiveness parameters?
	Allows for timely response?
	Comprehensive—both initial and recurring costs for all relevant elements?

(Continued)

Table 3.4   (Continued)

	Consistent—allows proposed system to be compared to analogous system?
	Flexible—handles early, top level, and can evolve to more detail later?
	Simple—requires minimum data but can handle easy expansion?
	Usefulness—directly supports decision makers' needs for information?
	Completeness—includes all relevant cost elements?
	Valid—capable of providing logical repeatable results?
Data	All necessary input data have been identified?
	Sources of data have been identified?
	Data have been normalized and scrubbed for inconsistencies and reporting system-induced problems?
	Sources of all costs have been recorded and justified?
Calculations	Cost-generating activities identified and cost drivers stratified?
	Constant dollar factors used?
	Inflation, learning curves, price levels properly applied?
	Costs per year captured and projected into future?
	Element cost streams summarized into top-level profile?
Sensitivity	All critical parameters analyzed for sensitivity?
	Impact on all costs assessed?
	Impact on LCC summarized?
Risk	Has a range of LCC or Ao been developed, based on risk associated with MTBF and MTTR?
	Has the range of uncertainty associated with MTBF, MTTR, and even unit costs of logistics resources such as spare parts been used to form bounds of risk concerning LCC and Ao estimates?
Recommendations	Have specific recommendations been developed based on results of analysis of model runs?
	Are recommendations backed up by summary graphs showing results of analysis?
Reporting	Total analysis adequately documented?
	Facts and necessary caveats stated correctly?
	Executive summary state recommendations, backed up with description of methodology, input data, output run sheets, references, and enough information for analysis replication verification?

3.5.1.1 Objectives

The purpose of the analysis in this early phase is to establish an Ao baseline, which drives the selection of the applicable cost elements and the resulting model data input requirements. As a guide, use the checklist questions in Table 3.4 to ensure that the rationale for the Ao analysis has been thorough, accurately stated, and provides management with the information necessary to make informed decisions.

3.5.1.2 Data and Models

To model the baseline operational scenario, the analysis team and analysis agency should study the initial draft mission needs statement (ICD) and user inputs to:

■ Describe the mission frequency and duration
■ Determine the number of comparison systems in operation
■ Describe the current logistics support environment
■ Describe logistics resource numbers and costs used to support the comparison system

From operational data on the existing (baseline) system, the following should be obtained:

■ Describe the achieved Ao of current similar operational systems, subsystems, or components, including achieved reliability, maintainability (R&M), and supportability values.
■ Identify the costs of current operational systems, subsystems, or components.
■ Determine the readiness drivers of the current operational system.
■ Identify any special design requirements or extraordinary support system performance requirements.

From the systems engineering and research and development communities, obtain the following:

■ Identify technologies under development, including their expected maturity, their estimated timeframe for readiness for production, and their risks.
■ Determine the anticipated reliability of those technologies relative to the current technology.
■ Identify the operating environment in which the system is intended to function, together with the related mission or warfare objectives.
■ Establish mission effectiveness goals for the system based on the relationship of the system to its platform and the relationship of the system to other related systems on the platform.
■ Incorporate the technical operating characteristics required for the system based on the established operating environments in which the system will perform.

In addition, consider the following inputs as a means to determine the operational requirements for the system and a specification of a preliminary Ao threshold:

■ Detailed combat scenario data required for warfare analysis and simulation based on established general operational scenarios approved for such planning purposes.
■ A mission profile, as was described in Section 3.4.

■ Technical and engineering data in the appropriate Systems Command, in military laboratories, and in external technical databases to establish basic engineering relationships of the system to the platform and to other systems.

■ Relationships to other systems must be established via reliability block diagrams or other methods, such as the work breakdown structure (WBS). Delineation of system redundancy, parallel or series structure, and the impact of system degradation must be a part of the information provided.

■ Collect specific technical operating characteristics of the system, drawn generally from the threat assessment documentation and program documents on existing/similar systems, including the baseline comparison system (BCS).

In summary, the operating environmental data, the platform availability data, the system mission effectiveness data, and the system technical operating characteristics data will jointly determine the tentative Ao threshold for the system.

3.5.1.3 Ao Analysis

The Ao analysis process for this early phase includes:

1. Define the purpose of the Ao analysis.
2. Identify the baseline and alternatives.
   a. Establish the initial baseline Ao for comparable systems, which will become the baseline point of reference for later analysis and evaluation.
   b. Establish the Ao requirement for the proposed system.
3. Develop the ground rules and assumptions.
4. Select the relevant cost elements and structure.
5. Determine the cost estimating technique.
6. Select or construct a cost model.
7. Identify the input data sources and collect the data.
8. Estimate and evaluate the relevant costs.
9. Perform a sensitivity analysis and identify or verify the major cost drivers
10. Perform a risk and uncertainty analysis.
11. Develop a set of recommendations.
12. Document the analysis.

There are six steps to the analysis in this first phase:

1. Select or create a baseline comparison system (BCS). Often this is the existing system that the fleet needs to replace or subsystems that need replacement. In some cases a notional system or composite system must be created to represent a notional baseline representing a point of comparison for alternatives under study.
2. Identify deficiencies in the existing/similar system(s) that make them inadequate to counter the threat or that are considered potentially unsupportable due to parts obsolescence, diminishing manufacturing sources, or excessive operating and support costs.
3. Establish the tentative Ao threshold based on the results of the related warfare analysis supporting the overall system requirements. In the absence of such documented analysis, the

judgment of fleet commanders in chief (CINCs) representative should be used. Generally, the minimum level of Ao acceptable for combat systems has been 0.80.

4. Ensure that the Ao of a system or subsystem is consistent with the overall system/platform readiness objective.

5. Create a baseline reliability block diagram (RBD) or notional work breakdown structure (WBS) for the platform in a top-down approach by allocating the platform readiness requirement to the subsystems and components.

6. Ensure that Ao requirements are scenario dependent by relating them to the readiness requirements of their host platforms (see Table 3.5). To establish preliminary Ao thresholds on the basis of mission effectiveness for systems (subsystems or equipment) being acquired for a platform, the program team will need to distinguish between three cases:
   - A replacement system with upgraded capability
   - A new system with new capability
   - A replacement system with improved supportability or a redundant system

3.5.1.3.1 Evaluation and Approval of the Analysis

Perform these steps for the evaluation and approval of the Ao analysis:

- Model the combat environment in sufficient detail to clearly establish both the technical operating characteristics of the system and the mission effectiveness required of the system. Include, for example, a definition of the battle group configuration, location, threat mix, engagement probabilities, engagement duration, specific mission probabilities, platform attrition rates, response, and counterresponse probabilities.
- Establish the specific mission effectiveness required for the system and its host platform(s) within the established combat environment. This effectiveness, which may be specified as warfare measures of merit, must be operational in nature and may include target kills, sortie success rates, etc. Evaluate the results of the warfare analysis to ensure that the objective or goal established for a specific measure of merit is met by the system under consideration.
- Ensure that the underlying assumptions of the simulation or other analytical methodology are consistent with current tactical and strategic planning for the weapons platform(s) and the system itself. Verify that deployment cycles, flying hour projections, platform availability goals, sortie rates, hours per sortie, theater utilization rates, aircraft inventories, etc., are reasonably represented in the assumptions used to conduct the warfare analysis.
- Evaluate alternative systems configurations, with varying operating characteristics and mission effectiveness, to determine the cost-benefit trade-offs of the system and to relate these trade-offs to specific tentative Ao thresholds.

3.5.1.3.2 Cost-Effectiveness Portion of the Analysis

Perform these steps for the cost-effectiveness portion of the Ao analysis:

- Describe the mission frequency and duration, and other measures of merit.
- Describe the perceived threat, including technologically achievable threats over the planned life of the system.
- Describe the capabilities required for both mission performance and supportability.

- Identify the anticipated number of systems to be procured.
- Identify the users' preferred direction regarding logistics support.
- Create the initial estimates of what resources might be available to procure the system and its support.

From operational data on existing (baseline) systems:

- Identify the achievable Ao of current, similar operational systems, subsystems, or components, including achieved reliability, maintainability, and supportability values.
- Obtain costs of current operational systems, subsystems, or components. This information is often available from item managers or in-service engineering agent (ISEA) agencies.
- Determine readiness drivers of current operational systems (the systems experiencing the most failures or consuming the most maintenance man-hours).
- Identify any special design requirements or extraordinary support system performance requirements.

Obtain the following information from systems engineering and research and development communities:

- Determine technologies under development, including their expected maturity, their estimated timeframe for readiness for production, and any known risk areas.
- Identify anticipated reliability of the emerging technology systems, subsystems, and components.

Analyze tentative Ao thresholds and establish the baseline:

- Review and validate mission effectiveness and Ao relationships.
- Establish mission effectiveness and Ao relationships.
- Review analytical results of the Ao warfare analysis.

The life cycle cost of a system is closely connected with Ao achieved by a system, and normally the higher the Ao required of a system the higher the life cycle cost.

3.5.1.3.3 Analyzing the Operational Scenario

Perform these steps to analyze the operational scenario:

- Develop the mission profile.
- Identify the following factors in the new system pertaining to Ao.
  - The number of missions per unit of time
  - Mission duration, number of operating days, miles, hours, flights or cycles per unit of time
  - Peacetime and wartime employment, operating scenario, basing concept, and operating environment
- To clarify the general guidance of the initial capabilities document (ICD), identify the following:
  - The type of system, e.g., antiair warfare (AAW), antisubmarine warfare (ASW), antisurface warfare (ASUW)

Table 3.5 Ao and Platform Relationship

	A Replacement System with Upgraded Capability	A New System with New Capability	A Replacement System with Improved Supportability or a Redundant System
Example	A new radar replaces an older model on an aircraft.	A new self-defense system is added to a ship currently without one.	An additional power unit is added to a ship to back up an emergency power supply or to reduce logistics support costs.
1. Block diagram or WBS available	Old block diagram/ WBS valid with substitution of new system for replaced system.	Old block diagram/ WBS must be modified to incorporate this series addition. Platform readiness will decrease when system is added in series.	Old block diagram/WBS must be modified to incorporate this parallel addition. Platform readiness will increase when system is added in parallel.
a. If platform readiness measure was just satisfied prior to adding the new system	Cannot go below replaced system's Ao.	Must make new system's Ao as high as posible. Platform readiness will drop unless other systems are improved. Should request total platform reanalysis to reallocate Ao's to all systems.	Any system Ao will improve platform readiness.
b. If platform readiness measure was not satisfied prior to adding this new system	Should consider increasing new system's Ao to make up deficiency.		Should consider using new system's Ao to make up deficiency.
2. Block diagram/ WBS not available	Assume new system will replace old system in exactly the same operational availability relationship to either system on the platform. Assume new system Ao must be at least equal to old system Ao.	Establish an operating environment and scenario for the new system in terms of required system effectiveness or performance (kill rate, acquisition time/ accuracy, range, etc.). Base new system Ao on costs and system effectiveness trade-offs in intended operating environment for new systems in isolation from platform.	

- The category of platform that employs the system, e.g., surface ship, submarine, or aircraft, and the type of platform within that category: aircraft carrier, cruiser, frigate
- The concept of operations, e.g., carrier battle group, surface battle group, independent operations
- The type of threat, e.g., stand-off air-delivered missile, stand-off surface-delivered missile, submarine
- The key capabilities required, e.g., over-the-horizon ASW, AAW out to 200 miles and up to 50,000 feet altitude
- ■ Logistic planning requirements, e.g., unique maintenance concepts; 15 days continuous, independent operations isolated from resupply; continuous availability for a 75-day operating cycle

After identifying the factors pertaining to the Ao, the next step is to conduct an associated analysis of alternatives (AoA) study. The initial requirement is to identify all existing systems similar to the system described by the ICD. The ICD quantifies the Ao and provides the basis for deriving the required system MTBF, MTTR, and MLDT. It will confirm or contradict critical assumptions about operational use, critical design considerations, and support concepts. Analysis of historical data on the AoA provides quantifiable statistics that form the baseline for satisfying an estimation of the achievable Ao and costs.

3.5.1.3.4 Estimating Achievable Ao and Costs

The analysis agency will prepare an associated analysis of alternatives (AoA) to provide the program team with the lower bound of achievable capability. On nearly all existing systems the program management office or in-service engineering agent has accomplished an assessment of the system that reports the system's performance in terms of reliability (MTBF), maintainability (MTTR), and supportability (MLDT), as well as manpower requirements and operating costs. These reports usually identify readiness drivers within the system, provide critical parts usage/failures and system characteristics, and identify other data sources. The program team can use these data to develop baseline statistics necessary to perform the comparative analysis required to respond to the ICD.

The program management office should also be able to furnish the maintenance plan, logistics support plan, and reliability block diagrams. These provide the program team with a baseline maintenance concept, supply concept, and a diagram of the functional relationships among the major components of the baseline system. The military supply Systems Command can provide the dollar value of a set of spares and repair parts for the comparative system and also mean logistics support times. The program office maintains data on the operational, maintenance, and support costs of operational ships, aircraft, and systems, and can also provide costing factors that can be used for cost estimation purposes. The research and development community is able to furnish any advances in technology that provide enhancements to the capabilities of the comparative system.

The program team selects and rejects alternatives on the basis of achievability, satisfaction of the capabilities in the ICD, acceptable risk, and cost. In effect, the program team is conducting a marginal analysis of reliability and supportability to determine the effects on Ao by varying the two elements. The lower bound of Ao is what is currently being achieved with current reliability and supportability. The upper bound of Ao is the alternative that meets the capabilities but exceeds the affordability constraints or represents unacceptable technological risk.

3.5.1.4 Documentation

Applicable policy states that an ICD must be prepared for the initial milestone (milestone A—concept studies approval) at which the milestone decision authorities' (MDA) approval will be sought to proceed with the early concept and technology exploration. Furthermore, policy requires operational requirements to be evolutionary in nature and become more refined as the program proceeds. The ICD and its associated analysis of alternatives (AoA) provide the general framework for the derivation of the key performance parameters at the appropriate approval milestone. An initial test and evaluation master plan (TEMP) will be prepared to describe the next phase (concept and technology development) tests to identify promising concepts and technologies. Some major systems, comprised of several major systems, will require a capstone requirements document (CRD) to be developed before the initial milestone decision meeting. The ICD, CRD, and TEMP documents provide the key performance parameters (KPPs), including Ao and life cycle costs (LCCs).

The minimum documentation required from the program team by the program milestone decision authorities (MDA) is:

- Initial capabilities document (ICD)
- Mission area assessment (MAA)*
- Capstone requirements document (CRD)
- Initial test and evaluation master plan (TEMP)
- Analysis of alternatives (AoA)

The commanders in chief (CINCs) provide the mission needs statement (ICD). The objective is to verify the need of the ICD against the mission area assessment (MAA). This is accomplished by performing short-term concept studies to consider whether the mission need can be satisfied by nonmaterial solutions. The program team and the resource cost and performance team draft the initial program objectives memorandum (POM) and begin staffing it through the planning, programming, and budgeting system (PPBS). The acquisition program baseline (APB) is susceptible to change during this process. Compromises are highly possible and are tied to affordability issues.

This early phase ends with both the approval of the ICD and resources in the program objectives memorandum (POM). The program team is given a level of funding, the year that funding will become available, and what thresholds the new system will achieve—or a range of thresholds (in the case of developmental programs)—that will become fixed later in the development phase of the acquisition cycle. This constitutes the authorization for the program team to proceed to the next phase: concept and technology development.

3.5.2 Concept and Technology Development Phase

The purpose of the concept and technology development phase is to evaluate the feasibility of alternative concepts for satisfying the need in the ICD, search for opportunities to apply advanced technology, and perform preliminary design of the material solution. The feasibility studies are performed in order to identify the feasible alternatives, identify the preferred alternatives, and prepare a report that will support a decision by the milestone decision authority (MDA) to proceed

---

* The Major Commands (MAJCOMs) identify mission needs through a mission area assessment (MAA) process.

with the preferred alternative. Part of this decision support documentation is to present the Ao estimates for the baseline comparison system, or other feasible alternatives, along with the preferred alternative. The justification for the preferred alternative will be that it satisfies the key mission requirement and can achieve the highest Ao and lowest LCC.

In this phase, the system concepts are developed into design specifications for individual equipment components. These individual components in combination achieve the performance and Ao of the complete system. The phase has two primary objectives. First, the contractors develop the system design concept to a level of design detail that proves the required system technology can be achieved at the end of the phase. The second objective is to validate that the detailed system design can achieve the expected performance and threshold requirements. The validation of the Ao threshold capability is accomplished through both engineering analysis and equipment test.

This phase develops a balance between the mission profile and Ao objectives and what can be achieved based on fleet experience and technological state of the art. The phase establishes the reality of the Ao thresholds through a combination of technical analyses, cost-benefit trade-offs, and test and evaluation. The objective of the technical effort is to identify and eliminate any problems from the system concept design that can prevent achievement of the Ao threshold. Early developmental testing (DT) data are collected and used in the Ao models. Most of the discussion concerning the use of DT data is deferred to the next phase (Section 3.5.3). To minimize duplication, the reader should refer to that section to get a balanced discussion of Ao analysis and use of DT data.

3.5.2.1 Objectives

During this phase, the analysis agency will perform studies and a decision support analysis to help determine the most promising solutions that satisfy the needs of the customer. All of the functions of alternative systems will be identified and analyzed. The first draft of the description of the functional baseline will be prepared. The updated analysis of alternatives (AoA) and the acquisition program baseline (APB) will be prepared, which fully documents the preferred or recommended alternative along with the comparisons to other alternatives studied, including the baseline comparison system (BCS). The objectives for this phase are to:

- Expand the mission profile to define the operational and logistics requirements and environmental conditions at the system and subsystem levels of indenture for each alternative studied
- Quantify the components of Ao of a set of system design concepts in order to evaluate system feasibility against mission success and cost
- Collect and use DT data in the Ao analysis; use negative impact information to help influence the design in specific configuration items to improve Ao or reduce LCC
- Begin to expand the Ao analysis to include detailed analysis at the subsystem levels of the work breakdown structure (WBS) wherever the design progress makes this feasible
- Refine the Ao thresholds in the program documentation

3.5.2.2 Data and Models

During this phase, a Functional Needs Analysis (FNA) and concept and technology development phase analysis of alternatives (AoA) typically consist of competitive, parallel, short-term concept studies. The focus of these studies is to define and evaluate the feasibility of alternative concepts and to provide a basis for assessing the relative merits (i.e., advantages and disadvantages, degree of risk, etc.) of these concepts. The AoA shall be used as appropriate to facilitate comparisons of alternate concepts. Evaluation of the design concepts requires a definition of the functional and performance demands of the required mission and an assessment of the capabilities of current or achievable technology to meet these demands. The studies use engineering models, preliminary development models, and preliminary research efforts initiated in critical technology areas. Evaluations are focused on the performance and capability demands on the system design, with evaluation of the Ao parameters required for this capability and the associated life cycle costs.

Cost estimates are derived from an underlying set of assumptions about the utilization, support concept, and financial requirements for each alternative design concept. In addition to the operational and support data, which are derived in the mission profile definition, specific financial data are obtained, including:

- A definition of the elements of the operating and support costs that will be program cost drivers. The allocated reliability and maintainability (R&M) values that are developed by the design engineer are modeled, and the preliminary DT data are also run through the Ao models to identify candidates for attention. The reliability growth chart in Chapter 4 of this book gives an indication of the growth being assessed and managed.
- Identification of the elements of the work breakdown structure (WBS) to which the costs are associated. The allocated R&M values that are developed by the design engineer are modeled, and the preliminary DT data are also run through the Ao models to identify candidates for attention.
- Models for estimating, tracking, and assessing life cycle costs (LCCs).
- Inputs to government-generated or -controlled cost models, such as operating personnel, labor, and overhead costs of government maintenance, cost of inventory introduction and maintenance, and costs of training.
- A definition of the expected production unit cost goal along with unit costs of systems, subsystems, and components (for analysis purposes). Where this information is considered competition sensitive, use triangle function estimates with ranges, such as low, expected, and high.
- Production cost elements to be considered, such as recurring, nonrecurring, labor, overhead, subcontracts, general and administrative, and profit.
- Anticipated production quantity, rate of production, production schedule, increments of production, and provisions for accommodating changes to these factors.
- A provision for accommodation of changing economic conditions, including constant dollar base year, or indices to be used to deflate out-year dollars.
- Required system reliability.
- Required system maintenance characteristics.
- Baseline maintenance concept.
- Quantitative contract support system requirements.
- Qualitative contract support system requirements, such as levels of supply support, levels of repair, and spares allocation.
- Logistics element baselines.
- Requirements for built-in test/built-in test equipment (BIT/BITE), automatic test equipment (ATE), and other specialized support equipment.

This phase includes testing to verify achievement of the reliability, maintainability, and supportability values derived through technical analysis. Most testing in this phase is for developmental test and evaluation (DT&E). The results of DT&E are used to either verify or modify the results of the technical analyses as well as qualification and acceptance of the technology and design concepts. This development test program is utilized to derive engineering information on the components of Ao and to assess equipment growth toward the threshold requirements for reliability, maintainability, and supportability.

Test and evaluation (T&E) plans are established to develop a database for quantitatively assessing the achievement of support-related thresholds, the adequacy of support plans and resources, and the impact on cost and readiness objectives. Responsibility is assigned and sufficient test assets are programmed and budgeted to provide independent assessments for both DT&E and operational testing and evaluation (OT&E). Technical thresholds (validated by DT&E) and operational thresholds (validated by OT&E) are established for reliability and maintainability, inherent availability, and Ao.

3.5.2.3 Ao Analysis

3.5.2.3.1 Expand the Mission Profile

A complete mission profile consists of an operational profile and a logistic profile that covers nominal, contingency, and emergency modes of utilization from factory acceptance through end of useful life. A complete mission profile is defined by these elements:

1. Operational profile: Describes the conditions, circumstances, and influences that affect an item during the period of time that it is on an operational mission. Different levels of operational stress are described, and the worst-case set of stresses is defined in terms of the portion of the deployed mission that this condition exists.
2. Logistic profile: Describes the conditions, circumstances, and influences that affect an item during the periods of time from government acceptance until issuance to a user organization, and from return by the user organization for storage, repair, or overhaul until reissue to a user organization.
3. Environmental profile: Describes the specific natural and induced nominal and worst-case environments associated with the operations, events, functions, situations, and parameters defined by the mission profile.
   a. Define the specific system stress conditions that are required by the mission objectives. Prior to this phase, the general, functional, and Ao requirements to support the mission were defined and documented in the mission needs statement (ICD). Deriving a complete mission profile requires evaluation of specific design characteristics of the system. This process continues throughout the acquisition life cycle and even after deployment.
   b. Development of a mission profile begins with the operational mission profile. The operational requirements are established as a series of events. The multimission capability of complex weapon systems often results in many profiles describing the complete range of mission capabilities and requirements. When a range of alternate missions is possible, each is examined as a distinct event sequence, and each is separated into phases.

c. Define the logistic mission profile, which includes mobility requirements, deployment scenarios, mission frequency and duration, basing concepts, anticipated service life, interactions with the systems/end items, operation environment, and human capabilities and limitations. Peacetime and wartime employment are considered when identifying the supportability factors.

d. Military systems and subsystems must be designed to survive and function in the operating or combat environment. Therefore, specifications governing the design must reflect this need. These specifications must also provide for system survivability in the punishing transportation and storage environments encountered during the system's life. Specific environmental conditions for the systems and subsystems must be developed in detail in order to formulate detailed specifications.

e. Determine the expected effect of mission stress on the predicted levels of system, subsystem, and component reliability. K-factor* the mean time between failures (MTBF) values based on such stress factors as catapult launches, hard landings, extreme vibrations, and environmental factors. Document the rationale used to justify the K-factors.

3.5.2.3.2 Identify the Technological Opportunities

Alternative system design concepts are explored within the system's mission need and program objectives. Benefits are optimized by a competitive exploration of alternative system design concepts with trade-offs among mission capability, Ao parameters, schedule, and cost. During the initial steps of the acquisition process, the program team avoids restricting alternative solutions to mission needs or program objectives to systems or products that might limit consideration of alternatives and opportunities to leverage advanced technology. Alternative system design concepts are solicited from a broad base of qualified firms. Emphasis is placed on innovation and competition for achieving the best system solution.

3.5.2.3.3 Quantify the Components of Ao

Each concept evaluation includes estimates of both the quantitative and the qualitative parameter of the system concept for reliability, maintainability, and supportability characteristics. The quantitative parameters of MTBF, MTTR, and MLDT are supported by qualitative factors, such as failure mode descriptions, criticality of failures, space requirements for maintenance, and tools and repair part descriptions. These qualitative parameters are required to define the components of Ao in realistic terms for evaluation of alternate design concepts. This activity includes the definition of special logistics problems and an estimate of the current supportability characteristics that may apply in their solution. Current support capability is defined as existing procedures, repair facilities skills, and equipment that could accommodate a new requirement. Trade-off studies are performed to evaluate alternatives to satisfying those requirements that cannot be satisfied by existing support capabilities. The best support concept is selected and is included in the logistics support plan, along with appropriate requirements to be levied on the contractors.

Chapters 4 to 6 in this book provide explanations of engineering analyses and technical evaluations that are performed to determine the reliability, maintainability, and supportability characteristics of a system design.

---

* The K-factor for a value allows for a percentage increase or decrease (variance) in the value.

3.5.2.3.4 Cost-Benefit Trade-Off Analysis to Support the Ao Requirement

The program team's objective is to deliver a system that achieves a specific mission objective at the lowest cost. Ao is a prime determinant of a system's probability for mission success. The primary objective of Ao calculations is to develop a basis for trade-offs among reliability, maintainability, and supportability characteristics of each design-related decision. The relationship of the components of Ao allows evaluation of both mission effectiveness and life cycle costing. Cost-benefit trade-off analyses are conducted through the accomplishment of a number of key actions:

■ Perform various types of cost-to-benefit curves that will be continuously refined throughout development.
■ Identify preliminary thresholds for each alternative under consideration.
■ Allocate key parameters to all levels in the work breakdown structure (WBS).
■ Evaluate design reliability at the equipment level.
■ Evaluate equipment design maintainability.
■ Evaluate supportability "design to" requirements, focusing on design features critical to Ao.
■ Ensure that reliability and maintainability, and any supportability design requirements, are addressed in demonstration testing.
■ Determine the optimum design and support concepts.

The reliability and maintainability requirements, established prior to this phase, are evaluated to ensure that the thresholds are realistic. Reliability and maintainability thresholds are evaluated against current experience with similar fleet systems, and the expected technological advantage developed in this phase. Supportability requirements, characteristics, and thresholds, established in the integrated logistics support plan, are updated through the refined and upgraded specifications for the system maintenance and support concepts.

The threshold values for the components of Ao must be realistic. An overly high threshold value may incur excessive costs in attempts or achievements; it may degrade the effectiveness of logistics planning; it may adversely impact program plans and schedule; or it may lead to a compromise on a lower value later in development. A low threshold, established early in design, may later lead to excessive support costs and require costly redesign.

Throughout this phase, the program team monitors development of the design concept in order to evaluate factors related to Ao. The team must monitor system reliability, maintainability, and supportability. Monitoring is achieved through evaluating the results of technical analyses and developmental testing. An integrated logistics support management team (logistics IPT) may support the program team in this phase. Logistics IPT membership is tailored to the program and can include representatives from the program office, the Systems Command (SYSCOM) functional logistics element teams, and the Program Support Inventory Control Point (PSICP).

3.5.2.3.5 Develop Cost-Benefit Curves

While there is no standard required approach to a cost-benefit analysis (CBA) for Ao, two general approaches to CBA are recommended:

■ Cost change evaluation
■ Detailed concept cost analysis

These two approaches differ in the required design detail and in the accuracy of the resultant cost estimates. The cost change evaluation method is more frequently used.

3.5.2.3.6 Developing Recommended Preliminary Thresholds for Alternatives

The evaluation of preliminary Ao thresholds is performed in two steps. First, an analysis of alternatives (AoA) is established for cost comparison. The most likely baseline, which is called the baseline comparison system (BCS), is an operational system having a current mission profile similar to the design concept profile and operating requirement. An AoA is normally the process used in performing the BCS analysis. The baseline system must have well-defined cost factors. The second step is comparing each alternative system design concept with the baseline system. Use a form similar to Table 3.6 to evaluate the cost changes between alternatives. The program team will need to judge the difference between the baseline and the alternative system design factors and then estimate the expected change in Ao and cost. The degree of change in Ao is a nonlinear function of cost. This Ao vs. cost relationship is illustrated in Figure 3.7. The curve is derived from a traditional S-shaped logistics function, which illustrates that a higher Ao is achievable through an exponentially higher cost.

3.5.2.3.7 Select the Most Cost-Effective Design Alternative

The program team's analysis action for this phase is to select the most cost-effective design alternative. Applying design-to-cost (DTC) and cost-benefit analysis (CBA) trade-offs is recommended. Do not necessarily be limited to the specific cost goals established in the previous phase. The cost goals for this phase can be viewed as targets by which visibility into the cost consequences of alternate design features can be measured and assessed for Ao achievement. The cost-effectiveness of the reliability, maintainability, and supportability design characteristics is assessed in terms of the DTC goals in order to arrive at an optimum mix of system effectiveness and costs. Use Table 3.7 as a guide. The CBA allows the program team to select the most cost-effective Ao threshold for the selected design alternative.

3.5.2.4 Documentation

The minimum documentation required from the program team by the program milestone decision authorities (MDA) includes:

■ A mission profile
■ Cost as an independent variable (CAIV) objective, key performance parameters (KPPs), and other system performance parameters
■ An initial acquisition program baseline (APB)
■ A preliminary test and evaluation master plan (TEMP)
■ An initial acquisition strategy
■ Draft system performance specifications for reliability and maintainability (R&M)
■ A logistics support planning document
■ Logistics management information (LMI), formerly called the logistic data repository (LSAR)

Table 3.6 Cost Change Evaluation Form

Design Concept Alternative 1: % Change from Mission Needs Statement (ICD) and Analysis of Alternatives (AoA)	Design Factor	Reliability	Maintainability	Manpower and Personnel	Supply Support: Replenishment Spares	Support Equipment	Technical Data: Manuals & Publications	Training	Computer Resources	Facilities	Packaging, Handling, Storage, and Transportation	Design Implementation
Cost factor (percent contribution to life cycle cost)												
Research and development cost (e.g., 8%)												
Investment: Acquisition cost (e.g., 22%)												
Operation and support cost (e.g., 70%)												
Total life cycle cost (LCC)												

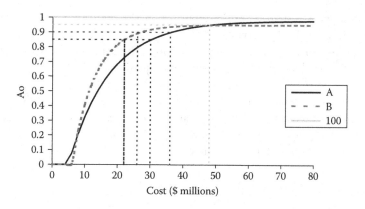

Figure 3.7   Cost vs. Ao curve.

Table 3.7   Ao Trade-Off Threshold Requirements Form

Ao Component	Threshold
Reliability MTBF Mission reliability Mission duration (hours)	
Maintainability MTTR Corrective maintenance	
Supportability (preventive maintenance) Frequency (per day/week/month)	
Built-in-test (BIT) Detection rate Isolation rate False alarm rate	

Operational availability (Ao)
Calculations used to estimate Ao must be
  shown using the specified MTBF and MTTR
  values and describing the other parameters
  (MLDT, etc.) used.	

3.5.3 *System Development and Demonstration Phase*

The purpose of this third phase, systems development and demonstration, is to develop the system, reduce program risk, ensure operational supportability, design for production (producibility), ensure affordability, and demonstrate system integration, interoperability, and utility. This is the phase in which the system design for quantity production is completed and a limited production system is built and tested in the intended fleet environment. In this phase, the system requirements are developed into firm product specifications (drawings, schematics, and manufacturing instructions) and actual hardware and computer programs.

The logistics support system design, established in the logistics support plan and logistics management information in the previous phase, is completed. Logistics support is implemented for operational testing and its transition to production. The equipment designs are tested by the contractor for design evaluation and for operational qualification. The system and logistic elements are tested within the fleet by the program team. Finally, the system is delivered to the fleet representative from the Operational Test and Evaluation Force (OPTEVFOR) for a full operational test supporting the production decision at the next phase. The Ao analysis for this phase contains a heavy discussion of developmental testing. Much of the discussion is also applicable to the previous phase but was not duplicated there.

3.5.3.1 Objectives

The objectives of the Ao analysis for this phase are to:

- Refine the Ao requirement by performing an analysis at the detailed subsystem level
- Update and expand the design reliability, maintainability (R&M), and supportability analyses
- Verify R&M specifications through testing
- Perform maintenance planning and document maintenance plan documents
- Develop and refine logistic planning documentation

The program team in this phase updates the design reliability, maintainability, and supportability analyses to include both the latest predictions and results of developmental test and evaluation (DT&E). This action verifies that the Ao threshold is achievable. Engineering analyses conducted in this phase transform the functional specifications established at the previous phase into firm designs described in product specifications.

Most analytical efforts in this phase are for the further definition of detailed logistics support concepts and resource requirements as the system/equipment design progresses. The time requirements, levels and locations of actions, and the requirements for spares and repair parts, facilities, personnel, training, training equipment, technical data, tools, and test equipment are refined for established configurations. The logistics planning is expanded to reflect the activities for test support, preoperational support, and implementation of each element, and to establish performance and reporting requirements for monitoring logistics activity progress.

3.5.3.2 Data and Models

3.5.3.2.1 Supportability Analysis Database

The primary sources of technical data on the components of Ao during this phase are the results of engineering analysis and the Logistics Management Information (LMI). During this phase an analysis of Ao must be conducted using historic data from existing similar weapon systems along with the results of developmental testing.

3.5.3.2.2 Developmental Test (DT) Data

Testing and evaluation of a system during its development is an evolutionary process that becomes more detailed, controlled, and specific as the item design matures. Early Ao developmental testing, called phase I or DT-I, is performed prior to this phase. Its purpose is to validate engineering analyses, develop information on a specific design or technology, and "grow" the reliability and maintainability configuration of the design. This type of early developmental testing may continue into this phase. DT-I determines and records the critical parameters of a design related to Ao. These tests evaluate the actual functions of an item against its intended functions established through engineering analyses. If adequate design evaluations have been conducted by highly effective engineers and logisticians, the design should be expected to function as intended with minimal effort in DT required.

During the previous phase and early in this phase, the designer should be given considerable latitude to work out and correct problems and design deficiencies so that a satisfactory design evolves. This allows the designer to design, test, modify, redesign, and retest until the hardware design is as good as he can get it within time and resource constraints. As the equipment design progresses, developmental tests are performed on models, breadboard circuits, parts, or other items to establish basic design parameters and determine functional capabilities. The important element in this development or growth testing is to obtain and document the engineering data that ensure achievement of reliability, maintainability, and supportability in the final product. Refer to Chapter 4 in this book for additional discussion of reliability growth.

3.5.3.2.3 Using DT Data to Influence the Design for Supportability

Data obtained during test and inspection are utilized to provide feedback for changes in design. This establishes the final design that will achieve the desired Ao threshold. The information on the Ao component characteristics of the product design is established in the Logistics Management Information (LMI) database and in the logistics plan. These specifications of reliability, maintainability, and supportability characteristics of the system design, with past DT-I records, are the primary input to the next phase of developmental testing (called phase II or DT-II). DT-II, which is discussed in more detail below, is the developmental test and evaluation (DT&E) process that is conducted to support the limited rate production decision. The Ao analysis using achieved reliability values from DT will allow the supportability engineer to help focus design improvements where they provide the best payoff.

The increased role of the system design agent in the cost-benefit trade-off analyses during this phase necessitates that specific contractual requirements be established in solicitations. At this stage, production costs, key support cost factors, and quantity relationships are derived and compared with available resources. These early cost estimates are iterated as primary parameters during the formulation of minimum essential performance and Ao requirements for the new system or equipment. Such cost-benefit relationships are the primary vehicle for the supportability engineer to identify design deficiencies and areas where support cost savings are feasible. The contract must call for delivery of this valuable cost and Ao information to all analysis agencies.

3.5.3.3 Ao Analysis

3.5.3.3.1 Update and Verify the Reliability, Maintainability, and Supportability Analyses

The engineering analysis of the components of Ao during this phase is comprised of those analytical techniques that cannot be performed without a detailed design description, such as drawings, schematics, or a description of parts and materials. This description must include updated reliability and unit cost estimates for each system, subsystem, and repairable candidate. Contractors are understandably reluctant to provide preliminary cost information for a variety of legitimate reasons. The contract should call for analysis purposes estimates that include triangular ranges (low, most probable, high) in the cost vs. risk analysis.

The program team's objective is to complete the engineering analysis for reliability, maintainability (R&M), and supportability as early as possible in the development cycle to serve as a basis for design decisions. At this phase, the inherent R&M design characteristics and requirements are well established in the equipment-level development specifications. The R&M engineering analyses in this phase are intended for parts selection and detailed design checks to assess design capability against fixed R&M specifications. Not until this phase is the analytical effort in logistics expanded to define the supportability requirements of a specific design configuration at the subsystem level.

3.5.3.3.2 Complete the Logistics Planning

A complete Acquisition Logistics Support Plan (ALSP) should be available by the end of this phase. The supply support portion of the ALSP is of critical importance to the achievement of Ao requirements because it is the basis of the spares budget. The planning factors included in the ALSP along with factors in the maintenance plan are used in preprovisioning supply support planning. The program logistics team is responsible for developing the logistics planning documentation. The Program Support Inventory Control Point (PSICP) must also be included in the development of these plans and their review prior to publication. The production ALSP is to identify specific support resources to meet installation and checkout requirements and fleet operational needs. At this same time, logistic test and evaluation criteria are developed to support the test and evaluation master plan (TEMP) and must be consistent with the logistics test and evaluation described in the logistics plan. Developmental testing should be sufficiently rigorous to identify any logistics problems to ready the logistics support system before operational test and evaluation (OPEVAL).

The level of repair analysis (LORA) is refined to include updated and detailed design information. The LORA is conducted in conjunction with the logistics supportability analysis process. LORA is particularly important because it provides the initial basis for maintenance and supply support planning. As mentioned earlier, LORA enables economic and other maintenance considerations to support decisions on repair, replacements, or discard of components. LORA determines the sites and reasonable skill categories for performing the appropriate level of maintenance. The Program Support Inventory Control Point (PSICP) needs this information to complete the provisioning process for the system and equipment, to load failure rate predictions to its inventory model programs, and to determine stocking levels. By the end of this phase, the LORA should be completed for each system and subsystem.

The maintenance plans should also be completed. Often a major weapon system will have an entire family of maintenance plans at the subsystem level. From the maintenance plan, supply policies and procedures are established for use during the contractor (interim) support phase.

3.5.3.3.3 Monitor and Evaluate the Ao

The program team's key action in monitoring Ao during this phase is to ensure proper testing of the Ao components. Developmental test and evaluation (DT&E) is conducted during this phase to validate the engineering analyses performed for the components of Ao and to ensure that the equipment achieves the Ao threshold. DT-II (developmental testing phase II) is conducted during this phase to support the limited rate production decision. DT-II demonstrates that the design meets its performance, reliability, maintainability, and logistics supportability specifications. The development testing conducted during DT-II is usually performed in two discrete phases (DT-IIA and DT-IIB) comprising two types of developing testing. The concept and technology development phases of DT-II comprise a formal technical evaluation (TECHEVAL) of the product conducted with the hardware and validated software. It identifies technical deficiencies and determines whether the design meets the technical specifications and requirements. TECHEVAL also provides a major source of data for the certification of readiness for operational test and evaluation (OPEVAL) and limited rate production.

3.5.3.3.4 Monitor the DT Testing

The developmental testing process must be monitored during this phase to identify critical deficiencies, to correct the deficiencies, and to perform an engineering evaluation and reliability qualification. The process involves the series of analytical tests that are discussed in this section.

3.5.3.3.4.1 Reliability Growth Testing — Reliability growth testing is an essential element of the DT-II program. Once the feasibility of the design concept to achieve the Ao threshold is verified, engineering evaluation tests are planned and implemented to identify and remove significant failure modes in the design configuration. Testing exercises the product and its elements over a spectrum of life cycle usage conditions and operational demands to increase the probability of detecting and identifying inherent failure modes. These reliability growth tests are implemented with a vigorous test, analyze, and fix (TAAF) program. The level of design maturity achieved during this phase is largely determined by the success in debugging the design during the engineering evaluation tests of DT-II.

3.5.3.3.4.2 Reliability Qualification Testing — Reliability qualification tests are to demonstrate that the design can meet or exceed Ao requirements in the operational environment. Qualification tests are conducted to the environmental extremes demanded by the mission profile. Test conditions involve the most severe levels, combinations, and sequences of functional stress identified in the design specifications. The reliability qualification test program is structured so that, upon completion, the risk of failing any reliability demonstration testing can be certified as very low.

Reliability qualification testing to the environmental extremes identified in the mission profile is a long-standing best practice. The engineering evaluation tests conducted in DT-II evaluate the capability of a design to meet the operational and environmental stresses of the mission profile. Qualification testing at or above these stress levels provides maximum assurance that the product will meet reliability requirements. If failures occur during qualification testing, the failures and failure modes are analyzed and compared with qualification criteria to determine the need for corrective action and any follow-on retest.

The optimum reliability qualification test program requires qualification testing at various indenture levels (parts, components, subsystem, and system levels). Generally, these tests are performed at the highest practicable level. If a given item is to be procured from two or more contractors, samples from each source are qualified. If there is a change in the configuration of an item subsequent to its qualifications, the nature of the change is examined to determine the need for requalification.

3.5.3.3.4.3 Demonstration and Acceptance Testing — For system acquisition programs with moderate to high technical risks, phase II developmental testing (DT-II) often involves the fabrication and testing of one or more engineering development models (EDMs). EDMs are followed by the fabrication and test of one or more pilot production models. Programs of lesser risk may involve pilot production models only. EDMs are prototypes of the complex system that are functional equivalents of the system, built for one or more iterations of the test-fix-test process to establish such system attributes as reliability, maintainability, supportability, and safety. An EDM may not have the exact physical configuration of the planned production system. DT&E is performed on EDMs to reduce the design risks and uncertainties prior to fabrication of a more representative production model. It also verifies attainment of technical performance objectives in the components, subsystem, interfaces, and finally, at the total system level.

3.5.3.3.4.4 Reliability Demonstration Testing — Reliability demonstration tests determine contractor compliance with the contractual requirements for system reliability. These tests are performed on the prototype configuration (EDM or pilot production unit) that is specified in the contract. Reliability demonstration is performed after completion of all qualification tests and when analysis of engineering data indicates that the specified reliability requirements can be achieved by the product. The program team ensures that the test scoring rules, such as failure definition and test times, are formalized and representative of service use. The tests are conducted under environmental and operational conditions, including preventative maintenance, in accordance with the specified mission profile. Testing by the military or by the contractor using platforms assigned on loan from the military is an acceptable alternative to factory test cell mission profile simulation. Results of the test are documented in a written report.

The program team is aware of the limitations of reliability demonstration tests and the resources required. Since reliability demonstration tests indicate that the product will perform reliably under service use, the environmental conditions and operational demands invoked on the product during these tests must be compatible with the conditions and demands of the mission profile. Reliability demonstrations are usually conducted in the contractor's facility. Test conditions cannot exactly duplicate the fleet's environment; therefore, results may be optimistic and misleading. Typical test plans require the definition of four parameters: (1) the specified mean time between failures (MTBF), (2) the minimum acceptable MTBF, (3) the consumer's risk, and (4) the producer's risk. The program team either specifies the test plan in the contract or equipment specification, or reviews and approves the contractor-developed test plan.

3.5.3.3.4.5 Maintainability Demonstration Testing — Maintainability demonstration tests indicate that maintainability characteristics of the product meet contractual maintainability requirements. The specific approach used can range from limited controlled tests to an extensive controlled field test of the product. These tests provide quantitative estimates of such maintainability parameters as corrective maintenance downtime, fault isolation time, failed item replacement, and checkout time. The tests are witnessed and verified by the government and documented in a written test report.

Maintenance skills, spares provisioning, sequence of fault occurrences, and other relevant conditions must represent expected conditions for the operational fleet system. The validity of these demonstrations is highly dependent upon the degree to which these environmental resources and skills are representative of those in actual service use. The program team supplies information that is based on operational and other constraints, which provides a basis for defining the test procedures. As a minimum, this information includes the maintenance philosophy, descriptions of the maintenance environments, the modes of operation for the test, and the levels of maintenance to be demonstrated.

The program team determines the need, type, and scoring of this formal maintainability demonstration. The scoring criteria are based on mission requirements, cost of tests, and the type of equipment being developed. A maintainability demonstration test does not guarantee achievement of the required maintainability requirements. However, it focuses the contractor's attention on incorporation of maintainability features in the design. The program team should not require a maintainability demonstration test if any of these three conditions apply:

1. Quantitative maintainability characteristics can be determined through analytical techniques.
2. Proper facilities and resources cannot be made available as needed.
3. The system or subsystem shows evidence of compliance with allocated maintainability requirements.

3.5.3.3.4.6 Operational Test and Evaluation (OT&E)

— The final phase of developmental test and evaluation (DT&E) of the pilot production model is technical evaluation (TECHEVAL), which is conducted in the system's intended operational environment. As an example, the TECHEVAL for shipboard systems is usually conducted in an active fleet ship in at-sea exercises. TECHEVAL has two purposes: to verify that the system design that is planned for production meets technical performance requirements, and to verify that the system is ready for operational test and evaluation (OPEVAL). As stated previously, TECHEVAL is generally the last DT&E event of this program, conducted in the system's planned operational environment. The operations and tests performed during TECHEVAL are structured to assess the components of Ao achieved by the total system in the field.

The final phase of OT&E is OPEVAL, conducted in the intended operational environment. OPEVAL is usually conducted on the same hardware as TECHEVAL. It starts about a month after the completion of TECHEVAL to allow for the analysis of TECHEVAL results and the military System Command (SYSCOM) certification to the chief of military operations (CMO) of readiness for OPEVAL. The results of TECHEVAL are used by the Operational Test Readiness Review Board to judge whether the system is ready for OPEVAL. The program team has to ensure that the TECHEVAL report is available to support the review board, which is approximately 2 weeks prior to OPEVAL.

The Operational Test and Evaluation Force's (OPTEVFOR) goal is to issue the final OPEVAL report within 90 days of test completion. This final report is provided to the SYSCOM director for review. The results of this review are presented to the Acquisition Review Board chairman with a recommendation to support this request for production that the program team plans to make at milestone C.

3.5.3.3.5 DT-II Test Data

Phase II developmental testing (DT-II) provides data to support the continuing design effort in this phase, and to provide assurance that the design configuration meets specification requirements established in this phase. The DT-II test program (early engineering evaluation tests and reliability qualification tests) is structured to include a reasonable assessment of Ao characteristics of the product. This is done in order to approach the demonstration testing effort of the technical evaluation (TECHEVAL) with significantly more assurance. Experience gained in an expanded qualification test program may indicate that a reduction in reliability demonstration testing is feasible.

Test data from the development tests mentioned above (including test conditions, significant events, and problems) are meticulously recorded, analyzed, and maintained in the integrated data system in order to plan logistics support based on achieved vs. predicted reliability. DT-II engineering evaluation tests assess the degree to which the design configuration, components, and materials meet equipment development specifications. DT-II tests also determine the effects of varying stress levels or combinations and sequences of environments; they validate the failure mode, effects, and criticality analysis (FMECA); and they verify that reliability, maintainability, and supportability requirements have been met. DT-II tests are performed on the highest prototype and production assembly levels practicable to represent intended production items as closely as possible.

3.5.3.3.6 Conduct a Cost-Benefit Trade-Off Analysis

This system development and demonstration phase has two significant characteristics affecting the cost-benefit analysis process:

- As the system design progresses from a description of required equipment functions to required physical characteristics, the latitude to change the design diminishes.
- As the design of the system and the logistics support become more definite, the ability to accurately estimate life cycle costs increases.

Therefore, in this phase the program team is in a position in which previous rough cost estimates become fixed. The ability to change cost factors without an unacceptable cost burden no longer exists. Another significant factor in this phase is the evaluation of the system and equipment design, and the system definition changes from mission operations concepts and functional descriptions to detailed engineering descriptions (drawings, materials, and dimensions). The system design agent becomes the primary source of system description. Therefore, during this phase the contractor's role in cost estimation and the cost-benefit analysis (CBA) is increased and assumes functions that were performed by the program team in earlier phases of development.

3.5.3.4 Documentation

The documents that should be created or updated during this phase include:

- Logistics plans
- An acquisition strategy
- Acquisition program baseline (APB)
- Exit criteria for the next milestone
- Test and evaluation master plan (TEMP)
- Level of repair analysis (LORA)
- Maintenance plan
- Logistics support summary reports
- Logistics assessment review (LAR) documentation

The data obtained during test and inspection are utilized to provide feedback documentation for changes in the system design. This establishes a final design that will achieve the Ao threshold. The information on the Ao component characteristics of the product design is established in the Logistics Management Information (LMI) database and in the logistics plan. These specifications of reliability, maintainability, and supportability characteristics of the system design, along with past development testing DT-I records, are the primary input to DT-II.

The specific output of the cost-benefit analysis and trade-off process is the life cycle cost (LCC) estimate, which is established and presented at milestone C for the production decision. The LCC estimate at milestone C includes a DTC goal for the acquisition cost component, and a separate DTC component for operating and support (O&S) costs. The process through which the LCC estimate is derived is basically that which is described in Chapter 9. During this phase, the LCC cost estimates are based on the most detailed of the three procedures for cost estimation, the industrial engineering method.

Results of the Ao analysis are reported to the chief of military operations staff, as well as recommendations for actions necessary to exceed Ao thresholds and achieve Ao goals. Reports are made to the resource cost/performance team on previously unbudgeted costs and any extraordinary support requirements, indicated by the analyses. Alternative courses of action with associated Ao expectations and cost considerations are also provided.

If the analyses determine that Ao goals cannot be met, the program team reviews its options very carefully. Engineering and logistic analyses evaluate all alternatives, such as improved reliability (MTBF), maintainability (MTTR), and supportability (MLDT, MAdmDT, and MOADT), to determine what is required. They must not immediately come to the conclusion that a greater repair parts investment is required. It is possible, regardless of the amount of investment in repair parts, that the Ao goal will never be achieved. If additional spare parts and repair parts are the answer, the program team investigates the possibility of applying the readiness-based sparing (RBS) model.

Data obtained during test and inspection are utilized to provide feedback for changes in design. This establishes a final design that will achieve the Ao threshold. The information on the Ao component characteristics of the product design is established in the LMI and in the logistics plan. These specifications of reliability, maintainability, and supportability characteristics of the system design, with past DT-I records, are the primary input to DT-II.

These actions establish cost goals for Ao and LCC that can be validated and refined for use as primary design parameters, equal to performance in priority. As the program progresses through this phase, some cost (production and support) and performance trade-off flexibility is needed to permit development of an acceptable system within the cost constraints. This contract must be structured to require the contractor to conduct cost-benefit trade-offs based on Ao.

The specific output of the cost-benefit analysis and trade-off process is the LCC estimate, which is established and presented at the production milestone (C). The LCC estimate at milestone C includes a design-to-cost (DTC) goal for the acquisition cost component, and a separate DTC component for operating and support (O&S) costs. The LCC cost estimates for this phase are based on detailed cost estimates.

A copy of the TECHEVAL report is also sent for information. Policy requires the Systems Command (SYSCOM) to provide certification of the readiness of each system to enter its OPEVAL. It is policy not to enter OPEVAL until the readiness criteria have been satisfied, and it is certified that the system will pass OPEVAL. The assessment of the system to provide certification for OPEVAL is performed by the test and evaluation (T&E) people with support from specialists to assess reliability, maintainability, and supportability.

Certification and the decision to approve OPEVAL are based on completion of these steps related to Ao by the program team:

1. The test and evaluation master plan (TEMP) is current and approved.
2. All TEMP-specified prerequisite DT-II data have been completed and the reports are published.
3. All developmental test and evaluation (DT&E) objectives and performance thresholds have been met.
4. System operating and maintenance documents, including preliminary allowance parts lists, have been distributed for OPEVAL.
5. The logistics plans and necessary supporting detailed technical documentation, such as failure mode, effects, and criticality analysis (FMECA), LORA, LCC, and supportability analysis, have been provided to the test and evaluation force (OPTEVFOR).
6. Adequate logistics support, including spares and repair parts, are available for OPEVAL, and the logistics support system is representative of that which will support the production system.
7. The OPEVAL manning of the system is the same (numbers, rates, ratings, and experience level) as that planned for the fleet systems under normal operating conditions.
8. The test plan has been approved and provided to OPTEVFOR.
9. Required training for personnel who will operate and maintain the system during OPEVAL (including OPTEVFOR personnel) has been completed, and this training is representative of that planned for the fleet units having the system.

3.5.4 Production and Deployment Phase

The purpose of the production and deployment phase is to achieve the operational capability that satisfies mission needs. This phase provides a key window of time for achieving the Ao requirements at the lowest possible life cycle cost (LCC). During the production contract years, systems are being delivered to the user and real operational data are collected concerning system failure rates and maintainability (maintenance repair times) experience. The data must be aggressively collected, an analysis performed, and corrective action decisions made with an aggressive and cooperative approach. Once the production contract is ended, the ability to affect corrective actions in a timely fashion becomes much more challenging.

3.5.4.1 Objectives

This phase has three principal objectives with regard to Ao. They are to execute the program plans to achieve the design Ao in production, to monitor the program Ao to identify any deviations from the plans and determine the degree of deviation, and to take corrective action caused by changes to the plans in order to attain the required Ao in the deployed systems. The following five actions are to be accomplished in this phase:

1. The system production is funded, and funding for the support during operations is put into place in the budget.
2. All key program documentation is approved.
3. Performance standards concerning reliability, maintainability, logistics supportability, and Ao thresholds are well established.

4. The system has been demonstrated, tested, and accepted as worthy of commitment to production.
5. All logistics resources required to support the Ao requirements of the system users are identified and fully funded in the budget at the lowest reasonable LCC.

What remains is to produce the system on the production line, deploy the system in the fleet, and establish the support structure so that the system meets the design specifications and operational requirements in the fleet. This phase of the acquisition concentrates on production, deployment, and follow-on support of the system. It includes these steps:

1. Validate the Ao and LCC estimates with actual fleet feedback data.
2. Attain the required thresholds in the production models of the system rather than establish Ao requirements.
3. Establish the refined baseline for Ao and total ownership cost reduction (TOC-R) during the operating and maintenance phases of the system life cycle.
4. Confirm achievement of the Ao requirement with currently funded logistics resources.
5. Identify any Ao impacting shortfalls.
6. Approve the postfielding Ao monitoring plan. The program Ao monitoring plan explains how actual systems performance data will be collected and analyzed. Critical elements of the Ao calculation (MTBF, MTTR, MLDT) must be monitored over the life of the program.
7. Confirm the achievement of Ao during early fielding. Measure the achieved Ao.
8. Update the appropriate documentation to reflect the demonstrated Ao.
9. Assess the impact of deviations from the logistics plans, maintenance plan, and transition plan on achievable Ao.
10. Manage the changes or modifications in the design, configuration, or support resource that impact the achievement of the Ao threshold.
11. Develop plans and identify resources to improve Ao, if the Ao threshold is not being achieved.
12. Plan for postproduction support.

3.5.4.2 Data and Models

In the previous phases, only predictions and developmental testing (DT) test data were available to model the achievement of Ao objectives and thresholds. During this phase, however, actual operational test and fleet feedback data are collected for model inputs. These data include:

- Provisioning technical documentation
- Test and evaluation data and reports
- Casualty reports
- Commanding officer narrative reports
- Maintenance Data System (MDS) data, also referred to as 3M data
- Visibility and Management of Operating and Support Costs (VAMOSC) program data and reports
- In-service engineering agent (ISEA) failure rate analysis reports, including information concerning failure trends from intermediate and depot data
- Engineering change proposals

- Logistics Management Information (LMI) prime contractor analysis reports
- Maintenance plans
- Logistics plans
- Operational Logistics Support Summary (OLSS)

3.5.4.3 Ao Analysis

The Ao analysis process for this fourth phase includes:

- Ensure that the system production model provides the same characteristics as those to which the prototype was designed, developed, and tested.
- Ensure that the configuration, installation, and operation of the system are consistent with the product specifications and the use study from which the system was developed.
- Manage and coordinate the execution of key fleet introduction plans.

3.5.4.3.1 Monitor the Achieved Ao from Early Fleet Reporting

Until now, Ao has been used as a threshold or objective function. The program team now begins to consider Ao as both a process and a measure of achievement. The process is the measuring of the interdependent impacts of shortfalls in reliability, maintainability, or supportability upon each other, the Ao of the components of the system, and ultimately the material readiness of the system. The monitoring of the achieved Ao can be displayed in a matrix, similar to that shown in Table 3.8, with its major components on one axis and the components of Ao and their subelements on the second axis. The matrix shown in Table 3.8 should be viewed on three planes overlaying each other. The three planes of the matrix are the threshold values, schedules, and costs. The objective of this type of matrix is to provide continuous and consistent monitoring of production system performance, and to focus attention on those critical resources that adversely impact Ao, reliability, maintainability, and supportability thresholds.

The program team needs to monitor the key Ao driving indicators. The team manages those critical path items and resource requirements that vary from the required levels of performance. The program office staff coordinates the various commands contributing to the acquisition, production, deployment, and support of the system. The staff also ensures the integration of contractor and government tasks. Each member of the staff manages the program segments and completes the applicable portions of the program team's Ao matrix. The program team concentrates management attention on those variances from the system specifications. The program team assesses the impact of a variance in one component of material readiness upon other components of Ao that are dependent upon the element out of tolerance. The dependent relationships become keys to analysis of problems in the deployed operational system.

3.5.4.3.2 Update the Appropriate Documentation to Reflect the Demonstrated Ao

Changes to the program plans approved at the previous phase decision point will occur throughout the production, fielding/deployment, and operational support phases of the system. These changes must continue to be reflected in four documents that are crucial to program coordination throughout this phase:

Table 3.8   Subsystem/System to Elements of Ao Matrix

Duty Cycle = Operating Hours/ Calendar Hours K = 2.0	Subsystem A	Subsystem B	Subsystem C	Total System
Reliability (MTBF)	1,200 h	2,000 h	16,000 h	1,000 h
Maintainability (MTTR) • Maintenance plan LOR	0.5 h	1.5 h	15 h	3 h
Supportability (MLDT) • Maintenance planning • Manpower and personnel • Supply support • Technical data • Training and training support • Facilities • Packaging, handling, storage, and transportation Design interface	269 h	269 h	269 h	269 h
Ao	≥0.90	≥0.95	≥0.98	≥0.88

a. The maintenance plan
b. The provisioning computation
c. The logistics plan
d. The initial operational capability (IOC) date

These four references are continually monitored by the team and updated as changes occur. The entire support establishment and the fleet use these documents for scheduling, budgeting, and planning. Changes to these documents can significantly impact the achievable Ao upon deployment of the system. For example, a decision to change the maintenance concept from piece part repair to modular replacement can change:

■ The technical manuals
■ The maintenance technicians
■ The allowance parts list (APL)

- The Program Support Inventory Control Point (PSICP) weapon system file data
- The technical skills required of the shipboard maintenance personnel
- The intermediate maintenance activity and depot overhaul point workload schedule
- The budgets
- The packaging, handling, storage, and transportation plan
- The IOC date

While this example is a drastic change to a system maintenance concept, it demonstrates that a change to one area of a system can have significant impacts across the entire spectrum of support for the system.

3.5.4.3.3 Assess the Impact of Deviations, Changes, and Modifications

During the design process, the requirements for deviations from specifications and the need for modifications or engineering change proposals become evident. These deviations will naturally change the allocation of the Ao parameters for reliability, maintainability, and supportability among the components of the system being designed. Each of these three Ao parameters is discussed below.

Concerning the *reliability* parameter, the developmental test and evaluation (DT&E) and the operational test and evaluation (OT&E) processes will have confirmed that the system design and its prototype model provide the capabilities and meet the thresholds established for this system. However, this does not guarantee the same for the production model. Mean time between failures (MTBF) is the largest single contributor to system material readiness. It is the most intractable and most expensive to alter, impacting virtually all elements of material readiness when changes do occur. This component of Ao is the most critical factor that the program team will have to manage. Change to the system design at any level of indenture must receive the program team's immediate attention. The team determines the impact of the change upon all other dependent elements, assesses the costs, benefits, and risks of that change to the system configuration, and reestablishes control of all elements that have changed. Required engineering changes to a system design costs time, money, and readiness in terms of:

- The modifications to technical manuals, training plans, parts allowance documents, test procedures, retrofit planning, and the other support elements
- The cost of retrofit installations, the procurement of new spares, the purge of stocks of obsolete parts, the purchase of new test equipment, publications, retraining, and possibly contending with litigation depending on the terms of the contract
- A decreased readiness until the fixes are in place, and the turmoil to the support establishment

A configuration change requires the same level of management attention, coordination, and planning that the original system configuration required.

With respect to the *maintainability* parameter of Ao, the maintenance plan drives all of the other supportability elements of the system. Second only to configuration changes, the maintenance plan impacts every logistics element. If the program team waits to develop and publish the maintenance plan until after the initial operational capability (IOC) date, the team is really acting too late. The maintenance plan is dependent upon the reliability and configuration of the system. However, all other elements of logistics are dependent upon the maintenance plan, so that the support system required to maintain the system and restore it to operation when it fails can be designed and in place when the system is first deployed. Maintainability (MTTR) is not as mathematically significant as MTBF and MLDT in the computation of Ao. MTTR is usually 3 hours or less. The MTTR threshold was established at milestone B and updated at milestone C.

Throughout the production, fielding/deployment, and operational support phase, the program team should be sensitive to any changes in configuration, form, fit, and function of the system or its component parts that require maintenance personnel to take longer than the MTTR threshold to restore the system to full operation. Although the MTTR threshold is an average for all maintenance actions, any action that substantially exceeds the threshold should be reviewed by the program team.

Concerning the *supportability* parameter of Ao, the program team in this phase must have an experienced and dedicated logistics team. The logistics team is required to coordinate and control the many interdependent elements of logistics support, each managed by different commands, and each comprised of innumerable factors, codes, and data elements. The logistics elements are merged into the Logistics Management Information (LMI) database through the logistics plans. The logistics team orchestrates this process, reduces uncertainty in support planning, ensures the compatibility of resources, diminishes the duplication of action, and coordinates the transition of support tasks from the contractor.

In this phase, the reliability and maintainability parameters of Ao should be locked into the system design. As long as this stability in the parameters is maintained, the consistency between the various planning documents, the scheduled development and delivery of the support elements, and the budgeted cost of each element will track as planned. This ensures that the system is installed, trained personnel are on site, and resources required to sustain inherent performance of the system are simultaneously positioned. However, no program is immune to changes that will improve system reliability, maintainability, or supportability. The logistics team's functions are fourfold:

1. *Maintain the supportability analysis.* The program team should continue to document all parameters used to determine the resource support requirements and relate those parameters to the program thresholds. The team should be knowledgeable of the changes to the program plans and whether a change is at the system level or the piece part level.
2. *Establish interdependencies among the program elements.* The logistics team should be able to identify the impact of a change in one area to any other element.
3. *Identify critical tasks.* The start-up of some tasks is dependent upon the completion of other tasks. All tasks are tied to budget cycles. Tasks requiring operations and maintenance funds are particularly susceptible to changes in the schedule.
4. *Assess and reduce risk.* Risk is a function of both the probability and the consequence of failure. The logistics team cannot eliminate changes to schedules, configuration, budgets, or other deviations from the program plans. The team is expected to identify the impact of those changes on other program elements and to minimize or prevent degradation to the system Ao at the time of deployment caused by inconsistent or out-of-phase support elements.

Each element of support requires a specified response time to plan, budget, and execute. This is the lead time. The logistics team knows when an increment of each element of support is required to be positioned and responsive to the fleet requirements. These support data are advanced by a period of time equal to the response time, giving the logistics team the latest date that data and documentation must be provided in order for that element of support to be in place to support the operational system. Any changes subsequent to that date produce a risk of degraded Ao in the fielded system. This can only be offset by extraordinary management attention to reduce the response time. For example, suppose that 12 months before the first production model is delivered, a major repairable module is changed from a remove and replace maintenance concept to a lower level of indenture (e.g., circuit card) remove and replace concept. This change to a circuit card will provide a reduced operation and maintenance cost to the fleet. It also will increase the repair capability at the shipboard level of maintenance. However, the logistics team should immediately be aware that:

- Technical manuals do not address these new maintenance procedures, and technical manuals often require 18 months to reprint and distribute.
- Maintenance courses have already graduated personnel who were trained in the former maintenance procedure.
- Test equipment to fault isolate to the circuit card level have not been bought, and the procurement and production lead time for this specialized support equipment is 2 years.
- The allowance parts list (APL) designates the module as an on-board spare part, but the individual circuit cards are nonstandard stock. This leads to cataloging the circuit cards and procuring them in 26 months.
- The sole source of supply for the circuit cards has only enough capacity to support the production line.
- The vendor requires a time period of 1 year to increase capacity.
- The circuit cards use proprietary manufacturing techniques that are held only by the sole source vendor.

Situations similar to the above occur frequently throughout the production, fielding/deployment, and operational support phases of acquisition. The serial impact of the change upon other elements of support is not exaggerated. The program team has to be aware of the multiplier effect of any variance from the program plans, schedule, or budgets. The team has to take immediate action to maintain consistency and coordination among the various support elements to ensure that system material readiness is sustained at the threshold value.

3.5.4.3.4 Develop Plans to Sustain Ao

The final test of whether the program team has maintained the system design Ao through production is the Ao achieved by the system when it is deployed in the operational environment. In order to do this, the program team has to:

- Develop a continuing and consistent reporting system to monitor system performance.
- Determine responsibility for compiling those reports and how the program manager can monitor the system performance.
- Manage the variation in Ao from the established thresholds.

The team should maintain all of the baseline documentation, going all the way back to when the program was initiated. This establishes the evolution of the system parameters to those of the production baseline configuration. The test and evaluation master plan (TEMP) together with the results of the developmental test and evaluation (DT&E), operational test and evaluation

(OT&E), and follow-on operational test and evaluation (FOT&E) form the baseline for comparing the achieved Ao in the testing environment with the actual fleet experience. The fleet will provide casualty reports (CASREPs), Maintenance Data System (MDS) data reports, allowance change requests (ACRs), commanding officer narratives (CONARs), and any other special reports specified by the program team. Also available to the program team are failure analyses compiled by the in-service engineering agent (ISEA), the designated overhaul point (DOP), shore intermediate maintenance activities (SIMAs), parts usage and failure rate data, configuration data from the program records as well as those maintained by the ISEA, not operationally ready supply (NORS), and CASREP data from the inventory control point (ICP) or aviation support office (ASO).

A newly deployed system will experience problems. During the first several systems years of operation, CASREPs will be high, work hours per maintenance action will be high, Ao will be lower than specified, and utilization will be high. The program team has to anticipate and expect such results. The fleet will exercise a new system at every opportunity and under every possible condition. The maintenance personnel want to utilize their training and determine how the system is constructed. Inevitably, parts allowances will have holes in them, and just as inevitably, the parts required to restore operation will be for items not in stock. The program team's immediate concerns during this initial operational period will be:

- Problem definition
- Assessment of impact
- Feedback

Throughout the operational cycle of the system, the program team's first and most critical task is to define the problem when the system fails to meet the performance parameters. When does the program team take corrective action, and when does the team continue to monitor the system's Ao performance but not take action? Throughout the acquisition of a system, each component of Ao has been individually tested and validated as achievable. These threshold values are the baseline values against which the system's performance in the fleet is compared. A problem exists when any of these components falls below the threshold value. However, the objective of the acquisition has been to deliver a system to the fleet that provides enhanced capability. One of the critical criteria by which that system is measured is Ao. The system Ao can be met with many combinations of the mean time between failures (MTBF), mean time to repair (MTTR), and mean logistics delay time (MLDT) values. For example, a 20% shortfall in reliability may be offset by a 25% gain in supportability, and the system Ao threshold could still be met. The options for a thorough analysis and development of the fix for the shortfall are available. So, there is no real need for crisis management, but the program team would need to take action in determining the cause of any shortfall in the reliability.

Before the program team deploys the first system, the methodology for monitoring system performance must be in place and functioning. The sophistication of the reporting and monitoring system depends upon the complexity of the system and the level of detail necessary to identify and isolate any problems for testing, analyzing, and fixing (TAAF). A well-managed, complex system can have a very detailed monitoring and reporting system. One example is the Material Readiness Database (MRDB), which monitors:

- Total system Ao
- Reliability (mean time between failures—MTBF)
- Maintainability (mean time to repair—MTTR)

- Supportability (mean logistic downtime—MLDT, mean administrative delay time—MAdmDT, and mean awaiting outside assist time—MOADT)
- Uptime and downtime, and deployed and nondeployed periods, for each fleet in which the system is installed
- Subsystem equipment and components experiencing reliability problems
- High usage repair parts and supply system response times to provide those parts

The reporting system can display the data in matrix form, pie charts, timeline progressions, and narrative form. This requires special reporting by the fleet, special compilation and drafting by the responsible activity, and printing and distribution costs.

The sophistication of the above tracking and monitoring system is not required for all programs. A readiness assessment can be as simple as dividing calendar time free of casualty reports (CASREPs) by total calendar time for each installation and averaging the results across all installations. This is a gross calculation for Ao, but it may be sufficiently accurate for an auxiliary generator. Ao for a missile is computed as the number of successful launches divided by the number of attempts, since the missile is a nonrecoverable system. The disadvantage of this method of monitoring is that it does not isolate problems to the components of reliability, maintainability, or supportability. The program team knows only that the material readiness of the system/equipment is degraded and then has to isolate the cause of the degradation through additional testing and analysis. This method of monitoring could be costly. The program team would have to assess the requirement for a given level of detail and determine whether the costs to obtain and compile data over the period of time to system maturation are worth it. The program team should minimize the reporting requirements on the fleet and maximize the use of the existing reporting system, while satisfying the requirements to measure the achievement of readiness thresholds.

When shortfalls in the achievement of readiness thresholds occur, the program team identifies the cause, assesses the impact, determines the fix, and executes the solution. Identification of the cause is the most difficult of these to accomplish. The more complex the system, the more difficult the job of isolating the problem becomes. As a general rule, readiness problems are initially manifested as supply support problems. When parts fail faster than the supply system can replace them, a supply support problem exists, and the thread to problem resolution unravels. On the surface, the fleet correctly reports that the supply support is unsatisfactory. The system is nonoperational due to lack of repair parts. Once the parts are provided, the system will be repaired. If the problem is that the supply system bought an insufficient inventory, or the procurement lead times increased significantly, then the degradation to the system availability is a supply support problem.

If the program team begins with the premise that readiness problems are manifested initially as supply problems, then they continue the analysis to determine if the supply support problem is masking a more serious long-term reliability or other logistics support problem. The initial analysis by the program team should be to correlate the predicted replacement rate with the actual replacement rate in the fleet.

The product specifications provide a design replacement factor, or failure rate, for each part in the system. The program team obtains the actual failure rates for the parts that are causing the most frequent CASREPs, have the most backorders in the supply system, or are otherwise identified by the fleet as supply problems. These failure data are available from both the Program Support Inventory Control Point (PSICP) and the 3M Maintenance Data System (MDS). Both sources of data are obtained and compared. The 3M data indicate actual failure rates unique to the system. The PSICP usage rates indicate total demands against the supply system, and identify the activities using those parts. Comparing the data from these sources reveals whether the lack of parts is caused by higher than predicted failures in the system, by other systems using common repair parts, or by intermediate- or depot-level activities that are using more parts than predicted. These two data sources will identify which parts are causing support problems. When compared with predicted replacement rates, the data will focus the actions of the program team's toward parts reliability, maintenance, or supply support solutions.

Frequently, parts problems are caused by fleet maintenance practices. Repair parts with higher than predicted use can be caused by:

■ *Poor fault isolation detection procedures or equipment.* If the technician can only isolate failures to an ambiguity group of three parts with available test equipment, then the only means available to identify the actual failure is to replace each of those three parts until the system is fixed. If two of those parts have very low failure rates but are experiencing very high demand, then the program team needs to assess fixes to the fault isolation procedures.

■ *Unplanned usage* is where cover plates, shims, leads, gaskets, insulators, and other parts are experiencing higher usage than predicted. Corrective maintenance procedures may require the removal or even destruction of these parts of the system. Any time a part is removed, the chance for it to be damaged, destroyed, or lost increases. If that part is critical to safe operation of the equipment, its actual failure rate may not have been predicted and it would not have been stocked.

■ *Increased system utilization* is where the system was designed to be used a specified number of hours per month, and planned maintenance cycles and parts usage per year were based upon that utilization rate. If the parts usage dramatically increases, then the program team should determine and compare the actual fleet system utilization rate. The fleet may have discovered new capabilities not anticipated, or the predicted utilization rate may have been grossly understated. In this situation the system is faultless, except that the failure rates require recomputation, and the supply system needs to increase inventory levels to accommodate the higher demand caused by greater system operating hours.

■ *Technical data errors* frequently cause a higher than normal demand for parts when the technical manual identifies the incorrect part, the part number to the National Stock Number (NSN) cross-reference list misidentifies the correct NSN, or the part has been modified, making it useless in older configurations of the equipment, but it still has the same NSN as the obsolete configuration. The fleet will continue to order and recorder the same item until the data problem is highlighted and corrected.

The above examples of relationships among reliability, maintainability, and logistics elements are indicative of difficulties confronting the program team in attempting to identify the real system degradation problem. The point is not to be misled by the initial problem identification, but to continue to analyze the problem until satisfied that the actual degradation has been identified and a fix developed.

When the real problem is determined, the program team still must contend with the lead time to develop, procure, and deploy the fix, and to assess the interdependent impacts on other elements of maintainability and supportability until the fix is in place.

The immediate degradation may not significantly impact interfacing parts, equipment, or subsystems, but a prolonged degradation may have a deteriorating effect. The program team therefore considers time factors as well as funding and hardware considerations in prioritizing the fix.

3.5.4.4 Documentation

The documents that should be created or updated during this phase include:

    a. Logistics Management Information (LMI) reports
    b. Maintenance plan
    c. Provisioning computation
    d. Logistics support plan
    e. Initial operational capability (IOC) and chief of military operations pre-IOC logistics readiness reviews (LRRs)
    f. Postproduction support plan
    g. Transition plan

The postproduction support plan and the transition plan require further discussion.

3.5.4.4.1 Postproduction Support Plan

Development of a plan for postproduction support begins at milestone C and is updated throughout the production cycle. This plan provides for continued support for the life cycle of the system after the production line is closed. The postproduction support plan should include:

- The schedule for program production line closing
- Whether continuing contractual coverage is required for proprietary hardware or software
- Whether the government will buy those rights in data
- Whether the government will make a "lifetime buy" of all proprietary piece parts to support the system throughout its life cycle
- Whether the system will be supported by the contractor depot, or whether transition to an organic MRO depot is required
- Procurement of all system technical specifications in sufficient level of detail for reprocurement from capable sources in a competitive mode
- Disposal/demilitarization

3.5.4.4.2 Transition Plan

The transition plan provides the schedule, responsibilities, and strategy for transitioning supply- and depot-level maintenance support from the contractor to the military. This plan accommodates budget cycles, administrative and procurement lead times, and the orderly transfer of engineering and technical data required for military activities to have the support in place on the date of transition.

3.5.5 Sustainment Phase

The sustainment phase in a system's life cycle is where the system support program is implemented. The target is to meet the operational performance requirements of the system in the most cost-effective manner. However, there are several forces acting on the system Ao during the sustainment phase that warrant constant management attention:

- Physics of failure causes can in turn cause reductions in systems reliability.
- Aging factors can cause reductions in systems reliability.

- Maintenance-induced failures can cause reductions in systems reliability.
- Environmental conditions can contribute to the above three.

3.5.5.1 Objectives

Given these failures and conditions, there are three principle objectives for this phase:

1. To achieve the design Ao in production
2. To monitor the program Ao to identify deviations from plans, and to determine the degree of deviation
3. To identify the corrective actions to maintain the required Ao in the deployed system

In order to accomplish these objectives, seven actions are recommended:

1. Validate the Ao estimates with actual fleet feedback data.
2. Identify specific subsystems and components that are driving the Ao problems.
3. Provide decision support analysis and recommendations for system improvements.
4. Confirm the achievement of Ao during early fielding and remeasure the achieved Ao.
5. Manage any changes or modifications in design, configuration, or support resources that impact the achievement of the Ao threshold.
6. Identify resources to improve Ao, if the Ao threshold is not being achieved.
7. Identify postproduction support issues.

3.5.5.2 Data and Models

In the previous phases only prediction test data were available to model the achievement of the Ao objectives and thresholds. During this phase, actual fleet feedback data are collected for model inputs.

- Visibility and Management of Operating and Support Costs (VAMOSC) program data and reports
- Casualty reports (CASREPs)
- Commanding officer narrative reports
- 3M Maintenance Data System (MDS) data
- In-service engineering agent (ISEA) failure rate analysis reports, including information concerning failure trends from intermediate and depot data
- Engineering change proposals
- Prime contractor analysis reports

3.5.5.3 Ao Analysis

The Ao analysis process for this phase includes:

- Ensure that the fielded system continues to provide the required Ao characteristics.
- Ensure that the configuration, installation, and fleet operation of the system are consistent with the product specifications from which the system was developed.
- Perform Ao studies and analysis to support the recommendations for system upgrades, modernization, new technology insertion, and other engineering modifications.

3.5.5.3.1 Monitor the Achieved Ao from Fleet Reports

The first step in the Ao analysis for this phase is to use fleet reports to monitor and study the interdependent impacts of the shortfalls in reliability, maintainability, and supportability upon the Ao of the components of the system. The system can be displayed in a matrix with its major components on one axis and the components of Ao and their subelements on the second axis, similar to what's shown in Table 3.8, which was used for the previous phase. The matrix in that table continues to be applicable in the sustainment phase and should be viewed on three planes overlaying each other. The three planes of the matrix are threshold values, schedules, and costs. The objective of this type of matrix is to provide continuous and consistent monitoring of production system performance and to focus attention on those critical resources that adversely impact Ao, reliability, maintainability, and supportability thresholds.

The program team should continue to monitor the key indicators, including those critical path items and resource requirements that vary from the required levels of performance. The program team should assess the impact of a variance in one component of material readiness upon other components of Ao that are dependent upon the element out of tolerance. The dependent relationships are important to the program team because they become keys to an analysis of problems in the deployed operational system.

3.5.5.3.2 Assess the Impact of Deviations, Changes, and Modifications

During the sustainment phase, the need for modifications or engineering change proposals becomes evident. These will naturally change the allocation of the three Ao driving parameters, reliability, maintainability, and supportability, among the components of the system being designed. Each of the three parameters is discussed below.

The *reliability* parameter, mean time between failures (MTBF), is the largest single contributor to system material readiness. It is the most intractable and most expensive to alter, impacting virtually all elements of material readiness when changes occur. This component of Ao is the most critical factor the program team manages. Change to the system design at any level of indenture must receive the program team's immediate attention. The team must determine the impact of the change upon all other dependent elements, assess the costs, benefits, and risks of that change to the system configuration, and reestablish control of all elements that have changed.

Engineering changes to the system design continue to cost time, money, and readiness in terms of:

- Modifications to technical manuals, training plans, parts allowance documents, test procedures, retrofit planning, and the other support elements
- Cost for retrofit installations, procurement of new spares, purge in stocks of obsolete parts, purchase of new test equipment, printing of publications, retraining, and possibly contending with litigation
- Decreased readiness until the fixes are in place, and the turmoil to the support establishment levels out

Configuration changes require the same level of management attention, techniques, coordination, and planning that the original system configuration required.

The *maintainability* parameter, mean time to repair (MTTR), is sensitive to any changes in configuration, form, fit, and function of the system or its component parts. These changes require maintenance personnel to take longer than the MTTR threshold to restore the system to full operation. Although the MTTR threshold is an average for all maintenance actions, any action that substantially exceeds the threshold should be reviewed by the program team.

The *supportability* parameters, mean logistic downtime (MLDT), mean administrative delay (MAdmDT), and mean awaiting outside assist time (MOADT), require that the program team have an experienced and dedicated logistics group. The logistics group is required to coordinate and control the many interdependent elements of logistics support. Each element should be managed by the different commands, and each should be comprised of innumerable factors, codes, and data elements. The logistics elements are merged into the Logistics Management Information (LMI) database through the logistics plans. The group orchestrates this process, reduces uncertainty in support planning, ensures the compatibility of resources, diminishes the duplication of action, and coordinates the transition of support tasks from the contractor.

In this acquisition phase reliability and maintainability should be locked into the system design. As long as that stability is maintained, the consistency between and among the various planning documents, the scheduled development and delivery of the support elements, and the budgeted cost of each element will track as planned. This ensures that the system is installed, trained personnel are on site, and resources required to sustain inherent performance of the system are simultaneously positioned.

All programs need to continuously consider changes that improve system reliability, maintainability, or supportability. The logistics group's functions are:

1. *To maintain the supportability analysis.* The group should continue to document all parameters used to determine support resource requirements and relate those parameters to the program thresholds. The group should be knowledgeable of changes to the program plans and whether a change is at the system level or the piece part level.
2. *To establish interdependencies among the program elements.* The logistics group should be able to identify the impact of a change in one area to any other element.
3. *To identify critical tasks.* The start-up of some tasks is dependent upon the completion of other tasks. All tasks are tied to budget cycles. Tasks requiring operations and maintenance funds are particularly susceptible to changes in schedule that modify the fiscal year in which the task is begun.
4. *To assess and reduce risk.* Risk is a function of both the probability and the consequences of failure. The logistics group cannot eliminate changes to schedules, configuration, budgets, or other deviations from the program plans. The group is expected to identify the impact of those changes on other program elements and to minimize or prevent degradation to system Ao at the time of deployment caused by inconsistent or out-of-phase support elements.

3.5.5.3.3 Execute the Plan to Sustain Ao

The final test of whether the program team has maintained the system design Ao through production is the Ao achieved by the system when it is deployed in the operational environment. The success of having achieved the desired Ao depends on:

■ A continuous and consistent reporting system to monitor the system performance
■ Good management of any variance from the Ao thresholds

All systems will experience problems during the sustainment phase. During the first several systems years of operation, the casualty reports (CASREPs) will be high, work hours per maintenance action will be high, and Ao will be lower than specified. Why? Because operators tend to exercise a new system at every opportunity and under every possible condition, and because maintenance personnel like to utilize their new training and are curious how the system is constructed. In addition, it is very likely that some parts required to sustain the system will not be in stock. Thus, the program team should focus on:

- Problem definition: Being proactive rather than reactive
- Assessing the impact of problems and changes

Throughout the operational cycle of the system, the program team's first and most critical task is to define the problem when the system fails to meet the performance parameter. When does the program team take corrective action? When does the team continue to monitor the system's performance but not take action? When shortfalls in the achievement of readiness thresholds occur, the program team must identify the cause, assess the impact, determine the fix, and execute the solution. Identification of the cause is the most difficult of these to accomplish. The more complex the system, the more difficult the job of isolating the problem becomes. As a general rule, readiness problems are initially manifested as supply support problems. When the system fails, parts fail. When parts fail faster than the supply system can replace them, a supply support problem exists and the thread to problem resolution unravels. On the surface, the user is correctly reporting that the supply support is unsatisfactory. The system is nonoperational due to lack of repair parts. Once the parts are provided, the system will be repaired. If the problem is that the supply system bought an insufficient inventory or the procurement lead times increased significantly, then the degradation to the system availability is a supply support problem.

If the program team begins with the premise that readiness problems are manifested initially as supply problems, then the team should assess the impact of the problem to determine if the supply support problem is masking a more serious long-term reliability or other logistics support problem. The initial analysis should be to correlate the predicted replacement rate with the actual replacement rate in the fleet. The product specifications provided a design replacement factor or failure rate for each part in the system. The team needs to monitor the actual failure rates for the parts that are causing the most frequent CASREPs, have the most backorders in the supply system, or are otherwise identified by the user as supply problems. These failure data are available from both the Program Support Inventory Control Point (PSICP) and the 3M Maintenance Data System (MDS). Comparing the data from these sources reveals whether the lack of parts is caused by higher than predicted failures in the system, by other systems using common repair parts, or by intermediate- or depot-level activities that are using more parts than predicted. These two data sources will identify which parts are causing support problems and, when compared with predicted replacement rates, will focus the actions of the program team toward a parts reliability, maintenance, or supply support solution.

Frequently, parts problems are caused by fleet maintenance practices. Repair parts with higher than predicted use can be caused by:

- *Poor fault isolation detection procedures or equipment.* If the technician can only isolate failures to an ambiguity group of three parts with available test equipment, then the only means available to identify the actual failure is to replace each of those three parts until the system is fixed. If two of those parts have very low failure rates but are experiencing very high demand, then the program team needs to assess fixes to the fault isolation procedures.

■ *Unplanned usage* is where cover plates, shims, leads, gaskets, insulators, and other parts are experiencing higher usage than predicted. Corrective maintenance procedures may require the removal or even destruction of these parts of the system. Any time a part is removed, the chance for it to be damaged, destroyed, or lost increases. If that part is critical to safe operation of the equipment, its actual failure rate may not have been predicted and it would not have been stocked.

■ *Increased system utilization* is where the system was designed to be used a specified number of hours per month, and planned maintenance cycles and parts usage per year were based upon that utilization rate. If the parts usage dramatically increases, then the program team should determine and compare the actual fleet system utilization rate. The fleet may have discovered new capabilities not anticipated, or the predicted utilization rate may have been grossly understated. In this situation, the system is faultless, except that the failure rates require recomputation, and the supply system needs to increase inventory levels to accommodate the higher demand caused by greater system operating hours.

■ *Technical data errors* frequently cause a higher than normal demand for parts when the technical manual identifies the incorrect part, the part number to the National Stock Number (NSN) cross-reference list misidentifies the correct NSN, or the part has been modified, making it useless in older configurations of the equipment, but it still has the same NSN as the obsolete configuration. The fleet user will continue to order and reorder the same item until the data problem is highlighted and corrected.

The above examples of relationships among reliability, maintainability, and logistics elements are indicative of difficulties confronting the program team in attempting to identify the real system degradation problem. The point is to continue to analyze until the team is satisfied that the actual degradation has been identified and a fix developed. When the problem is identified, the program team still must contend with the lead time to develop, procure, deploy the fix, and assess the interdependent impacts on other elements of maintainability and supportability until the fix is in place. The immediate degradation may not significantly impact interfacing parts, equipment, or subsystems, but a prolonged degradation may have a deteriorating effect. The program team therefore considers time factors as well as funding and hardware considerations in prioritizing the back-fitting of the fix.

3.5.5.4 Documentation

The documentation for this phase should report on tracking and monitoring the Ao in the operational environment. The documentation should:

■ Show how any changes or modifications in the system design, configuration, or support are managed
■ Assess the impact on the Ao of these changes from the configuration
■ Identify the resources to improve the Ao, if the Ao threshold was not achieved

3.6 Conclusion

The operational availability (Ao) of a system is the probability that the system will be ready to perform satisfactorily in its intended operational environment. Ao is the primary measure of material readiness for weapon systems and equipment. Specific equations and models that are commonly used in the analysis of Ao and its individual elements have been provided in this chapter. The truest measure of Ao is expressed in Equation 3.10, which is repeated here:

$$Ao = \frac{MTBF}{MTBF + MTTR + MLDT + MAdmDT + MOADT}$$

where:

MTBF = mean time between failures (an index of system reliability)
MTTR = mean time to repair (an index of system maintainability)
MLDT = mean logistic delay time (an index of system supportability)
MAdmDT = mean administrative delay time (an index of system supportability)
MOADT = mean awaiting outside assist delay time (an index of system supportability)

This expression is useful throughout the life cycle of the system from concept development through disposal. In this expression, the factors affecting each variable are quantified, and the analyst has established a process for evaluating the effects of changes to a specific variable on Ao. The utility of this expression is that it requires that the program team:

- Determine whether a variable affects reliability, maintainability, or supportability
- If possible, quantify that variable
- Consistently measure performance against the baseline
- Identify those factors that affect Ao whenever a significant change to reliability, maintainability, or supportability occurs

The expressions and analysis methods for Ao given in this chapter provide decision makers with the necessary tools and common logic for determining if Ao estimates are accurate and how each of the controllable components of Ao contributes to, or limits, a system's operational availability.

While there is no cookbook approach to satisfying all of the requirements that achieve the Ao threshold, this chapter has provided techniques that are applicable to the specific requirements of a program in the various phases of the acquisition cycle. Each acquisition program is unique. A program team develops its own management matrix, risk assessment process, and milestones that are specifically tailored to the requirements of the program. This chapter was prepared as a practical guide for the analysis supporting the program manager and sponsor. There is no expert on all aspects of a system acquisition or the sustainability of the system, but there are many experts on specific aspects of acquisition and sustainment. But if one utilizes all of the tools that are available to effectively manage the acquisition and sustainment process for a system, then that individual truly becomes an expert on that specific system.

Suggested Reading

Blanchard, Benjamin S. 1998. *Logistics engineering and management.* Upper Saddle River, NJ: Prentice Hall.

Blanchard, Benjamin S., and Wolter J. Fabrycky. 1998. *Systems engineering and analysis.* Upper Saddle River, NJ: Prentice Hall.

Blanchard, Benjamin S., Dinesh Verma, and Elmer L. Peterson. 1995. *Maintainability: A key to effective serviceability and maintenance management.* New York: Wiley-Interscience.

Defense Systems Management College. 1990, January. *Systems engineering management guide.* Fort Belvoir, VA: U.S. Department of Defense.

Defense Systems Management College. 1997, December. *Acquisition logistics guide.* 3rd ed. Fort Belvoir, VA: U.S. Department of Defense.

Defense Systems Management College. 2001, January. *Systems engineering fundamentals.* Fort Belvoir, VA: U.S. Department of Defense.

Eccles, Rear Admiral Henry E. 1959. *Logistics in the national defense.* Harrisburg, PA: Stackpole Press.

International Council on Systems Engineering (INCOSE). 2000. Systems engineering. *Journal of the International Council on Systems Engineering* 3(1).

Manary, Joel M. 2001, February. *Operational availability and cost effectiveness handbook, a practical guide for military systems, sub-systems, and equipment under acquisition reform.* U.S. Navy Report OPNAVINST 3000.12A-Draft#3.

Reliability Analysis Center (RAC). 1999a. *Reliability toolkit.*

Reliability Analysis Center (RAC). 1999b. *Introduction to operational availability.*

Thorp, Col. George C. 1917. *Pure logistics: The science of war preparation.* Newport, RI: Naval War College.

U.S. Department of Defense (DoD). 2003, May. *Defense acquisition guidebook.* DoD Directive 5000.1.

Chapter 4

Reliability

Preface

As is the case with many disciplines, availability, reliability, maintainability, and supportability are all related to dependability. Dependability is the ability to deliver a system or service that can be trusted. It is a collective term used to describe performance and its influencing factors: availability performance, reliability performance, maintainability performance, and maintenance support performance. Thus, dependability is a system property that integrates all of these disciplines. None can be treated as stand-alone. For this reason, availability, reliability, maintainability, supportability, and all of the related disciplines should be incorporated into an overall systems engineering approach.

Currently, in the defense and commercial sectors, the systems approach is implemented as the integrated product and process development (IPPD) process. IPPD is a systems engineering process integrated with sound business practices and commonsense decision making. Under IPPD, all essential sustainment activities are simultaneously integrated through the use of multidisciplinary teams, the integrated product teams (IPTs), to optimize the design, manufacturing, business, and supportability processes. IPPD is a fundamental shift from sequential development, in which separate groups operating independently design the product, then the manufacturing processes, and then the support system. IPPD evolved from the concurrent engineering approach to system design, and is often called integrated product development (IPD).

This chapter is the first in the series of three chapters on dependability. The objective is to develop an improved understanding of reliability strategies being used in both government and commercial sustainment enterprises in order to identify innovative solutions for improving the performance of depot-based maintenance, repair, and overhaul (MRO) operations.

4.1 Introduction to Reliability

Two standard definitions for reliability are:

1. The ability of a system and its parts to perform its mission without failure, degradation, or demand on the support system.
2. The probability that an item can perform its intended function for a specified interval under stated conditions. For nonredundant items, this is equivalent to definition 1. For redundant items, this is equivalent to the definition of mission reliability.

To measure the operational availability (Ao) of a system under development, the program manager must be capable of assessing system reliability both quantitatively and qualitatively. A quantitative assessment of reliability requires knowledge of system and equipment failure frequency, expressed as mean time between failures (MTBF). A qualitative assessment of system reliability requires the system program manager to understand the system's probable failure modes, effect of failures on the mission, and the design engineering effort required to eliminate unacceptable failure modes. Ao is established through a combination of the reliability and maintainability design characteristics of the subsystem, the equipment, and the support system design. It is essential that the program manager be capable of accurately assessing system reliability during design when the reliability elements of Ao are established. The Ao of a system can never exceed the inherent design reliability of the equipment, no matter how good the production, quality, or maintenance program may be. The design disciplines and analyses that are discussed in this chapter are intended to identify and focus attention on equipment design weaknesses, so that they may be corrected, protected against, or accepted after consideration in Ao trade-off analyses. They also provide a means of ensuring that a design will meet specified MTBF (reliability) requirements prior to production commitments. This approach is known as reliability by design, which is the subject of Section 4.3.

4.1.1 The Mathematics of Reliability

The reliability of an item is generally expressed as the probability that the item will satisfactorily perform its intended function for a given period of time under specified conditions of use. The mathematical expressions for components of a system represented by series elements are given in Figure 4.1. The expressions for parallel elements are given in Figure 4.2. These series-parallel functional relationships are utilized as building blocks to a model for the equipment or system level.

R is the reliability of the input/output system.

$$R_{series} = P_A P_B P_C P_D P_E \tag{4.1}$$

If all the elements are identical, then

$$R = P^n \tag{4.2}$$

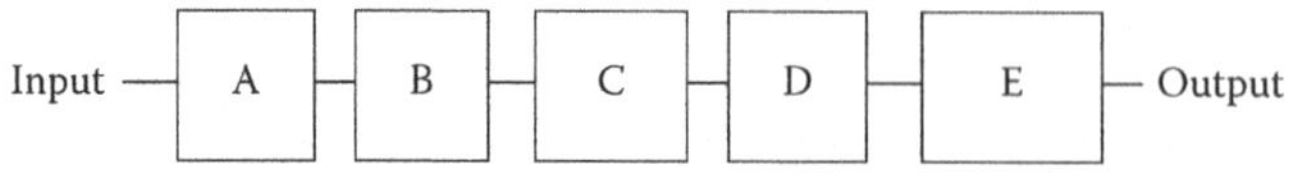

Figure 4.1 Reliability by design process.

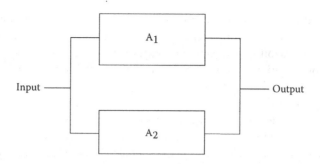

Figure 4.2   Series block diagram.

---

where n = number of elements. As an example: If $P_A = P_B = P_C = P_D = P_E = 0.98$, what is the system reliability? Answer: $R = P^n = (0.98)^5 = 0.9039$.

Assume that λ is the failure rate of the input/output system.

$$\lambda_{series} = \lambda_A + \lambda_B + \lambda_C + \lambda_D + \lambda_E \tag{4.3}$$

If all elements are identical, then $\lambda_{series} = n \times \lambda$, where n = number of elements. As an example: If $\lambda_A = \lambda_B = \lambda_C = \lambda_D = \lambda_E = 0.02$, what is the system failure rate? Answer: $\lambda_{series} = n \times \lambda = 5 \times 0.02 = 0.1$.

R is the reliability of the input/output system.

$$R_{parallel} = P_1 + P_2 - P_1 P_2 \tag{4.4}$$

As an example: If $P_1 = P_2 = 0.90$, all n elements are in parallel, and all n elements are identical, what is the system reliability? Answer: $R = P_1 + P_2 - P_1 P_2 = 0.90 + 0.90 - 0.81 = 0.99$.

$$R = 1 - q^n \tag{4.5}$$

where q = the unreliability, or $1 - R$. Thus:

$$R = 1 - (1 - R)^n \tag{4.6}$$

$$R = 1 - (1 - 0.9)^2 = 0.99 \tag{4.7}$$

The level of detail in a reliability model depends on the stage of system development and the detail that is available on the system and equipment design. Therefore, a model of the system's reliability characteristics must reflect the system design and operating characteristics. The detailed mathematical model, which is constructed to serve as the basis of allocation, prediction, and engineering, must relate reliability to design configuration, modes of operation, duty cycles, and use conditions.

Two important mathematical parameters in a reliability model are the unit of measure of reliability and the independence of failure events. Units of measure for reliability depend on system/equipment utilization. The equipment involved in a system usually can be broken down into three major categories determined by their mode of operation: continuous, intermittent, and impulse operations. The reliability of continuous-use equipment, such as computers and radar or electronic equipment, is defined in terms of the reliability parameter of failures per unit time, or MTBF. The reliability of intermittent-use equipment, such as magazines or load and launch equipment, is defined in terms of the reliability parameter of failures per cycle. Impulse operations, or go/no-go events where time of operation is very short, as in fuse or squib operations, are defined by the number of successes per number of attempts.

The mathematics applied in the relatively simple models presented here is based on assumptions of statistical independence between the elements of the system described in the reliability block diagrams, as illustrated in Figures 4.1 and 4.2. Failure of one component of the system is assumed to be independent of failures of other components. It is not necessary in the modeling for independence to exist, but the mathematics become increasingly difficult if independence of failure events is not assumed. Although the simplification of assuming independence of failure events may not apply to all equipment, most reliability mathematical models are built on this assumption. Independence of failures is generally true for electronic components, but may not be true for mechanical failures. For example, the failure of a lube oil pump may cause a bearing to overheat and become a secondary failure.

4.1.2 Reliability Modeling

Reliability modeling is an integral part of almost all reliability program plans. A reliability model of the system or equipment is required for making numerical apportionments and estimates of reliability. A system model is mandatory for evaluating complex series-parallel equipment arrangements usually existing in military systems. It is common practice to define a basic reliability model and a mission reliability model. The basic reliability model is a series model used for estimating the demand for maintenance and logistics support caused by the system and its component parts. In the basic reliability model, all elements of the system, even those elements provided for redundancy, or alternate modes of operation, are modeled in series. In other words, the basic reliability model consists of a reliability block diagram, with all the blocks in series, and an associated mathematical expression relating failure rate, duty factor, and mission duration data to failures in the series of elements. The mission reliability model, on the other hand, consists of a reliability block diagram and associated mathematical description that depicts the intended utilization of the system to achieve mission success. Elements of the system, provided for by redundancy or alternate modes of operation, are shown in the reliability block diagram in a parallel configuration appropriate to the mission phase or mission application.

Reliability modeling efforts are useful at all stages in system development. In early development stages, they are needed to translate operational requirements for the system into a set of meaningful reliability requirements for each component through the allocation process. In later stages of development, as the design progresses, the modeling efforts are useful in assessing the degree to which the system reliability requirements are being met. Modeling efforts are also useful in the evaluation of alternative design approaches to achieve system functions. The model may be useful in evaluating the effects of proposed changes to the system, even after production and deployment.

The basic information for a reliability model is derived from functional or schematic descriptions of the system that depict the relationship or system components. The reliability model reorients the diagrams into a series/parallel network of blocks (a reliability block diagram) showing the reliability relationships among the various components of the system. These diagrams, together with the appropriate duty cycle, mission duration, and component failure rate data, are used to develop mathematical expressions that provide estimates of mission reliability.

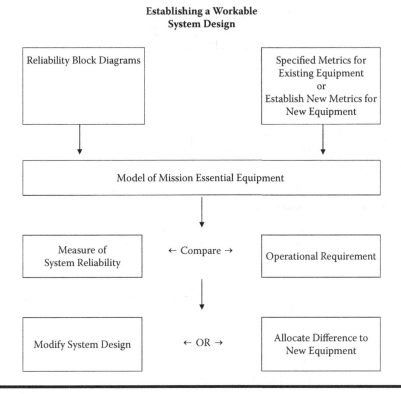

Figure 4.3   **Parallel block diagram.**

4.1.3 Application of the Reliability Model

Figure 4.3 illustrates the process by which a reliability modeling effort may be used to generate a set of reliability requirements for components to achieve the operational reliability requirement for the system. The basic reliability model is developed by the application of expected component failure rates to the reliability block diagram.

The levels of indenture for the system, subsystem, and component block diagrams are illustrated in Figure 4.4. An estimate of system reliability is derived by mathematical computation of the associated reliability model, through either a manual process for simple systems or computer simulation.

In the concept and technology development phases of system developments, the specific equipment may not yet be selected or designed. Specific failure rates cannot be established at this time. However, reliability assessment can be accomplished by assuming the failure rates of equipment in existing systems with similar functions.

4.2 Reliability by Design

The reliability by design approach differs from traditional reliability programs in several areas. The emphasis is on making reliability an integral part of the design process rather than something done by a group of reliability experts separate from the designers. The objective is to get designers to consider those factors affecting component life with the same emphasis as those factors affecting

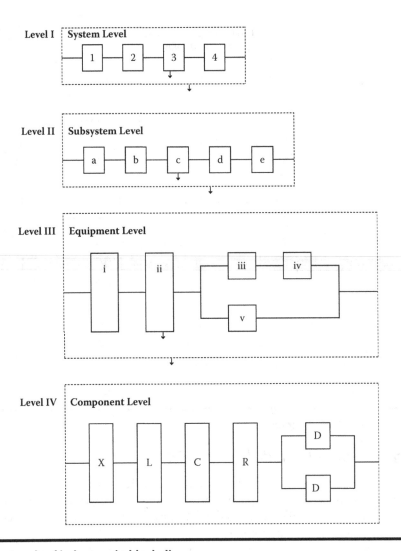

Figure 4.4 Levels of indenture in block diagrams.

system performance. Accomplishing this objective entails the translation of operational reliability requirements into meaningful design requirements. The reliability by design approach differs in another major way from the traditional reliability approach. Since the emphasis is on the design itself, there is a resulting deemphasis on program plans and formal reliability demonstration testing. There is a greater payoff in spending more time and resources on performing the design process than on testing the design to determine if it complies with requirements. There is a very sound basis for this reasoning. First, there are analytical techniques allowing assessment of reliability before hardware buildup, when changes can be easily instituted. Second, as reliability requirements increase in magnitude, the practicality of demonstrating them through testing diminishes because of extremely long and costly test times required to do so. For instance, it would take over 11,000 h of test time to demonstrate a 5,000 h MTBF with 90% confidence under optimum conditions (zero failures). The impact on program schedules, coupled with the expense of corrective action late in system development, when hardware is available for test, may make reliability demonstrations infeasible.

The level of confidence that a program manager has in his or her ability to assess design reliability, and also in the data derived in the assessment, depends directly on his or her level of understanding of the reliability by design process. The following sections briefly describe the basic tools of the process: concentrating on establishing reliability requirements (allocation), assessing the inherent design reliability (prediction), and identifying and correcting design weaknesses through a failure mode, effects, and criticality analysis (FMECA). The first step in performing all of these analyses is development of a design reliability model. Because design reliability assessment is properly performed early in the system design process, the program manager does not yet have a system available to perform the analysis. Therefore, he or she must create a realistic model of the system suitable to be exercised for reliability allocation, prediction, and design analysis.

4.2.1 Reliability Allocation

4.2.1.1 Objective of the Allocation

After the reliability model is established and functional relationships are defined, the system program manager is able to determine the reliability values required of each subsystem in order to achieve the level of system reliability demanded by the Ao objectives. This process is reliability allocation. Reliability allocation represents the assignment of reliability thresholds to subsystems in such a manner that the system reliability requirements will be satisfied. Allocation employs the reliability model by proceeding from system reliability requirements to compatible subsystem thresholds. Allocated reliability requirements are useful in directing reliability effort along profitable channels, and for compatibility among the various development efforts. A few important uses of reliability allocation are:

- During the conceptual phase, allocation of proposed reliability requirements aids in the determination of technical feasibility.
- When various subsystems are developed by different contractors, allocation provides compatible contractual reliability requirements.
- Allocation provides the prime contractor and government monitors with a means of evaluating subcontractor reliability achievements.
- Allocated reliability requirements may be used as developmental goals for parts and subsystems. Reliability growth progress can be monitored for subsystems to avert problem areas, reallocate resources and efforts, or initiate appropriate reliability trade-offs.

When the allocation is combined in consonance with the reliability model, the allocated thresholds must yield a system reliability that is not less than the requirements specified in the system specifications. The resulting reliability goals provide the basis for establishing comparisons of requirements with predictions. Such comparisons serve as a measure for detecting potential problem areas for adjusting the reliability thresholds. The allocation process is an approximation. The reliability parameters apportioned to the subsystems are used as guidelines to determine design feasibility. If the allocated reliability for a specific subsystem cannot be achieved at the current state of technology, the system design must be modified and the reliability of the subsystems reallocated. This procedure is repeated until an allocation is achieved that satisfies the system-level requirements, accommodates all constraints, and results in subsystems that can be designed within the current or achievable technology.

If it is found that even with reallocation some of the individual subsystem requirements cannot be met with current technology, the designer may use one or any number of the following approaches (assuming that they are not mutually exclusive) in order to achieve the desired reliability:

1. Find a more reliable design or use more reliable component parts.
2. Simplify the design by using fewer component parts, if this is possible without degrading performance.
3. Apply component derating techniques to reduce the estimated failure rates.
4. Use graceful degradation or redundancy for those cases in which approaches 1, 2, and 3 cannot produce the desired reliability.
5. Reassess the baseline operational scenario (BOS) and operational requirements document (ORD).

4.2.1.2 Practical Considerations in Reliability Allocation

The ideal apportionment would allocate reliability design requirements to achieve the most economical use of resources, including time and cost. Allocation of reliability is a trade-off between the reliabilities of the system's individual components to achieve specified total system reliability. By imposing high requirements on those units in which reliability is easier to attain, and lower requirements in those more difficult and more costly areas, the overall cost of system development may be controlled. A few important factors for consideration are:

■ The complexity of the system will have an effect on the achievable reliability. The more complex the system, the greater the number of subassemblies and modules, and the more difficult and costly it is to achieve a high reliability. Imposing an unrealistically high reliability on a more complex system increases the cost disproportionately when compared with the effect of increasing the reliability requirement for a simpler system.
■ The amount of development and research required to produce the system will greatly influence the time and cost of development. Imposition of a high reliability requirement on a system under development will increase the development time, the length of tests required to demonstrate the reliability, and the overall cost.
■ The intended operational environment will determine the achievable reliability. For example, a system to be used in a rugged environment will cost more to develop than a similar one to be used under less severe conditions for example, with an equal reliability.
■ The mission's length and the time the equipment is required to perform influence the achievable reliability. It requires more development effort. It costs more to produce a system capable of operating for a long time without failure than to develop one for a shorter period of use.
■ A component's high reliability is based on the importance of its operation. A component whose failure would not jeopardize the accomplishment of the mission need not be highly reliable. To the extent that failures can be tolerated, lowered reliability requirements may be imposed.

4.2.1.3 Reliability Allocation Methods

There are a number of approaches to allocating reliability requirements. Two of these are designated as the equal, or fair share, allocation method, and the other is allocation by complexity, or the weighted allocation method.

4.2.1.3.1 Equal Allocation Method

In the absence of definitive information on the system, other than the fact that a subsystem is to be used in series, equal allocation to each subsystem is reasonable. In this case, the *n*th root of the system reliability would be allocated to each of the *n* subsystems. The equal allocation technique assumes a series of *n* subsystems, each of which is assigned the same reliability threshold. A prime weakness of the method is that the subsystem thresholds are not assigned in accordance with the degree of difficulty associated with achievement of these requirements. For this technique the model is

$$R_s = \prod_{i=1}^{n} R_i \tag{4.8}$$

$$R_i = (R_s)^{1/n} \text{ for } i = 1, 2, \ldots, n \tag{4.9}$$

where R_s is the required system reliability and R_i is the reliability apportioned to subsystem *i*. As an example, consider a proposed communication system that consists of three subsystems (transmitter, receiver, and coder), each of which must function if the system is to operate. Each subsystem is developed independently. Assuming each is equally expensive to develop, what reliability requirement should be assigned to each subsystem in order to meet a system requirement of 0.729? The apportioned subsystem requirements are found as

$$R_T = R_R = R_C = (R_S)^{1/n} = (0.729)^{1/3} = 0.90 \tag{4.10}$$

Thus, a reliability requirement of 0.90 would be assigned to each subsystem.

4.2.1.3.2 Allocation by Complexity

The allocation by complexity method assumes the subsystems are in series with constant failure rates in a series such that any subsystem failure causes system failure. Also, subsystem mission time is equal to system mission time. This allocation technique requires an expression of reliability requirements in terms of failure rate. The steps are:

Step 1: The objective is to choose λ_i such that:

$$\sum_{i=1}^{n} \lambda_i \leq \lambda \tag{4.11}$$

where λ_i is the failure rate allocated to subsystem *i*, and λ is the required system failure rate.
Step 2: Determine an initial value of the subsystem failure rates λ_i from past observations or estimation. Assign a weighting factor w_i to each subsystem according to Equation 4.12:

$$w_i = \frac{\lambda_i}{\sum_{i=1}^{n} \lambda_i} \tag{4.12}$$

Step 3: Allocate (recalculate) the subsystem failure rate requirements:

$$\lambda_i = w_i \lambda \tag{4.13}$$

To illustrate this method, consider a system composed of three subsystems with predicted failure rates of $\lambda_1 = 0.003$, $\lambda_2 = 0.001$, and $\lambda_3 = 0.004$ failures per hour, respectively. The system has a mission time of 20 h, and 0.90 reliability is required. Assume that system reliability is defined by the exponential equation

$$R(t) = e^{-\lambda t} \tag{4.14}$$

Find the subsystem requirements λ_i. The apportioned failure rates and reliability goals are calculated as:

Step 1: Calculate λ: Since $R(20) = e^{-\lambda(20)} = 0.90$, then $\lambda = 0.005$ failures per hour.
Step 2: Calculate w_i: $\lambda_1 = 0.003$, $\lambda_2 = 0.001$, $\lambda_3 = 0.004$:

$$w_1 = \frac{0.003}{0.003 + 0.001 + 0.004} = 0.375$$

$$w_2 = \frac{0.001}{0.003 + 0.001 + 0.004} = 0.125$$

$$w_3 = \frac{0.004}{0.003 + 0.001 + 0.004} = 0.5$$

Step 3: Allocate (recalculate) λ_i:

$$\lambda_1 = 0.375(0.005) = 0.001875$$

$$\lambda_2 = 0.125(0.005) = 0.000625$$

$$\lambda_3 = 0.500(0.005) = 0.002500$$

The corresponding allocated subsystem reliability requirements are:

$$R1\ (20) = \exp\ [-(0.001875)20] = 0.96$$

$$R2\ (20) = \exp\ [-(0.000625)20] = 0.99$$

$$R3\ (20) = \exp\ [-(0.002500)20] = 0.95$$

4.2.1.3.3 Other Allocation Techniques

There are a number of more complex techniques that are available for the allocation of reliability requirements to the components of a system. Among these are:

1. The agree technique, which considers both the complexity and relative importance of each subsystem
2. The minimization of effort technique, which considers minimizing the total effort expended to meet the system reliability requirements
3. The dynamic programming technique, which provides an approach to the reliability allocation with minimum effort expenditure when the subsystem is subject to different effort functions

4.2.2 Reliability Prediction

4.2.2.1 Objective of Prediction

The operational availability, Ao, achieved by a military system depends upon the type of reliability program implemented in the equipment design. The early design phase is the optimum time, from an economic standpoint, for evaluating a design, incorporating design modifications, and establishing long-term reliability characteristics. During the design phase, reliability predictions are performed on the system to identify those components that may cause system failure in operational units. Formal reliability prediction is also necessary in the early design phase of a system to determine if it will be capable of achieving operational availability requirements.

Reliability prediction is the process of quantitatively assessing whether a proposed, or actual, equipment/system design will meet a specified reliability requirement. The primary objective of reliability prediction is to provide guidance for engineering and management decisions, based on the assessment of inherent reliability of a given design. Therefore, the real value of the quantitative expression lies in the information conveyed with this value and the information's use. Predictions alone do not contribute to system reliability without additional actions. Predictions constitute decision criteria for selecting courses of action that affect reliability. Specific objectives of reliability assessment during development are to (1) provide continuous, up-to-date information concerning the attainment of reliability requirements, (2) identify design weaknesses in sufficient detail so corrective action can be instituted, and (3) provide a reasonable assessment of design reliability prior to production.

The reliability assessment program starts early and continues throughout the life of the equipment. It is important to identify as soon as possible the failure modes of the equipment, progress in meeting certain criteria, and equipment design weaknesses. The sooner these design characteristics are identified, the easier and more cost-effective it is to make any necessary adjustments. During design and development, predictions serve as quantitative guides against which design alternatives can be judged on reliability. The purposes of reliability prediction include feasibility evaluation, comparison of alternative configurations, identification of potential problems during design review, logistics support planning and cost studies, determination of data deficiencies, trade-off decisions, allocation of requirements, and definition of the baseline for reliability growth and demonstration testing.

4.2.2.2 Reliability Prediction Procedures

In general, there is a hierarchy of reliability prediction techniques available to the designer depending upon two factors: (1) the depth of knowledge of the design, and (2) the availability of historical data on equipment and component part reliabilities. As the system design proceeds from the conceptual phase through development to the production phase, data describing the system design evolve from a qualitative description of systems functions to detailed specifications and drawings suitable for hardware production. A hierarchy of reliability prediction techniques is developed to accommodate the different reliability study and analysis objectives, and the availability of detailed data as the system design progresses.

Basically, the reliability prediction process involves the application of individual component failure rates to the reliability model that was developed and is updated as the design progresses. In general, reliability prediction requires: (1) development of an accurate model of system performance and reliability, and (2) derivation of adequate data to forecast failure frequency for each system component. As described in Section 4.1.2, the system reliability model must replicate the functional performance of the system based on a description of design engineering parameters. The model must also realistically describe all possible failure modes and their effects on the system. The failure data utilized in the model must be derived from equipment that is similar to the system's mission profile in design characteristics, environmental conditions, and operational use.

Reliability prediction techniques can be classified in five categories, depending on the type of data and information available for the analysis:

1. *Similar equipment technique.* The equipment under consideration is compared with similar equipment of known reliability in estimating the probable level or achievable reliability.
2. *Similar complexity technique.* The reliability of a new design is estimated as a function of the relative complexity of the subject item with respect to a typical item of similar type.
3. *Prediction by functional technique.* Previously demonstrated correlations between equipment function and reliability are considered in obtaining reliability predictions for a new design.
4. *Part count technique.* Equipment reliability is estimated as a function of the number of parts in the equipment, in each of several part classes.
5. *Stress analysis technique.* The equipment failure rate is determined as a function of all individual part failure rates, considering part type, operational stress level, and derating characteristics of each part.

Another procedure for reliability prediction is the use of a computer program to perform the calculation. Reliability predictions for complex systems frequently require a large amount of tedious computation, and a number of off-the-shelf software programs have been developed for performing reliability predictions. However, prediction through a computer program utilizes the basic reliability model structure previously described, written in digital program form, and one of the five basic prediction techniques. The system program manager should check his computer installation to determine which programs are available or should be obtained before performing any laborious manual calculations.

The most common techniques for prediction of reliability, such as those described in the military standards and handbooks, have been developed for analysis of electronic equipment. Therefore, current contractual documentation for military equipment usually requires reliability predictions to be determined through methods corresponding to electronic design engineering practices. Reliability prediction is an integral part of the design process and requires coordinated effort between design engineering and reliability engineering activities. In order to be effective, reliability prediction techniques must relate reliability engineering procedures and data to the mission profile and design engineering parameters. Utilization of electronics-oriented procedures for reliability prediction of mechanical systems usually limits the accuracy of the quantitative results. The difficulty of reliability prediction for mechanical equipment is the result of several factors inherent to nonelectronic technology, which increases the complexity of model development and limits opportunities for data collection.

The level of confidence a program manager has in a predicted reliability value depends on his or her level of understanding of the procedures employed in the prediction process. In comparison to the analysis of electronic systems, confidence in reliability predictions for mechanical systems is generally low because a single, widely accepted approach for mechanical reliability prediction does not exist. The difficulty of establishing standard procedures for mechanical reliability prediction is due, in part, to the complexity of developing realistic models for mechanical systems and the lack of accurate specific failure data on most mechanical equipment.

4.2.3 Failure Mode, Effects, and Criticality Analysis (FMECA)

4.2.3.1 FMECA Objectives

A number of different techniques are available for reliability design analysis to assure the program manager that inadequate design evaluation has been conducted, ensuring reliable material will be designed and produced. FMECA is one of these disciplines and is a structured approach to evaluating the reliability of a design by considering potential failures and the resulting effect on the system. FMECA is presented as an example of a reliability design analysis technique because it incorporates the procedures described for modeling and predictions. It may also be utilized for analysis of systems maintenance and logistics support.

The procedures of an FMECA are to identify potential design weaknesses through systematic documented consideration of all likely ways in which a component or equipment can fail, causes for each mode, and the effects of each failure on the system, which may be different for each mission phase. The primary objective of this design discipline is to iteratively examine all potential failure modes, their causes, and their effects so that the designer will have information on areas where the design may be strengthened. FEMCA should be initiated at the system level as soon as preliminary design information is available. Early identification of all catastrophic and critical failure possibilities allows them to be eliminated or minimized through design correction at the earliest possible time. The FMECA then becomes an iterative process as the design continues through lower levels of development. A properly performed FMECA is invaluable to program decisions regarding the feasibility and adequacy of a design approach. The extent of effort and sophistication of the approach used in an FMECA will be dependent upon the nature and requirements of the program and the system technology. Therefore, it is necessary to tailor the requirements for FMECA to each individual program.

4.2.3.2 Application of the FMECA

The FMECA is a well-documented analysis tool that is utilized for reliability analyses in both defense and commercial industries. For example, commercial aircraft manufacturers use the FMECA process to certify for the Federal Aviation Administration that a new aircraft design is suitable for flight. The tabular FMECA is the grandfather of all other failure effects analysis techniques. The tabular FMECA employs a simple approach. A table or worksheet is used to itemize every probable failure mode and its resulting effect. This analysis is generally referred to as a failure mode and effects analysis (FMEA). The specific information contained on the worksheet can be tailored to the individual system, but usually includes item identification, failure mode, probable failure causes, failure effect, method of fault detection, and remarks concerning corrective actions or design changes. Table 4.1 presents a standard worksheet for FMEA.

Table 4.1   An FMECA Worksheet

System_____ Indenture level_____ Reference drawing_____ Mission_____								Date_____ Sheet_____ of_____ Compiled by_____ Approved by_____			
					Failure Effects						
Identification Number	Item/Function Identification (Nomenclature)	Function	Failure Modes and Causes	Mission Phase/Operational Mode	Local Effects	Next Higher Level	End Effects	Failure Detection Method	Compensating Provisions	Severity Class	Remarks

The level of detail contained in the analysis is determined by the availability of information and the intended application of the results. The analysis can also include an evaluation of the relative importance of failure modes based upon the severity of their effect on the system and their probability of occurrence. This procedure is called criticality analysis (CA). Table 4.2 is a sample CA worksheet. The combined analysis, FMEA and CA, is an FMECA. FMECA is a versatile technique that can be used to analyze any system at any stage in its design.

Basically, the analysis consists of identifying and tabulating the modes by which a system, component, or part may fail, along with the effect of a failure in this mode. It is performed primarily to isolate and identify weaknesses in the design. FMECA may be applied at any level, from complete systems to individual parts. Its purpose is to describe or identify each possible way (the failure mode) an item can fail to perform its function. For a tracking radar system, the function of tracking may not be performed due to failure of any of several items, such as the input power, transmitter, receiver, or tracking servo loop. Each single-item failure is considered as the only failure in the system while its impacts are analyzed. Where a single-item failure is nondetectable, the analysis is extended to determine the effects of a second failure, which, in combination with the first undetectable failure, could result in a catastrophic or critical failure condition. Passive and multiple failures that may result in catastrophic or critical conditions are also being identified.

It is important that the program manager understand the criticality of scheduling the FMECA. As in most reliability analyses, FMECA must be performed as early as possible in the systems development in order to be able to impact design reliability.

Table 4.2   Example of a Criticality Analysis Worksheet

System_____ Indenture level_____ Reference drawing_____ Mission_____		Date_____ Sheet_____ of_____ Compiled by_____ Approved by_____

Identification Number	Item/Function Identification (Nomenclature)	Function	Failure Modes and Causes	Mission Phase/Operational Mode	Severity Class	Failure Rate Data Source	Failure Probability	Failure Effect Probability (P)	Failure Mode Ratio	Failure Rate	Operating Time (T)	Failure Mode Criticality	Item Criticality	Remarks

4.2.3.3 FMECA Procedures

These are standard basic procedures for performing an FMECA:

1. *Define the system to be analyzed.* A complete system definition includes identification of internal and interface functions, expected performance at all indenture levels, system constraints, and failure definitions. Functional narratives of the system should include descriptions of each mission in terms of functions that identify tasks to be performed for each mission, mission phase, and operational mode. Narratives should describe the environmental profiles, expected mission times, and equipment utilization, and the functions and outputs of each item.
2. *Construct the block diagrams.* Construct functional reliability block diagrams that illustrate the operation, interrelationships, and interdependencies of functional entities for each item configuration involved in the system's use. All system interfaces are indicated.
3. *Identify the failure modes.* Identify all potential items and interface modes and define their effects on the immediate function or item, on the system, and on the mission to be performed.
4. *Classify the failure modes.* Evaluate each failure mode in terms of the worst potential consequences. Assign a severity classification category.
5. *Fault detection and compensation.* Identify failure detection methods and compensating provisions for each failure mode.

6. *Correct the design.* Identify corrective design or other actions required to eliminate the failure or control the risk.
7. *Reevaluate corrective actions.* Identify effects of corrective actions or other system attributes, such as requirements for logistics support.
8. *Document the results.* Document the analysis and summarize the problems that could not be corrected by design. Identify the special controls necessary to reduce failure risk.

These general procedures may be tailored to the individual system under analysis and the specific objectives of the analysis.

4.3 Reliability Design Approaches

There are essentially three design approaches or strategies that can be used to satisfy system-level reliability requirements: (1) use of highly reliable equipment, (2) graceful degradation, and (3) redundancy. These strategies are limited by several factors, including acquisition costs, scheduled manning levels, weight and space, and logistics constraints. The approaches are listed in the order that would usually be most preferable to the program manager. Selection of highly reliable equipment and parts for the system is usually the most beneficial design approach, but the program manager must consider the higher initial cost offset. At the other extreme, use of redundant equipment in parallel is usually the last choice of reliability improvement, due to increased cost and the maintenance or logistic burdens. Each system has unique requirements that drive the program manager and the designer toward selection of specific design approaches.

4.3.1 High Reliability Configuration and Component Design

The most straightforward design approach that can be used to achieve system reliability requirements is the use of highly reliable equipment or components. No single method can be described for this technique. Basically, this is the application of good design practices to meet an accurate equipment mission profile, with a conservative safety margin in the selection of equipment stress ratings against anticipated stress levels. The process to achieve this design objective and to assess design status can only be described through the entirety of the reliability engineering discipline. The advantages of this approach include lower support cost, reduced maintenance, reduced spares and weight, and perhaps reduced initial acquisition cost. Use of high reliability equipment or components is a preferred design approach for achievement of Ao requirements. The drawbacks to this approach are increased development time if the requisite technology is not currently available, increased development costs, and possible risks associated with pushing the state of the art in component manufacturing technology.

4.3.2 System Graceful Degradation

The implementation of the latest state-of-the-art design, engineering, and manufacturing procedures and processes cannot guarantee reliability in today's advanced, highly complex weapon systems. To ensure the highest reliability and operational readiness, a building block approach to system design can be utilized. The basic blocks are interconnected so that a malfunction, either equipment failure or battle damage, will not degrade or inhibit the operation of the total system. This multiple-function design approach, redundancy, or "graceful degradation" enhances total system reliability by allowing a minimum number of functions to be performed that permit mission completion.

Graceful degradation is utilized in a system design that employs a network of similar items. Parallel paths within a network are capable of carrying an additional load when elements fail. This can result in degradation to tolerable output. In other words, an element failure in a parallel path does not always cause complete equipment failure, but instead degrades equipment performance. The allowable degree of degradation depends on the number of alternate paths available. When a mission can still be accomplished using equipment whose output is degraded, the definition of failure can be relaxed to accommodate degradation. Naturally, finite values of degradation must be built by an array of elements configured into an antenna or an array of detectors configured into a receiver. In either case, individual elements may fail, reducing resolution, but if a minimum number operate, resolution remains great enough to identify a target.

This technique requires application of such design considerations as load sharing, functional modularization, reconfiguration, and selective redundancy. These design considerations achieve basic system performance characteristics with a minimal increase in complexity, providing a pay-off in high system reliability.

The Aegis Ballistic Missile Defense AN/SPY-1 radar system* exemplifies the graceful degradation concept inherent in the total system. The AN/SPY-1 transmitter provides full transmitted power through multiple separate radio frequency (RF) power channels. The loss of a channel does not greatly degrade system performance. The online maintenance capability of the radar allows for repairs to be performed by normal maintenance procedures with no system downtime. This feature allows the radar to achieve the required Ao even though a malfunction has occurred.

Graceful degradation is also a feature of the multiple computer system of Aegis. The three computers, each consisting of four bays, have automatic reload/reconfiguration ability. If a malfunction or failure involves a computer program error, automatic detection by the executive program initiates a computer decision to automatically reload the program from disc. If there is a hardware failure, the executive program isolates the failure to a bay and automatically reloads a reduced program into the three remaining operational bays. For all computer failures, restoration of system performance may be accomplished in less than 15 s.

The successful application of this technique requires extensive planning during preliminary design to ensure that interfacing system designs, such as air conditioning, power, or compressed air, on the larger system is designed to support the graceful degradation. Switching networks can also become complex and expensive. They can make a significant contribution to system unreliability, unless they are treated with the same attention as the primary system.

4.3.3 Redundancy

The reliability of a system can be significantly enhanced through redundancy. Redundancy involves designing one or more alternate functional paths into the system through addition of parallel elements. Redundancy has been extensively applied in airborne systems. For example, the electronic multiplexing system for the U.S. Air Force B-1 bomber used a redundant design. Redundant computers control the main switching buses. Normally, one of the two computers is active and feeds the two main buses controlling all switching functions, while the other continuously performs

---

* The Aegis Ballistic Missile Defense system was jointly developed by the U.S. Missile Defense Agency and the U.S. Navy as part of the nation's Ballistic Missile Defense System (BMDS). The Aegis weapon system is currently deployed on eighty-one ships around the globe with more than twenty-five additional ships planned or under contract. In addition to the United States, Aegis is the maritime weapon system of choice for Japan, South Korea, Norway, Spain, and Australia.

the same function and compares its output with that of the active computer. If the active computer malfunctions, the standby automatically takes over. Another example is the modern antenna systems in radar sets, where hundreds of transmitter/receiver (TR) modules are used to form the desired bean pattern. This technology offers a method of directing the radar beam without changing the position of the fixed antenna. Often many of the TR modules can fail with a graceful degradation effect instead of single-point failure.

The following treatment of redundancy is not meant to be comprehensive. Rather, it points out the concepts that are important to equipment design and cautions the designer that the application of redundancy has some drawbacks.

4.3.3.1 Redundancy Techniques

Mission reliability can be increased through redundancy at the cost of increasing unscheduled maintenance. The unscheduled maintenance increase accompanying redundancy may be offset by improving reliability through use of component improvement techniques, such as parts screening, derating, and design simplification. Depending on the specific applications, a number of approaches are available to improve reliability through redundant design. These design approaches can be classified on the basis of how the redundant elements are introduced into the system to provide a parallel function path. In general, there are two major classes of redundancy:

1. *Active redundancy.* External elements are not required to perform detection, decision, and switching when an element or path in the structure fails.
2. *Standby redundancy.* External elements are required to detect, make a decision, and switch to another element or path as a replacement for a failed element or path.

Techniques related to each of these two classes are depicted in the tree structure shown in Figure 4.5.

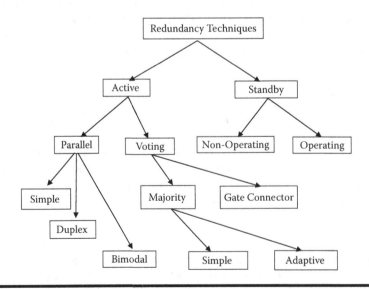

Figure 4.5   Types of redundancy.

Figure 4.6 presents the basic redundancy technique based on design configuration, such as simple parallel redundancy. Although not readily apparent, redundancy does not lend itself to a categorization exclusively by element complexity. The configurations shown in Figure 4.6 are more applicable to the circuit level than to the equipment level, not because of inherent limitations of the particular configuration, but rather supporting factors such as cost, weight, and complexity.

The decision to use redundant design techniques must be based on a careful analysis of the trade-offs involved. Redundancy may be the only available method when other techniques of improving reliability have been exhausted, or when methods of equipment or part improvement are more costly than duplications. Its use may benefit maintenance planning, since the existence of redundant equipment can allow for repair without system downtime. Occasionally, there are

Simple Parallel Redundancy

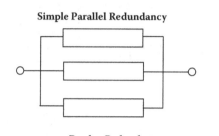

In its simplest terms, redundancy consists of a simple parallel combination of elements. If any element fails open, identical paths exist through parallel redundant elements.

Duplex Redundancy

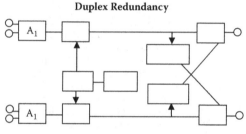

The Duplex technique is applied to redundant logic sections, such as A_1 and A_2 operating in parallel. It is primarily used in computer applications where A_1 and A_2 can be used in duplex or active redundant modes are a separate element. An error detector at the output of each logic section detects non-coincident outputs and starts a diagnostic routine to determine and disable the faulty element.

Bimodal Parallel/Series Redundancy

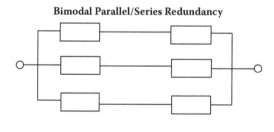

A parallel connection of series redundant elements provides protection against shorts and opens. Direct short across the network due to a single element shorting is prevented by a redundant element in series. An open across the network is prevented by the parallel element. This network is useful when primary element failure mode is open.

Bimodal Series/Parallel Redundancy

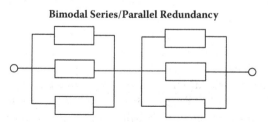

A series connection of parallel redundant elements provides protection against shorts and opens. Direct short across the network due to a single element shorting is prevented by a redundant element in series. An open across the network is prevented by the parallel element. This network is useful when the primary element failure mode is short.

Figure 4.6   Redundancy techniques.

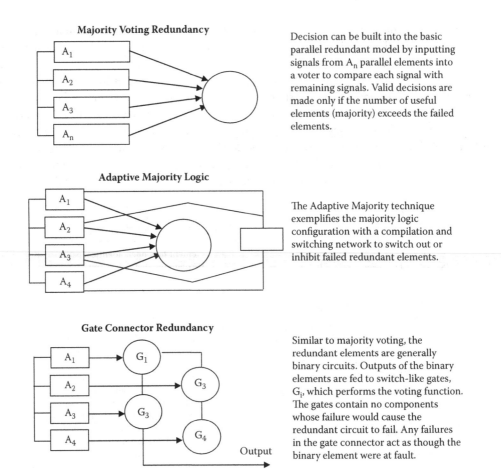

Majority Voting Redundancy

Decision can be built into the basic parallel redundant model by inputting signals from A_n parallel elements into a voter to compare each signal with remaining signals. Valid decisions are made only if the number of useful elements (majority) exceeds the failed elements.

Adaptive Majority Logic

The Adaptive Majority technique exemplifies the majority logic configuration with a compilation and switching network to switch out or inhibit failed redundant elements.

Gate Connector Redundancy

Similar to majority voting, the redundant elements are generally binary circuits. Outputs of the binary elements are fed to switch-like gates, G_i, which performs the voting function. The gates contain no components whose failure would cause the redundant circuit to fail. Any failures in the gate connector act as though the binary element were at fault.

Figure 4.6   Continued.

situations when equipment cannot be maintained, such as satellites. In such cases, redundant elements may prolong operating time significantly.

4.3.3.2 Redundancy Disadvantages

The application of redundancy has disadvantages. It increases weight, space, complexity, cost, and time to a design. The reliability gain for additional redundant elements decreases rapidly for additions beyond a few parallel elements. As illustrated by Figure 4.7 for simple parallel redundancy, there is a diminishing gain in reliability as the number of redundant elements is increased beyond the first one or two additional redundant elements to a system. The greatest gain in reliability is actually achieved through the addition of the first redundant element. This gain is equivalent to a 50% increase in the system MTBF, as shown for the simple parallel case in Figure 4.8. In addition to increased maintenance costs for repair of the additional elements, reliability of certain redundant configurations may actually be less. This is due to the serial reliability of switching or other peripheral devices needed to implement the particular redundancy configuration that was illustrated in Figure 4.6.

Standby Redundancy

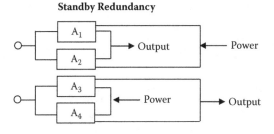

A particular redundant element of a parallel configuration can be switched into an active circuit by connecting outputs of each element to switch poles. Two switching configurations are possible.

1) The element may be activated by the switch until switching is completed and power is applied to the element in the switching operation.

2) All redundant elements are continuously connected to the circuit and the single redundant element activated by switching power to it.

Operating Redundancy

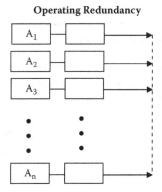

In this application, all redundant units operate simultaneously. A sensor on each unit detects failures. When a unit fails, a switch at the output transfers to the exit and remains there until failure.

Figure 4.6   Continued.

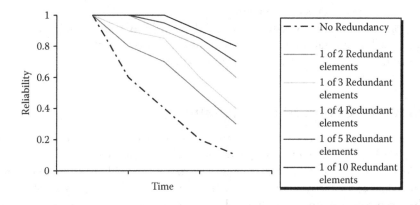

Figure 4.7   Decreasing gain in reliability for 1 of *n* redundant elements.

The effectiveness of certain redundancy techniques (especially standby) can be enhanced by repair. Standby redundancy allows repair of the failed unit, while operation of the good unit continues uninterrupted, by virtue of the switching function built into the standby redundant configuration. The switchover function can readily provide an indication that failure had occurred and operation is continuing on the alternate channel. With a positive failure indication, delays in

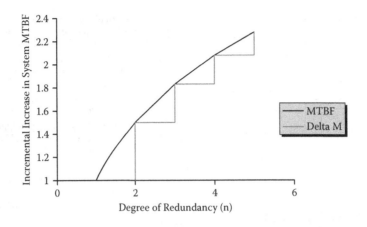

Figure 4.8 Incremental increase in system MTBF for *n* redundant elements.

repair are minimized. A further advantage of switching is related to built-in test (BIT). BIT can be readily incorporated into a sensing and switchover network for ease of maintenance.

The achievement of increased reliability brought about by incorporation of redundancy is dependent on the effective isolation of redundant elements. Isolation is necessary to prevent failure effects from adversely impacting other parts of the redundant network. The susceptibility of a particular redundant design to failure propagation may be assessed by application of FMEA. The particular techniques addressed in the previous section on FMECA offer an effective method of identifying likely fault propagation paths.

Interdependency is most successfully achieved through standby redundancy, as represented by configurations classified as decisions with switching, where the redundant element is disconnected until a failure is sensed. Design based on such techniques must provide protection against switching transients and consider effects of switching.

Furthermore, care must be exercised to ensure that reliability gains from redundancy are not offset by increased failure rates due to switching devices, error detectors, and other peripheral devices needed to implement the redundant configurations.

4.4 Reliability-Centered Maintenance

Reliability-centered maintenance (RCM) is an analytical method for matching the preventive maintenance (PM) capabilities of an organization to the design characteristics of the product. RCM provides a framework for organizing and directing technical knowledge to ensure that all PM is essential and cost-effective. Preventive maintenance is one of the two types of maintenance, the other being corrective maintenance (CM). PM is elective downtime. In certain cases, some PM may possibly be performed with the product operating. PM consists of actions meant to prolong the product's operational life and keep it safe to use. An ideal product would require no PM, and the probability of failure would be remote, or redundancy would make failure acceptable. Then, only corrective maintenance would be required infrequently (although verifying the operational status of redundant items before use would be a PM task).

Corrective maintenance includes those activities required to return failed equipment to acceptable operational status. CM consists of recognizing that a failure has occurred (fault detection), determining what has failed (fault isolation), accessing and replacing or repairing the failed component, and confirming that the failure has been corrected. It is the maintainability engineer's responsibility to strike the best balance between PM and CM, keeping in mind such factors as safety, availability requirements, and the customer's operating and support concepts.

Most often, failure is not a remote possibility, and most products of any complexity require some PM, even if that is only cleaning. PM is primarily concerned with wear-out failures. Ideally, PM tasks are performed immediately prior to a failure. The goal is to identify only that PM that is absolutely necessary and cost-effective.

Figure 4.9 summarizes the steps in an RCM approach to identifying PM. It is important to note that before beginning the RCM process, a configuration management system should be in place. Also, RCM analysis used to be performed after the design was frozen, and was used only to determine the PM program. Increasingly, it is being used earlier in the design process to help optimize the design for maintainability.

Preventive maintenance for a product may be scheduled based on condition (e.g., corrosion), a number of events (e.g., cycles of operation), the seasonal time period (e.g., desert operations), operational profile changes (e.g., surge operations), and sometimes as the result of the failure of other equipment. For example, aircraft manufacturers recommend a range of takeoff and landing cycle-based and time-based PM. The initial overall maintenance program should reflect the RCM-based schedule for PM. After fielding, the time intervals between PM tasks should be optimized based on experience.

RCM is based on six precepts:

1. The consequences of a failure determine its priority.
2. The selection of a PM task should be based on an item's failure pattern.
3. Scheduled maintenance is required for an item when the failure of that item to perform its function or the nature of the failure mode has possible safety consequences.
4. Redesign is required for safety-related items when PM cannot reduce the risk of failure to an acceptable level.
5. PM for failures not having safety consequences must be justified on an economic basis. It is less costly to perform PM than to run the item to failure.
6. PM cannot improve the designed-in reliability.

PM tasks should be both applicable and effective in order to be considered as part of an RCM program. Table 4.3 provides some insight into determining if specific types of PM tasks are applicable and effective. Note that lubrication tasks are omitted. Such tasks are common maintenance. To simplify the decision structure used in RCM analysis, such tasks are omitted, but not forgotten.

RCM basically consists of answering a series of questions for each failure. These questions are:

1. How or why does a failure occur?
2. What are the consequences of the failure?
3. Will PM eliminate or reduce the probability of the failure, improve safety, or reduce costs?
4. What PM tasks are needed and can be performed?
5. Which PM tasks should be performed?
6. What PM tasks must be performed?

For question 2, Table 4.4 summarizes the categories of potential consequences of failure. Questions 4 and 5 pertain to applicability and effectiveness, respectively, as addressed in Table 4.3. Figure 4.10 illustrates a portion of the decision logic used in identifying PM tasks (question 4) using RCM.

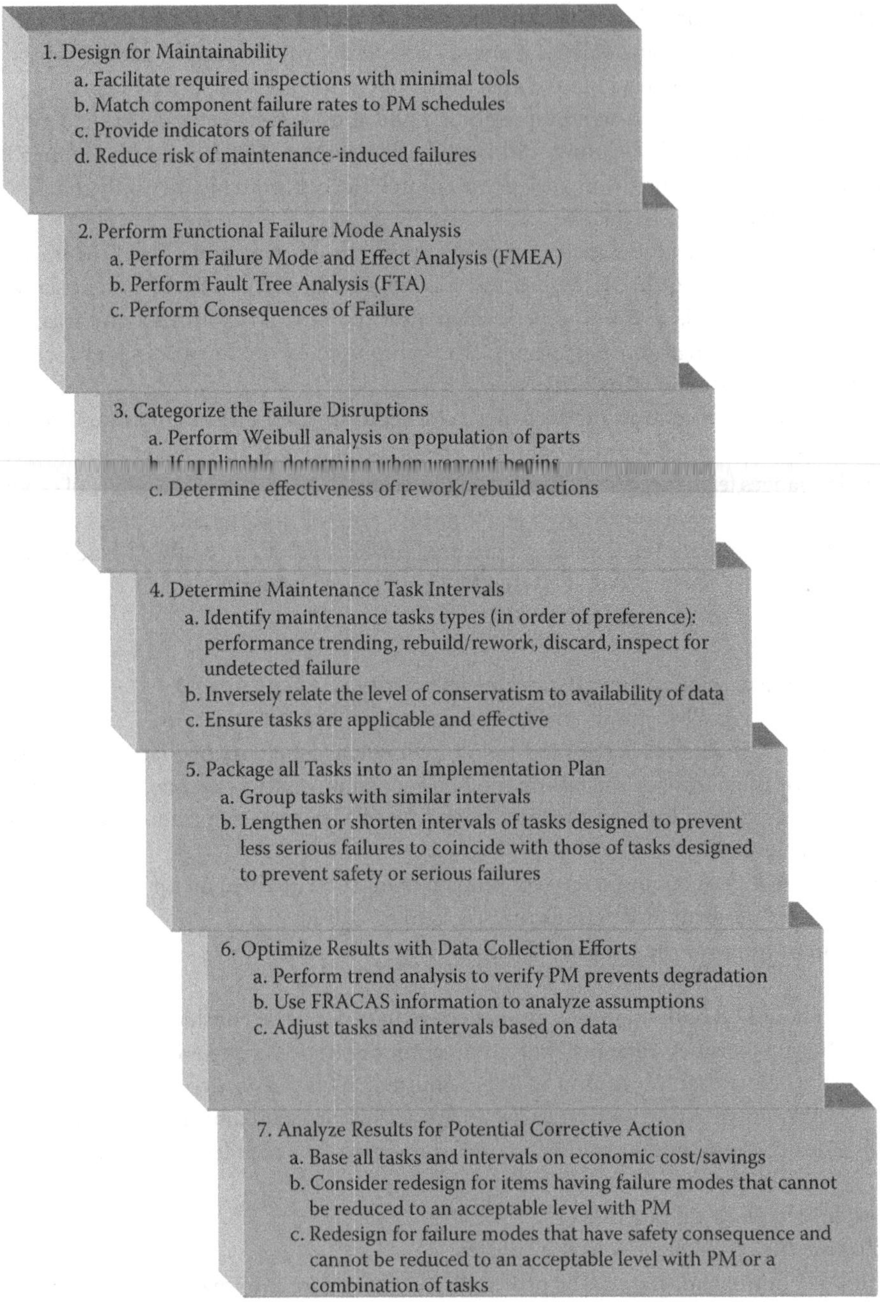

Figure 4.9   Steps in an RCM approach to identifying PM.

Failures can be either functional or potential. A functional failure is one that prevents or impairs the capability of an item to perform its intended function. Such failures are usually reported by the operator. The function of the item must be clearly defined.

Table 4.3 PM Task Applicability and Effectiveness Criteria

Task Type	Applicability Criteria	Effectiveness Criteria
• Performance trending	• Reduced failure resistance can be detected (potential failure) • Consistent time between potential failure and functional failure	• Task reduces failure to an acceptable level • Cost of scheduled PM is less expensive than corrective maintenance (CM) and the cost of failure without PM
• Rework/ rebuild	• Components/assemblies exhibit a distinct wear-out period ($\beta > 1$[a]) • Most components/assemblies survive to this time • Performance trending task not applicable and effective	• Task reduces failure to an acceptable level • Cost of scheduled PM is less expensive than CM and the cost of failure without PM • Rework/rebuild will restore item to like new condition and failure resistance
• Discard	• Components/assemblies exhibit a distinct wear-out period ($\beta > 1$) • Most components/assemblies survive to this time • Performance trending task or rework task not applicable and effective	• Task reduces risk of failure to an acceptable level • Cost of scheduled PM is less expensive than CM and the cost of failure without PM
• Failure identification	• Failure is not evident to operators of equipment • Failure results in increased risk of failure to other components • Performance trending task, rework, or discard task not applicable and effective	• Task reduces risk of multiple failures to an acceptable level • Cost of scheduled PM is less expensive than CM and the cost of failure without PM

[a] Based on analyzing failure data using Weibull analysis or based on experience. Weibull analysis is discussed in Section 9.3.9.

A potential failure is one where the physical condition of the item indicates that a functional failure is imminent. Such a failure is usually uncovered by maintenance personnel. If no action is taken, a potential failure will become a functional failure.

Examples of potential failures are cracks in structures, excessive vibration in bearings or gears, and metal particles in a gearbox indicating wear.

Reference has been made in Table 4.3 to performance trending. Performance trending, also called predictive maintenance or performance monitoring, is a process whereby one or more parameters are unobtrusively monitored and trended over time. These parameters must be directly related to the "health" of the equipment being monitored. On the basis of some threshold value (determined through analysis or experience) of a parameter or combination of parameters, the equipment will be repaired or replaced prior to any actual failure. The performance trending approach to scheduling PM can significantly reduce costs, prevent failures, and increase safety.

Table 4.4   Categories of Consequences of Failure

Category	Consequences	Can Be Addressed by
Safety	Possible loss of equipment; possible injury or death of operators, maintenance personnel, or bystanders	Redundancy
Operational	Indirect economic loss (e.g., inability to carry passengers) and direct cost of repair	PM given appropriate failure pattern
Nonoperational	Direct cost of repair	PM given appropriate failure pattern
Hidden failure	Multiple failures as a result of the undetected failure of a function (e.g., undetected loss of oil in an automobile can lead to severe engine damage)	Instrumentation, wear indicators, gauges, etc.

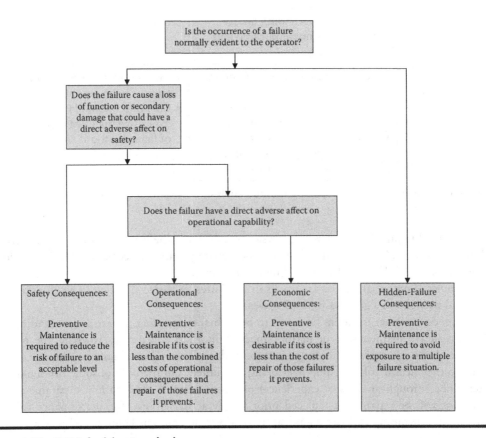

Figure 4.10   RCM decision tree logic.

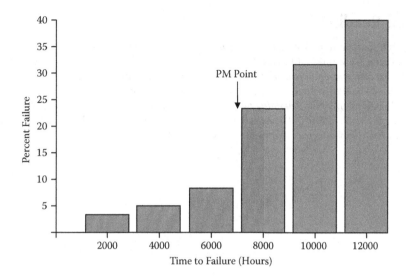

Figure 4.11   Determination of the optimum PM point.

This approach has long been used to detect an impending problem in rotating machinery by monitoring vibration. Other performance trending tasks include:

■ Oil analysis to detect wear metals in lubricating oil
■ Nondestructive inspection (dye penetrant, ultrasonic, etc.)
■ Visual inspection
■ Measurements (e.g., of the length of a crack)

Improvements in sensors and recording devices, and an understanding of which parameters truly indicate health, have increased the number of applications of performance trending. One such device, developed under Air Force sponsorship, is the time stress measurement device (TSMD). The TSMD collects, records, and stores stress data for subsequent analysis. Although studied as a method of dealing with false alarms, TSMDs can be used with appropriate sensors to record health-related parameters. The recorded levels of the parameters can be compared with preestablished limits. If the limits are exceeded or the data indicate that the limits will be exceeded in the near future, an inspection can be performed to confirm that a failure is imminent. If the inspection confirms the analysis, then appropriate PM can be performed before an actual failure occurs. If the inspection shows that no problem exists, it may be necessary to revise the preestablished limits.

The histogram shown in Figure 4.11 represents an optimal PM point for a representative RCM analysis. Before implementation of a PM task and associated task interval, an economic justification should be performed. The cost of performing the PM should be less than the cost of running to failure.

Maintenance expenditures throughout a product's lifetime often exceed the purchase price. Careful planning of a scheduled PM program, using RCM, can greatly reduce the cost of ownership. Dedicated application of the steps of an RCM analysis can potentially save money and optimize system availability. Chapter 5 in this volume, on maintainability, discusses RCM analysis in greater depth.

Suggested Reading

ARINC Research Corporation. 1995. *Product reliability, maintainability, and supportability handbook*, ed. Michael Pecht. New York: CRC Press.

Lewis, E. E. 1996. *Introduction to reliability engineering*. New York: John Wiley & Sons.

Moubray, J. 1992. *Reliability-centered maintenance*. New York: Industrial Press Inc.

Reliability Analysis Center. 1994. *Reliability toolkit: Commercial practices edition*. Rome, NY.

Reliability Analysis Center. 1996–1997. *Reliability blueprints*. A series of six guidebooks. Rome, NY.

Smith, A. 1993. *Reliability-centered maintenance*. New York: McGraw-Hill.

Chapter 5

Maintainability

Preface

Maintainability is the measure of the ability of a system or item to be retained in or restored to operable condition. It is meant to be a design characteristic that measures the capacity of a design to reduce system/equipment downtime. System reliability is impacted by maintainability, since maintenance is intended to reduce the risk of equipment wear-out and failure. System supportability is impacted by maintainability design characteristics that determine the requirements for maintenance manning level, training, tools, and spare parts. Thus, maintainability, reliability, and supportability are all interrelated to dependability, which is the ability to deliver a system or service that can be trusted. This chapter is the second in the series on dependability that attempts to develop an improved understanding of the strategies being used in both government and commercial sustainment enterprises to identify innovative solutions for improving the performance of depot-based maintenance, repair, and overhaul (MRO) operations.

5.1 Overview

Maintainability is measured as mean time to repair (MTTR). It is the average time required to perform maintenance on all of the removable items in a system. In maintainability prediction analyses, it is how long repair and maintenance tasks will take in the event of a system failure. Maintainability is a significant determinant of the operational availability (Ao) of the system. Its design characteristics have a direct impact on reliability, which is measured by mean time between failures (MTBF), and on supportability, which is measured by the mean logistic downtime (MLDT). Although maintainability is usually measured only in terms of the MTTR portion of equipment downtime, maintainability design characteristics, and ultimately the system maintenance plan, influence many of the logistics support requirements for the system. Thus, the system program manager must ensure that an adequate maintainability analysis is performed to allow the maintainability design characteristics be in balance with the requirements for reliability and logistics support. This is referred to as a trade-off analysis.

Design trade-off analyses are conducted as an iterative process, but with a definite order of precedence. Reliability vs. maintainability trade-off analyses are performed initially to determine equipment design characteristics and configuration. Maintainability vs. supportability analyses are then conducted to determine the logistics support system that is required to meet equipment design characteristics. Because the system program manager's primary measure of effectiveness is system Ao, these design trade-off analyses are iterated to determine the effect of each design action on the Ao components of reliability, maintainability, and supportability.

Maintainability trade-offs are conducted to achieve an optimum balance, within mission and resource requirements, between the frequency of failures and the downtime and resources required for maintenance. Usually, reliability improvements have an associated cost increase. The system program manager determines, within specific mission requirements for Ao, the most cost-effective mix of inherent design reliability and maintenance requirements. The procedures for reliability and maintainability design and trade-off analyses are significantly different between preventive maintenance actions and corrective maintenance actions.

5.1.1 Preventive Maintenance vs. Corrective Maintenance

Maintenance actions are grouped into two categories:

1. Preventive or scheduled maintenance tasks are implemented for an item to be retained in a specified condition.
2. Corrective or unscheduled maintenance tasks are required for an item to be restored to a specified condition.

Preventive maintenance actions are performed to enhance overall system reliability and to reduce the risk of failure. The objective of preventive maintenance analysis is to determine the optimum resource allocation for scheduled maintenance against the reliability improvement, which is gained. The analysis of preventive maintenance employs a standardized analytical technique, called reliability-centered maintenance (RCM) analysis. RCM analysis, which was introduced in the previous chapter, is a decision logic process that identifies those maintenance actions that improve system reliability and are cost-effective. Scheduled maintenance actions must be performed on any item whose loss of function or mode of failure could have safety consequences. The selection of scheduled actions is initially constrained by fixed requirements for system safety and mission success. If preventive tasks cannot reduce the risk of such failures to an acceptable level, the item is redesigned to alter its failure consequences. Scheduled maintenance is also required for any item whose functional failure will not be evident to the operator, and therefore cannot be reported for corrective maintenance action. In all other cases in which the consequences of failure are either cost increase or degradation of functions, scheduled tasks are directed at preventing failures and justified on the grounds of cost or mission enhancement. An RCM analysis program leading to the identification of all preventive maintenance requirements includes only those tasks that satisfy the criteria for both applicability and effectiveness. The applicability of a task is determined by the technical characteristics of the item, and its effectiveness is defined in terms of failure prevention and reliability improvement.

Corrective maintenance analysis has two objectives. First, the equipment design is assessed in order to evaluate its reliability and maintainability characteristics. In this trade-off analysis, undesirable characteristics are identified as design problems and fed back to the design team for correction or improvement. Second, during a maintainability vs. logistics trade-off analysis, tentative maintenance levels for each maintenance task and tentative support equipment requirements are identified. Corrective maintenance requirements are then subjected to both task and skills analysis and timeline analysis. The system program manager should understand that this grouping of trade-off analyses is not always clear or required. During the reliability/maintainability trade-off analysis, the practicality of logistics support must be considered in addition to MTBF and MTTR. Logistics support requirements for tools, spares, and training will be determined by the equipment design characteristics that are established to achieve the values of MTBF and MTTR.

5.1.2 Inherent Availability

The objective of reliability vs. maintainability trade-off analyses, which are conducted for corrective maintenance actions, is to determine a balance between resource allocation for reliability improvement, cost of maintenance, and the penalty of equipment downtime. These analyses measure the resources required to perform the maintenance action and to eliminate or reduce the frequency of the failure mode in the equipment design. In the early design phase, before detailed results are available from the evaluation of logistics support requirements, time is used as the primary measure of reliability and maintainability. The basic relationship for reliability/maintainability trade-off is based on the inherent availability (Ai) of the system. Ai is the probability that an item is in an operable state at any time, and is based on a combination of MTBF and MTTR:

$$Ai = \frac{MTBF}{MTBF + MTTR} \tag{5.1}$$

Thus, in addition to MTTR being used as a measure of reliability, it can be used in a reliability prediction in order to calculate the availability of a product or system. The system program manager must realize that this level of reliability vs. maintainability trade-off analysis does not provide assurance that the system will achieve an optimum level of Ao. And it should be noted that this stage of analysis ignores MLDT, a measure of supportability, which may be the most significant factor in achievement of operational availability. Chapter 6 in this volume, on supportability, will address MLDT.

5.2 Preventive Maintenance

5.2.1 Objective of Preventive Maintenance

Maintainability impacts system reliability. One preventive maintenance analysis technique that helps improve system and equipment reliability is reliability-centered maintenance (RCM). RCM was introduced in Chapter 4. It employs an established analytical method of analysis for matching the preventive maintenance capabilities of an organization to the design characteristics of the product. The concept was established by the commercial airline industry in the early 1960s as a tool for the development of an effective preventive maintenance program. The industry found that many preventive maintenance actions had no effect on the actual failure rate of equipment, and may even have been detrimental, due to maintenance errors and maintenance-induced failures. It had always been the underlying assumption of aircraft maintenance theory that there is a fundamental cause-and-effect relationship between scheduled maintenance and operating reliability. This assumption was based on the intuitive belief that because mechanical parts wear out, if the equipment was overhauled, it was better protected against the likelihood of failure. The only decision to be made for scheduled maintenance was in determining the equipment age limit for maintenance, which was necessary to ensure reliable operation. The RCM concept allowed the application of more decision factors than time in the development of an effective scheduled maintenance program.

The objective of RCM is to determine the minimum set of preventive maintenance tasks that will allow the equipment to achieve inherent reliability at minimum costs. Each scheduled maintenance task in an RCM program is generated for an identifiable and explicit reason. The consequences of each failure possibility are evaluated, and the failures are then classified according to the severity of their consequences. Proposed tasks for all significant items that would hinder operating safety or preclude mission success are then evaluated according to specific criteria of applicability and effectiveness. The resulting preventive maintenance program includes all the tasks necessary to protect operating reliability, and only the tasks that will accomplish this objective.

5.2.2 The RCM Analysis Process

To perform an RCM analysis, this information must be derived:

1. A determination of significant items
2. A failure mode and effects analysis (FMEA)
3. A method for partitioning the system to a workable level
4. An evaluation of failure consequences
5. An evaluation of proposed maintenance tasks

These requirements are input into the maintenance planning and logistics support analysis process. The key to the complete process for determining preventive maintenance requirements is the use of an RCM decision logic diagram (Figure 5.1). The first three questions determine the consequences of failure for every failure mode of each significant item. Next, depending on the consequence of failure, the proposed maintenance tasks to satisfy each failure mode are evaluated for applicability and effectiveness. This logic diagram generally provides a clear path to follow. In cases where a yes or a no answer is not evident, default logic is provided. The default logic specifies which path to follow in cases of uncertainty.

The information to be channeled into RCM decisions requires analysis under two different sets of conditions: (1) the development of an initial maintenance program on the basis of limited information, and (2) modification of these initial requirements as information becomes available from operating experience. As information accumulates, it becomes easier to make decisions. In a new program, however, there are many areas in which there is insufficient information for an ultimate yes or no answer. To provide for decision making under these circumstances, it is necessary to have a backup default strategy dictating the course of action. The default decisions are shown in Table 5.1.

Table 5.1 displays, for each of the decision questions, which answer must be chosen in case of uncertainty. In each case the default answer is based on protection of the equipment against serious consequences. This default approach can conceivably lead to more preventive maintenance than necessary. Some tasks will be included as protection against nonexistent hazards and others may be scheduled too frequently. The means of eliminating excessive maintenance costs are provided

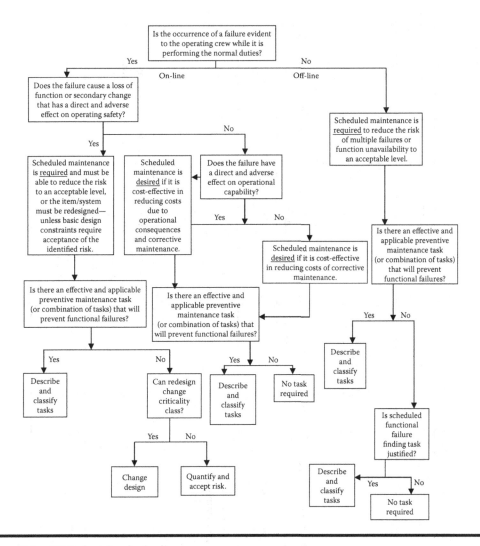

Figure 5.1   RCM decision logic diagram.

by the age exploration studies, which begin when the equipment goes into service. Through this process, the information needed to refine the initial RCM decisions and make necessary revisions is gathered systematically for evaluation.

5.2.2.1 Types of Preventive Maintenance

RCM requirements consist of tasks selected on the basis of actual reliability characteristics of the equipment they are designed to protect. The tasks are one of two general types of preventive maintenance, either scheduled inspections or scheduled removals. A scheduled inspection may be accomplished at any level of maintenance. It could be an inspection to detect impending failures or to detect functional failures that have occurred. Scheduled removals fall into two areas, removal for rework or reconditioning, or removal for throwaway. Functional failures, reconditioning, and throwaway tasks are directed at preventing single failures. Failure-finding

Table 5.1　Default Decisions for Reliability-Centered Maintenance

The default answers to be used in developing an initial preventive maintenance program in the absence of data from actual operating experience

Decision Question	Default Answer to Be Used in Case of Uncertainty	Initial Program	Ongoing Program	Possible Adverse Consequences of Default Decision	Default Consequences Eliminated with Subsequent Operating Information
		Stage at Which Questions Can Be Answered			
Identification of significant items: Is the item clearly nonsignificant?	No: Actually, item has significance.	X	X	Unnecessary analysis	No
Evaluation of failure consequences: Is an occurrence of a failure evident to the operating crew during performance of normal duties?	No (except for critical secondary damage): Classify function as hidden.	X	X	Unnecessary inspections that are not effective	Yes
Does the failure cause a loss of function of secondary damage that could have a direct adverse effect on operating safety?	Yes: Classify consequences as critical.	X	X	Unnecessary redesign or preventive maintenance that is not effective	No for redesign; yes for preventive maintenance
Does the failure have a direct adverse effect on the operational capability?	Yes: Classify consequences as operational.	X	X	Preventive maintenance that is not cost-effective	Yes

Evaluation of proposed tasks	Action			Consequence	Decision
Evaluation of proposed tasks: Is an on-condition task to detect potential failures applicable?	Yes: Include on-condition tasks in program.	X	X	Preventive maintenance that is not cost-effective	Yes
If an on-condition task is applicable, is it effective?	Yes: Assign inspection intervals when enough to make task effective.	X	X	Preventive maintenance that is not cost-effective	Yes
Is a rework task to reduce the failure rate applicable?	No (unless there are real and applicable data): Assign items to no preventive maintenance.	–	–	Delay in updating opportunity to reduce cost	Yes
If a rework task is applicable, is it effective?	No (unless there are real and applicable data): Assign items to no preventive maintenance.	–	X	Unnecessary redesign (safety) or delay in exploring opportunity to reduce cost	No for redesign; yes for preventive maintenance
Is altered task to avoid failures or reduce the failure rate applicable?	No (except for solo life items): Assign item to no preventive maintenance.	X (solo life only)	X (solo life only)	Delay in exploring opportunity to reduce costs	Yes
If an altered task is applicable, is it effective?	No (except for solo life items): Assign item to no preventive maintenance.	X (solo life only)	X (solo life only)	Delay in exploring opportunity to reduce costs	Yes

tasks are directed at preventing multiple failures. The development of a preventive maintenance program consists of determining which of these four tasks, if any, are applicable and effective. Applicability depends on the failure characteristics of the item. An inspection for potential failures can be applicable only if an item has characteristics that define a potential failure condition. Similarly, an age limit task will be applicable only if the failures at which the task is directed are related to age. Effectiveness is a measure of the results of the task objective, which depends on the failure consequences involved. A proposed task might appear useful if it promises to reduce the overall failure rate, but it could not be considered effective if the purpose of applying it was to avoid all functional failures. A summary of applicability and effectiveness criteria for all tasks is provided in Table 5.2.

For inspection tasks, the distinction between applicability and effectiveness is usually obvious. The item does not have characteristics that make such a task applicable. For age limit tasks, the distinction is sometimes blurred by the intuitive belief that the task is always applicable, and therefore effective. In reality, imposing an age limit on an item does not guarantee that its failure rate will be reduced. The issue is not whether the task can be done, but whether doing it will enable the item to achieve its inherent reliability.

5.2.2.2 Scheduled On-Condition Tasks

Scheduled inspections to detect potential failures are termed on-condition tasks, since they call for the removal or repair of individual units of an item on the condition that they do not meet the required standard. These tasks are directed at specific failure modes and are based on the feasibility of defining some identifiable physical evidence of a reduced resistance to the type of failure in question. Each unit is inspected at regular intervals and remains in service until its failure resistance falls below a defined level, that is, until a potential failure is discovered. Since on-condition tasks discriminate between units that require corrective maintenance to forestall a functional failure, and those units that will probably survive to the next inspection, they permit all units of the item to realize most of their useful lives. Many routine servicing tasks, such as checking oil quantity and air pressure, are on-condition tasks. The applicability of an on-condition task depends on both maintenance technology and the design of the equipment. For example, bore scope and radioisotope techniques have been developed for inspecting turbine engines, but these techniques are of value chiefly because the engines have been designed to facilitate their use. Whenever an on-condition task is applicable, it is the most desirable type of preventive maintenance. It avoids the premature removal of units that are still in satisfactory condition, and the cost of correcting potential failures is often far less than the cost of correcting functional failures, especially those that cause extensive secondary damage. For this reason, on-condition inspection tasks are steadily replacing older practices.

5.2.2.3 Scheduled Rework Tasks

Many single-celled and simple items display wear-out characteristics—that is, the probability of their failure becomes significantly greater after a certain operating age. When an item does not have an identifiable wear-out age, its overall failure rate can sometimes be reduced by imposing a hard time limit on all units to prevent operation at the ages of higher failure frequency. If an item's original failure can be repaired by rework or remanufacture, the necessary rework task may be scheduled at appropriate intervals. For example, an aircraft tire could have been scheduled for rework after a specified number of landings, since retreading restores the original failure resistance.

Table 5.2 Applicability and Effectiveness Criteria Summary

Task	Safety	Operational	Economic	Hidden Failure
Effectiveness				
All	Must reduce risk of failure to acceptable level	Must be cost-effective; cost of scheduled maintenance must be less than combined cost of loss of operation and repair	Must be cost-effective; cost of scheduled maintenance must be less than cost of repair	Insure level of availability to reduce risk of multiple failures to acceptable level
Applicability				
On condition	Possible to detect reduced failure resistance Possible to define potential failure condition that can be detected by an explicit task Consistent age between potential failure and functional failure	Same	Same	Same
Schedule rework	Identify age with rapid increase in conditional probability of failure Large percentage must survive to this age Possible to restore original failure resistance by rework	Same	Same	Same

(Continued)

Table 5.2　(Continued)

Task	Safety	Operational	Economic	Hidden Failure
Schedule discard	Must be critical failure Specified age limit below which no failures occur	Failure has major operational consequences Identify age with rapid increase in conditional probability of failure Large portion must survive to this age	Same as operational	Must be critical multiple failure Specified age limit below which no failure occurs
Failure finding	—	—	—	Must be a hidden function No other task is applicable or effective

However, this would have resulted in the retreading of all tires at the specified age limit, whether they needed it or not, and would not have prevented functional failures in those tires that failed earlier than anticipated. A rework task may be applicable, either for a simple item or to control a specific failure mode in a complex item. Although the age limit will be wasteful for some units and ineffective for others, the net effect on the entire population of that item will be favorable. This does not apply to complete rework of a complex item. Failures in complex items are the result of many different failure modes, each of which may occur at a different average age. Consequently, the overall failure rate of such items remains relatively constant. In some cases reliability decreases gradually with age, but there is no particular age that can be identified as a wear-out zone. Unless there is a dominant wear-out failure mode that is eliminated in the course of rework, complete rework of a complex item will have little or no effect on the overall failure rate.

5.2.2.4 Scheduled Discard Tasks

The scheduled rework of items at a specified age limit is one type of hard time task. The other is scheduled discard of items or their parts at some specified operating age. Such tasks are frequently termed life limit tasks. Life limits may be established to avoid critical failures, in which case they are called safe life limits. They may also be established because they are cost-effective in preventing noncritical failures, in which case they are called economic life limits.

5.2.2.5 Safe Life Limits

A safe life limit is imposed on an item only when safety is involved and there is no observable condition that can be defined as a potential failure. The item is removed at or before the specified maximum age and is either discarded or disassembled for discard of a specific part. This practice is most useful for simple items or individual parts of complex items, such as pyrotechnic devices in ejection seats (which have a limited shelf life) or turbine engine disks and nonredundant structural members (which are subject to metal fatigue). The safe life limit is usually established by the equipment manufacturer on the basis of developmental testing. Initially, a component whose failure would be critical is designed to have an extensive life. It is then tested in a simulated operating environment to determine what average life has actually been achieved, and a conservatively safe fraction of this average life is used as the safe life limit.

5.2.2.6 Economic Life Limits

Occasionally extensive operating experience may indicate that scheduled discard of an item is desirable on purely economic grounds. An economic life limit, however, is established in the same manner as an age limit for scheduled rework. It is based on the actual age–reliability relationship of the item, rather than on some fraction of the average age at failure. The objective of a safe life limit is to avoid accumulating any failure data. The only justification for an economic life limit is cost-effectiveness. The failure rate must be known in order to predict how the total number of scheduled removals at various age limits would affect the cost-benefit ratio.

5.2.2.7 Scheduled Failure Finding Tasks

A scheduled task may be necessary to protect the availability of a functional failure that is not evident to the operator. Hidden functional failures, by definition, have no immediate consequences;

yet undetected failures increase the risk of multiple failures. If no other type of maintenance task is applicable and effective, hidden function items are assigned scheduled inspections for hidden failures. Although such tasks are intended to locate functional failures rather than potential failures, they can be viewed as a type of on-condition maintenance, since the failure of a hidden function item can also be viewed as a potential multiple failure. The chief difference is in the level of item considered; a functional failure of one item may be only a potential failure for the equipment as a whole.

5.2.3 Age Exploration Program

Any preventive maintenance program can be developed and implemented with incomplete information. Generally there are limited data on the variation of failure resistance with age, variation of conditional probability of failure with age, and the operational values of failure symptoms. An important element of RCM is age exploration—a procedure for systematically gathering the information necessary to determine the applicability and effectiveness of particular maintenance tasks. As this information accumulates, the RCM decision diagram provides a means of revising and refining the initial program. Much of this information is already available for equipment that has been in service for some time, although the specific data needed may have to be retrieved from several different information systems. The remaining useful life of the equipment will be a factor in certain decisions. RCM analysis under these circumstances will result in fewer default decisions and more efficient preventive maintenance requirements. Such programs usually include more maintenance requirements and usually include a larger number of on-condition inspections than a program arrived at under other policies, and fewer of the scheduled rework tasks. Age exploration is an integral part of the RCM program and consists of two parts: (1) to detect decreases in reliability, and (2) to validate or determine the criteria for applicability and effectiveness of the four basic preventive maintenance tasks. Decreases in reliability can be detected through examination of in-service equipment to determine if the degradation is caused by increases in the rates of known failure modes or failure modes not anticipated. Data to support this part of age exploration can be found in engineering investigations, depot maintenance data, and operator discrepancy reports. The determination or validation of applicability and effectiveness criteria, the second part of age exploration, almost always requires special data collection programs. Since extra data collection imposes a greater workload on maintenance organizations, only essential data should be required, and only for a period long enough to establish or validate the uncertain parameters.

5.3 Corrective Maintenance

5.3.1 Objective of Corrective Maintenance

The purpose of corrective maintenance trade-off analysis is to optimize repair characteristics associated with hardware at all levels of indenture, from system to component. Optimization of repair characteristics is usually accomplished by three methods:

1. Reduce the amount of downtime that results from repair actions. The reduction of unscheduled maintenance downtime is a significant consideration, not only for Ao but also to

increase the probability of mission success by restoring a failed item. The cost of corrective maintenance is measured by reduction in availability of the system and by the support resources required to restore the system to a specified level of operation.

2. Simplify maintenance procedures by designing for ease in performing the interchange of parts and to minimize the complexity of diagnosis, both of which can reduce skill- and training-level requirements for maintenance personnel. Simplified maintenance may also reduce the numerical value for MTTR and maintenance man-hours per operating hour. This objective serves to create an atmosphere in which maintenance work can be accomplished with greater reliability and accuracy.

3. Design for an optimum mix of spare parts for unscheduled organizational repairs. The range of design options can be illustrated with a description of the two extreme choices for maintenance at the operational site. The first design choice is replacement of the entire subsystem or major equipment item upon failure. This choice requires full redundancy of each subsystem and is usually prohibitive in terms of resources available. The other extreme design method is the capability to pinpoint and replace the exact source of every failure at the operational site. This choice is usually prohibitive in both excessive downtime of the subsystem and overall support cost.

5.3.2 Techniques for Corrective Maintenance

There are a number of design techniques that may be implemented to improve the repair maintainability characteristics of equipment. These techniques may be classified into three general categories:

1. *Equipment configuration methods* such as standardization, accessibility, modularity, unionization, and interchangeability are well-established methods for reducing maintenance time. Standardization reduces waiting time for parts by decreasing the variety of parts that must be produced, stored, and shipped. Accessibility decreases both corrective and preventive maintenance times by allowing failure parts to be accessed more quickly. Modularity, unionization, and interchangeability decrease the number and type of assemblies that are diagnosed, removed, and replaced. Other configuration techniques include the design and location of controls, displays, inspection points, and lubrication points. Packaging and structure design also have a significant impact on maintainability.

2. *Maintenance concepts and methods* are another aspect of maintainability design. These techniques include modular replacement, automatic reconfiguration, remove and discard, and interchangeability.

3. *Test and diagnosis* are an important aspect of maintainability. Before repair can begin, the part of the equipment that has failed must be identified. As part of diagnosis, test points will often need to be used. If testability is designed into the item, then diagnosis will be quicker and more efficient. The concepts of built-in test equipment (BITE) and automatic test equipment (ATE) make diagnosis easier.

5.3.3 Repair Maintainability Procedures

The tasks of modeling, allocation, and prediction are analytical techniques that allow the engineer to simulate the maintainability characteristics for equipment in order to determine subsystem requirements and to evaluate design progress. Operational requirements are translated into design goals through the use of modeling. Allocation and prediction can then be performed to optimize maintainability characteristics under given constraints. Maintainability models are used to determine the effect that a change in one variable has on system cost, maintainability, or maintenance performance characteristics. The models should relate to, or be consistent with, cost and system readiness models and other appropriate logistics support models. They may be used to determine the impacts of change in fault detection probability, proportion of failure isolation, frequency of failure, critical percentile to repair, or maintenance hours per flying or operating hour.

Maintainability allocation follows a process very similar to that of reliability allocation. The reliability allocation involves the establishment of MTBF design goals for the various subelements of the system. Maintainability allocation is a method of apportioning the system MTTR requirement to all of the functional subelements of the system. The maintainability allocation is performed after the reliability allocation and prediction because it requires estimates of subsystem or equipment failure rates that are the logical result of the reliability analysis. To start the process, the engineer must make rough estimates of subsystem or equipment MTTR values. These estimates or rough predications often must be obtained from the engineer's subjective judgments that are based on the maintenance concept, the diagnostic capabilities, and all interfacing logistic policies. Once these estimates have been made, the procedure is rather simple to determine whether or not the system MTTR requirement can be met.

Although the modeling and allocation techniques for maintainability are similar to the reliability engineering techniques, the prediction process for maintainability is quite different. Reliability engineering and prediction is a specific technique through which the engineer can apply general engineering principles and good design practices to establish and assist the inherent failure rate. Maintainability, however, is more of an art than a science. An individual's talent and experience are often more valuable than established principles. For example, maintainability prediction procedures only provide techniques through which the analyst can summarize and average the estimated times for elementary maintenance tasks. The derivation of task time estimates is left to the analyst.

The system program manager should be aware that the most practical means of ensuring consideration in the design process of all qualitative factors that influence maintainability design is to establish a dialogue between experienced maintenance and logistic specialists and the design engineers. The most effective methods of formally implementing the required dialogue are design reviews, maintenance engineering checklists, and FMECA.

Maintainability design reviews provide an excellent means of exchange and evaluation of information related to both the design and maintenance of equipment. Early in the design state, equipment configuration may be adjusted to allow achievement of performance and reliability, and also to evaluate reliability/maintainability trade-offs. Maintainability design reviews may be conducted separately from formal program reviews in order to allow full attention to maintainability design without being overshadowed by concerns of schedule, budget, or other program requirements.

Maintainability design checklists are used throughout the design process to help the analyst think systematically and ensure consideration of the minimum design requirements. Checklists are developed by the maintenance specialist to describe to the equipment designer specific design features, such as quick-release fasteners and self-alignment bearings. Checklists are most useful if they are tailored to the specific equipment and its general maintainability design.

The FMECA provides an excellent source of information for maintainability analyses and trade-off. It also provides a formal means of information transfer between the maintenance specialist, the design engineer, and the reliability engineer/analyst. The maintenance specialist may utilize the FMECA to identify failure modes with the associated maintenance tasks, both preventive and corrective. The FMECA allows tracking of the effects of maintenance actions. It will then directly correlate maintenance with systematic failure ranking of the criticality of maintenance actions for proper management of design changes.

5.4 Testability and Diagnostics

Testability, an important component of maintainability, is a design characteristic that allows the status of an item to be determined and facilitates the timely and efficient isolation of faults within the item. It is insufficient to make a design testable. Testing must efficiently detect and isolate only faulty items, with no removal of good items. Removing good items is a problem in many industries, with obvious impacts on troubleshooting times and support costs.

Diagnostics include the tests for detecting and isolating faults and the means by which tests are performed. Achieving good diagnostics involves determining the diagnostic capability required in a product. A diagnostic capability can be defined as all capabilities associated with the detection, isolation, and reporting of faults, including testing, technical information, personnel, and training. Commonly used approaches to providing a diagnostics capability include the use of built-in test (BIT), external test equipment, and manual troubleshooting.

For what type of products are testability and diagnostics important? Any product that is to be used for an extended period of time and is repairable should have good testability characteristics and effective diagnostics. For products where safety is concerned, testability and diagnostics are very important. Even for nonrepairable products, good testability and diagnostics are needed to warn the operator or maintainer when the product is not functioning properly.

For repairable products, detecting and isolating a fault can be the most time-consuming portion of the total repair time. Figure 5.2 shows the elements of a repair action. Modern, complex products often incorporate electronics and microprocessors, complicating fault isolation. The omnipresence of software further complicates fault isolation.

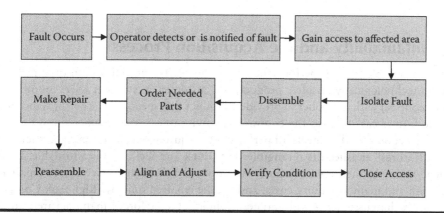

Figure 5.2   Elements of a repair action.

5.5 Maintainability and Logistics Requirements

Logistics requirements are greatly affected by maintainability design decisions. Logistics managers use the results of maintainability analyses in planning for six major categories of logistics:

1. Manpower and personnel
2. Support and test equipment
3. Facilities requirements
4. Training development
5. Sparing
6. Technical manuals

Conversely, the logistics provided for a product will affect the degree to which the inherent maintainability of a product is realized in actual use. That is, even if the inherent maintainability meets or exceeds the design requirement, the observed operational maintainability will be as expected only if the required logistics are available. Furthermore, the support concept and any customer constraints or requirements regarding technical data, support equipment, training (initial, recurring, and due to personnel turnover), field engineering support, spares procurement, contractor depot support, mobility, and support personnel must be understood and considered during all design trade-offs and analyses.

An increasingly more critical aspect of logistics is obsolescence of piece parts. Sometimes these parts are no longer available because the underlying manufacturing processes are eliminated for ecological or economic reasons. Sometimes, the parts themselves are displaced by ones that incorporate new technology but are not identical in form, fit, and function (F^3). Whatever the reason, parts and process obsolescence is an often overlooked and critical issue. Life buys are one way of coping with obsolescence.

Table 5.3 summarizes four key support infrastructure factors that influence operational maintainability in the military. Many of these factors, sometimes all of them, also influence the operational maintainability of commercial products. Just as the maintenance concept affects operational maintainability, so does the operating concept (i.e., the manner in which it will be operated). Included in the operating concept are the types of mission, deployment requirements, the need for operations at austere bases, etc. Although designers try to account for the operating concept, they often do not do so adequately, or the operating concept may change.

5.6 Maintainability and the Acquisition Process

Maintainability is a customer performance requirement. In the acquisition of a new product to replace a technologically obsolete product, the customer must either select an off-the-shelf product or contract with a supplier to provide a product that meets all the performance requirements. The former case typifies the commercial environment. A customer shops around, for example, for a computer that meets all performance requirements (e.g., speed, capacity, portability, and features), satisfies the intangibles (e.g., look and feel), and is affordable. Even customers who maintain their own computers want one that is inexpensive to have repaired (i.e., low operation and maintainability costs) and can be repaired quickly (high Ao). Competition not only gives the customer a wide range of choice, but it forces manufacturers to design and build computers that are maintainable and reliable. Individual customers do not develop

Table 5.3 Support Infrastructure Factors Affecting Military Operational Maintainability

Factors	Description
Airlift available for deployment	Mobility has always been a critical element of system effectiveness and is even more important to U.S. forces today. Mobility is without doubt affected by the operational reliability and maintainability (R&M) performance of a product. The types and quantities of spares needed to support operations and the size and quantity of support equipment are directly related to how well the product has been designed to be reliable and maintainable. In turn, the spares and support equipment needed to sustain an aircraft squadron determine the airlift capacity needed to deploy a squadron. Without the needed airlift, the spares and other logistics needs will not be available, and the measured availability (a function of R&M) will suffer.
Maintenance manning	Within reasonable ranges of maintainability performance, manning is insensitive to changes in maintainability and vice versa. However, if manning (or the assumed skill levels of personnel) falls below a certain level (not always well defined), availability will suffer because repairs will not be made in a timely manner and maintenance-induced failures may increase in frequency.
Depot pipeline time	The frequency with which a product fails (and requires depot maintenance) and the time required for the product or a component thereof to be sent from a base to the depot, be repaired, and be received back at the base determine how many spares are needed to sustain a given level of operations. By making the line repairable unit (LRU) or shop repairable unit (SRU) more reliable, by making it easier to repair (repairs can be made more quickly), or by shortening the shipping times, the number of required spares can be reduced. Conversely, if the depot pipeline time exceeds what was expected and planned for, repairs will not be made in a timely manner and availability will suffer.
Maintenance concept	The maintenance concept can affect mobility, manning, pipeline time, required spares, and the availability of the product. The viability of a given maintenance concept depends in part on the R&M characteristics of the product. For example, a two-level concept basically consists of remove and replace (R&R) actions at the organizational level. Replaced components (sometimes the product itself) are then sent back to a depot-level facility for repair. Such a concept can reduce manning requirements and improve mobility. But, if the organizational-level diagnostic capability is poor, a two-level concept would be uneconomical because a large number of spares would be required to keep the pipeline full. Decentralized depot concepts also can improve mobility and increase operational efficiency. Again, the viability of such concepts depends partly on the maintainability characteristics of the product. Conversely, because it can affect the number of spares required and mobility, an ineffective or poorly implemented concept will decrease availability, effectively reducing the observed (compared with the designed) maintainability.

design requirements and specifications, contract for the development of a new model, or otherwise directly participate in the development. Instead, the manufacturer must determine the requirements through customer surveys, warranty information, and benchmarking of competitors' products.

Likewise, when purchasing commercial off-the-shelf (COTS)* products, the military services do not directly participate in the development of those products. For example, the military services purchase personal computers for office use from the same manufacturers as does the general public. These PCs come off the same production lines used to manufacture PCs for the commercial marketplace, have the same design, use the same parts, and often come with the same warranty. So, for a COTS purchase, no design is involved, and hence design maintainability is not always an issue.[†] The use of COTS items does, however, have implications for supportability. Since customers using COTS items are essentially purchasing on a form, fit, function, and interface (F^3I) basis, they will not have configuration control of or data describing the internal design of a COTS item. Without configuration control or design data, the customer will have no way to develop and maintain maintenance procedures for repairing the COTS item. Consequently, the support concept will be one of removing and replacing the failed COTS item and sending it back to the supplier for repair.

When the military needs a product not used in the commercial marketplace, or which is similar to a commercial product but must meet much more severe requirements, a new military acquisition program begins. The program may be to develop a completely new product or to modify an existing one. In either case, the customer must explicitly identify to potential suppliers the performance requirements for the product. When more than one supplier is capable of providing the product, these requirements are included in a Request for Proposal (RFP) that is issued by the military customer's procuring activity. Maintainability must be addressed in the RFP.

5.7 Maintainability and the Manufacturing Process

The manufacturing processes used to transform the design to a tangible product determine if the inherent design maintainability of the product is achieved. It is essential that manufacturing requirements do not compromise the designed maintainability, so manufacturing engineers and planners must be involved in the design effort. Without their involvement, maintainability design features or approaches may make the product difficult or too expensive to manufacture. For example, access panels that were included to ensure maintainability requirements are met might be placed in an area where the mold line of the product has compound curves. Moving the panel to an area that is flat or has a simpler surface might still allow good access and improve manufacturability.

The eventual quality of a product is directly related to the processes used in the manufacture of the product. Today, process capability is an important indication of how well a process is controlled. Every process has some variation in its output. Supposedly identical manufactured

---

* COTS is used to mean either "commercial off the shelf" or "commercial item."
[†] Design of interfaces when the COTS product is a component or subsystem of a larger product being developed for the customer is, of course, another matter. For example, the ability to detect that the COTS item has failed, providing access to remove and replace the item, identifying any tools or support equipment needed to calibrate the item, and developing the procedures associated with these activities will be major maintainability concerns.

products will vary in size, strength, and defect content, and seemingly identical services will vary in time to performance and effectiveness. In either case, the greater the variation, the less often the customer will be satisfied. So long as the process is stable, random samples of the output will measure values randomly distributed in a defined range. According to the central limit theorem in statistics, the sample measurements should be normally distributed about the mean of the process and their variation. Controlling the process within acceptable limits is critical. Such control is monitored by statistical process control (SPC) charts. The range of expected variation is generally set at ±3 sigma, the standard deviation of the sample around the target value, though exceptions are sometimes made (e.g., 4 is used in the automotive industry). The 3 sigma variation around the mean has led to the development of Six Sigma quality control techniques. So long as the sample values vary randomly in this range, the process is "in control" and should not be adjusted. When there exits a trend pattern (e.g., a series of consecutive points constantly rising or falling), or when the values range outside the control limits, there is some factor at work that must be identified and corrected to restore the expected variation. In most cases, if we wish to control the values of a variable, we also wish to control the variation in the parameter between units. For example, if we wish to achieve a comfortable room temperature, we would not be happy with a figure obtained by averaging very hot and very cold measurements. For this reason, plotting the mean value of the samples in a control chart is often accompanied by a chart that plots the range.

The control charts are used to monitor a process to ensure it remains in control, i.e., stable. It is important to note that "in control" is not the same as "in specification." When in control, the process is showing only its inherent variation, and hence doing the best that it can. This may not be good enough if the typical variation is beyond the specification limits. When a process is in control, but not in specification, only a change to the process can reduce the proportion of defective products.

The first task in measuring variation is to determine the parameters that most impact the customer's satisfaction. These will be the measures of quality. Some possibilities are:

- *Physical*: Size (length, width, height), weight, strength
- *Performance*: Gain, frequency, power output
- *Failure related*: Service life, failure rate, defect rate, reject rate
- *Cycle time*: Time to produce, time from order to delivery, design cycle
- *Cost*: Cost to produce, warranty costs, scrap produced, rework costs, overhead rate

5.8 Maintainability and Safety

In designing for maintainability, the maintainability engineer must be constantly aware of the relationship between maintainability and safety. Maintenance can be hazardous to personnel. It can involve working on high-power electrical equipment or high-pressure hydraulic or pneumatic equipment. Maintenance must sometimes be performed in tight areas where adequate ventilation can be a problem. Mistakes in procedures can result in injury and damage to products. So safety is a concern. Safety includes designing the product and maintenance procedures to minimize the possibility of damage to the product during servicing and maintenance, and to minimize the possibility of harm to maintenance and operating personnel. Safety procedures usually come with warning labels, precautionary information for maintenance and operating manuals, and the procedures for disposing of hazardous materials and product waste.

The principal objective of a system safety program is to ensure that safety, consistent with functional requirements, is designed into systems, subsystems, equipment and facilities, and their interfaces. Military handbooks, such as MIL-HDBK-338B, *Electronic Reliability Design Handbook* (U.S. Department of Defense 1998), contain detailed treatments of safety issues. Much of the discussion is based on the handbook MIL-STD-882C, *System Safety Program Requirements* (U.S. Department of Defense 1993). This handbook provides uniform guidelines for:

- Developing and implementing a comprehensive system safety program for identifying the hazards of a system
- Imposing design requirements and management controls to prevent mishaps by eliminating hazards or reducing the associated risk to a level acceptable to the managing activity

From a maintainability perspective, the safety terms listed in Table 5.4 are important. Many different types of safety analyses can be performed for a large, complex product.

Table 5.4 Maintainability-Related Safety Terms

Term	Description
Fail safe	A design feature that either ensures that the system remains safe or, in the event of a failure, will revert to a state that will not cause a mishap. Fail-safe features are important during maintenance, just as they are during operation. For example, aircraft have a device that prevents inadvertent operation of the landing gear while the aircraft is on the ground.
Hazard	A condition that is prerequisite to a mishap. Preventing injury or death to maintainers begins with identifying potential hazards. For example, foreign object debris (FOD) is a hazard around aircraft operations.
Hazard probability	The aggregate probability of occurrence of the individual events that create a specific hazard.
Hazardous material	Any material that due to its chemical, physical, or biological nature causes safety, public health, or environmental concerns.
Mishap	An unplanned event (accident) or series of events that result in death, injury, occupational illness, or damage to or loss of equipment or property or damage to the environment.
Risk	An expression of the possibility of a mishap in terms of hazard severity and hazard probability.
Risk assessment	A comprehensive evaluation of the risk and its associated impact.
Safety	Freedom from those conditions that can cause death, injury, occupational illness, or damage to or loss of equipment or property or damage to the environment.

(Continued)

Table 5.4 (Continued)

Term	Description
Safety critical	A term applied to a condition, event, operation, process, or item of whose proper recognition, control, performance, or tolerance is essential to safe operation or use, e.g., safety-critical function, safety-critical path, or safety-critical component.
Safety-critical computer software components	Those computer software components and units whose errors can result in a potential hazard, or loss of predictability or control of a system.

Table 5.5 Safety Analyses Most Applicable to Maintainability

Name of Analysis	Comment
System Hazard Analysis (SHA)	The SHA documents the primary safety problem areas of the total system design, including potential safety-critical human errors. It should identify design areas that can pose hazards to personnel during maintenance.
Operating and Support Hazard Analysis (O&SHA)	The O&SHA identifies associated hazards and recommends alternatives that may be used during all phases of intended system use. It should identify hazards that could exist during maintenance.
Occupational Health Hazard Assessment (OHHA)	The OHHA identifies human health hazards and proposes protective measures to reduce the associated risks to levels acceptable to the managing activity. It should identify potential health hazards during maintenance.

Those most closely applicable to maintainability are listed in Table 5.5.

In addition to analyzing the hazards posed by a product's design and its operation and support, it is important to identify potential hazards facing personnel during maintenance tests and demonstrations. Evaluating these hazards is part of evaluating test and evaluation (T&E) safety. The purpose of evaluating T&E safety is to ensure that safety is considered (and safety responsibility assigned) in test and evaluation, to provide existing analysis reports and other safety data, and to respond to all safety requirements necessary for testing in-house, at other supplier facilities, and at government ranges, centers, or laboratories.

In addition to the safety analyses made of the final design, subsequent analysis should be made of proposed changes to the design. All engineering change proposals and requests for deviation/waiver should be evaluated to determine the safety impact, if any, upon the product.

Finally, maintenance of products containing pyrotechnic or other explosive devices is an especially hazardous activity. Consequently, these devices should be analyzed to assign an explosive hazard classification (EHC) to new or modified ammunition, explosives (including solid propellants), and devices containing explosives, and to develop hazard characteristics data for these devices.

References

U.S. Department of Defense. 1993, January19. *Military standard system safety program requirements.* MIL-STD-882C.

U.S. Department of Defense. 1998, October 1. *Electronic reliability design handbook. MIL-HDBK-338B.* Superseding MIL-HDBK-338A (October 12, 1988).

Chapter 6

Supportability

Preface

Supportability is the ability to restore a failed system back to its operational state as quickly and effortlessly as possible. The more inherent qualities a system possesses to help restore it back to a working condition, the more supportable the system. Thus, supportability focuses on the design characteristics of the system. These characteristics include designing for reliability, designing for maintainability, technical support data, and maintenance procedures. Its purpose is to facilitate detection, isolation, and timely repair/replacement of system anomalies. It includes diagnostics, prognostics, real-time maintenance data collection, corrosion protection and mitigation, reduced logistics footprint, and other factors that contribute to an optimum environment for developing and sustaining a stable, operational system. To minimize system failures, the supportability posture should be designed in (DAU 2008).

Supportability is a design characteristic. It is impacted by reliability and maintainability. Reliability, maintainability, and supportability are all interrelated to dependability, which is the ability to deliver a system or service that can be trusted. This chapter is the third in the series on dependability that attempts to develop an improved understanding of the strategies being used in both government and commercial sustainment enterprises to identify innovative solutions for improving the performance of depot-based maintenance, repair, and overhaul (MRO) operations.

6.1 Supportability Metrics

Supportability is the average time needed to satisfy material and administrative requirements associated with restoring a failed system to operation using available administrative and logistics channels. This time is expressed as the mean logistics downtime (MLDT). Except for the actual repair time, which is the mean time to repair (MTTR), all logistics metrics should be included in supportability as some subset of MLDT. Mean logistics delay time (MLDT) is the sum of these logistics submetrics, such as mean downtime for outside assistance (MOADT) and mean supply response time (MSRT).

177

6.1.1 Mean Downtime for Outside Assistance (MOADT)

The average downtime per maintenance action that is awaiting outside assistance is MOADT. This is normally caused by the lack of test equipment, tools, or skills beyond those available at the operational level (e.g., on board a ship). This also occurs when repairs require the use of special facilities, such as a dry dock or floating crane. Every system experiences some MOADT. The system program manager should be particularly sensitive during the maintainability and supportability analyses to the requirements of the maintenance plan, and the requirements to replace any readiness-driving parts that fail. The objective of the system program manager is to eliminate any requirement for outside assistance, except for catastrophic failure. The maintenance plan is reviewed for consistency with the number and skill level of both operating and maintenance personnel. Any requirements for test equipment must be consistent with the equipment lists. The system program manager should also review the maintenance code* of any spare or repair part that is Military Essentiality Code 1 (MEC 1).† A MEC 1 code assigned to a part designates that part as a readiness-driver. If that part fails, its next higher assembly fails. If the failure of the next higher assembly causes a system failure, then the maintenance level at which that part can be replaced and the skills, tools, test equipment, and accessibility of that part become critical factors to eliminating the need for outside assistance for a system failure.

6.1.2 Mean Downtime for Documentation (MDTD)

The average downtime per maintenance action to obtain documentation needed for fault isolation, maintenance, and checkout is MDTD. This is normally an insignificant portion of the mean logistics delay time, but it occurs each time the system fails, and is therefore inversely proportional to the reliability of the system. High MDTD normally is caused by technical publications that are not applicable to the configuration of the system installed, or by errors in the technical documentation. The system program manager should be sensitive to consistency between configura-

---

* The maintenance code is the third position in the U.S. Joint Services Uniform Source, Maintenance, and Recoverability (SM&R) codes. The SM&R code is a five-position code that reflects supply maintenance decisions made during the logistic planning process. The first two positions are the source code that indicates the means of acquiring the item for replacement purposes. The third position is the maintenance code that indicates the lowest level of maintenance authorized by the maintenance plan to remove, replace, or use the item. The third position of the SM&R code is the code that the system program manager reviews for all MEC 1 items to ensure that critical readiness-driver repair parts are replaceable at the operational level, and that the supply system considers that item as a candidate on-board allowance item; then an APL is computed. The fourth position is a maintenance code that indicates whether the item is to be repaired, and identifies the lowest level of maintenance authorized by the maintenance plan to return the item to serviceable condition from some or all failure modes. The fifth position is the recoverability code that indicates the approved condemnation level.
† The repair parts code system is the Military Essentiality Code (MEC). Any repair part with a MEC of 1 is potentially a readiness-driving part. A MEC 1 means that when that part fails, its next higher assembly fails. If the loss of the next higher assembly causes failure of the system or equipment, then the part that initiated the chain of failures is a critical readiness-driving repair part. A MEC 5 means that part is required for safe operation of the equipment. For purposes of parts sparing, a MEC 5 repair part is treated like a MEC 1 repair part. The system program manager needs to ensure that any MEC 1 item that will cause total system failure is capable of being replaced at the operational level. If that part is not capable of being replaced, then a major deterrent to Ao exists when the system is deployed.

tion, maintenance procedures, and part identification in the illustrated parts breakdown and the allowance parts lists (APLs).

6.1.3 Mean Downtime for Training (MDTT)

The average delay time per maintenance action due to lack of training is MDTT. This is rarely a factor in the achievement of the operational availability (Ao) threshold and normally occurs when all trained maintenance personnel have been transferred or are otherwise unavailable. The principal requirements for the system program manager are to ensure consistency between the planned and corrective maintenance actions required at the user level, and the curriculum in the technical training courses.

6.1.4 Mean Supply Response Time (MSRT)

The average delay time per maintenance action to obtain spare and repair parts is MSRT. MSRT is the single greatest driver of MLDT. The MSRT component of the MLDT requirement is compared to normal supply response time to determine if it is reasonably attainable with the standard supply system.

6.1.5 Mean Requisition Response Time (MRRT)

The approximation of supply system response times whenever a part is not available and it must be requisitioned from the supply system is MRRT. The computation of MRRT requires that the system program manager determine these percentages for the system being analyzed:

- The percentage of maintenance actions requiring parts that are allowed in stock at the operational level (e.g., on board ship)
- The percentage of allowed parts requirements that are normally satisfied from operational stock

Depending on the developmental stage of the system, these percentages can be obtained from empirical information on a similar existing system, from the 3M database, from casualty report (CASREP) data, or from APL data.

6.1.6 Mean Downtime for Other Reasons (MDTOR)

The average downtime per maintenance action for reasons not otherwise identified, including administrative time, is MDTOR. It is common practice to provide for 10 h of MDTOR, and include MDTD and MDTT in MDTOR when these values are insignificant.

6.2 Determining Mean Logistics Downtime

The supportability of a system, as measured by MLDT, can be estimated by summing its submetrics using a decision tree. A decision tree (or tree diagram) is a decision support tool that uses a graph or model of the decisions, their probabilities, and their possible consequences.

The tree includes the outcomes, the probabilities of the outcomes, and the resource costs or benefits. A decision tree is used to identify the strategy that is most likely to reach an established goal.

6.2.1 MLDT Calculation Using a Decision Tree

MLDT is a function of the percentage of maintenance actions that require parts (MRRT) and the mean supply response time (MSRT) to obtain those parts. The MRRT value can be estimated using a decision tree, as illustrated in Figure 6.1.

Figure 6.1 is an example of an approximation of the MRRT time for a part that is not available on board a U.S. Navy ship and must be requisitioned from the supply system. The 45.9 h delay awaiting the part from off the ship is based upon the assumption that the wholesale supply system is funded to satisfy 85% of the requisitions it receives. The remaining 15% of all requisitions that are referred to the wholesale supply system cannot be filled. The times to fill requisitions for deployed and nondeployed units used example supply system timeframes. The decision tree

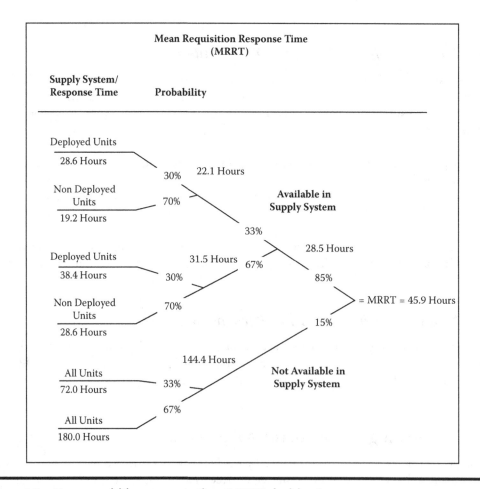

Figure 6.1   Mean requisition response time (MRRT) decision tree.

concludes that, to the degree that the input assumptions and probabilities are valid for any specific system being analyzed, it takes 45.9 h on average to satisfy an off-ship requisition.

Figure 6.2 is the decision tree for computing MSRT, the weighted average response times to satisfy repair parts requirements from both shipboard inventories and the supply system. The MSRT value of 23.9 h assumes a 60% allowance for stock at the operational level (i.e., on board ship).

Finally, the decision tree in Figure 6.3 calculates the approximation for MLDT given the inputs from the MRRT and MSRT tree diagrams. The MLDT value of 20.3 h is based on the assumption that 85% of the maintenance actions will require parts. Not all maintenance actions do require repair parts. A greater percentage of maintenance actions on electronics equipment require parts than maintenance actions on structural or mechanical equipment. So, analysts must adjust the probabilities to reflect the type of parts required.

6.2.2 Probabilities Used in Estimating MLDT

The above estimation of the supportability parameters MRRT and MSRT demonstrates that the derivation of MLDT is subject to a number of percentages that impact these parameters. These percentages can differ significantly from one system to another. Although it is possible to actually measure supply response times and the percentage of maintenance actions requiring parts, MLDT information is not generally available as a distinct data element from statistical data files. Instead, the methodology requires an estimation of MLDT through calculations that

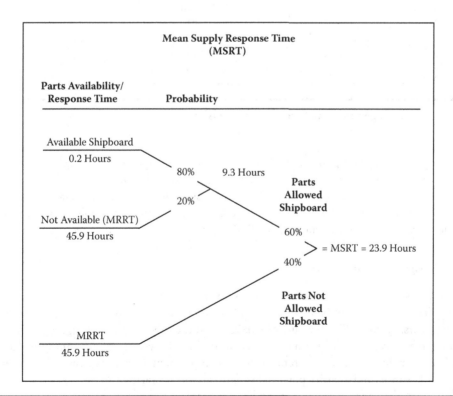

Figure 6.2 Mean supply response time (MSRT) decision tree.

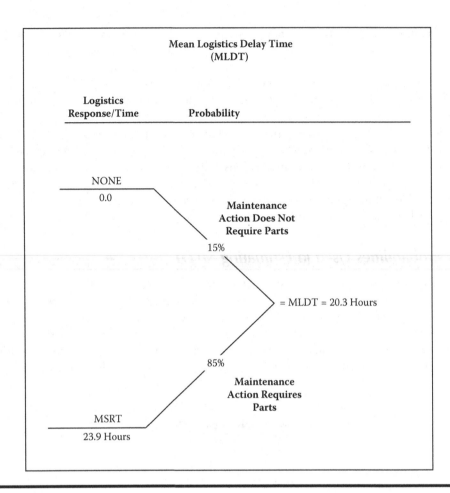

Figure 6.3   Mean logistics delay time (MLDT) decision tree.

use fundamental supply support statistical information and reasonable default values for the probabilities. A set of reasonable default values are given in Table 6.1. They reflect Department of Defense (DoD) policy, funding levels, authorized stock levels at various echelons for supply, supply material availability (SMA) levels from the supply system, and supply response times for requisitions from the casualty reports (CASREPs) for critical maintenance requirements.

6.2.3 Replacement Rates

All repair parts have a reliability factor that is provided by the manufacturer at the time of provisioning. This may initially be expressed as mean cycles between failures, failures per million operating hours, or the MTBF measure of reliability. At the time of provisioning, this is converted to an annual replacement rate, so that all parts in the supply system use a common replacement factor. Replacement rates are important to the system program manager because they determine inventory allowances and identify potential supply support problems.

All military allowance computation models use a replacement factor as a key variable to determine the inventory of spares and repair parts to support organizational-level maintenance. Some

Table 6.1 Default Values for Calculating MLDT

		Default Value
Percentage of corrective maintenance actions that require parts	Hull, mechanical, and electrical (HM&E)	60%
	Electronic systems	85%
Percentage of maintenance actions requiring parts that are satisfied from operational stocks	Hull, mechanical, and electrical (HM&E)	65%
	Electronic systems	60%
Percentage of parts requirements for allowed on-board items that are satisfied from on-board stocks	All systems	80%
Time required to obtain a part from on-board stocks	All systems	2 h

allowance models weigh this demand rate more heavily than others. The concern is whether the replacement factor continues to reflect the actual replacement rate throughout the life cycle of the system. If a part is identified as a supply support problem, the first check the system program manager should make is to compare actual replacements in the fleet against the replacement factor used by the supply system to compute allowances.

In the design phases of system development, the replacement factor for each part should be compared with the U.S. Joint Services Uniform Source, Maintenance, and Recoverability (SM&R) coding and the Military Essentiality Code (MEC). Any part with a high replacement rate that is a MEC 1 coded item, but is not coded for organizational-level removal or replacement, requires close scrutiny by the system program manager, since it is a key warning of a future readiness problem.

6.2.4 Alternatives When the MLDT Is Insufficient

When the system program manager has calculated the optimum mean response times that the standard supply system can attain, and the MLDT is not sufficient toward achieving the operational availability (Ao) threshold, what alternatives does he or she have? Since MSRT and reliability (MTBF) are the two major drivers in the attainment of the Ao thresholds, these two variables become the focus of action.

MSRT can be improved when it has been determined that standard military sparing will not provide the response time required to achieve the Ao thresholds. For example, the U.S. Navy Office of the Chief of Naval Operations (OpNav) has approved the general use of an allowance computation model that optimizes the supply support required to achieve Ao. Also, the military has approved the use of several forms of readiness-based sparing (RBS) models. The Aviation Readiness Requirements Oriented to Weapon Replaceable Assemblies (ARROWS) model is in wide use to support the U.S Naval Air (NAVAIR) systems readiness requirements. RBS is designed to satisfy the mean supply response time required to achieve the Ao threshold, and it is the only alternative available to the system program manager to deviate from standard military sparing policy. The time required to complete this process, including approval, the program objectives memorandum (POM) and budget cycles, procurement lead times, and positioning the inventory in the fleet, is about 3 years. The determination that extraordinary supply support is necessary must be made as soon in the acquisition process as possible.

6.3 Designing for Supportability

Designing for supportability refers to those actions and activities that are involved in providing the parts, materials, services, training, and documentation required to maintain the maximum performance capabilities of a product or system. The goal is to reduce life cycle costs through the minimization of product/system downtime. The initial system acquisition cost is not the largest contributor to total life cycle costs. In fact, some studies indicate that the cost of operation and support of a fielded system account for more than half of its total life cycle costs (DAU 2008), which reinforces the importance of designing systems for supportability.

System supportability should be dealt with from the very beginning in the conceptual design stage. The concern should be with identifying those aspects of the system design that will reduce the effort and cost associated with keeping a system in a maximum state of readiness. It also involves identifying and developing the necessary support services, training, and documentation that will aid in the effective operation and maintenance of the fielded system. The planning and definition of the product/system support requirements are essential to achieving high levels of supportability. By designing for product/system supportability, one seeks to prevent the occurrence of unanticipated support requirements and provide a lower-cost, highly supportable final product/system. With this goal in mind, realize that downtime minimization can be accomplished if the integrated product team (IPT) addresses supportability considerations up front during the design stage, not after the fact. Some of these considerations include (DAU 2008):

- The operational use of the product/system
- The environmental conditions during operation (i.e., temperature, humidity, etc.)
- Expected or required reliability: failure rates on subsystems and components
- Personnel requirements (operational and support)
- Expected or required maintainability: projected updates and configuration changes

To increase supportability, the IPT must begin by identifying potential system failures and working toward a design that:

- Eliminates/reduces their potential causes
- Increases the MTBF
- Minimizes the impact and criticality of failures

The IPT should also consider ways to quickly return inoperable systems to full operation. This will require direct consideration of system maintainability and testability. Testability is the capability of the product/system to be checked for proper operation to ensure maximum readiness or to diagnose anomalous performance. Finally, processes must be established to provide feedback to the IPT on the operation of fielded systems. This is necessary to provide valuable information on necessary changes and enhancements (i.e., hardware, software, services, etc.) that would improve present and future systems (DAU 2008).

6.4 Trade-Off Analyses

Supportability considerations must be balanced against other system/product requirements, such as reliability and maintainability. To assess the overall impact of the system on these other abilities, trade-off analyses are recommended. The following discussion addresses one of these trade-off design analyses. Chapter 9 in this volume addresses another: the trade-off with costs and affordability.

6.4.1 Level of Repair Analysis (LORA)

The LORA is a specialized maintainability/supportability trade-off design analysis. The analysis is intended to determine the optimum facility at which a specified maintenance action should be performed. It seeks to answer the question: Should repair be performed at an operational (organizational) facility, intermediate facility, or depot? As an example, in the U.S. Navy, aircraft maintenance is divided into three levels: organizational, intermediate, and depot. Organizational maintenance is repair work performed by the operating units, such as a squadron, on a day-to-day basis. This work consists of inspecting, servicing, lubricating, adjusting, and replacing parts, minor assemblies, and subassemblies. Intermediate maintenance is work performed at centrally located facilities in support of the operating units. This work consists of calibration, repair, or replacement of damaged or unserviceable parts, components, or assemblies, limited manufacture of parts, and technical assistance. Depot maintenance is performed at large industrial-type facilities, such as a Naval Aviation Depot (NADEP), and it includes major overhaul and major repair or modifications to aircraft, components, and equipment, and the manufacture of parts.

The LORA utilizes standardized computer models and cost factors. The Logistics Management Information (LMI) database (described in the next section) is utilized in conducting the LORA. The maintainability design characteristics, utilized as inputs to the LORA, include maintenance procedures described in task, skills, and timeline analyses. These technical characteristics are examples of the maintenance factors that are utilized in conducting a LORA:

- *Life cycle*: The entry in this field is the total number of years (including the base year) that the equipment is operational and for which logistics support costs are to be calculated in deriving LORA recommendations.
- *Gross removal factor* (GRF): The expected number of items removed from the next higher assembly, including false removals.
- *Unit cost*: The estimated unit procurement cost of the item.
- *MTBF*: The predicted mean time between failures, in terms of operating hours.
- *MTTR*: The predicted mean time to repair the item, in elapsed hours. This factor is used to compute the Ao of the equipment and to provide estimates of maintenance shop workloads.
- *Repair cycle*: The average number of days required for shop repair. Separate entries are made for organizational-, intermediate-, and depot-level maintenance.
- *Beyond capability of maintenance rate*: The percentage of failures that cannot be repaired at the indicated maintenance level and are sent to a higher-level maintenance activity for repair or condemnation. Separate entries are provided for organizational- and intermediate-level maintenance sites.

■ *Scrap rates*: Fractions of failures that cannot be repaired and are scrapped at the indicated maintenance level. Different values are used for the organizational-, intermediate-, and depot-level maintenance sites.
■ *First removal rates*: Percentages, which are multiplied by the number of real failures, to give the number of false removals of the item. Different values are used for the organizational-, intermediate-, and depot-level maintenance sites.
■ *False removal detection rates*: Percentages, which are multiplied by the number of false removals, to give the number of such removals indicated as false. Different values are used for the organizational-, intermediate-, and depot-level maintenance sites.

The basis for each of these technical factors is dependent upon the type of equipment: system or support equipment. The inventory control point (ICP) that will be supporting the item can normally provide approximations of these rates for similar existing items.

The LORA is conducted as an integral part of the maintenance planning and analysis process. LORA models attempt to simulate the planned maintenance practices and procedures for the system. They provide an advanced look at intermediate and depot support costs. The system program manager must ensure that a LORA does not result in uncoordinated changes to the supportability analysis. The LORA may be conducted as a computer-based model, or by manual computation for simple systems. If computer-based analysis is required, the contractor may request existing level of repair computer programs through the system program manager. Subsequently, the designated activity will provide level of repair computer programs, user's guides, and other such program documentation that will enable the contractor to meet the processing requirements.

The system program manager may also require level of repair analysis using noneconomic factors, including safety, repair feasibility, and mission success. This analysis, if required, is accomplished without cost as the prime consideration and is performed prior to the LORA economic analysis. Any LORA recommendations that are based on noneconomic analysis may also include an economic analysis in order to assign some economic value to the noneconomic recommendation.

Additional data are developed in the analysis that are not a direct part of the LORA. A contractor can use the results from LORA, from government-furnished information, and from maintenance planning data to select source, maintenance, and recoverability (SM&R) codes for the items in which a LORA analysis was conducted. In addition, the contractor can use the analytical data, the government-furnished information, and the maintenance planning data to compute the technical factors associated with maintenance plans.

6.4.2 The Logistics Management Information (LMI) Database

Maintainability/supportability trade-off analyses, such as the LORA, require large amounts of data on all elements of the integrated logistics support (ILS) components of the system being evaluated. The Logistics Management Information (LMI) system provides a database that may be used to:

■ Determine the impact of design features on logistics support
■ Determine the impact of the proposed logistics support systems on the Ao and maintainability goals
■ Provide data for trade-off studies, life cycle costing, and logistics support modeling
■ Exchange data among functional organizations

- Influence the system design
- Provide data for the preparation of logistic products specified by data item descriptions (DIDs)
- Provide the means to assess supportability of the fielded item
- Provide the means to evaluate the impact of engineering change, product improvement, major modifications, or alternative proposals

The LMI system is intended to provide the data through which design decisions can be made to balance system cost, schedule, performance, and supportability. The LMI data elements of interest in a maintainability/supportability trade-off analysis would include:

- Maintenance
- Manpower and personnel
- Supply support
- Support equipment
- Technical data
- Training and training support
- Computer resources support
- Facilities
- Packing, handling, storage, and transportation
- Design interface

U.S. Department of Defense documents MIL-PRF-49506 (U.S. DoD 1996) and MIL-HDBK-502 (U.S. DoD 1997) are helpful to an analyst in a trade-off analysis. They contain the standard procedure for the evaluation of the ILS elements of the weapon system. MIL-PRF-49506 describes the information required by the government to perform acquisition logistics management functions. Its principal focus is on providing the DoD with a contractual method for acquiring support and support-related engineering and logistics data from contractors. Appendix A of the document identifies eight types of supportability analysis summaries in broad, general terms, and Worksheet 1 can be used to identify the content of the summaries. Appendix B identifies definitions, data codes, and field formats of 159 data products (previously identified as data element definitions in MIL-STD-1388-2B, Appendix E). MIL-HDBK-502 provides the general requirements and descriptions of tasks for a supportability trade-off analysis. It establishes data element definitions, data field lengths, and data formats. In addition, the document contains an application guidance appendix that may be used by the system program manager for selection and tailoring of the tasks to meet program objectives in a cost-effective manner.

References

Defense Acquisition University (DAU). 2008. Supportability. In *Defense acquisition guidebook*. Chapter 4.4.9. https://akss.dau.mil/dag/. Retrieved October 25, 2008.

U.S. Department of Defense. 1996, November 11. *Logistics management information [data products]*. MIL-PRF-49506.

U.S. Department of Defense. 1997, May 30. *Acquisition logistics*. MIL-HDBK-502.

Chapter 7

Capability: Performance-Based Logistics

Performance Based Logistics (PBL) is DoD's preferred approach for product support implementation.*

Preface

Capability is the ability to perform an action. For the purposes of this book, this ability is about identifying a framework of performance metrics, performance measurement, and performance management for assessing the effectiveness of actions in the military sustainment enterprise. Performance metrics are the units or standards of measure for the overall quantitative or qualitative characterization of performance. Performance measurement is the process of collecting, analyzing, and the proper reporting of the performance metric data to identify opportunities for system and process improvements. Performance management is the translation of the performance measurement data to useful information and the techniques that will be used to drive continuous performance improvement of the actions.

This chapter fulfills a need for guidance to identifying the performance metrics, the performance measurement, and the performance management techniques that should be used in sustainment programs. The guidance will describe how performance is linked to the achievement of short-term goals, long-term strategic objectives, and enterprise-wide improvements. The U.S. Department of Defense (DoD) has issued a number of policy directives on performance-based initiatives. One of these initiatives is performance-based logistics (PBL). PBL is a widely recognized and recommended management approach for improved performance, improved system readiness, and reduced cost through the implementation of government-industry partnerships. The essence of PBL is to provide incentives, not barriers, for the achievement of objectives, and to measure

---

* U.S Department of Defense (DoD). Office of the Inspector General-Audit. The Military Department's Implementation of Performance-Based Logistics in Support of Weapon Systems. Report No. D-2004-110. August 23, 2004. 1.

performance by collecting, analyzing, and reporting performance data and using the resulting information to drive improved quality.

As the PBL concept has evolved over the years, most applications have been at the subsystem or equipment levels, where a small number of performance metrics have been applied. Recently, the DoD has mandated that major acquisition projects move toward a weapon-system-level approach to PBL. But, little guidance exists to guide program staff members in selecting the right types and numbers of metrics to satisfy program-level objectives, which are tied to enterprise objectives, and are applicable over the life cycle of a weapon system. As a result, this chapter was written to fill this void. It integrates the concepts, methods, and models described in the literature concerning performance measurement, balanced scorecard, and performance-based logistics, and other research findings that concern performance metrics and measurement. It describes a methodology for identifying a framework of measures and metrics that facilitate performance management of major DoD weapon system acquisition projects over the life cycle of the weapon system, and to link these metrics to strategic enterprise objectives. The focus is on performance measurement and the management of performance at all levels of a sustainment program. The chapter is meant to be a source reference to project-level and enterprise-wide documents related to performance-based management. Two observations guided the development of this chapter:

1. Most PBL experience has been limited to relatively simple component-level applications.
2. More comprehensive guidance is needed for major systems-level applications of PBL.

One of the key tenants of PBL is the use of performance metrics for determining satisfactory performance of product support service providers. Chapter 8 in this volume addresses this tenet.

7.1 Introduction

7.1.1 Purpose and Scope

This chapter presents an overview of performance-based logistics with a foundation in performance management. The general guidance can be tailored to the appropriate level of detail for small, medium, or large program applications. This tailoring is discussed further in Section 7.2. The scope is focused on DoD applications, but it is also generally applicable to wider use of the subject matter. These are some key points to consider:

■ The fundamental purpose of performance measurement is to identify opportunities for systems and process improvement. An enterprise-wide systems approach to process improvement is recommended.
■ Performance management activities are performed by people at all levels in the program organization. Many of these individuals will view and use measurement information in ways specifically applicable to their particular function and will focus on performance measures applicable to that function. It is important that all members of the enterprise/program understand the overall integrated use of performance information and the leading/lagging linkages of the measures.
■ Performance metric tracking has been applied in various parts of the organization, but generally it is not integrated within the enterprise. For example, maintenance data analysis

was a bottom-up performance management process, with selected reports being reviewed above the flying unit level. PBL, on the other hand, has been a primarily top-down performance measurement process focusing on contractor performance. In the current era of total life cycle program management, a comprehensive enterprise-wide performance management process should integrate performance management information at all levels of the enterprise.

■ PBL programs should create a tailored metrics handbook. Selected material from this chapter can form the foundation of this handbook. It should be prepared as a companion document to a program-specific PBL implementation plan (PBL-IP). The PBL-IP should contain a framework of PBL program activities, such as those described in Section 7.2.

7.1.2 Definitions

7.1.2.1 Metrics and Measures

Many related terms and concepts are defined in this chapter, but two key terms, *metrics* and *measures*, are defined now because they are frequently used interchangeably:

■ *Performance metric*: A description of the unit or standard of measure (e.g., man-hours, dollars, percentage). The definition of a metric often has three components that are common to metrics and measures: name, definition, and the method of calculation.
■ *Performance measure*: A description of the overall quantitative or qualitative characterization of performance. The description of a measure may have as many as ten or more components.

7.1.2.2 Performance-Based Management

Performance-based management is a systematic approach to performance improvement through an ongoing process of establishing strategic performance objectives. It involves: measuring performance; collecting, analyzing, reviewing, and reporting performance data; and using that data to drive process improvement.

7.1.2.3 Performance-Based Measurement and Performance-Based Management

One can become confused by the differences between performance measurement and performance management. Performance measurement is the comparison of actual levels of performance to preestablished target levels of performance. To be effective, performance measurement must be linked to the organizational strategic plan. Performance management uses the performance measurement information to manage and improve performance and to demonstrate what has been accomplished. Performance measurement is a critical component of performance-based management.

7.1.2.4 Performance-Based Logistics

Performance-based logistics is a performance-based sustainment or acquisition strategy to improve performance, operational availability, and total ownership cost reduction through the strategic implementation of varying degrees of government-industry partnerships. The essence of PBL is buying measurable performance of a system by aligning DoD strategic objectives with customer requirements. The purpose is to provide incentives for the achievement of objectives, to measure performance by collecting, analyzing, and reporting performance information, and to use that information to drive improvement.

7.1.3 The Third Wave

The central role of performance measurement in managing an organization to achieve its desired performance goals has long been recognized. The *first wave* of performance measurement focused on management accounting and financial data analysis. This first wave was prevalent from the early days of the industrial revolution to well into the 1970s. The changing global competitive environment of the past several decades compelled organizations to broaden their perspective beyond mere financial performance. Industry recognized the need for improvements in quality, speed, and flexibility. The *second wave* of performance measurement saw an expansion of the use of performance measurement, but was still focused primarily on personnel performance measurement in addition to organizational financial performance. The use of information technology was primarily devoted to financial control systems and the insertion of information technology into physical assets and products. The information age environment for both manufacturing and service organizations ushered in new capabilities for competitive success. The term *third wave* is generally applied to the leveraging of information technology in the creation of more efficient processes and products. The third wave of performance measurement zeros in on the use of computer-based software applications and tools specifically designed to gather, integrate, analyze, format, and facilitate the sharing of performance measurement information in ways that are faster, less manpower-intensive, and counters the effects of information overload.

Traditional data collection and reporting involves manually collecting performance data on forms, looking for trends in the data, and summarizing the results in printed management reports. However, this traditional method reporting is rapidly being replaced by automated software that relies on a computer's processing power to help collect, analyze, process, and communicate management information in real time and in both visual and printed form.

A new class of software—performance information systems—is appearing. Software systems in this category take advantage of more sophisticated features available from client/server-based information systems, such as querying and reporting, data mining and data warehousing, and multidimensional analysis. These more sophisticated systems typically incorporate additional information technology components, such as executive information systems, graphical user interfaces, advanced reporting features, drill-down reporting to gain access to the underlying data, and linkages to databases at multiple locations. These systems are most applicable in situations where sophisticated trend analysis or forecasting (e.g., leading indicators) is required, or where enterprise-wide information systems are being developed to manage and integrate not just performance information, but other corporate information as well.

The sophistication of the collection and reporting system should be matched to the mission needs of the organization. Clearly, the information technology investment must return benefits to the organization that exceed the investment costs. These benefits should be mission related, and they will typically accrue in terms of improved information accuracy, security, accessibility, timeliness, and cost-effectiveness.

7.1.4 The Foundations of PBL

The roots of modern performance-based management and PBL are in the Government Performance Results Act (GPRA) of 1993. The GPRA requires federal agencies to set strategic goals, measure performance, and use performance information to identify and correct deficiencies. The National Performance Review (NPR) and the GPRA were the results of studies and public laws issued in 1993. The NPR and GPRA have been implemented by a number of more recent DoD initiatives. Among these are the Defense Reform Initiatives, the Quadrennial Defense Review, and an evolving set of implementation concepts. These concepts have resulted in a wide range of related defense transformation initiatives. The concepts are listed in Table 7.1 in order to broaden the boundaries of leveraging benchmarking information opportunities and sources available for PBL development, tailoring, and evolutionary improvement. How well an enterprise accomplishes its objectives is determined by the achievement of discrete measurable results that flow from business processes. In order to take a strategic approach to PBL, a broad understanding of these concepts is recommended.

To provide a useful frame of reference as they studied performance measurement in best-in-class organizations, the NPR performance measurement study team built a model of the performance measurement process used in the federal context. This performance measurement process model, shown in Figure 7.1, was published in the team's June 1997 report (NPR 1997). A close review of the NPR model activities will reveal that it forms a solid enduring process for setting up an enterprise-level performance measurement program.

To complement its strategic planning study, NPR commissioned the first-ever intergovernmental benchmarking consortium involving not only U.S. federal agencies, but also local governments and

Table 7.1 Transformation Implementation Concepts and Components Matrix

	Concepts				
Components of the Concept	*PBL*	*Performance Management*	*Business Process Improvement*	*Balanced Scorecard*	*Lean Enterprise Architecting (Mathaisel et al. 2005)*
Strategic planning	X	X	X	X	X
Performance objectives	X	X	X	X	X
Performance measures	X	X	X	X	X
Data collection	X	X	X	X	X
Analysis and review	X	X	X	X	X
Continuous improvement	X	X	X	X	X

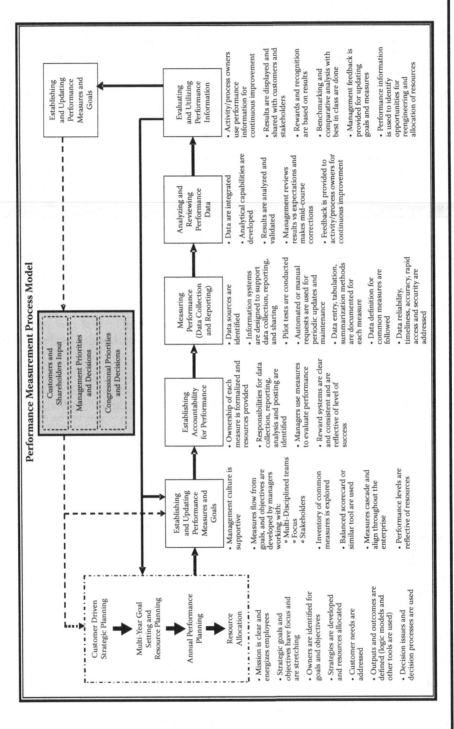

Figure 7.1 Performance measurement process model. (Source: NPR 1997.)

the government of Canada, in a collaborative study of performance measurement. As documented in its June 1997 report, the NPR performance measurement study team found that the best performance measurement, management systems, and practices work within a context of strategic planning that takes its cue from customer needs and customer service. They found that:

1. *Leadership* is critical in designing and deploying effective performance measurement and management systems.
2. A *conceptual framework* is needed for the performance measurement and management system.
3. Effective internal and external *communications* are the keys to successful performance measurement.
4. *Accountability* for results must be clearly assigned and well understood.
5. Performance measurement systems must provide intelligent *decision support* information for decision makers, not just compile data.
6. Compensation, rewards, and *recognition* should be linked to performance measurement.
7. Performance measurement systems should be *positive*, not punitive.
8. Results and progress toward program commitments should be *openly shared* with employees, customers, and stakeholders.

7.2 PBL Program Activities

PBL is implemented by following a sequence of activities. The activities are provided in Table 7.2. The subparagraph numbering that follows matches the activity numbering in the table. All activities should be applied, in some tailored form, to a full program or weapon system-level PBL initiative. A smaller subsystem- or component-level PBL initiative may select a more limited application, and apply only selected activities.

Table 7.2 PBL Program Activities

Activity	Activity Title	Full	Limited
1	Define program requirements	X	X
2	Define stakeholder objectives	X	
3	Establish the PBL team and define roles	X	X
4	Perform strategic planning	X	
5	Identify PBL candidates and opportunities	X	X
6	Define the program performance baseline	X	
7	Formalize a performance-based agreement (PBA)	X	X
8	Identify the product support providers/allocate workload	X	
9	Perform a business case analysis (BCA)	X	
10	Define roles of the product support manager (PSM) and product support providers (PSIs)	X	

(Continued)

Table 7.2   (Continued)

Activity	Activity Title	Full	Limited
11	Establish the product support provider (PSI)	X	
12	Identify a metrics/architecture	X	X
13	Integrate key processes	X	
14	Define the performance data and reporting schema	X	X
15	Define win-win incentives	X	
16	Define a dispute resolution process	X	
17	Define the contract/tasking approach	X	
18	Monitor performance and identify actions	X	X
19	Conduct formal performance reviews	X	
20	Identify opportunities for improvement	X	X

7.2.1 Define Program Requirements

PBL is designed to support operational requirements of the warfighter in terms of:

1. Defense systems operational availability (Ao), expressed as the mission-capable (MC) rate for aircraft systems
2. Affordability, expressed as the reduced life cycle cost (LCC) with focus on high operating and support (O&S) cost drivers
3. Reduced footprint, which are the logistics resources, primarily in theater of operations
4. Reduced cycle times in the supply chain in terms of minimizing the mean logistics delay time (MLDT)
5. Use of performance-based contracting and performance-based management to link all logistics activity to performance agreements with the warfighter, and to measure and control the performance of logistics resource providers

7.2.2 Define Stakeholder Objectives

Applicable performance objectives, parameters, and measures are considered warfighter requirements and are documented in program requirement documents. In August 2004, the Office of the Secretary of Defense (OSD) described performance in terms of the following five objectives, and charged programs to tailor and develop metrics that support and map to these desired objectives:

1. Achieve *operational availability* targets: The percent of time that a weapon system is available for a mission or ability to sustain operations tempo.
2. Improve *system operational reliability*: The measure of a system in meeting mission success objectives (percent of objectives met, by weapon system). Depending on the weapon system, a mission objective would be a sortie, tour, launch, destination reached, or capability.

3. Reduced *cost per unit of usage*: The total operating costs divided by the appropriate unit of measurement for a weapon system. The unit of measure could be flight hour, steaming hour, or miles.
4. Reduction of the *logistics footprint*: The government or contractor presence of logistics support required to deploy, sustain, and move a weapon system. Measurable elements include inventory, equipment, personnel, facilities, transportation assets, and real estate.
5. Improved *logistics response times*: This is the period of time from when the logistics demand signal was sent to the satisfaction of that demand. Logistics demand refers to systems, components, or resources, including labor, that are required for weapons systems logistics support.

7.2.3 Establish the PBL Team and Define Roles

Establish the PBL Team. A critical early step in any PBL effort is establishing a team to develop and manage the implementation. Although the program manager (PM) is the total life cycle system manager, the foundation of PBL strategies relies on ensuring the participation and consensus of all stakeholders, especially the customer, in developing the optimum sustainment strategy. The team, led by the PM or the PM's product support manager (PSM), may consist of government and private sector functional experts and should include all appropriate stakeholders, including warfighter representatives, as shown in Figure 7.2. However, it is important that members are able to work across organizational boundaries.

Team building to support PBL is similar to traditional integrated logistics support management, except the focus on individual support elements is diminished and replaced by a system orientation focused on performance outcomes. The structure of the team may vary, depending on the maturity and the mission of the program. For instance, during the system development and demonstration

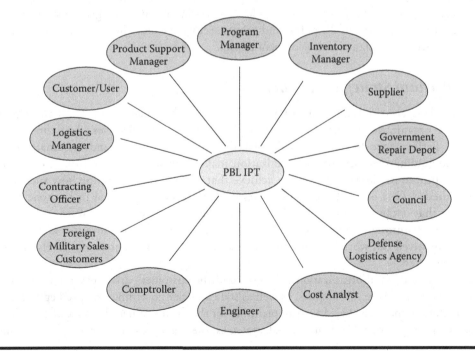

Figure 7.2   National PBL team.

(SDD) phase of a new project, systems design for operational effectiveness has the biggest impact on life cycle sustainment. The PM must know where the system is at in the life cycle, understand what major milestones are approaching, and provide useful information to the decision makers for the program to move forward through the life cycle successfully. Before a team can be established, the PM must establish the achievable goals. By knowing what must be accomplished, the PM can best choose who should be on the team to do the work, keeping resource impacts to a minimum. A bad approach is for a PM to establish a team, and then look to the team to establish goals. This is an example of "having a solution that is looking for a problem," and provides no initial team focus. By having the goals known up front, the PM can take a competency-based approach to team building (eliminating the stovepipes of function-based organizations), achieve system orientation, and build a management infrastructure.

7.2.3.1 Integrating across Traditional Stovepipe Organizational Boundaries

Team membership may need to include representatives from component command headquarters and logistics representatives from supply, maintenance, and transportation. It may also need to include representatives from operational commands or defense agencies, as well as engineering, technical, procurement, comptroller, information technology organizations, and contract support. After the team is organized, the members establish their goals, develop plans of action and milestones, and obtain adequate resources.

7.2.3.2 Establishing the Public/Private Support Strategy IPT

These integrated government and industry integrated product teams (IPTs) will ensure consideration of all factors and criteria necessary to achieve an optimum PBL strategy. The strategy should utilize the best capabilities of the public and private sectors in a cost-effective manner throughout the support strategy design and development phases.

7.2.4 Perform Strategic Planning

Strategic plans are the foundation of performance-based management. The first step is to define the organizational mission and strategic performance objectives. As defined by the National Performance Review, strategic planning is "a continuous and systematic process where the guiding members of an organization make decisions about its future, develop the necessary procedures and operations to achieve that future, and determine how success is to be measured."* One of the benefits of strategic planning, as established in the tenets of the GPRA, is that it can be an opportunity to unify the management, employees, stakeholders, and customers through a common understanding of where the organization is going, how everyone involved can work to that common purpose, and how progress and levels of success will be measured.

For many successful organizations, the "voice of the customer" drives operations and charts the course for the future. Companies, as well as state and city governments, have begun focusing on customers as one of the key drivers in planning for the future. When the voice of the customer becomes an integral part of organizational strategies, the organization becomes what is termed a

---

* National Performance Review (1997).

customer-driven organization. A customer-driven organization is "one that maintains a focus on the needs and expectations, both spoken and unspoken, of customers, both present and future, in the creation and/or improvement of the product or service provided."*

7.2.4.1 Setting Strategic Directions

Components integral to setting a strategic direction are:

- A *mission statement* that identifies the purpose for which the organization is organized or the function that is now carried out in the business world.
- A *vision* of the future business environment and the organization within it.
- A *values statement* of the organization's code of ethics or the values it espouses related to teamwork, quality, and protection of the environment and community in which it operates.
- *Assumptions* about the business environmental conditions that should be expected to exist in the future.
- *Business strategies* or broad statements of how objectives are to be accomplished, e.g., a growth strategy.

7.2.4.2 Setting Strategic Objectives, Goals, Targets, and Initiatives

A program vision statement could include:

- A team working with mutual trust and respect
- To provide an effective, suitable, and affordable weapon system to the warfighter

Some of the key program objectives related to this vision include:

- Maintain a shared vision, goals, and objectives
- Focus on affordability and cycle time reduction
- Improve products, processes, and people
- Apply best practices
- Conduct periodic assessments
- Manage through common/shared databases

7.2.4.3 PBL Strategic Planning

Strategic planning involves long-range vision setting. Vision setting is defining the direction(s) that will achieve a predictable future state of organizational or program success. One example of a PBL vision-setting statement is:

> The program logistics support providers have implemented a mature performance management environment that is delivering required operational availability of aircraft at a reduced life cycle cost and deployed logistics footprint than was experienced on predecessor systems. The program has achieved a balanced logistics support

---

* Ibid.

structure between the extremes of all organic (internal to the military) support and all contractor logistics support (CLS). This balance would involve:

- Depot and wholesale supply operations would be an integrated partnership of organic and industry providers. They would provide a variety of wholesale-level sustainment and management products/services along with the collection, reporting, and analysis of performance measurement metrics.
- Elimination of the need for intermediate-level (I-level) maintenance, through reliability improvements, would be a strategic objective of the program. As an interim measure, I-level operations would be an integrated partnership of organic and industry providers who support the need for skilled organic personnel for deployed operational-level (O-level) maintenance and I-level operations. For some designated items, I-level operations would be a full repair operation. Major phased inspections would be performed at the I-level sites. Only minimum scheduled maintenance inspections would be conducted, with the major phased inspections performed at the I-level sites.
- O-level support in all operating locations would use organic military personnel with one exception. Logistics support would be performed by contractor logistics support (CLS) for nondeployable training equipment and for training and testing equipment at training and testing sites. The requirements for agile and flexible deployment operations dictate that O-level manning remain organic military.
- Fleet support team detachments (FST-Dets) at the continental U.S. (CONUS) operating locations would be an integrated partnership of organic and industry personnel who are providing needed technical support to fleet customers along with gathering, analyzing, and reporting O- and I-level performance metrics.

7.2.4.4 PBL Tactical Planning

Tactical planning is the act of defining the short-term activities/initiatives that will position the organization to achieve its strategic direction and objectives. The PBL tactical plan is to implement the process activities defined in Table 7.2 and to identify the short-term initiatives needed to correct deficiencies identified during reviews of the metric reports.

7.2.4.5 Beyond the Strategic Plan

Flowing out of the strategic plan are two performance-based products that further define and validate organizational or individual strategic performance objectives. These two products are (1) performance plans and (2) performance agreements. These documents aid in the development of the strategic performance measures covered in Section 7.2.12. The performance plan is described here, and the performance agreement is described in Section 7.2.7.

Performance plans outline organizational and individual commitments to achieving specific results against the goals, objectives, and metrics of the organizational strategic plan for the resources requested in the budget. In other words, performance plans state what is going to be accomplished for the budgeted money. Performance plans are used to establish performance agreements and for comparing planned results to actual performance results.

Table 7.3   Levels and Codes of PBL Applications

	All Elements of a System	*Multiple Elements of a System*	*Single Elements of a System*
System level	(S1) All ILS elements for an entire system	(S2) Multiple ILS elements for an entire system	(S3) A single ILS element for an entire system
Subsystem level	(Sub 1) All ILS elements for an entire subsystem	(Sub 2) Multiple ILS elements for an entire subsystem	(Sub 3) A single ILS element for an entire subsystem
Component level	(C1) All ILS elements for a single component	(C2) Multiple ILS elements for a single component	(C3) A single ILS element for a single component

7.2.5 Identify the PBL Candidates and Opportunities

Two DoD references require programs to identify PBL candidates in two contexts: (1) which systems, subsystems, and components will be coded for application of PBL, and (2) which subsystems and components should be the focus for near-term improvement initiatives.

7.2.5.1 Coding to Identify Candidates for the Application of PBL

Programs can use the coding in Table 7.3 to identify candidates for a PBL application. Many major programs, such as the V-22 Osprey, are beginning to select the S2 strategy, which specifies a PBL application for multiple integrated logistics support (ILS) elements within the system.

7.2.5.2 Identifying PBL Opportunities

The program should periodically review the PBL strategy to identify near-term opportunities to improve systems readiness, reduce cost of ownership, and reduce the deployed logistics footprint. The PBL IPT should review information provided on a PBL candidate listing, like the one shown in Figure 7.3. The opportunity index column will identify candidates with the greatest potential for improving system performance in satisfying warfighter requirements.

7.2.6 Define the Performance Baseline

7.2.6.1 Current Baseline Support Concept

The current support concept is that planned before application of a major PBL strategy. This baseline forms the reference point for any analysis applicable to changes in cost or footprint resulting from the implementation of PBL. This support baseline forms the reference point, in terms of life cycle cost (LCC), which is utilized to analyze changes in LCC as a result of implementing PBL.

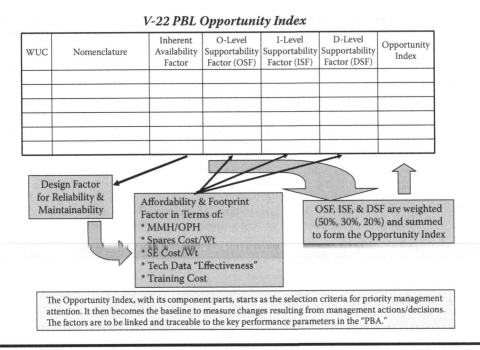

V-22 PBL Opportunity Index

WUC	Nomenclature	Inherent Availability Factor	O-Level Supportability Factor (OSF)	I-Level Supportability Factor (ISF)	D-Level Supportability Factor (DSF)	Opportunity Index

Design Factor for Reliability & Maintainability

Affordability & Footprint Factor in Terms of:
* MMH/OPH
* Spares Cost/Wt
* SE Cost/Wt
* Tech Data "Effectiveness"
* Training Cost

OSF, ISF, & DSF are weighted (50%, 30%, 20%) and summed to form the Opportunity Index

The Opportunity Index, with its component parts, starts as the selection criteria for priority management attention. It then becomes the baseline to measure changes resulting from management actions/decisions. The factors are to be linked and traceable to the key performance parameters in the "PBA."

Figure 7.3   Example of a PBL opportunity index.

7.2.6.2 Maintenance Concept

The maintenance support plan can employ the traditional organic three-level maintenance concept—operational, intermediate, and depot (O-I-D)—or the U.S. Air Force standard two-level (O-D) maintenance concept.

7.2.6.3 Baseline Performance and Cost

A baseline performance plan should be developed to form a basis for comparison of alternatives for product and process improvement. Three evolutionary baselines can be developed. Each should be with respect to the five objectives/measures described in Section 7.2.2. The first baseline for comparison is the legacy system being replaced. The second baseline for comparison is the traditional logistics support infrastructure. The third baseline is a rolling baseline using an opportunity index, such as described in Figure 7.3. The baselines should have a minimum of three elements: (1) a baseline operational availability (Ao), as described in Chapter 3 of this book; (2) a baseline life cycle cost, as described in Chapter 9 of this book; and (3) a baseline logistics footprint.

The PBL opportunity index table shown in Figure 7.3 is used to display the baseline of performance and cost information. The information in this table will be drawn from data in the supportability analysis (SA) databases for the candidate subsystems along with associated models and data sources. These data will represent the latest estimates resulting from the considerable developmental and operational test data. This information is to be formulated into a set of top-level factors, which link the capability resulting from the system design and the primary supportability environment to the key performance parameters in the program requirements documents and agreements with the warfighter.

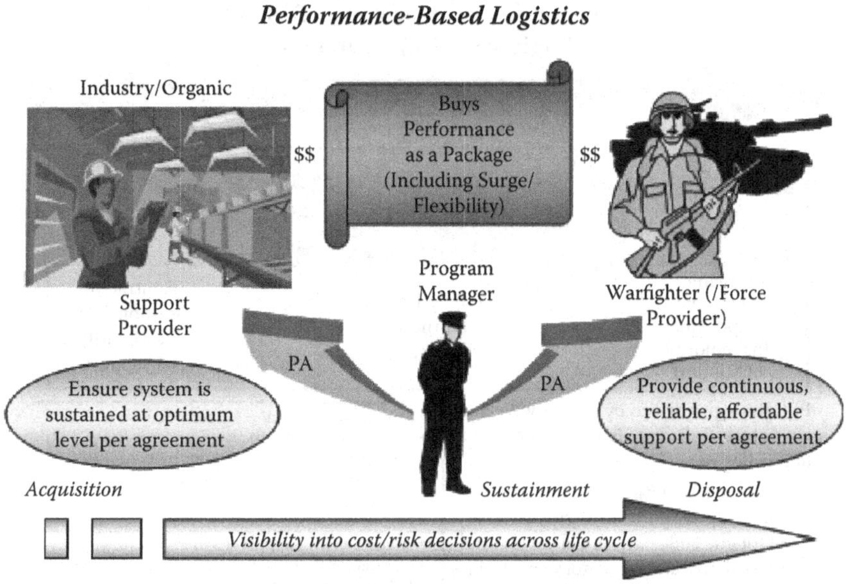

Performance-Based Logistics

Figure 7.4   Types of performance-based agreements.

7.2.7 *Formalize a Performance-Based Agreement*

There are two types of performance-based agreements (PBAs): an agreement with the warfighter, and an agreement with the support provider. Both are illustrated in Figure 7.4. The first is a PBA between the program office and the headquarters representative of the warfighter. It is usually in the format of a memorandum of understanding (MOU). The second type is the PBA between logistics representatives of support providers and the program office. This type of PBA is generally in the form of a contract tasking document, which contains performance-based metrics applicable to the specific support provider.

Performance agreements are designed, in partnership with management and those actually doing the work, to provide a process for measuring performance and, therein, for establishing accountability. The agreements state expectations for each party signing the agreement. They help improve communication with customers and stakeholders, and they make transparent the conduct of an organization or individual. Agreements written in plain and concise format with specific annual deliverables allow customers and stakeholders to know what they are getting for their money, as well as give them an opportunity to influence organizational priorities. The reader should refer to the *Performance Based Logistics (PBL) Guidance Document* (SECNAV 2003) for an example approach to developing performance agreements.

7.2.8 *Identify Product Support Providers and Allocate Workload*

DoD policy requires that "sustainment strategies shall include the best use of public and private sector capabilities through government/industry partnering initiatives, in accordance with statutory requirements."* An effective support strategy considers best competencies and partnering opportunities as shown in Figure 7.5.

---

* U.S. DoD, OSD, PBL Guidebook, March 2005.

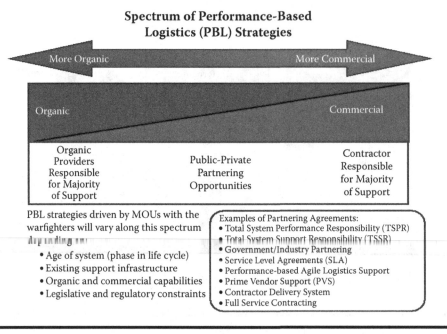

Figure 7.5   PBL performance strategies.

To that end, a workload allocation/sourcing plan identifies what is best for each support function in terms of capability, skills, infrastructure, opportunities for partnering, compliance with PBL Title 10 (e.g., the 50/50 rule), public/private flexibility, and affordability.

7.2.9 Perform a Business Case Analysis (BCA)

Policy and guidance documents describe the use of a business case analysis (BCA) for three purposes: (1) initial evaluation of a PBL provider strategy, (2) an evaluation to support decisions concerning PBL incentives, and (3) recurring evaluations of initiatives to improve performance. A BCA can be performed to help establish the merit and cost-effectiveness of the basic mix of organic, private, and partnership approaches to the program PBL implementation strategy. As an example, the V-22 Osprey Program performed an extensive BCA in 2001 as part of a study entitled "Support Alternatives Analysis Team (SAAT) Study." The study found that each of the sustainment alternatives evaluated could provide satisfactory V-22 support. Evaluated costs of the alternatives were very close to each other, and they were within the error of the estimate. The selection of an approach should therefore not be on the evaluation of cost.

A follow-up comprehensive business case analysis of the U.S. Marine MV-22 and U.S. Air Force CV-22 weapon systems was performed as part of the Joint Sustainment Strategy Study (JSSS). This study also concluded that each of the sustainment alternatives could provide satisfactory V-22 support. The JSSS BCA report also found that life cycle costs for each sustainment alternative were very close, and that cost was not a differentiator for PBL strategy selection at the weapon system level. The BCAs described in the *PBL Guidebook* (DoD 2005) and the *Performance Based Logistics (PBL) Guidance Document* (SECNAV 2003) should be completed when:

- There is significant change concerning competition between logistics service providers
- A change in the support will require a significant change in funding investment
- An infrastructure change will likely be controversial and require cost vs. benefit justification

A description of a business case analysis and an example BCA spreadsheet are provided in Chapter 9.

7.2.10 Define the Roles

The program manager's responsibilities for oversight and management of the product support function are delegated to a product support manager (PSM). A PSM is an overarching term characterizing the various service function titles, such as a system support manager. A PSM leads the development and implementation of the product support and PBL strategies and ensures achievement of desired support outcomes during sustainment. The PSM employs a product support integrator (PSI), or a number of PSIs as appropriate, to achieve those outcomes. The program manager's oversight role includes developing the PBL implementation plan and performance assessment plan, monitoring performance, and revising the product support strategy and PBAs as necessary. The program manager also acts as the agent for the warfighter, certifying PSI performance. The PSM is expected to take a hands-on approach and not assume that the contracts or agreements will be self-regulating.

The product support integrator (PSI) is an entity performing as an agent charged with integrating all sources of support, public and private, defined within the scope of the PBL agreements to achieve the documented outcomes. PSIs are fully responsible for meeting the metrics defined in the performance-based agreements and PBL contracts. In the V-22 program, for example, the horizontal concept of product support integration is envisioned with multiple PSIs. At a minimum, two primary contractor PSIs are (1) Rolls Royce for the engines and (2) at least one other primary PSI for a whole range of subsystems and sustainment responsibilities. Dependent on the PBL scope, current PBLs in force for common items/systems may continue to be utilized, resulting in additional PSIs.

7.2.11 Establish the Product Support Integrator

As mentioned in DoD PBL guidance documents, "the program manager (PM) is to assign a Product Support Integrator (PSI) from either the DoD or private sector."* Activities coordinated by the PSI can include:

- Which support functions will be provided by which organic organizations
- Which support functions will be provided by which private sector companies
- How partnerships between organic providers and industry providers will be formulated and administered, as illustrated in Figure 7.6
- Perform as the decision authority concerning changes to the support infrastructure
- Perform as the decision authority concerning any disputes associated with provider selections and performance-related issues

---

* DoD, OSD, PBL Guidebook, March 2005.

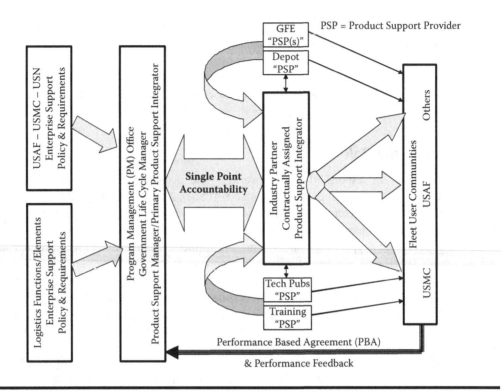

Figure 7.6 Product support integration (PSI) relationships.

Additionally, the seven functions below are considered basic functions of a PSI:

1. Overall wholesale-level material management
2. Supply chain management
3. Depot-level maintenance management
4. Reliability improvement management
5. Parts obsolescence management
6. Configuration management
7. Engineering support management

7.2.12 Identify the Performance Metrics Architecture

The scorecard used in the V-22 Osprey Program, shown in Figure 7.7, is a representative architecture for identifying the performance metrics. A variety of performance measures and metrics have proved useful in analyzing and controlling PBL efforts at the different levels of management, and each logistics support service provider performs a role as the program moves from the development phase into the production, deployment, and sustainment phases.

Each measure is to be fully described on a measure description sheet, such as the example in Table 7.4. Information concerning the measure name, measure definition, measure objective, measure owner, and planned changes in thresholds and targets is essential for fully understanding measure data that are to be collected and used to satisfy program objectives.

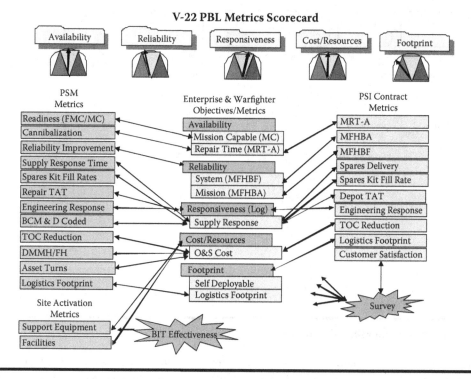

Figure 7.7   PBL metrics scorecard used on the V-22 program.

Table 7.4   Performance Measure Description Form

Measure Name:	
Metric:	
Definition:	
Calculation Method / Formula:	
Measure Objective:	
Measure Owner:	
Measure Data Are Available in Data Source:	
Planned Report Format:	
Update Frequency:	

Year:	2013	2014	2015	2016	2017	2018	2019	2020
Target:								
Threshold:								

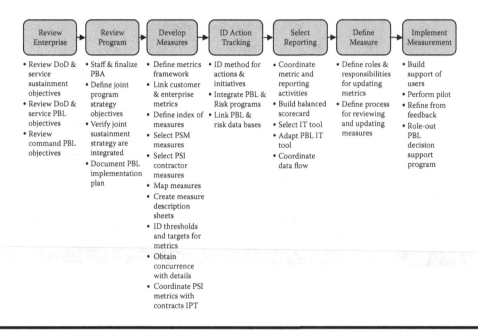

Figure 7.8 Metric identification process.

Each of the logistics element support service providers, wherever they are in the logistics service value chain, will select specific measures that link to the top-level performance measures identified in the PBA. The tree of measures illustrated in Figure 7.8 shows the linkage from the top-level measures, through the measures described in the performance-based contract and tasking statements, to the measures used to manage lower-level processes and activities that satisfy the work statements in the tasking/contracting documents.

A round of top-down and bottom-up coordination reviews will need to be performed to identify the set of linking measures. Once the comprehensive metric linkage matrix is developed, a key subset of these measures will need to be selected to be defined in contracting/tasking documents between the program and service providers.

Performance measurement systems succeed when the organization's strategy and performance measures are in alignment and when senior managers convey the organization's mission, vision, values, and strategic direction to employees and external stakeholders. The performance measures give life to the mission, vision, and strategy by providing a focus that lets each employee know how he or she contributes to the success of the company and its stakeholders' measurable expectations. Integration makes it possible for performance measures to be effective agents for change. If the measures quantify results of an activity, one only need compare the measured data with the desired goals to know if actions are needed. In other words, the measures should carry the message.

Inappropriate measures are often the result of random selection methods. For example, brainstorming exercises can get people thinking about what is possible and provide long lists of what could be measured. Unfortunately, such efforts by themselves do not provide reliable lists of what should be measured. Unless the measures are firmly connected to results from a defined process, it is difficult to know what corrective actions to take as well as be able to predict with confidence what effects those changes will have. In order to be able to identify effective corrective actions to improve products and services, results of all key processes must be measured. In this way, specific processes that need to change can be identified when progress is not satisfactory.

7.2.12.2.1 The Conceptual Framework

A conceptual framework can help in deciding what to measure. For example, measuring organizational performance can be linked to the strategic planning process. Or you can use a balanced set of measures to ensure that senior leaders can get a quick comprehensive assessment of the organization in a single report. A family of measures can be used to align measurement across levels of the organizations (NPR 1997). These and other frameworks are discussed later in this section.

When you are developing or updating your performance measures, you should consider conceptual frameworks to stimulate thought about what should be measured. Experience has shown that a framework is needed to organize your thoughts, identify common vocabulary, and ensure appropriate coverage for your performance measurement system. This is particularly important when you are developing a measurement system for the first time. If you are just developing your performance measurement system, select one framework and use it. Although some frameworks fit particular organizations better than others, any framework will help get you started. When updating your performance measures, it is useful to review other frameworks to identify new ideas and approaches that might improve your system.

7.2.12.2.2 Scorecard Structure

In his evaluation of several performance measurement frameworks, Vikram Mahidhar (2005) makes the statement: "The Balanced Scorecard, the most widely used performance measurement framework, restricts performance measurement to four predetermined buckets." This statement is incorrect. While many examples of the application of the balanced scorecard (BSC) framework do use the basic four perspectives (predetermined buckets), Robert Kaplan and David Norton (1996) clearly state that an organization or business unit should create a BSC that focuses on translating strategy into a set of tangible objectives and measures. The management team creates a BSC structure that matches the organization's enterprise and lower-level objectives. Figure 7.9 demonstrates this idea.

The performance measurement framework that you select will help you determine your strategic focus as you begin to develop your performance measures. However, before you go about this task, you need to get yourself organized. Specific steps to take in getting organized are:

- *Establish the performance measurement team.* The team should be made up of the people who actually do the work to be measured and the people who are very familiar with the work to be measured. It is important that each person understands the task before him or her and his or her role in its accomplishment.
- *Gain an understanding of the jargon.* Performance measurement jargon can be very confusing, but needs to be understood and agreed to by the performance measurement team.
- *Consider the considerations.* The considerations are: keep the number of performance measures at each management level to a minimum; develop clear and understandable objectives and performance measures; determine if the cost of the measure is worth the gain; consider performing a risk evaluation; consider the weight of conflicting performance measures and develop consistent performance measures that promote teamwork.

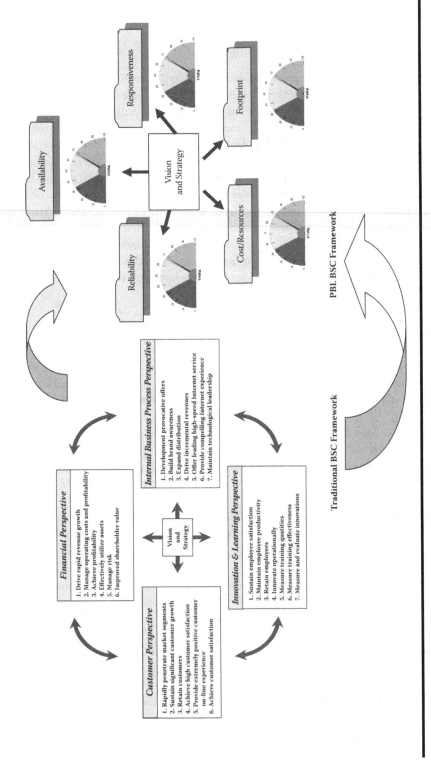

Figure 7.9 Adapting the traditional BSC framework to a PBL BSC framework.

- *Know how to check/test your measures.* After you have developed your performance measures, you will need to check/test them for soundness (i.e., completeness, applicably, usefulness, etc.). Knowing how to perform these checks/tests, and thus knowing what to look for in a performance measure, will help your team develop sound performance measures from the start.
- *Take a look at how other organizations measure performance.* Now that your team is organized and ready to develop its performance measures, take one last important step: look at what other organizations similar to yours have done and are doing with regard to their performance measurement.

Various authors have discussed measures in terms of elements, which are the component parts of a complete description of the measure. These complete descriptions provide the detail needed for all stakeholders to fully understand the design of the measure. Some authors have provided performance measure description sheets that provide a consistent format/view of the different elements of the measure. The *Performance-Based Management Handbook* by Oak Ridge Associated Universities (ORAU 2001) shows two such measure description sheets with element fill-in descriptions. The measure description sheet in Table 7.4 shows how this concept was applied to a PBL program.

Performance measures can be broadly classified by three dimensions: measure type, tense, and focus. *Measure type* refers to the primary classification of the measure, such as financial measures, process measures, customer measures, and organizational growth measures. *Tense* refers to the concept of leading vs. lagging indicators. *Focus* refers to the internal vs. external characteristics of the measure with respect to parts of the organization or group of organizations.

Performance measure levels refer to either levels of the organization or levels of the work breakdown structure (WBS) of the project or system that is the subject of performance measurement. This concept is frequently expressed as the drill-down levels of detail, which are aggregated into top-level measures. Many times, a top-level measure, such as "average customer wait time for parts or services," will be more useful when it can be drilled down to the specific part, service, or location that is aggregated into the top-level measure.

Performance measures should be limited to those that relate to strategic organizational goals and objectives, and those that provide timely, relevant, and concise information for managers at all levels to assess progress toward achieving predetermined goals. In general, a good performance measure:

- Is defined, i.e., is simple, understandable, logical, unambiguous, and repeatable
- Is accepted by and meaningful to the client/customer
- Tells how well goals and objectives are being met
- Allows for economical data collection
- Is timely, sensitive, shows a trend
- Has accountability assigned
- Drives appropriate action by providing decision support information

A complete description of the measure includes:

- A specific target goal or objective—tangible and measurable
- Data requirements, data sources, and frequency of measurement
- Calculation methodology, such as an equation and definitions of variables/terms
- Description of reporting scheme
- Any other relevant rationale for the measure

Other key definitions:

- *Strategic goal*: Statement of guidelines on how the organization will achieve the vision.
- *Performance goals/objectives*: A set of statements that summarize what must be achieved to make the strategic vision a reality. They describe the critical success factors that together form the strategy of the organization.
- *Performance initiative*: The key near-term actions or programs required to achieve improvements toward performance targets. The initiatives are planned, scheduled, resourced, and tracked as part of the annual performance plan in support of the organizational strategic plan.
- *Performance target*: The level of performance or rate of improvement needed.

During a seminar on collecting and reporting the right measures, John Crager of the American Productivity and Quality Center highlighted the importance of selecting the right kind, the right number, and the right balance of measures. Among the many points to consider when creating metrics, he stresses the importance of selecting the right number—and right type—of measures, what he calls the Goldilocks syndrome. He warns, "Most managers, and this includes middle-managers, supervisors, and upper-level managers, cannot effectively track and make decisions on more than 12 to 14 measures ... unless all they do is measurement and they don't manage or lead in the organization." * On the other hand, there is the significant danger of selecting a single, over-arching measure, an "übermeasure." Relying on one key metric can create an environment where the lack of a broader perspective inadvertently encourages the achievement of goals by undesirable means. Crager says, "One thing that measurement does is it drives behavior."†

The key to creating measures is to strive for balance. The concept of balancing performance measures took root in 1996 when Robert Kaplan and David Norton first introduced the balanced scorecard (Kaplan and Norton 1996). The gist of the concept is to translate business mission accomplishment into a critical set of measures distributed among an equally critical and focused set of business perspectives. Since Kaplan and Norton introduced the balanced scorecard concept, many variations of the concept have surfaced, due mainly to the fact that no two organizations are alike, and their need for balanced measures and their identified business perspectives vary. Regardless of the framework, the two key components are (1) a balanced set of measures and (2) a set of strategically focused business perspectives. Four frameworks that use the balanced approach are the balanced scorecard, the "critical few" set of measures, performance dashboards, and the Malcolm Baldrige National Quality Award criteria.

7.2.12.8.1 The Balanced Scorecard

The balanced scorecard (Kaplan and Norton 1996) concept is a way of motivating and measuring an organization's performance. The concept takes a systematic approach to assessing internal results while probing the external environment. It focuses as much on the process of arriving at successful results as on the results themselves. Under the balanced scorecard methodology, the processes that contribute to desired results are viewed cross-functionally. Measures that make

---

* John Crager, "How to Collect and Report the Right Measures—Practical Steps to Overcome Measurement Challenges. The Goldilocks Syndrome versus the Ubermeasure," presented by American Productivity & Quality Center, February 27, 2004, http://www.bettermanagement.com, retrieved November 1, 2008.
† Ibid.

one function look good while deflating another are avoided, thus minimizing negative competition between individuals and functions. The scorecard asks questions from four interconnected business perspectives:

1. *Financial*: How do we look to our stakeholders?
2. *Customer*: How well do we satisfy our internal and external customers' needs?
3. *Internal business process*: How well do we perform at key internal business processes?
4. *Learning and growth*: Are we able to sustain innovation, change, and continuous improvement?

The balanced scorecard provides a way for management to look at the well-being of their organization from the four identified perspectives. Each perspective is directly tied to organizational strategy, and strategically linked performance objectives and measures flow from these perspectives, providing the user with an integrated performance measurement system.

7.2.12.8.2 The "Critical Few" Performance Measures

Having too many measures—therefore generating a large amount of routine data—could distract senior management's focus from those measures that are the most critical to organizational success. The process of simplifying and distilling a large number of performance measures across the organization to select a critical few that drive strategic success should be viewed as part of the performance measurement process itself. It helps sharpen understanding of the strategic plan and its supporting objectives.

The selection of a critical few set of performance measures highlights the need for a balance between internal and external requirements, as well as financial and nonfinancial measures. Although there is not a magical right number of strategic measures, best practice companies typically have defined a working number of measures of between three and fifteen at each level within the organization, depending on the complexities of the organization. As with the balanced scorecard, the critical few framework develops strategically focused business perspectives and then identifies performance objectives and measures for each perspective; others develop performance indices* to report performance levels for a particular perspective. These indices take data from many measurement sources and "roll them up" into a single, meaningful, reportable number.

7.2.12.8.3 Performance Dashboards

A performance dashboard is an executive information system that captures financial and nonfinancial measures as indicators of successful strategy deployment. In France, companies have developed and used the Tableau de Bord, a dashboard of key indicators of organizational success, for more than two decades. The Tableau de Bord is designed to help employees "pilot" the organization by identifying key success factors, especially those that can be measured as physical variables. Many dashboards are indexed measures that roll-up performance in a weighted manner to a few select gauges based on many measures, or inputs.

---

* See the Oak Ridge Associated Universities, Performance-Based Management Handbook: Analyzing and Reviewing Performance Data, Vol. 5, 2001, for more information.

7.2.12.8.4 Malcolm Baldrige National Quality Award

In 1987, jump-starting a small, slowly growing U.S. quality movement, Congress established the Malcolm Baldrige National Quality Award to promote quality awareness, to recognize quality and business achievements of U.S. organizations, and to publicize these organizations' successful performance strategies. Now America's highest honor for performance excellence, the Baldrige Award is presented annually to U.S. organizations by the president of the United States. Awards are given in manufacturing, service, small business, education, health care, and nonprofits. In conjunction with the private sector, the National Institute of Standards and Technology designed and manages the award and the Baldrige National Quality Program.*

To empower performance-based management program stakeholders in maintaining and improving the use of measures and metrics, a uniform set of measure definitions should be identified. As experience with the use of measures is gained, measurement information users will likely have a need to recommend changes in the set of measures being used. Reference to a standard measures dictionary will make communication on this subject much more efficient. An example of a measures dictionary is provided in Chapter 8 of this book. This dictionary is tailored to the subject of PBL for DoD aircraft systems, though many of the measures are applicable to other uses.

At various times during the life cycle of a program/project, there will be a need to modify the measures that are being used. There will be a review of the applicability and utility of measures annually during the formal performance reviews. Nonuseful measures will be eliminated from use, and new measures will be drawn from the measures dictionary located in Chapter 8.

7.2.13 Integrate Key Processes

Two key processes will need to be integrated on most any size PBL effort: (1) the supply chain/supply information flow and (2) the flow of various funding sources and appropriations of funding. Many of the PBL team members will need to come to consensus on how the PBL arrangement will modify, but be fully integrated with, the traditional organic supply chain flows. Presenting this information in graphical form has been most successful in getting everyone involved to get a common understanding of the concepts. An example is shown in Figure 7.10.

Funding flows is always a sensitive issue, and no one on the PBL team will be empowered to agree on program implementation until the funding sources and flows are fully defined and agreed. This issue can get more complex as the number of PBL participating agencies multiplies. This topic can be a "show stopper" when different operating/sponsoring organizations are involved. Some PBL initiatives involve different services, and even different allied nations.

The V-22 program is a good example of the need to clarify and document agreements in this area, since the program is funded by numerous sponsors in the USN, USMC, and USAF. Figure 7.11 shows one recommended alternative for describing this example. In the diagram, the Navy and Marine Corps entities are on the left, the Program Manager Air (PMA) is shown in the middle, and the U.S. Air Force entities are on the right. This recommendation, while not adopted, showed funding from numerous sources flowing through the program office to the Naval Inventory Control Point (NAVICP), who was to award and manage the PBL contract with the industry contractor. Defining all of the players and acronyms is not important to this discussion. Suffice to say that the flow of funding from the numerous sources had to be fully understood and agreed upon for the PBL program to proceed.

---

* National Institute of Standards and Technology (NIST), http://www.nist.gov/public_affairs/factsheet/mbnqa. htm, retrieved November 1, 2008.

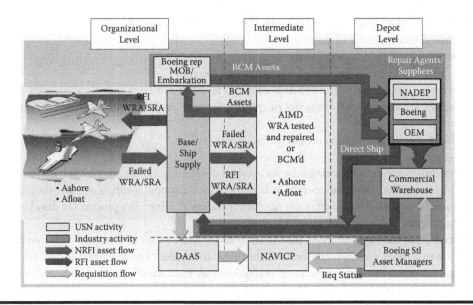

Figure 7.10   Supply chain flows example.

Recommended Funding Flow

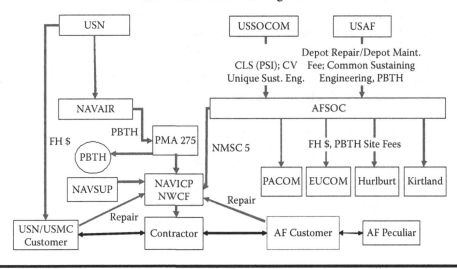

Figure 7.11   Funding flows example.

7.2.14 Define a Performance Data and Reporting Schema

The terms *performance measurement, digital dashboards,* and *balanced scorecards* have come to be used interchangeably. The features of these tools include:

■ Acquire data from a variety of sources and formats: databases, spreadsheets, flat files
■ Filter data according to logical (business) rules
■ Perform complex math or statistical operations (summing, averaging, and forecasting)

- Transform data to a variety of formats (forms, graphs, graphics)
- Make displays via the Internet
- Data staging in a data warehouse
- Information security associated with data and displays
- Two-way interaction to include drill-down to layers of raw data and supporting data
- Tag information with comments or queries to serve as the foundation for efficient problem solving
- Automatically generate reports in different formats

The performance data reporting schema involves developing an integrated information sharing system. An integrated information system is the key to situational awareness, asset visibility, and performance data collection, assessment, and information sharing. The process for developing the reporting schema is shown in Figure 7.12.

Developers of the data collection plan need to concentrate on identifying the data that decision makers use to operate the organization, and then need to conduct a survey of what data are already available. If they start by defining what is available rather than what is needed, the emphasis is put in the wrong place, and inevitably, a large data collection exercise is under way before the purpose of the data collection effort is clearly defined. Taking the time to define the purpose of the data collection and reporting the effort up front can yield benefits down the road as well. For instance, line management could have fewer objections to narrowly defined data collection requirements that impact their daily operations. Thus, the first step in data collection is to list the performance objectives and accompanying performance measures for which data are needed.

It is important to look beyond your own organization for performance measures and data requirements. The nesting of strategic and performance plans is vital to ensuring that the data collected are consistent across the organization and are provided in a timely manner. The organization's strategic and performance plans are the primary management documents from which performance measures are developed. Within any organization there are several subordinate

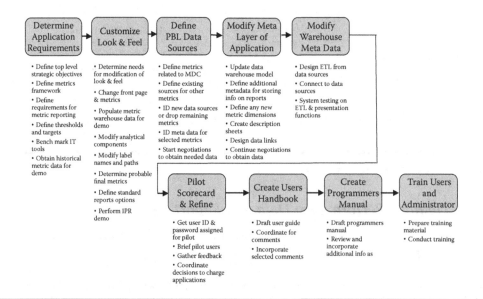

Figure 7.12   Reporting tool development process.

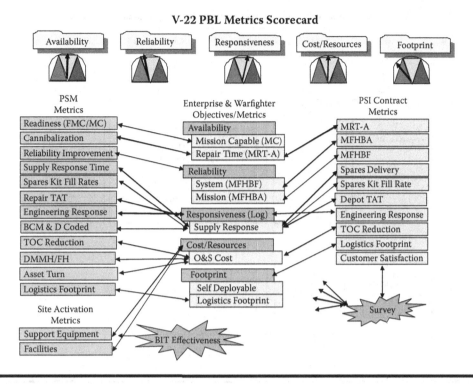

V-22 PBL Metrics Scorecard

Figure 7.13   Metrics mapping example.

organizations, each with its own strategic or performance plans. It is incumbent upon each subordinate organization to develop its plans such that they are in alignment with the organizational plans above them.

The linkage of measures to source data is described in the next chapter, and on the individual measure description sheets, which are also illustrated in Chapter 8.

Figure 7.13 shows how the government product support manager (PSM) and the contractor product support integrator (PSI) metrics are linked to enterprise-level objectives.

7.2.14.1 Metric Linking in the Reporting Scorecard Structure

Figure 7.14 shows how the metrics at lower levels of indenture are linked for the roll-up to higher levels of reporting.

7.2.14.2 Non-Automated Graphic Presentations

Figures 7.15 and 7.16 are two examples of how metrics can be displayed for reporting in a nonautomated format. These graphic displays are often used in program review meetings.

7.2.14.3 Automated Measurement Data Sharing

As discussed earlier, performance management activities are performed by numerous people at all levels of the program organization. Many of these individuals will view and use measurement information in ways specifically applicable to their particular function, and will focus

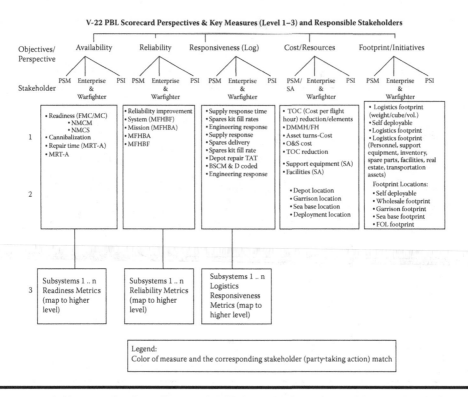

Figure 7.14 Linking metrics for roll-up and drill-down in the automated reporting tool.

on performance measures applicable to that function. It is important that all members of the program understand the overall integrated use of performance information, and the leading/lagging linkages of the measures defined in Sections 7.4 and 7.5. Historically, performance metric tracking has been applied in various parts of an organization, but generally not integrated within the enterprise. Figure 7.17 is a notional representation of the sustainment enterprise for military systems. Performance reporting has historically been conducted by any number of work centers in this enterprise environment. Now, the move is to link all of these measurement activities to enterprise strategic objectives, and to share the measurement information via Web-based information integration. Figures 7.18 to 7.20 show various segments of this shared data environment.

7.2.14.4 Selecting a Reporting Schema

There are basically two prevalent methods for reporting performance information. The first is the nonautomated method, where reports are created manually and distributed to a distribution list. The second uses specially created software applications, which can produce numerous standard and custom reports to be either pushed or pulled via the Web.

Government Computer News contains a good, concise article concerning executive dashboards. The article makes it clear that the terms *dashboard* and *scorecard* can be used interchangeably. The article listed the features of effective dashboards that were provided in Section 7.2.14.

Bell/Boeing Supportability Scorecard
Performance Matrix
Program: MV-22
Cumulative through November 2004

A & M "Imperatives"	Key Metrics	Description	% Weight	Scoring Criteria (YTD Relative Performance to Plan)									
				10-Stretch	9	8	7-Goal	6	5*	4	3	2	1
Financials OP Plan	TLCLS CPI	IMICS	10.0%	113.0%	109.0%	104.0%	100.0%	96%	91%	87%	82%	77%	72%
	TLCLS SPI	IMICS	10.0%	113.0%	109.0%	104.0%	100.0%	96%	91%	87%	82%	77%	72%
Customer Satisfaction	Customer Satisfaction	IPAR Score	7.5%	10	9	8	7	6	5	4	3	2	1
Performance	Blk A IETM	% Completed Blk A IETM	7.5%	115.0%	110.0%	105.0%	100.0%	95.0%	90.0%	85.0%	80.0%	75.0%	70.0%
	Baseline IETM	Critical Processes	7.5%	107.5%	105.0%	102.5%	100.0%	97.5%	95.0%	92.5%	90.0%	87.5%	85.0%
	Support Equipment SERDS	% filled	5.0%	115%	110%	105%	100%	95%	90%	85%	80%	75%	70%
	Tech Assist	Days TAT	15.0%	5.0	6.0	6.5	7.0	8.0	8.5	9.0	9.5	10.0	105
	DFSR/TARS TAT	Hours	15.0%	17	18	19	20	21	22	23	24	25	26
	Spares Delivery	On Time Delivery	5.0%	100%	98%	96%	94%	92%	90%	88%	86%	84%	82%
	ROR/TAT Fleet Support	Days TAT	5.0%	45	50	55	60	65	70	75	80	85	90
Reliability	Reliability	Mean Flight Hours Between Abort	2.5%	20	19	18	17	15	13	11	9	7	5
	Reliability	Mean Flight Hours Between Failure	2.5%	1.2	1.1	1.0	0.9	0.8	0.7	0.6	0.5	0.4	0.2
Maintainability	Maintainability	Maintenance Manhour Per Flight Hour	2.5%	17	18	19	20	21	22	23	24	25	26
	Maintainability	Mean Repair Time Between Aborts	2.5%	1.8	2.8	3.8	4.8	5.8	6.8	7.8	8.8	9.8	10.8
Strengthen the Team	Recognize & Reward	% of Personnel Recognized	2.5%	109%	106%	103%	100%	97%	94%	91%	88%	85%	82%
			100.0%										

2001 Trend:	Jan	Feb	Mar	Apr	May	Jun	Jul	Aug	Sep	Oct	Nov	Dec
Current	YTD Score	0	0	0	0	0	6.7	6.3	6.7	5.5	5.8	60	0
Forecasted	YE Projection	0.0	0	0	0	0	6.7	6.6	70	6.2	6.2	6.5	0

Figure 7.15 Nonautomated metric scorecard example 1.

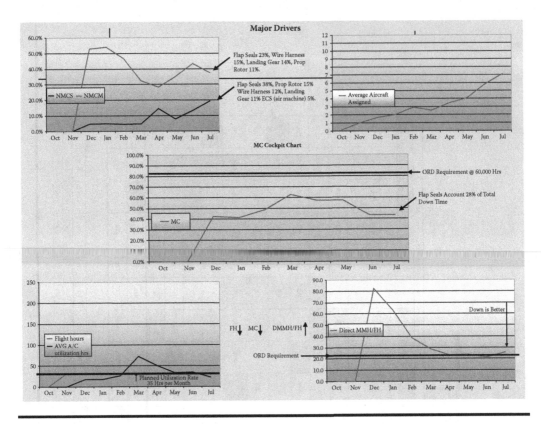

Figure 7.16 Nonautomated metric scorecard example 2.

Scores of software vendors offer balanced scorecard software applications. Many can be found through a Web search, and nearly all of the most widely used applications are on display at balanced scorecard conferences. *Government Computer News* lists fifteen examples of dashboard software with a wide range of features at an equally wide range of prices for server and user licensing. Demonstrations will show that most automated reporting tools show considerable benefits and useful features, which are vast improvements over nonautomated reporting methods. A review of available performance reporting tools will show that the annual licensing fees for these applications range between $3,000 and $30,000, depending on the number of user seats and other pricing criteria. This is a list of examples (in random order) from the many packages that are available:

- Dialog Strategy by Axsellit
- QPR Scorecard by QPR Software
- Balanced Scorecard Software by CorVu
- Pbviews 7.0 by Performance Soft
- Active Strategy Enterprise by Active Strategy
- Performance Plus by INPHASE
- Balance Scorecard by Rocket Software
- Host Scorecard by Host Analytics

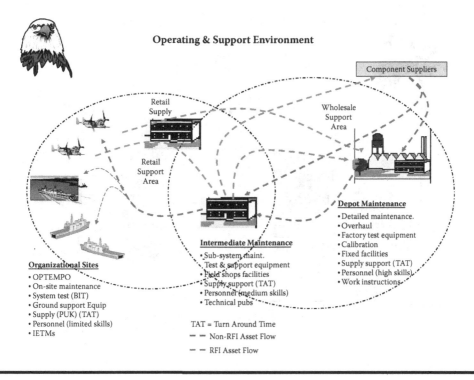

Figure 7.17 Operating and support reporting environment.

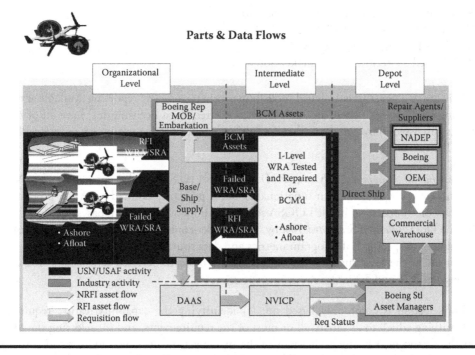

Figure 7.18 Parts and parts data flows—example program.

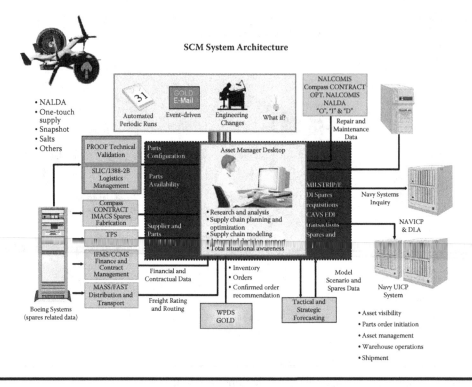

Figure 7.19   Supply chain management information architecture—example.

- Scorecard Software by Toolpack Consulting
- PM-EXPRESS by PM-EXPRESS
- SIMPLE by SIMPLE Systems
- Balanced Scorecard by Pathmaker Software

There are two government-owned tools for performance metric reporting available at the time of writing of this book. These are tools that do not require a licensing fee, have all of the PBL elements discussed above, and are therefore prime candidates for use by government PBL programs. The two are:

- *Post Fielding Support Analyzer (PFSA)* by LOGSA (U.S. Army's Logistics Support Agency). This tool provides excellent functionality but is primarily tailored for Army programs that draw on information in the LOGSA set of sustainment-related databases.
- The DoD *Balanced Scorecard Tool* by SAIC under contract to OSD. This tool can easily be tailored to specific PBL program metrics and data sources. This is the tool that was selected for use as the V-22 sustainment performance scorecard. Selected screenshots are shown in Figures 7.21 and 7.22.

Tool selection is commonly based on: (1) identifying the capability/feature requirements, (2) identifying which tools satisfy all or most of the requirements, and (3) selecting the tool that offers the best value. On-site evaluations of the two government-owned tools revealed that both tools had excellent capability. The PFSA was the best choice for U.S. Army programs, since it is

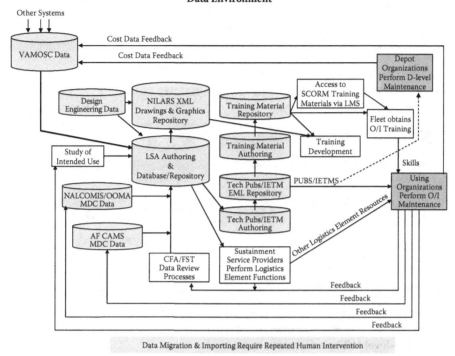

Figure 7.20 **Databases and data migration environment.**

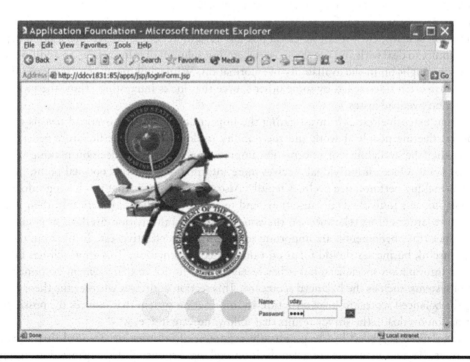

Figure 7.21 **Web-based log-in page for V-22 performance scorecard.**

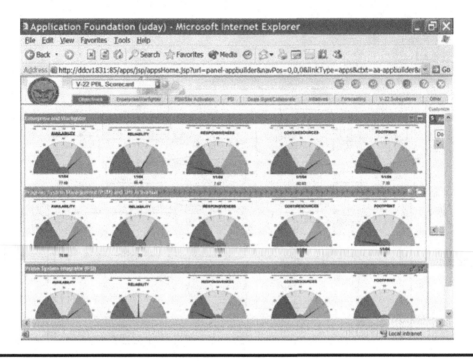

Figure 7.22 Top-level V-22 performance scorecard.

tailored to the U.S. Army logistics databases at LOGSA. The DoD Balanced Scorecard Tool is currently the best choice for adoption by most agencies.

In our society, we are confronted with more information every day—from the Internet, email, information systems, etc.—than we could possibly review. Yet our success at work often depends on our ability to deal with and use these overwhelming volumes of information. In addition, many people get caught up in the availability of information. While looking at one aspect of information, we are often sidetracked by some other source that looks interesting. Thus, the problem of information overload arises.

In fact, extensive research investigating the impact of information overload reveals that it is seriously affecting people at work and their ability to do their job. The literature generally recognizes that the availability of information improves an individual's decision making up to an optimal point. Once an individual receives more information than this optimal point, however, decision-making performance declines rapidly. Also, research shows that just having information available impacts individuals because they tend to incorporate the information in their decision making, regardless of its relevance. So the issues related to information overload or systems that help reduce this phenomenon are important for organization effectiveness. To filter out data that are not useful, businesses should focus on value-added information. This approach has been the focus of information specialists, but it has received little notice in management accounting and control systems, such as the balanced scorecard. This section addresses whether the theory underlying the balanced scorecard helps structure an information system that reduces the possibility of information overload. The survey results that follow indicate it does.

The balanced scorecard can help reduce the amount of information overload that a manager encounters. Because managers are given decision-making responsibilities, organizations use management account control systems to communicate information about the actions desired from these managers. Employment contracts include measures to encourage managers to undertake activities that are consistent with organizational interests. Traditionally, these measures have focused primarily on financial information that reflects the results of current performance. Therefore, managers are incentivized to make decisions that promote short-term value creation. Concern over this short-term focus has been an important issue for management accountants because it may cause the manager to underemphasize activities that create value for the future.

Robert Kaplan and David Norton (1996) developed the balanced scorecard as a performance measurement system to help mitigate this short-term decision-making focus. The balanced scorecard consists of measures linked to organization strategy and is structured to include a combination of financial measures that reflect past decisions and nonfinancial measures, which are indicators of future performance. Therefore, the balanced scorecard should encourage managers to balance their actions between a short- and long-term focus.

An organization's strategy can be thought of as a series of hypotheses concerning the cause-and-effect relationships among the performance measures and organizational objectives. The balanced scorecard's inclusion of both financial and nonfinancial measures provides a systematic way to manage and verify the relationships expected between the measures and performance drivers. The development of a direct link between these cause-and-effect relationships and organizational strategy enables managers to perform their work more effectively because the information provided helps managers obtain feedback about performance, thereby helping them pursue organizational objectives.

The balanced scorecard typically consists of four performance perspectives, each usually having between four and seven measures. This often results in up to twenty-eight performance measures. If this volume is compared to a traditional performance measurement system where only a few financial outcomes are used, a concern arises about a manager's ability to process outcome information across so many dimensions. Kaplan and Norton contend that the number of measures in the balanced scorecard will not result in a system that is so complicated that managers' decision making is impeded because the balanced scorecard directs actions toward the pursuit of a unified strategy. The balanced scorecard's inclusion of multiple perspectives enables managers to group measures, which facilitates information processing and, as a result, should improve decision making. Because the ability to process information is an important element of information overload, this suggests that the balanced scorecard may help reduce the amount of information overload that a manager encounters.

7.2.15 Define Win-Win Performance-Based Incentives

Effective application of contract/tasking incentives that positively influence the service providers is essential to a successful PBL program. The process shown in Figure 7.23 is an example that can be used to develop the PBL incentives plan.

7.2.16 Define a Dispute Resolution Process

There should be regular formal and informal reviews of performance information. Most decisions resulting from performance reviews will concern alternatives for improving achievement of warfighter objectives. Some more sensitive decisions concerning workload reassignment or other penalties could prove contentious. The application of performance-based contracting/tasking will involve the competitive selection of logistics service providers and the application of some positive rewards along with possible application of some penalties based on evaluation of performance. One common penalty, based on performance, has involved a change in service providers. These situations have the potential for differences of opinion. The players need to be assured that there is a standard and fair

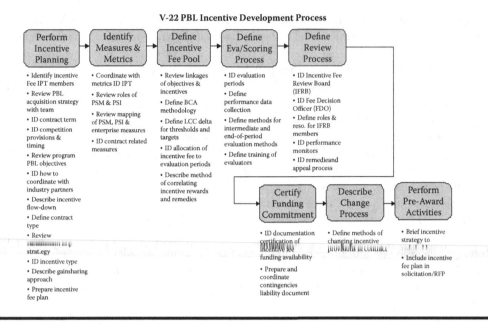

Figure 7.23   Example PBL incentives development process.

process for grievance submission and dispute resolution. PBL decisions are basically business decisions, and the fundamental rule of business law is to determine what is fair to the parties involved.

As an example, consider these three levels of dispute resolution:

1. The basic dispute resolution process involves a three- to five-person review board made up of members of the PBL-IPT and the maintenance strategy support team (MSST), who will review the dispute and document their decision in a decision memorandum. This memorandum will be approved or disapproved by the responsible government program manager.
2. An appeal from the basic process involves a five-person independent review board made up of at least two senior government officials, not assigned to the program office, and at least two senior private sector officials, not contractually involved in providing logistics sustainment to the program. The board reviews the dispute and documents their decision in a formal memorandum. This memorandum will be approved or disapproved by the government responsible program manager.
3. Contracts with private sector companies are subject to a standard contracts-related dispute and resolution process. Any PBL-related dispute should proceed from the basic process and the appeal process discussed above before proceeding through the formal contract dispute resolution process.

Typical dispute-related contract language might include the following:

This contract is subject to the Contract Disputes Act of 1978. Failure of the parties in this contract to reach agreement on any request for equitable adjustment, claim, appeal, or action arising under or relating to this contract shall be a dispute to be resolved in accordance with the clause at FAR 52.233-1, "Disputes," which is incorporated herein by reference. The contractor shall proceed diligently with performance of this contract, pending final resolution of any dispute arising under the contract.

7.2.17 Define the Performance Contracting and Tasking with Providers

PBL-related contracting and tasking documents should include work statements and descriptions of successful performance in measurable terms. Selected information concerning such subjects can be summarized in the statement of objectives (SOO) document for tailoring purposes:

- Applicable performance measures/metrics
- Metric objectives from the metric description forms (see Table 7.4).
- Performance data reporting
- Formal and informal performance reviews

In August 2004, the Office of the Secretary of Defense of the DoD issued guidance concerning the purchase of weapons system logistics support using performance-based criteria (DoD 2004). This is a summary of that guidance:

1. Follow the Federal Acquisition Regulations and Defense Federal Acquisition Regulations guidance concerning acquisition of logistics services and support.
2. Use of long-term contracts with incentives tied to performance is the preferred approach.
3. Use award term contracts, where possible, to incentivize optimal industry support.
4. Incentives should be tied to metrics.
5. Award and incentive contracts should include tailored cost and performance reporting to enable contract management and to facilitate future cost estimating and price analysis.
6. Include metrics definitions and a firm period of performance.
7. Use fixed price per system operating hour where possible.
8. Cost type contracts may be used in the early stages of PBL in order to establish maintenance and other performance data.
9. Full access to DoD demand data is to be incorporated into all PBL contracts.
10. PBL contracts should be competitively sourced wherever possible.
11. PBL contractors should be encouraged to use small and disadvantaged subcontractors (8A firms), and may be incentivized to do so to support agency goals in this area.

Contracts or tasking documents for product support providers should contain applicable top-level measures to be used to gauge successful performance. Two dimensions for these measures can be used in calculating a performance score for the performance period: (1) weight of the measure and (2) range score for each measure.

- *Weight of the measure*: Once the number of measures applicable to the effort is chosen, they are assigned percentage weights relative to each other. The total of these weights should equal 100%.
- *Range score for each measure*: For each measure a minimum threshold and stretch target are selected. The difference between these two numbers is divided into ten incremental step scores.

The final score is calculated by applying the weight to each of the measures and summing these individual weighted numbers to arrive at an overall score for the performance. Tables 7.5 and 7.6 are examples. The incentive fee pool is often a percentage of the contract or tasking funding total.

Table 7.5 Use of Performance Measures in Contracts

Metric	NMCS Non-NSN Items (%)	MICAP Delivery (Hrs)	RSP Kits ND (%)	Depot Delivery (Days)	Depot Aircraft Quality (# Disc)	Delinquent DRS (#)	WST Available (%)
Weight:	25	15	15	15	15	10	5
10	5.0–below	72–below	96	0.0–0.9	20–below	1	99
9	5.1–5.5	73–84	95		21–25	2	98
8	5.6–6.0	85–96	94	1.0–1.9	26–30	3	97
7	6.1–6.5	97–108	93		31–35	4	96
6	6.6–7.0	109–120	92	2.0–2.9	36–40	5	95
5	7.1–7.5	121–132	91		41–45	6	94
4	7.6–8.0	133–144	90	3.0–3.9	46–50	7	93
3	8.1–8.5	145–156	89		51–55	8	92
2	8.6–9.0	157–168	88	4.0–4.9	56–60	9	91
1	9.1–9.5	169–180	87		61–65	10	90
0	9.6 & Up	181 & Up	86	5.0 & Up	65 & Up	11 & Up	89

Table 7.6   Example Contractor Performance Metrics

Percent Available	Range	Performance
100%	380–400 Points	Standard of Excellence
90%	360–379	
80%	340–359	
70%	320–339	Acceptable
60%	300–319	
50%	280–299	
40%	260–279	
30%	240–259	Threshold
20%	220–239	
10%	200–219	
0%	<199	

This total fee amount may be divided into portions applicable to contract periods, such as annual increments. The amount of the annual incentive fee increment to be paid is determined by the annual total score, which will be a percentage value.

With the basic performance score concept defined, the next task is developing the actual key performance-level metrics. The performance-level metrics in Table 7.7 were used to monitor/measure contractor performance for purposes of administering a PBL contract and assessing incentive and award fees. These metrics were chosen with support of the warfighter to ensure their needs were met. A weighted objective point score (weight times score) is calculated for each of these performance metrics on a quarterly basis based on a 12-month rolling average. The objective score of 1,000 constitutes an award of 100% of the incentive fee for that period.

A business case analysis is performed to determine the amount of funding put into the budget and set aside to be awarded to the contractor based on the performance score for the contract performance period, usually annually. The F-117 example that was shown earlier in Table 7.4 has a 7% award fee pool.

In the illustration below (Tables 7.8 and 7.9), assume that the annual award fee amount is a maximum of $700,000. In example A of Table 7.9, the contractor gets the maximum score (10) in each of the seven weighted metrics. This results in the maximum award fee of $700,000. In example B, the achieved metrics (circled) are given in the scores to the left of each circle. The scores times the weight gives a subtotal score. The sum of the subtotals is 640 out of the maximum of 1,000. Therefore, the contractor is awarded 64% of the maximum award fee, or $448,000.

A PBL contract metrics scorecard is a tool to monitor/measure contractor performance for purposes of administering the contract and assessing incentive and award fees. As an illustration, the PBL contracts metrics scorecard for the V-22 Osprey program is shown in Table 7.10. Seven objective and three subjective metrics are chosen with support of the warfighter to ensure that their objectives are met. They were also chosen so that the contractor product support integrator (PSI) can have maximum control over the metrics. A weighted objective point score (weight times score) is calculated for each of the performance metrics on a quarterly basis based on a 12-month rolling

Table 7.7 Example Performance-Level Metrics

Not mission-capable supply (NMCS)	Measures the percent of possessed hours that aircraft are not capable of performing the primary mission because of a lack of repair parts. National Stock Number (NSN) and locally fabricated, assembled, and purchased items are excluded.
Mission capability (MICAP) deliveries	Measures the ability of the contractor to quickly respond and satisfy high-priority supply demands caused by aircraft being not mission capable for parts. NSN and locally fabricated, assembled, and purchased items are excluded.
Readiness spares packages (RSPs) kits ND	Measures the percent the kits are filled at any given time by the supply activities of the contractor. NSN, deployed kits, and locally fabricated, assembled, and purchased items are excluded. Kits returned from deployment are excluded from performance measurement for 00 days to allow for stock replenishment.
Depot aircraft quality	Measures the number of major or minor discrepancies (converted to points) found by the 49FW after the contractor has requested sign-off for closure. Documented and "do not work" discrepancies are excluded.
Depot delivery	Measures the number of days each modified aircraft fails to be delivered on time. There is no credit for early deliveries.
Delinquent product quality deficiency reports (PQDRs)	Measures whether the contractor responds within the targeted timeframe for any category 1 or category 2 deficiency.
Weapon system trainer (WST) availability	Measures the percent of the time the trainer is fully operational.

average. An objective score of 1,000 will constitute justification or an award of 100% of the incentive fee for the contract period.

7.2.18 Monitor Performance and Identify Actions

Performance metrics should be reported regularly, along with recommendations for improving the achievement of desired end states. Monthly reports should be made available via established digital information sharing networks. The PBL IPT should establish an analysis capability and ensure that reports contain conclusions, recommendations, and a tracking of action initiatives. Periodic reviews should be presented to decision forums, such as the maintenance strategy support team (MSST), who is the decision authority for recommendations involving major changes in support resources, such as support equipment, equipment modifications, and facilities. Only decisions concerning changes in sources of support in terms of major contract/tasking assignments will require a formal performance review.

7.2.19 Conduct Formal Performance Reviews

Formal technical reviews are a well established part of the systems engineering process. These reviews should be conducted throughout the program development phase. Formal performance

Table 7.8   Scores in the Seven Metric Areas

Metric Score:	NMCS Non-NSN Items (%) 25	MICAP Delivery (Hrs) 15	RSP Kits ND (%) 15	Depot Delivery (Days) 15	Depot Aircraft Quality (# Disc) 15	Delinquent DRS (#) 10	WST Available (%) 5
10	5.0-below	72-below	96	0.0-0.9	20-below	1	99
9	5.1-5.5	73-84	95		21-25	2	98
8	5.6-6.0	85-96	94	1.0-1.9	26-30	3	97
7	6.1-6.5	97-108	93		31-35	4	96
6	6.6-7.0	109-120	92	2.0-2.9	36-40	5	95
5	7.1-7.5	121-132	91		41-45	6	94
4	7.6-8.0	133-144	90	3.0-3.9	46-50	7	93
3	8.1-8.5	145-156	89		51-55	8	92
2	8.6-9.0	157-168	88	4.0-4.9	56-60	9	91
1	9.1-9.5	169-180	87		61-65	10	90
0	9.6 & Up	181 & Up	86	5.0 & Up	65 & Up	11 & Up	89

Table 7.9 Score Converted to Award Fee

Example A			Example B		
Score	Weight	Sub-Total	Score	Weight	Sub-Total
10	2.5	250	7	25	175
10	1.5	150	8	15	120
10	1.5	150	4	15	60
10	1.5	150	6	15	90
10	1.5	150	8	15	120
10	1.5	100	3	10	30
10	1.5	50	9	5	45
Total = 1000/1000 = 100%			Total = 640/1000 = 64%		
700K × 100% = 700K			700K × 64% = 448K		

reviews should be scheduled on a regular basis for the life of the PBL effort. A technical review is different. The purpose of a technical review is to assess if the system design satisfies program requirements as defined in program specifications and other documents, and to determine if issues and corrective actions warrant management and control. The primary purpose of a formal performance review is to assess if goals and objectives of the logistics effort are being achieved by the logistics service providers as specified in contracts and tasking statements, and to make a determination concerning incentive awards and penalties. The general process of a formal performance review is described in Figure 7.24. Table 7.11 outlines the basic actions in this process.

7.2.20 Identify Opportunities for Improvement

The implementation of performance improvement activities, whether at the enterprise level or the individual improvement initiative, requires two distinct management reporting methods: policy deployment reporting and measurement of the results.

The first method focuses on the implementation schedule and percent completion. The method used by most successful enterprises is called policy deployment. One of the more successful organizations, Danaher,* described it this way:

> The Danaher Business System has a policy deployment process in place that really takes the strategy and drives it throughout the organization with breakthrough objectives and measurable quality, delivery, cost and growth objectives, using the tools of lean to help achieve those (strategic) business objectives.

Lockheed-Martin calls its policy deployment reporting system TEMPO. A Navy organization uses the name STARS (Strategic to Tactical Activity Reporting System). STARS is a detailed, near-term management tracking, reporting, and sharing of progress of scheduled activities associated

* "Danaher Is a Paragon of Lean Success," *Manufacturing News*, Vol. 8, No. 12, June 29, 2001.

Table 7.10 PBL Contracts Metrics Scorecard for the V-22 Osprey Program

Metric	Spares On-time Delivery (h)	Readiness Spares Kits Fill (%)	Depot Repair TAT (days)	MFHBA (h)	MFHBF (h)	MRT-A (h)	Engineering Response Time (h)	TOC Reduction Index	LOG FP Reduction Index	Customer Satisfaction Index
	25%	10%	10%	10%	10%	10%	10%	5%	5%	5%
10	72	96	20	20	1.5	1.5	24	10	10	10
9	73–84	95	20–25	19–20	1.2–1.5	1.5–2	24–48	9	9	9
8	85–96	94	25–30	18–19	1.0–1.2	2–3	49–72	8	8	8
7	97–108	93	30–35	17–18	0.9–1.0	3–4	73–96	7	7	7
6	109–120	92	35–40	15–17	0.8–0.9	4–5	97–120	6	6	6
5	121–132	91	40–45	13–15	0.7–0.8	5–6	121–144	5	5	5
4	133–144	90	45–50	11–13	0.6–0.7	6–7	145–168	4	4	4
3	145–156	89	50–55	9–11	0.5–0.6	7–8	169–192	3	3	3
2	157–168	88	55–60	7–9	0.4–0.5	8–9	193–216	2	2	2
1	169–180	87	60–65	5–7	0.3–0.4	9–10	217–240	1	1	1
0	181 up	86 down	65 up	5 down	0.3 down	10 up	241 up	0	0	0

Metric definitions are given in Chapter 8.

Spares on-time delivery	Measures the percent of the spares kits that are filled at any given time by the supply-expediting activities of the contractor PSI. This assumes that contractor PSI representatives at the local (garrison and sea base) location are key members of the kit replenishment and parts replenishment team. Kits returned from deployments are to be excluded from performance measurement for 90 days to allow for stock replenishment.

(Continued)

Table 7.10 Continued

Metric definitions are given in Chapter 8.

Readiness spares kit fill rate	Measures the percent of the spares kits that are filled at any given time by the supply-expediting activities of the contractor PSI. This assumes that contractor PSI representatives at the local (garrison and sea base) location are key members of the kit replenishment and parts replenishment team. Kits returned from deployments are to be excluded from performance measurement for 90 days to allow for stock replenishment.
Depot repair turnaround time (TAT)	The average elapsed time (days or hours) from receipt of a failed item at a repair facility until the item is ready for reissue. Related directly to numbers and cost of spares needed for the pipeline, and related to ability of retail supply to support MC rate of aircraft.
Mean flight hours between aborts (MFHBA)	The mean flight hours between events that render an aircraft incapable of performing its mission. This metric focuses on mission reliability of the aircraft.
Mean flight hours between failures (MFHBF)	The basic measure of reliability for the aircraft. This metric focuses on logistics reliability and is directly related to mission capability.
Mean repair time—abort (MRT-A)	The basic measure of maintainability for the aircraft, but focused on those maintenance actions directly related to mission completion.
Engineering response time	Measures whether the contractor PSI responds within the targeted timeframe for any high-priority request for engineering assistance.
Total ownership cost reduction (TOC-R) index	A subjective measure of the contractor PSI involvement in identifying, and supporting through analysis, actions that can reduce the O&S cost per unit usage (flight hour). Low relative weight is because the contractor does not control all of the factors affecting approval and funding of many O&S cost drivers.
Logistics footprint (LOG FP) index	A subjective measure of the contractor PSI involvement in identifying, and supporting through analysis, actions that can reduce the unit load of spares, support equipment, and other logistics resources in the sea base and forward operation locations (FOLs). The need is for warfighter agility, but at the current life cycle phase, the contractor does not control the factors affecting selection of logistics resources for the FOL. This is the reason for the relatively small weight.
Customer satisfaction	A subjective measure based on surveys of a broad range of supportability-related stakeholders. The contractor PSI will participate in creation and maintenance of the survey contents aimed at identifying opportunities for sustainment process improvement and customer relationship management.

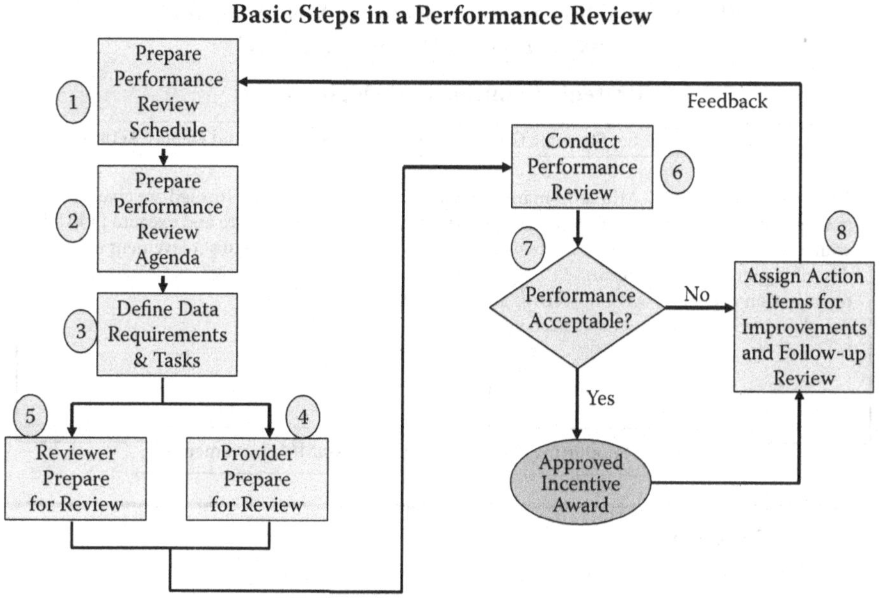

Basic Steps in a Performance Review

Figure 7.24 Formal performance review.

Table 7.11 Performance Review Process

Action	Description
1	Government project manager contractually establishes performance review requirements. The contractor prepares review schedules compatible with the master program milestone schedule.
2	The Product Support Integrator (PSI) prepares and distributes the agenda in advance of each review, defining: purpose and scope of the review; specific items to be reviewed, and date/time/place of the review.
3	The PSI defines applicable data to assist the support provider and reviewer in preparation for the review.
4	The support provider prepares for the review to include answers to questions (checklist) accompanying the agenda, description of the support services, requirements, analysis, performance results, problems, and recommended solutions.
5	The review team prepares for the review, selects focus areas in checklists, and formulates questions and suggestions.
6	The government project manager conducts the formal performance review meeting with the PSI and support provider participation and support.
7	The government team makes a decision concerning performance results or withholds approval decision pending corrective actions of deficiencies.
8	The government and contractor project managers assign action items that are agreed upon by the PSI team for performance improvemvent plans and corrective actions, and they establish a schedule for a follow-up review.

**Tracking Achievement of Strategic Vision Through
Focus on Tactical Details–"STARS"**

Strategic Planning and Deployment:

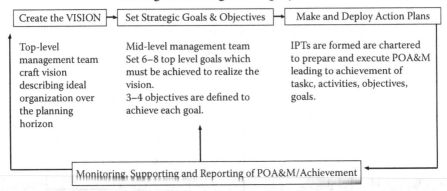

Create the VISION	Set Strategic Goals & Objectives	Make and Deploy Action Plans
Top-level management team craft vision describing ideal organization over the planning horizon	Mid-level management team Set 6–8 top level goals which must be achieved to realize the vision. 3–4 objectives are defined to achieve each goal.	IPTs are formed are chartered to prepare and execute POA&M leading to achievement of taskc, activities, objectives, goals.

Monitoring, Supporting and Reporting of POA&M/Achievement

Figure 7.25 STARS process.

with accomplishment of organizational strategic goals, objectives, projects, activities, and tasks. Figure 7.25 outlines the STARS process.

7.2.20.1 Measurement of the Results

The second management activity is to observe the changes to the linked (drill-down) metrics that result from the implementation of the change initiatives. The PBL performance measurement tool is one potential solution for a measurement reporting tool. A key factor in the need for a linked hierarchy or structure of measures is that change activities/initiatives are most often implemented on individual work processes, and the result of this change is measured in the short run at the local process level. In the longer run, changes in enterprise-level measures and objectives are analyzed with respect to these individual initiatives.

7.3 PBL Case Study: The V-22 Osprey

The following is a case study on the V-22 (Osprey) military aircraft (Figure 7.26). The V-22 has been in development for more than 25 years, but it has had some operational problems. Now, the U.S. Navy has deemed the V-22 operationally suitable and effective for fielding in 2007. The story of the Osprey was discussed with the author during site visits to the Naval Aviation (NAVAIR) Depot, North Island, San Diego, California. North Island is the Navy's West Coast aircraft depot specializing in the support of naval aircraft and related systems. Aircraft arrive at NAVAIR Depot North Island from fleet installations around the United States and the world for scheduled depot maintenance, major modification, or crash damage repair.

The V-22 Osprey is a dual-piloted, self-deployable, medium-lift aircraft for joint service application. Its multiengine tilt-rotor design combines the vertical flight capabilities of a helicopter with the speed and range of a fixed-wing airplane for conducting combat, combat support, and special operations missions worldwide. The tilt-rotor design combines the vertical flight capabilities of a helicopter with the speed and range of a turboprop and permits aerial refueling. It will operate

Figure 7.26   V-22 Osprey.

from aircraft-capable ships as well as shore sites. Capable of flying over 2,100 nautical miles with one aerial refueling, the V-22 provides the services and advantage of a V/STOL aircraft.

The Osprey is a high-wing, twin-engine, H-empennage, hybrid-composite airframe, with retractable tricycle landing gear. Its hybrid construction consists primarily of graphite-reinforced carbon epoxy composite structures with aluminum frames. The engine nacelles, powered by redundant hydraulic and electric actuators, rotate through a 97.5° range from horizontal (0°) to slightly aft of vertical. Nacelle position is a function of airspeed and normally programmed automatically by the flight control system. An automated blade folding and wing stowing system facilitates shipboard compatibility. A central integrated checkout (CIC) system including built-in test (BIT), and a vibration, structural life, and engine diagnostics (VSLED) system provide for a comprehensive on-board diagnostic capability. The BIT will diagnose the processors, memory, and communication links for faults and provide a pass or fail indication for each. The VSLED system provides a data collection, storage, and on-board analysis capability for the aircraft drive system and its associated support structure.

The V-22 weapon system is a multiservice, multimission, vertical/short-takeoff and landing (V/STOL) aircraft designed for these missions:

1. Marine assault vertical lift (MV-22)
2. Navy combat search and rescue (HV-22)
3. Air Force SOF (CV-22)

The primary mission of the U.S. Marine Corps MV-22B is to provide combat assault transport of Marines in the initial assault waves and follow-on stages of amphibious operations and subsequent operations ashore. The Air Force variant, the CV-22, will replace the MH-53J and MH-60G and augment the MC-130 fleet to provide a long-range vertical takeoff and landing insertion and extraction capability. The service life for the V-22 will be 10,000 flight hours with monthly flight hours of approximately 35 for the MV and HV, and 36 for the CV. The V-22 will be based and operated from Naval and Marine Corps air stations and Air Force bases, carriers, landing helicopter assault (LHA) and landing helicopter dock (LHD) ships, forward bases overseas, and world-wide austere sites. V-22 missions include both at-sea and ashore operational scenarios with home basing and deployments as indicated in the Joint Multi-Mission Vertical Lift Aircraft (JMVX) operational requirements document (ORD).

7.3.1 Maintenance Support Plan

The maintenance support plan for CV-22 and MV-22 common subsystems is to use the MV-22's three-level maintenance analysis as a baseline. Based on additional evaluations using the Joint Aviation Model (JAM) for repair level analysis (RLA), the RLAs will be tailored to expand O-level functions to include I-level capability and maximize a two-level maintenance philosophy. The JAM for RLA is an advanced joint service RLA program. The model is usable for acquisition programs that are Navy, Air Force, or joint Navy and Air Force programs. Commonality of support concepts will be a goal for the supportability program, and the final disposition will be made by the Maintenance Decision Board (MDB). For those subsystems unique to the CV-22, a three-level RLA and supportability analysis (SA) will be conducted for newly developed systems, while O-level SA only will be conducted for government-directed systems. Early involvement by the government will enable a more accurate assignment of maintenance level for given components.

7.3.1.1 Phased Maintenance

The V-22 maintenance concept is to fly to failure or to replace or restore in response to "on condition" failure indicators. Scheduled depot-level maintenance (SDLM) cycles are not planned for the V-22 aircraft. The design goals are 2.86 MMH/FH for unscheduled maintenance and 1.26 MMH/FH for scheduled maintenance. The V-22 program will take full advantage of scheduled maintenance principles as defined by reliability-centered maintenance (RCM). The RCM analysis has identified these goals:

1. Commercial aircraft-style walk-around preflights (turnaround inspection) with no daily inspection requirements
2. Thirty-five flight hours (monthly) schedule inspections
3. Eight hundred forty hours (24 month) phased maintenance cycle broken into four 210-hour (6-month) intervals
4. No required lubrication between phases (except for lubrication required after aircraft wash)

7.3.1.2 Interim Support

Interim support consists of both government and contractor support. It provides the basis for a smooth and timely transition from contractor to government support during initial operational activation, and will continue, when ordered by the government, in the production and deployment (P&D) phase. The objective of contractor and government interim support is to introduce the aircraft into the operational inventory while achieving and sustaining a high level of operational readiness at the first site, and providing a steady, incremental, and systematic growth in government support capability. The intent of the interim support program is to provide full, (government) organic O-level capability upon arrival of the first aircraft at the first operational site. Contractor interim logistics support will be utilized to provide I- and D-level maintenance until organic capability is phased in. Interim support provided by the contractor shall be based on, and traceable to, data developed in accordance with logistics support analysis, maintenance planning, and User Logistics Support Summary (ULSS).

7.3.1.3 Interim Contractor Support

Interim contractor support will be provided until each government site is fully transitioned to government organic maintenance and supply capability. As government-, organizational (O)-, intermediate (I)-, and depot (D)-level capability is established, contractor support will be phased out. Limited government O-level capability will be established prior to the arrival of the first aircraft in the fleet for operational evaluation (OPEVAL). Planning for interim contractor support will provide for adequate logistics response times during a phased transition from shared contractor and government support to complete government operational support. This transition of support will be addressed in the User Logistics Support Summary (ULSS).

7.3.1.4 Contractor Logistics Support (CLS)

During the low rate initial production (LRIP) periods the contractor will provide limited interim logistics support until the transition to organic support begins on a firm, phased schedule. Logistics support will begin a transition from contractor to government support, when the first unit is activated. It is anticipated that selected V-22 assets will be maintained by the contractor under contractor logistics support (CLS). Complete government O-level support capability will be established by arrival of the first aircraft at the first operational site. Complete government I-level capability was established 1 year prior to the first deployment. Complete D-level capability will be established by the government support date (GSD). After completion of the transition, logistics support will be totally government organic, except for selected components, for which CLS will be provided under separate contract provisions. Some CLS decisions have been implemented, as provided in Table 7.12. CLS contracts are administered and managed by NAVICP.

7.3.2 Baseline Performance Metrics

The PBL opportunity table, shown in Figure 7.3, was used to display the baseline performance metrics. The information in this table will be drawn from data in the supportability analysis (SA) databases for the candidate subsystems, along with associated models and data sources. These data will represent the latest estimates resulting from the considerable developmental and operational test data. This information is to be formulated into a set of top-level factors that link the capability resulting from the system design and the primary supportability environment to the key performance parameters (KPPs) in program requirements documents and agreements with the warfighter. The information gathered in an appropriately tailored formal maintainability demonstration is essential in establishing baseline performance and cost. Figure 7.27 shows the top-level relationship of the information to be collected in the opportunity table and the key performance metrics for the V-22 (shown in Table 7.13). The black TTM portion of the uptime/downtime line represents the design characteristics labeled *reliability* and *maintainability*. These make up Ai (inherent availability), which is column 3 of the opportunity table. The blue portion of the line

Table 7.12   CLS Support for the V-22

AE1107C engine	Rolls Royce
Forward-looking infrared radar (FLIR)	Raytheon
Flat-panel display, display electronics unit, digital map	EFW
Lightweight internal navigation system (LWINS)	Honeywell
Flight control computer	Lockheed Martin
Control display unit, remote frequency indicator	Honeywell
Keyboard unit, flight director panel	Honeywell
Auxiliary power unit (APU)	Hamilton Sundstrand

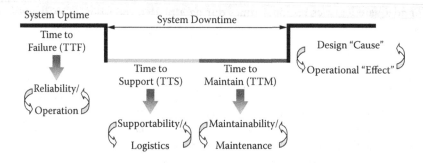

Figure 7.27   Relationship of design decisions and operational effects.

represents downtime associated with getting the part needed to fix the down system. This time is affected by the time it takes intermediate and depot levels of maintenance to get ready-for-issue (RFI) parts back into the supply system. This supportability/logistics information is what is collected in columns 4 to 6 of the opportunity table of Figure 7.3.

The time to maintain (TTM) is affected by at least three important factors: (1) the effectiveness of built-in test in identifying the single bad part needing to be fixed or replaced; (2) the design for accessibility, which makes it possible to quickly and easily fix the down system; and (3) the effectiveness of the technical manuals in helping the maintenance technician to identify and localize the defective part, and to quickly remove and replace that part. Numbers 1 and 2 are included in the Ai information in the opportunity table, while number 3 is included in columns 4 to 6 in the table.

7.3.3 PBL for the V-22

There are several unique features of the V-22 program that affect application of performance-based logistics. First, it is a joint program with Marine Corps, Air Force, and Navy involvement. The operating and support (O&S) scenarios, infrastructures, funding streams, and processes are different. Second, the V-22 is a unique new technology aircraft. It has been in development since 1982 and is now entering the production and deployment phase of the system life cycle. The third unique feature of the program is the very long, 25-year planned production program with a gradual buildup of operating aircraft, and a gradual phase-in of operating locations. The most

Table 7.13   Key Performance Metrics for the V-22 Osprey

Metric	Performance
Aircraft Availability	87% (T)* 82% (O)† @ 60,000 h
Reliability	0.9 h or > (T)* 1.2 h or > (O)† @ 60,000 h
Maintainability	20 h < (T)* 11 h < (O)†
	2.86 h (O)† unscheduled maintenance 1.26 h (O)† scheduled maintenance
Affordability	$806.11 per flight hour
Reduce wait time	Reduce retail customer wait time (CWT) to no more than 24 h Reduce wholesale customer wait time (CWT) to no more than 5 days

*(T) Threshold.
†(O) Objective.

recent V-22 Acquisition Logistics Support Plan (ALSP) reflects operating and support concepts for the Marine Corps, which are based on the traditional support doctrine. A fourth unique situation for the V-22 program is that sweeping changes in the logistics support doctrine are taking place, just as this program approaches the initial deployment phase.

Over the past 10 years, concurrent with the V-22 development, the application of performance-based management to DoD system acquisitions has been evolving. During the past 10 years specific support-related policy, directives, and guidance have emerged to describe the current stage of an evolving set of acquisition/logistics reform initiatives. The concepts of total life cycle systems management and performance-based logistics, and how these concept are to be applied on the V-22 program, is the specific purpose of the V-22 PBL Implementation Plan.

The following are key definitions and objectives of the PBL concept for the V-22. PBL is to support operational requirements of the warfighter in terms of:

1. Defense systems operational availability (Ao)—expressed as mission-capable (MC) rate for airplane systems.
2. Affordability (reduced LCC with focus on high O&S cost drivers).
3. Reduced footprint (logistics resources primarily in theater of operations).
4. Reduced cycle times (supply chain – minimizing mean logistics delay time).
5. Use of performance-based contracting and performance-based management, to link all logistics activity to performance agreements with the warfighter, and to measure and control the performance of logistics resource providers. This concept is illustrated in Figure 7.28.

7.3.4 PBL Strategic Planning

Strategic planning normally involves long-range vision. It is the act of defining the direction(s) that will achieve a predictable future state of organizational success. In the V-22 strategic plan,

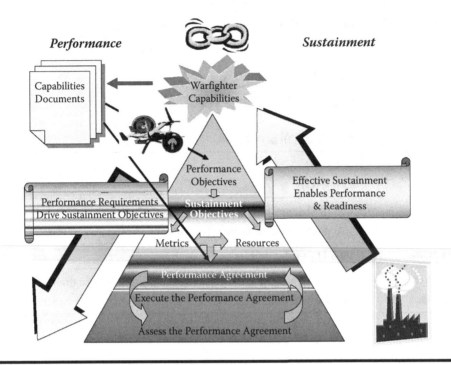

Figure 7.28 Performance and sustainment linkage.

logistics support providers have implemented a mature performance management environment, which is delivering required operational availability of aircraft at a reduced life cycle cost and deployed logistics footprint than was experienced on predecessor systems. The V-22 program has achieved a balanced logistics support structure between the extremes of all organic support and all contractor logistics support (CLS) (see Figure 7.29). This balance involves:

- Depot and wholesale supply operations are an integrated partnership of organic and industry providers. They provide a variety of wholesale-level sustainment products and services along with the collection, reporting, and analysis of performance measurement metrics.
- I-level CONUS operations ashore are an integrated partnership of organic and industry providers that supports the need for skilled organic personnel for deployed O-level and I-level afloat operations.
- O-level support in all operating locations is organic military personnel. The requirements for agile and flexible deployment operations dictate that O-level manning remain organic military.
- Fleet support team detachments (FST-Dets) at the CONUS operating locations are an integrated partnership of organic and industry personnel who are providing technical support to fleet customers along with gathering, analyzing, and reporting O- and I-level performance metrics.
- I-level afloat in aircraft-capable ships to include carriers, LHDs, and LHAs is organic military for the reasons discussed in the paragraph above. The I-level afloat operation is a Lean logistics footprint operation with more go/no-go checks and less full repair of equipment than the I-level ashore operation. Only minimum scheduled maintenance inspections are conducted with the major phased inspections performed at the I-level ashore sites.
- Logistics support is full CLS for nondeployable training equipment and for training and testing equipment at training and testing sites.

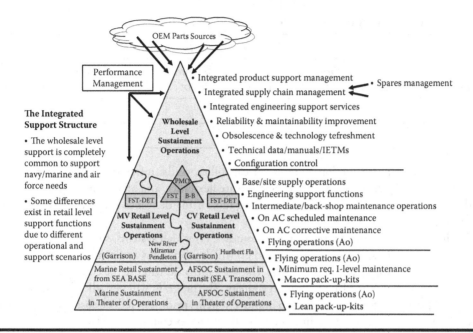

Figure 7.29   PBL strategic plan for the V-22 Osprey.

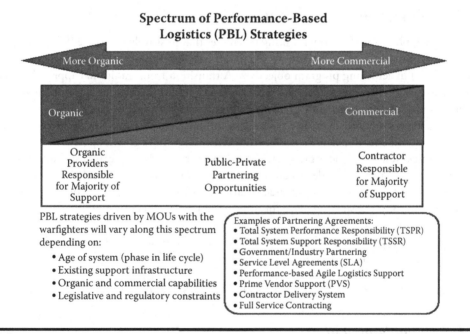

Figure 7.30   Spectrum of PBL strategies.

DoD policy requires that sustainment strategies include the best use of public and private sector capabilities through government-industry partnering initiatives in accordance with statutory requirements. An effective support strategy considers best competencies and partnering opportunities, as shown in Figure 7.30. To this end, a workload allocation/sourcing plan identifies what

Table 7.14 Workload Allocation Sourcing Template for the V-22

Sustainment Function	Product Support Provider/Source						
	Organic O-Level	Organic I-Level	Local	Organic Depot	Depot	Program Office	Other

is best for each support function in terms of capability, skills, infrastructure, opportunities for partnering, compliance with Title 10, public/private flexibility, and affordability.

The workload allocation/sourcing template (Table 7.14) describes the current V-22 logistics PBL strategy.

Candidates for PBL are identified in two contexts: (1) which systems, subsystems, and components will be coded for application of PBL, and (2) which subsystems and components should be the focus for near-term improvement initiatives. The V-22 program will use the coding that was shown in Table 7.3 to identify the PBL application strategy. The program will periodically review the PBL strategy to identify near-term initiatives to improve systems readiness, reduce cost of ownership, and reduce the deployed logistics footprint. The opportunity index column will identify candidates with the greatest potential for improving system performance in satisfying warfighter requirements.

7.3.5 Performance-Based Incentives

The effective application of contract tasking incentives that positively influence the service providers is essential to a successful PBL program. Not all past applications of contract incentives have been successful in achieving program objectives. A transition from traditional approaches to contracting and tasking to performance-based contracting and tasking requires cultural change, open collaborative communications, and a balanced approach to risks and rewards.

Focus groups made up of private sector and military logistics services providers should be formed to establish a set of performance-based incentives with the greatest potential for achieving successful outcomes. These focus groups will need to leverage recent research, studies, experience, and guidance documents in order to structure a set of incentives that result in achievement of objectives, rather than problematic provider relationships and undesired provider behavior. These two sources can form the starting place for information by the focus groups:

- "Constructing Successful Business Relationships: Innovation in Contractual Incentives," report on a major government and industry study (Science Applications International Corporation 1995)
- The DoD "Users Guide to Performance Based Payments" (DoD 2001)

7.3.6 PBL Implementation

The V-22 program-level PBL project is being implemented in four phases:

- *Phase A, the pre-PBL project phase, pre-CY 2004*: Supportability analysis conducted, including maintenance planning, supply support planning, and planning for other logistics elements, all based on the last-generation Marine Corps supportability doctrine.

■ *Phase B1, the comprehensive planning and analysis phase, CY 2004*: During 2004, the PM tasked the PBL IPT to create this plan and perform analysis described in this it. Several rounds of analysis, planning, and coordination are to be performed.

■ *Phase B2, the initial/pilot baseline definition phase, 2004–2007*: Initial PBL type contracts and funded tasking documents were awarded. Initial performance measurements will establish baseline points of reference based on actual operations and maintenance at the first operational fleet units. Ongoing performance assessments and annual formal performance reviews will result in a solid framework of expectations on the part of all stakeholders during this phase. During this phase adjustments to the maintenance concept and mix of organic and industry support service providers will be evolving.

■ *Phase C, the full program execution phase, 2007–2035*: Just before the first fleet deployments, and just before standing up second and third operational sites on the West Coast, the program will be ready to roll out a mature PBL support environment. Support provider assignments will be made based on the first 5 years of real-world experience. The performance measurement framework of measures and metrics will have been refined. The performance reporting via the digital data environment will have been adjusted to provide a mature information sharing capability. By the time 120 aircraft (one-fourth of anticipated production) have been delivered, the V-22 support concept will be leading the way in executing the USMC vision described in the strategic planning documents.

7.3.7 Regular Performance Monitoring and Feedback

Performance metrics will be reported regularly, along with recommendations for improving achievement of desired end states. Monthly reports will be made available via established digital data and information sharing networks. The PBL IPT will establish an analysis capability and ensure that reports contain conclusions, recommendations, and tracking of action initiatives. Periodic reviews will be presented to decision forums, such as the maintenance strategy support team (MSST) and others, who are the decision authority for recommendations involving major changes in support resources, such as support equipment, equipment modifications, and facilities. Only decisions concerning changes in sources of support in terms of major contract/tasking assignments will require a formal performance review.

7.3.8 Formal Technical Performance Reviews

Formal technical reviews are a well established part of the systems engineering process. These reviews have been conducted all through the V-22 development phase. Formal performance reviews will utilize the same process, and will be scheduled on a regular basis for the life of the PBL effort. The primary purpose of a *technical review* is to assess if the system design satisfies program requirements as defined in program specifications and other documents, and to determine if issues and corrective actions warrant management and control. The primary purpose of a *performance review* is to assess if goals and objectives of the logistics effort are being achieved by the logistics service providers as specified in contracts and tasking statements, and to make a determination concerning incentive awards and penalties.

7.3.9 Lessons Learned

The application of PBL concepts at the major defense systems level is relatively new. Since the V-22 program is a joint Navy, Marine Corps, and Air Force program, and joint support concepts are being studied, lessons learned from all applicable sources are being considered. Initial lessons learned are:

1. The DoD is moving to greater reliance on the private sector for the logistics support of new weapons systems and major upgrades. DoD has pilot programs under way to test various logistics support reengineering concepts that place greater reliance on the private sector. The Air Force has broader experience with contractor logistics support (CLS) than other services.

2. The CLS concept was providing extremely beneficial results at the CONUS home base of the flying units, but was causing problems for deployed units. Having total contractor support by fully qualified contractor personnel at O- and I-levels was achieving higher readiness at lower cost at the CONUS site. But deployed organic O-level support, concerning availability of qualified Air Force organic capability, was not yielding required readiness and results.

3. During 2001, the V-22 program office contracted to perform a study to identify and analyze different sustainment approaches associated with the wholesale supply system. A study team called the CV-22 Sustainment Alternatives Analysis Team (SAAT) performed a detailed 10-month study effort and produced a final study report in January 2002. The SAAT recommended that four distinct approaches to CV-22 sustainment be evaluated, reflecting support leadership from each of the four key organizations involved with the program: U.S. Air Force (USAF), U.S. Navy (USN), U.S. Special Operations Command (USSOCOM), and Bell-Boeing. In addition, the SAAT asked that they be given the freedom to suggest and evaluate hybrid sustainment alternatives based upon combinations or refinements of the four approaches, if this was indicated by the SAAT's analysis. The SAAT's recommendations were accepted by the Program Manager Air (PMA-275). Since each of the four primary alternatives centered on a specific organization's sustainment approach, the documents to be prepared to describe the approaches were called centric alternative descriptions (CADs). In each case, the sponsoring organizations were asked to include within their CAD a description of how they would recommend CV-22 wholesale support be provided. Each of the sustainment alternatives evaluated could provide satisfactory CV-22 support. However, the SAAT's evaluation identified specific qualitative and quantitative benefits offered by some approaches that need to be considered in the final decision. In accordance with PMA-275's direction, the SAAT results do not include a specific alternative recommendation for how the CV-22 should be supported, but rather provide information and analysis (both qualitative and quantitative) from which a recommendation can be formulated and supported.

4. All six of the concepts considered in this study are viable for the support of the CV-22. The concepts include a range of alternative support strategies and innovative approaches. All of the sponsor organizations will ultimately be involved in the support of the CV-22 to some degree, and all exhibited a broad understanding of CV-22 support considerations. The conduct of the SAAT effort stimulated a great deal of thinking and in-depth planning by all of the sponsors. As a result of this analysis and evaluation, much qualitative and cost information now exists on potential CV-22 sustainment options to support a selection of an approach. If, however, rather than selecting a single approach from among the alternatives presented, PMA-275 elects to blend the approaches by integrating the innovative ideas contained in the different CADs and hybrids into a new hybrid approach, the SAAT analysis will also assist in this activity.

References

Government Computer News. 2005, August. Executive dashboards. http://www.gcn.com/. Retrieved October 25, 2008.

Kaplan, Robert S., and David P. Norton. 1996. *The balanced scorecard—Translating strategy into action.* Boston: Harvard Business School Press.

Mahidhar, Vikram. 2005, September. Designing the Lean enterprise performance measurement system. Master's thesis, Massachusetts Institute of Technology.

Mathaisel, Dennis F. X., Timothy Cathcart, and Mario Agripino. 2005, February. *Sustaining the military enterprise: Architecture for a Lean transformation.* Defense Procurement Analysis Magazine.

National Performance Review (NPR) and Al Gore (VP of the United States). 1997, June. *Serving the American public: Best practices in performance measurement; benchmarking study report.*

Oak Ridge Associated Universities (ORAU). 2001. *The performance-based management handbook—A six volume compilation of tools and techniques for implementing the Government Performance Results Act (GPRA) of 1993.* Performance Based Management Interest Group.

Science Applications International Corporation. 1995. *Constructing successful business relationships: Innovation in contractual incentives.* Under Contract DASW01-95-D-0076, Delivery Order 45. For the deputy assistant secretary of the Army (Procurement). Retrieved from www.acquisition.gov/comp/seven_steps/library/DOAconstructing.pdf.

U.S. Department of Defense (DoD), Office of the Secretary of Defense (OSD). 2001, November. *Users guide to performance based payments.*

U.S. Department of Defense. 2003, May 23. *Supply chain management regulation.* DoD 4140.1-R.

U.S. Department of Defense, OSD. 2004, August 16. *Performance based logistics (PBL) performance criteria.*

U.S. Department of Defense, OSD. 2005, March. *PBL guidebook.*

U.S. Navy, Secretary of the Navy (SECNAV). 2003, January. *Performance based logistics (PBL) guidance document.*

Chapter 8

Capability: Performance Measures

Preface

The Department of Defense (DoD) acquisition guidebook states that "each program Performance Based Logistics (PBL) arrangement is unique and will vary from other PBL arrangements. A PBL arrangement may take many forms. There is no one-size-fits-all approach." The guidebook then gives this limited guidance on the selection of metrics:

> Many existing logistics and financial metrics can be related to top-level Warfighter performance outcomes. These include, but are not limited to, Not Mission Capable Supply (NMCS), ratio of supply chain costs to sales, maintenance Turn-Around-Time (TAT), depot cycle time, and negotiated time definite delivery of spares. While objective metrics form the bulk of the evaluation of a PBL providers performance, some elements of product support requirements might be more appropriately evaluated subjectively by the program management team, [the user, and other stakeholders].

A fundamental issue with performance measures centers on the question of how to define the critical few metrics that should be used to manage a project or enterprise. How many metrics should be included? The short answer is that performance measures should be limited to those that relate or link to strategic organizational goals and objectives, and that provide timely, relevant, and concise information for managers at all levels to assess progress toward achieving these predetermined goals. High-level metrics should be defined for the higher management levels in an enterprise. More detailed metrics should be defined at the operational levels. The number of measures should provide a balanced management approach to ensuring that all strategic organizational goals and objectives get appropriate management visibility.

This chapter provides an extra level of detail on metrics over that in Chapter 7 on performance. This chapter begins by providing a guide for performing a metric analysis of a project. It gives an example set of measures for aircraft maintenance, and it ends with a case study.

8.1 Introduction

The use of performance metrics has the potential to afford numerous benefits beyond simply providing status data. The effective use of metrics is a key feature for a successful project or enterprise. Metrics link processes and measurement. They are intrinsic to quality improvement programs, and they can be used to facilitate quality and continuous process improvement by communicating product, service, and process goals throughout the enterprise. They support risk management through early identification of deviations before major cost or schedule impacts come to pass. Metrics can also improve customer relations and satisfaction by providing insight into the technical solution, cost, and schedule.

World-class Lean enterprises in a wide array of industries are those that have developed and effectively communicated a clear and consistent set of enterprise-wide goals, objectives, and performance metrics that drive their performance at all levels and embracing all activities. Lean enterprises continuously focus on the customer. Goals concisely articulate the central long-term purpose and direction of the enterprise. Objectives define the strategic actionable thrusts for achieving the goals. Metrics represent a cascading set of consistent, repeatable, and valid measures of performance that enable assessment of progress toward the achievement of goals and objectives. Metrics foster understanding and motivate action for continuous improvement, and they facilitate comparative evaluation of performance relative to other enterprises (Massachusetts Institute of Technology 1998).

Performance metrics can be both qualitative and quantitative. They are expected to be more quantitative at finer levels of organizational or functional granularity. They must also be accompanied by a clear and complete set of planning assumptions, including the most likely anticipated future environment as well as constraints (e.g., physical, human, budgetary, technological). In the most effective organizations, the goals, objectives, and metrics are few in number and are clearly traceable from the top down. All stakeholders, ranging from their suppliers to their shop floor workers, know them and understand how their individual efforts contribute to the overall enterprise goals. They must also be sufficiently stable over time in order to induce the desired behavioral response and adaptation throughout the value stream. Conflicts must be eliminated, any variations explained, and subsequent changes must be effectively communicated to remove any appearance of inconsistency. Metrics, however defined and measured, will affect actions and decisions. Choosing the right metrics is critical to the overall success of an enterprise, but the challenge of developing good metrics is fraught with many pitfalls. To avoid these pitfalls, metrics, in short, should be directly tied to the organization's overall goals. They should be simple and easily understood as well as logical. They should be unambiguously defined, measurable, and should drive appropriate individual, team, or group behavior (Massachusetts Institute of Technology 1998).

8.1.1 The Selection of Performance Measures

Good performance metrics provide an indication of how well project and organizational goals and objectives are being met through processes and tasks, and they should provide the customer with the needed understanding of the project status. They should be simple, logical, understandable, unambiguous, and repeatable. The data for these metrics should be timely and economical to collect, analyze, and report. To be effective, the metrics must show trends, not just data, for a single point in time, and they should facilitate taking timely remedial actions. Some key factors in the selection of good performance metrics are:

- The assessment of the primary management and technical goals and objectives
- The identification of metrics that align with these goals and objectives
- A determination of the availability of data and personnel
- Tools to create the data needed to generate these metrics

8.1.2 Metric Frameworks

There are several frameworks that can be used for the development of good metrics that align organizational success and customer satisfaction. These frameworks include: quality function deployment; goal, question, metric; and Rome Laboratory Software Quality Framework.*

As described by Dr. Yoji Akao (1990), quality function deployment (QFD) is a "method to transform user demands into design quality, to deploy the functions forming quality, and to deploy methods for achieving the design quality into subsystems and component parts, and ultimately to specific elements of the manufacturing process."[†] Dr. Akao developed QFD in Japan in 1966, combining his work in quality assurance and quality control with function deployment that is used in value engineering. QFD uses graphs and matrices to help planners focus on the characteristics of a product or service from the viewpoints of market segments, company, or technology-development needs. QFD transforms customer needs into engineering characteristics and the appropriate test methods for a product or service. It prioritizes each product or service characteristic while simultaneously setting development targets.[‡]

Goal, question, metric (GQM) is an approach to software metrics that was developed by Victor Basili et al. (1994) of the University of Maryland, College Park, and the Software Engineering Laboratory at the NASA Goddard Space Flight Center. GQM defines a measurement on three levels:

1. Conceptual level (goal). A goal is defined for an object for a variety of reasons, with respect to various models of quality, from various points of view, and relative to a particular environment.
2. Operational level (question). A set of questions is used to define models of the object of study, and then it focuses on that object to characterize the assessment or achievement of a specific goal.
3. Quantitative level (metric). A set of metrics, based on the models, is associated with every question in order to answer it in a measurable way.

GQM is described in terms of a six-step process where the first three steps are about using business goals to drive the identification of the right metrics, and the last three steps are about

---

* Source: Wikipedia, retrieved November 1, 2008.

† Akao, Yoji, Development History of Quality Function Deployment, The Customer Driven Approach to Quality Planning and Deployment (Minato, Tokyo, Asian Productivity Organization, 1994), 339.

‡ Source: Wikipedia, retrieved November 1, 2008.

gathering the measurement data and making effective use of the measurement results to drive decision making and improvements. Basili described his six-step GQM process:

1. Develop a set of corporate, division, and project business goals and associated measurement goals for productivity and quality.
2. Generate questions (based on models) that define those goals as completely as possible in a quantifiable way.
3. Specify the measures needed to be collected to answer those questions and track process and product conformance to the goals.
4. Develop mechanisms for data collection.
5. Collect, validate, and analyze the data in real time to provide feedback to projects for corrective action.
6. Analyze the data in a postmortem fashion to assess conformance to the goals and to make recommendations for future improvements.

8.1.2.1 Rome Laboratory Software Quality Framework

Rome Laboratory (1985) at the U.S Air Force Materiel Command has been at the forefront of exploration and development techniques designed to improve software management with tools useful in improving the control and cost of software system development. Rome Laboratory has been working in the area of software quality since the earlier 1970s. The goal of the framework was to provide program managers a quantitative method for gaining insight into the quality of their software products (i.e., software requirements specification, preliminary design, detailed design, coding). The Rome Laboratory Software Quality Framework (RLSQF) is a three-tiered approach that associates a set of user-oriented software quality characteristics (quality factors) with their defining attributes (criterion), and these attributes, in turn, with measurable development activities (elements) at the lowest level. RLSQF contains a set of suggested data collection formats, procedures for beginning a metric program, and methods for selecting and training the measurement team.

8.1.3 Collection of Measurement Data

Metrics collection may be required by the customer, by a higher level organization, or at the discretion of project personnel. In any case, a plan for the collection of metrics should be developed. However, collection of metrics should not be constrained by the plan, if personnel responsible for the project determine conditions warrant additional metrics collection. The plan may be formal or informal, and it may be stand-alone or part of a larger document, such as the Systems Engineering Management Plan or Project Management Plan. The plan should contain the objectives, metrics definition, responsibilities, and timescales. The plan may also include references, support material, and a logbook for measurement activities.

The metrics collection activities start with identification of the input data required and the source of that data: typically the person or team that carries out the activity or produces the product/service being measured. Next, a coordination meeting should be held with involved personnel to work out logistics, schedules, and other issues. Then raw data can be collected according to the planned schedule or at additional times as required. The collection schedule should minimize disruption of the project, but data collection must be frequent enough to indicate meaningful changes in status and allow remedial action to take place in time to avoid major problems. Metric templates should be used to standardize and simplify this collection process. Typical components of these templates include project and metric identification and related information, source of raw data, collection times and responsibilities, tools, usage, reporting method, need-to-know personnel, and storage information.

After the data have been collected, it should be verified and entered into a database, spreadsheet, or chart for analysis and periodic reporting. These data should be retained as part of the project records.

8.1.4 Analysis of Measurement Data

Raw measurement data must be transformed into usable metrics and analyzed in a timely manner. Typically, the raw data must be converted to metrics though computation, normalization, or comparison with prior data. For example, estimated completion date can be converted into a schedule variance or cost to date into a budget variance. This process should be automated to reduce the level of effort to generate the metrics and for expediency.

After the metrics have been created, they must be compared with previous metrics, extrapolated, and interpreted. Metrics that fall outside acceptable limits or show unacceptable trends can then be used to determine the source of the problem and appropriate remedial actions.

8.1.5 Reporting of Measurement Information

To obtain the maximum benefit from metrics, it is necessary to effectively communicate the information provided by them in a timely fashion. The reporting of the metrics should be easy to understand and unambiguous. Graphical representation provides the best form of communication for these data through the use of histograms, line graphs, and control charts. Useful information from the data should be distributed as rapidly as possible to the personnel or teams that can benefit from taking action based on those data. This can be accomplished through the use of briefings, bulletin boards, or online posting.

8.2 General Performance Measures

Each project must establish a minimum set of metrics that provides the greatest cost-benefit for that project, taking into account any contract requirements. They must provide product and process insight, which permits rapid response to problems and drives appropriate corrective actions.

The International Council on Systems Engineering (INCOSE) provides a metrics guidebook.* The purpose of the guidebook for Integrated Systems and Product Development is threefold: (1) capture the experience represented in the INCOSE Metrics Working Groups, both local and national, where successful measurement programs have been implemented; (2) support groups establishing new metrics programs; and (3) open a dialog within the engineering community on relevant measurement in a systems or integrated product development (IPD) environment. The guidebook divides systems engineering metrics into three types: planning and control metrics, engineering process and quality metrics, and technical performance measures. Planning and control metrics are used to create the project plan based on the key measurable components of the

---

* Source: http://www.incose.org/ProductsPubs/products/metricsguidebook.aspx, retrieved November 1, 2008.

activities to be performed. Process and quality metrics are used to determine how well the work activities are being performed and the acceptability of the resulting products or services. Technical performance measurements provide information on whether the product or service can meet its technology-based criteria. Examples are:

1. Planning and control metrics:
   a. Budget variance: How many dollars or man-hours expended vs. project plan?
   b. Schedule variance: When will the task be completed vs. the project plan?
   c. Personnel variance: What staffing categories are used vs. project plan?
   d. Systems engineering personnel variance: How many systems engineering personnel are actually working on the project vs. the plan?
2. Process and quality metrics:
   a. Requirements volatility: How many requirements have changed vs. time?
   b. Design volatility: How many design changes have been approved vs. time?
   c. Test defects: How many defects have been detected by project and customer test personnel?
   d. Requirements defects: How many requirement defects (valid problems) have been detected by peer reviews of the requirements?
   e. Plans and procedures: What plans and procedures are being used vs. adopted process?
3. Technical performance measures:
   a. Response time: What is the system response time vs. planned or required response time?
   b. Critical resource utilization: How much of the critical systems resource is utilized during normal and peak operations (e.g., CPU, memory, DASD, bandwidth, weight, size, and power, as appropriate for the system, subsystem, or product)?
   c. System availability: When is the system available for full operation?

The selection of candidate metrics should begin with questions related to the what, how, and when of the project's processes, products, and services.

The following metrics were the most frequently used by Fortune 500 companies in their performance management systems, as reported by the Government Procurement Executives' Association.*

1. *Percent of customers satisfied with timeliness*: This measure captures the customer's degree of satisfaction with the timeliness of the delivery of products or services and other factors affecting the acquisition schedule. The timeliness category may include an assessment of the following:
   a. Are products and services delivered when needed?
   b. Are milestones consistently met?
   c. Is planning performed early in the acquisition process?
   d. Is communication consistent and effective?
   e. Does the acquisition office do a good job in preventing problems that may lead to delays?

---

* Government Procurement Executives' Association, Guide to a Balanced Scorecard Performance Management Methodology. Moving from Performance Measurement to Performance Management (1999), retrieved from http://management.energy.gov/documents/BalancedScorecardPerfAndMeth.pdf on November 26, 2008.

Data for this measure come from a customer survey.

2. *Percent of customers satisfied with quality*: This metric measures the customer's satisfaction with the quality of goods and services delivered. Quality also includes an assessment of whether or not contractors selected for awards offer the best combination of quality and price. Data for this measure come from a customer survey.

3. *Percent of customers satisfied with the responsiveness, cooperation, and communication skills of the acquisition office*: The perceptions, choices, and behavior of all participants in the acquisition process affect the outcome of any acquisition. This measure is based upon the degree of responsiveness of the acquisition team, the success of mechanisms that support teaming, and the degree of satisfaction with communications and problem solving. Data for this measure come from a customer survey.

4. *Cost-to-spend ratio*: This metric represents the cost for each office to spend one dollar of their customers' funds. This metric is calculated by dividing the operating cost of each office by the total obligations of that office. The amount for total obligations is taken from the Federal Procurement Data System (FPDS) feeder system. The cost of operating each office includes salaries, benefits, training, travel, information technology, and contractor support. It is recognized that these elements of cost may not capture the entire cost of the acquisition system, but the decision was made not to attempt to quantify the costs of developing statements of work, conducting inspections, and making payments. In addition, due to the variation in acquisition system organizational structures across the federal agencies, the result of this cost-to-spend measure may not be directly comparable, one agency to another. Cost-to-spend measurements should be looked at as only one of the indicators of the current status of the acquisition system's efficiency. The most important focus should be on improvements themselves. Benchmarking across, and outside of, federal agencies can provide avenues of inquiry for identifying best practices for possible adoption, and should also be one of the techniques used to facilitate performance improvement.

5. *Cost avoidance through the use of purchase cards*: This measure represents the number of purchase card transactions multiplied by the estimated costs avoided by using purchase cards vs. issuing a purchase order. Data for this measure may be extracted from data reported to the General Services Administration Federal Supply Service.

6. *Percent of prompt payment interest paid of total money disbursed*: This element represents the amount of interest penalties paid as a percentage of total disbursements by the agency. This element is calculated by taking the total interest penalties paid by each office divided by the amount of total disbursements paid. Data for this measure may be extracted from the U.S. Treasury's annual prompt pay report, or from local financial systems.

7. *Ratio of protests sustained by General Accounting Office (GAO) and the Court of Federal Claims (COFC)*: This measure captures the ratio of protests upheld by the GAO or COFC. For this measure, protest is defined as a written objection by a vendor concerning an acquisition.

8. *Number of actions using electronic commerce*: This metric represents the total number of acquisition actions through use of electronic commerce required by the Office of Management and Budget (OMB) to be reported quarterly to the General Services Administration vs. total number of award actions.

9. *Percent achievement of socioeconomic goals*: This measure tracks each agency's achievement of the socioeconomic goals established for the agency. This element will comprise several separate measures. For each defined category, the agency's achievements for that category, as reported to the Small Business Administration, are divided by the goal established for that category. The

individual measures for the categories are not averaged together. Data for this measure may be extracted from the files of the local Office of Small and Disadvantaged Business Utilization.

10. *Extent of reliable management information*: This measure captures the extent to which the managers of the procuring activities believe they have timely, accurate, and complete information to make management decisions. The measurement information will come from an appropriate survey instrument.

11. *Percent of employees meeting mandatory qualification standards*: This measure identifies the percentage of acquisition employees that meet the mandatory education, training, and experience requirements as identified in the Office of Personnel Management Contract Specialist Qualification Standards. It will be calculated by dividing the number of acquisition employees that meet the education, training, and experience requirements by the total number of acquisition employees in the organization. Data will be derived from the local Acquisition Career Development data system.

12. *Percent of employees satisfied with the work environment*: In order to retain high-quality acquisition professionals, and enhance worker performance, the work environment must be pleasant and include the necessary resources for accomplishment of work. This measure represents the employees' degree of satisfaction with items such as tools provided (e.g., information technology, reference material, etc.), working conditions, and reward mechanisms. Data for this measure come from an employee survey.

13. *Percent of employees satisfied with the professionalism, culture, values, and empowerment*: Management plays a vital role in the operation of each acquisition team by directing, motivating, and leading their personnel. Acquisition leadership should foster a professional environment that promotes the efficient and effective acquisition of goods and services from responsible contractors. This measure includes an assessment of the employee perception of organizational professionalism, culture, values, and empowerment. Data for this measure come from an employee survey.

8.3 Lean Measures

World-class Lean enterprises in a wide array of industries have developed and effectively communicated a clear and consistent set of enterprise-wide metrics driving their performance at all levels and embracing all activities, ranging from product development to customer support. Lean companies take a value stream (extended enterprise) view of their operations, embracing all of their support activities and suppliers, adding value to their end products, focused on satisfying their customers. Lean metrics represent a cascading set of consistent, repeatable, and valid measures of performance that enable assessment of progress toward the achievement of goals and objectives, foster understanding and motivate action for continuous improvement, and facilitate comparative evaluation of performance relative to other enterprises.

Vikram Mahidhar (2005) investigated key aspects of a Lean enterprise performance measurement system. Mahidhar recognized that the balanced scorecard (BSC) is currently the most widely used performance measurement framework, but he discounted it as a useful framework for a Lean enterprise. Mahidhar's observation was that the BSC restricts performance measurement to four predetermined buckets (perspectives). He pointed out that a number of measures concerning suppliers and employees were excluded from the four traditional BSC perspective areas. He quoted other similar research that also concluded that the four traditional BSC perspective areas restricted the inclusion of all needed measures into the four perspective categories.

This is a common misconception. Many researchers find that many applications of the BSC are implemented without any attempt to tailor the framework. Tailoring the framework to fit the strategic objectives of the organization is an essential step.

The following metrics were the most frequently used in presentations by organizations reporting on Lean success stories:

1. Reduction in cycle/wait time (most used measure by far)
2. Reduction in unit/product cost
3. Reduction in rework (first-pass yield)
4. On-time delivery
5. Process step reduction
6. Reduction in number of process hand-offs
7. Reduction of approvals/signatures
8. Reduction of process-related forms and paper
9. Co-location of process participants
10. Footprint reduction (floor space, transportation, inventory)

8.3.1 Lean Enterprise Measures

1. Order to delivery time
2. Product development cycle time
3. Workforce output
4. Inventory turns
5. Scrap or rework rate
6. Design changes (by project phase)

8.3.2 Enterprise Flow-Related Measures

1. Flow efficiency—actual work time divided by total flow/work time
2. Throughput
3. Order to point of use delivery cycle time
4. Total product design (PD) cycle time
5. Models established for evaluating flow processes
6. Flow paths reduction
7. Inventory reduction
8. Setup time reduction
9. Process owner inspections—throughout the value chain
10. Single piece flow—number or percentage
11. Space reduction
12. Travel distance reduction
13. Production and delivery synchronization
14. Unplanned flow stoppage due to need for equipment maintenance

8.3.3 Information Flow-Related Measures

1. Commonality of databases
2. Information retrieval time

3. Sharable information—supplier to customer
4. Visibility of process flow
5. Minimize amount of documentation, while ensuring information availability

8.3.4 Lean Leadership-Related Measures

1. Metric use/sharing at all levels of the enterprise
2. Metric flow-down and linkages to enterprise strategic objectives
3. Individual use of metrics and linkage to enterprise objectives
4. Total enterprise involvement in achieving strategic objectives and metrics
5. Involvement of workforce representatives, to include unions, in enterprise strategy

8.3.5 Other Lean-Related Measures

1. Lead time: The time it takes one piece to move all the way through a process or a value stream from start to finish. Envision timing a marked part as it moves from beginning to end.
2. Value-added time: Time of those work elements that actually transform the product in a way that the customer is willing to pay for.
3. Cycle time: How often a process, as timed by observation, actually completes a part or product. Also, the time it takes an operator to go through all of his or her work elements before repeating them.
4. Defect rate: A defect should never be passed to the next process. Do we know what creates a defect in the eyes of our customers? How many potential defects can be created on our product?
5. Distance moved: This metric focuses on the waste of transportation.
6. Space used: Focusing on reducing space eliminates transport waste and reduces handling and cost.
7. Setup times: A lower setup time allows more changeovers and increases the ability to reduce batch sizes and mix production.
8. Inventory levels or turns: This metric is a good overall picture of the reduction in overproduction.
9. Cost per piece: A decreasing trend shows that waste is being eliminated. Some companies use labor hours per piece (e.g., labor hours used to assemble a car). Make sure that this measurement spans the value stream and considers overhead allocation. We don't want to improve the cost per price in one small section of the value stream while dramatically driving it upwards in another for an overall negative impact.
10. Number of suggestions: This measure is an indicator of how much the employees are involved in improvements. Some companies also track how many suggestions were actually implemented, and sometimes the time taken to respond to the suggestions.

8.4 Process Improvement Measures

8.4.1 Common Process Improvement Measures

1. Structured process change tools established
2. Process analysis capability established

3. Data-driven process assessment capability established
4. Process improvement targets established
5. Number of repeat problems with a process

8.4.2 Organizational Design Measures

1. Number of organizational levels/layers
2. Number of levels of approval required for program/product decisions
3. Number of processes that enable decisions at the lowest practical level of the organization
4. Number of processs that expedite decision making

8.4.3 Process Development-Related Measures

1. Number of critical enterprise processes documented
2. Percent of critical enterprise processes documented
3. Number of enterprises in a digital/sharable process asset library (PAL)
4. Percent of enterprises in a digital/sharable process asset library (PAL)
5. Process architecture has capability for growth
6. Enterprise processes are tailored and utilized by product teams
7. Project/product teams document both product and process requirements

8.4.4 Process Capability Maturity-Related Measures

1. Number of Lean practices adopted in the enterprise
2. Number of suppliers certified
3. Scrap/rework/repair as percent of cost
4. Percent of enterprise processes defined and documented
5. Amount of cost/waste reduced in enterprise processes

8.4.5 Relationship Development-Related Measures

1. Number of projects with customers on strategy-related IPTs
2. Number of years in supplier-customer relationships
3. Percent of procurement dollars spent under long-term supplier relationships
4. Number of strategic alliance type suppliers vs. the total number of direct suppliers
5. Satisfaction with stable relationships
6. Number of labor-management partner relationships
7. Workforce employment stability
8. Stakeholder satisfaction with long-term relationships

8.4.6 Customer Focus-Related Measures

1. On-time delivery of product and support from source to point of delivery
2. Customer participation on IPTs
3. Customer access to supplier information
4. Stakeholder access to product/process flow information

5. Flexible reaction to changing requirements
6. Customer relationship management—in areas of requirements, product design, and product value

8.4.7 Enterprise Stability-Related Measures

1. Number of program schedule changes per assessment period
2. Number of organizational restructures per assessment period
3. Changes in product purchase quantities
4. Turnover in project personnel/management
5. Percent of changes that are planned and scheduled—vs. unplanned changes
6. Number of products where demand justifies/enables continuous flow
7. Percent of contracts that are multiyear
8. Number of cycle-time changes resulting from externally imposed changes
9. Program structures able to react/absorb changes
10. Program risk areas planned in noncritical flow path

8.4.8 Workforce Capability- and Utilization-Related Measures

1. Training hours per employee
2. Training budget as percent of enterprise budget
3. Output per employee
4. Skills development programs—applicable to skill categories
5. Skills certification—number/percent of personnel certified in critical skills
6. Skills requirements vs. skills inventory
7. Workforce skills broadening—skills-broadening assignments

8.4.9 Learning Environment-Related Measures

1. Number of benchmarking events documented during the period of assessment
2. Number of knowledge-sharing events performed during the assessment period
3. Experience/lessons learned sharing environment/system established
4. Number of supplier training programs conducted
5. Percent of workforce time spent in development/learning activities

8.5 Sustainability and Supportability Performance Measures

Sustainability and supportability are integral to the success of a system and will be considered equal in importance with cost, schedule, and performance. Some measures may be more applicable during the development, deployment, or support periods of the program life cycle. Some measures will apply to specific work centers. Provided below are examples of supportability-related measures of performance for each element of integrated logistics support (ILS). These metrics can be used to provide a quantitative means of ensuring the attainment of supportability goals for acquisition end items. There is no implication that any of these metrics are mandatory. Supportability metrics must be tailored for each individual acquisition program and for individual work centers in the sustainment organizations.

8.5.1 Readiness and Flying Hour Measures

1. *Primary aircraft inventory (PAI)*: This inventory represents aircraft available for flight. It can be a number of assigned aircraft minus backup aircraft inventory (BAI). A low PAI possessed forces a higher operating tempo on fewer aircraft.

2. *Backup aircraft inventory (BAI)*: Backup aircraft inventory shows the number of aircraft above primary mission inventory that permit scheduled and unscheduled maintenance, modifications, inspections, and sort time repair of aircraft without reduction of aircraft available for operational missions.

3. *Number of flying hours*: This metric is the total number of flying hours for the reporting period (week, month, quarter, year).

4. *Number of sorties flown*: This metric is the total number of sorties for the reporting period (week, month, quarter, year).

5. *Average sortie duration (ASD)*: This measure is the average time an aircraft stays airborne during an individual sortie. The computation is straightforward: total hours flown divided by total sorties flown.

6. *Total abort rate (leading)*: A unit's abort rate can be an indicator of both aircraft reliability and quality of maintenance performed. The Mobility Air Forces tracks material and non-material aborts through the Global Decision Support System and Air Mobility Command's History System via diversion codes *J* and *K*. A *J* divert is an abort due to an aircraft system malfunction, while a *K* divert is for nonmaterial reasons. Examine the abort rate in relation to system malfunctions. Look for trends, root causes, and lasting corrective actions. The focus should be on preventing as many aborts as possible. Adding a preventable or not preventable indicator on the chargeable deviations slide focuses attention on prevention. A high abort rate will drive the flying schedule effectiveness rate down. An air abort is really an operations call. Not all airborne malfunctions, however, result in an air abort. If an alternate mission is flown, then it's not an air abort. If there are a lot of air aborts, talk with operations. It may simply be a misunderstanding of the rules.

$$Air\ Aborts\ (J\ Diverts) + \frac{Local\ Training\ Aborts + Ground\ Aborts}{Total\ Sorties\ Attempted}(100)$$

$$Total\ Sorties\ Attempted = Sorties\ Flown + Ground\ Aborts \qquad (8.1)$$

7. *Mean flight hours between aborts*: The mean time in hours between events that render the aircraft incapable of performing its mission.

8. *Mean flight hours between failures—logistics*: A measure of system reliability related to demand for logistics support. For example, a system with redundant subsystems can have a failure but complete the mission. Even though there was no abort or mission failure, there is a demand for repairing the failure at the end of the mission.

9. *Fully-mission-capable (FMC) rate (lagging)*: Compare the FMC rate with the monthly mission-capable rate. A significant difference between the two indicates aircraft are flying with key systems partially inoperative and cannot perform all the designed operational capability statement missions. A low FMC rate may indicate a persistent parts-supportability problem.

$$\frac{FMC\ Hours}{Possessed\ Hours}(100)$$

$$Possessed\ Hours = 720\ hours\ (hours\ per\ month) \tag{8.2}$$

10. *Partially-mission-capable (PMC) rate*: An aircraft may be partially mission capable for either parts or maintenance, and the status indicates that the aircraft cannot perform all assigned missions. Good maintenance practice dictates all malfunctions be fixed as soon as possible, whether or not it's convenient.

$$\frac{PMCB\ Hours + PMCM\ Hours + PMCS\ Hours}{Possessed\ Hours}(100) \tag{8.3}$$

11. *Mission-capable (MC) rate (lagging)*: The time that an aircraft is up and ready to perform a mission. This metric is the sum of fully-mission-capable hours and partially-mission-capable hours. The MC rate is perhaps the best-known yardstick for measuring a unit's performance. This rate is very much a composite metric. That is, it is a broad indicator of many processes and metrics. A low MC rate may indicate a unit is experiencing many hard (long-fix) breaks that don't allow them to turn an aircraft for many hours or several days. It may also indicate serious parts supportability issues, poor job prioritization, lack of qualified technicians, or poor sense of urgency. The key here is to focus on the negative trends and top system problems that lower the MC rate.

$$\frac{FMC\ Hours + PMCB\ Hours + PMCM\ Hours + PMCS\ Hours}{Possessed\ Hours}(100) \tag{8.4}$$

12. *Operational reliability*: The measure (percent) of aircraft meeting mission success, meaning "mission complete." Depending on the aircraft type, mission complete may be equal to the destination reached or cargo/personnel delivered.

8.5.2 Maintenance Measures

1. *Total not-mission-capable maintenance (TNMCM) rate (lagging)*: Maintenance is responsible for keeping the TNMCM rate under control by fixing aircraft quickly and accurately. Prioritization of jobs, good workload distribution, adequate facilities, and robust coordination between the maintenance operations center, flight line, and intermediate-level/back shops are crucial to minimizing downtime. Look for a relationship between the report recovery, break, and fix rates to not-mission-capable maintenance (NMCM). A strong correlation could indicate heavy workloads (people are overtasked), poor management, training problems, or poor maintenance practices. Usually, if the TNMCM rate is too high, these other rates also indicate problems. The key is to be alert. When one is bad, automatically look at the others.

$$\frac{NMCM\ Hours + NMCB\ Hours}{Possessed\ Hours}(100) \tag{8.5}$$

2. *Total not-mission-capable supply (TNMCS) rate (lagging)*: TNMCS is driven principally by spare parts availability. However, maintenance can keep the rate lower by consolidating feasible cannibalizations (CANNs) to as few aircraft as practical. TNMCS is based on the number of airframes out for parts, instead of the number of parts that are mission capable (MICAP). It does not take long to see the link between the CANN rate and the TNMCS rate. The best situation is for both rates to be as low as possible. Another word of caution: TNMCS should not be held low at the expense of increased CANN actions. Maintenance should not be driven to make undesirable CANNs (those that may be labor-intensive or risk damaging the good part) just to keep the TNMCS rate low. Maintainers will let leaders know what they think if pressed to CANN a part that's not feasible just to consolidate all MICAPs on one aircraft. An easy mistake is just looking at the few components eating up huge chunks of time. Usually these are hard-to-obtain items across the Air Force or involve heavy maintenance. They are obvious, but little can be done about them. Try focusing on the items getting a lot of hits. They may be easy to get, but why are so many being ordered? Is the base stockage level high enough? Is there a trend or reason why so many need to be ordered in the first place? Another facet is the amount of time lost due to parts in transit. Are the parts easy to procure but sitting on pallets at some port? Are the folks on base getting the old parts turned in? Could the part be fixed on base, even though the current guidance says send it back to the depot? Can the status quo be challenged?

$$\frac{NMCS\ Hours + NMCB\ Hours}{Possessed\ Hours}(100) \tag{8.6}$$

3. *Repeat/recurring (R/R) rate (leading)*: R/R is perhaps the most important and accurate measure of the quality of maintenance performed in a unit. A repeat discrepancy is one occurring on the same system or subsystem on the first sortie or sortie attempt after originally reported. A recurring discrepancy occurs on the second through fourth sorties or attempted sortie after the original occurrence. A unit's goal should be no R/R. A high R/R rate may indicate lack of thorough troubleshooting, inordinate pressure to commit aircraft to the flying schedule for subsequent sorties, or a lack of experienced, qualified, or trained technicians. Examine each R/R discrepancy and seek root causes and lasting fixes.

$$\frac{Total\ Repeats + Total\ Recurs}{Total\ Pilot\ Reported\ Discrepancies}(100) \tag{8.7}$$

4. *Cannibalization (CANN) rate (lagging)*: The CANN rate is the average number of CANN actions per one hundred sorties flown. A CANN action is the removal of a serviceable part from an aircraft or engine to replace an unserviceable part on another aircraft or engine, or removal of a serviceable part to put into a readiness spares package for deployments. This rate includes all aircraft-to-aircraft and engine-to-aircraft CANN actions.

The measurement is used in conjunction with the supply issue effectiveness rate. In most cases, a CANN action takes place when base supply cannot deliver the part when needed and mission requirements demand the aircraft be returned to an MC status. Since supply relies on the depot for replenishment, this indicator can also be used, in part, to indicate depot support.

$$\frac{Number\ of\ Aircraft\text{-}to\text{-}Aircraft\ CANNs + Number\ of\ Engine\text{-}to\text{-}Aircraft\ CANNs}{Total\ Sorties\ Flown}(100)$$

(8.8)

5. *Average repair cycle time by segments (buckets of time)*: This metric is a more detailed look at the total repair cycle days. The total repair cycle is broken into three segments:
   a. Pre: The time a serviceable part is issued from supply until the broken part is received by the back shop for repair.
   b. Repair: The time a part remains in the shop until repaired, minus time spent awaiting parts (AWP).
   c. Post: The time it takes for the repaired part to be turned back into supply.

The sum of the three steps above equals the total repair cycle time. It measures the efficiency of the three major steps in a unit's repair cycle.

$$Pre\text{-}Maintenance\ Time = \frac{Total\ Number\ of\ Days\ in\ Pre\text{-}Maintenance}{Total\ Number\ of\ Items\ Repaired}$$

$$Repair\ Time = \frac{Total\ Number\ of\ Days\ in\ Repair - AWP\ Days}{Total\ Number\ of\ Items\ Repaired}$$

$$Post\text{-}Maintenance\ Time = \frac{Total\ Number\ of\ Days\ in\ Post\text{-}Maintenance}{Total\ Number\ of\ Items\ Repaired}$$

$$Total\ Repair\ Cycle\ Time = Pre\text{-}Maintenance\ Time + Repair\ Time + Post\text{-}Maintenance\ Time$$

$$\frac{Total\ Repair\ Cycle\ Time - Awaiting\ Parts\ Days}{Number\ of\ Items\ Turned\ In}$$

(8.9)

6. *Mean time to repair (MTTR)*: MTTR is a basic measure of maintainability. It is the sum of corrective maintenance times divided by the total number of failures within a particular

measurement interval under stated conditions. The measurement interval can be units of time, miles, rounds, cycles, or some other measure of life units.

$$MTTR = \frac{\text{Sum of Corrective Maintenance Times}}{\text{Number of Failures}} \qquad (8.10)$$

7. *Mean repair time—abort (MRT-A)*: Same as MTTR, but focused on systems and equipment that cause mission aborts. This focuses the basic measure on warfighter mission success. Calculated like above, but divide by the number of failures causing aborts.

$$MRT\text{-}A = \frac{\text{Sum of Corrective Maintenance Times}}{\text{Number of Failures Causing Aborts}} \qquad (8.11)$$

8. *Mean time to perform scheduled (periodic) maintenance*: This metric is a measure of the elapsed time from the start of scheduled maintenance from when the system is not ready for use to the time the system is restored to its operational state.

$$\frac{\text{Sum of Scheduled Maintenance Times}}{\text{Number of Scheduled Maintenance Actions}} \qquad (8.12)$$

9. *Mean time to repair by echelon*: A basic measure of maintainability. The sum of corrective maintenance times at any specific level or echelon of repair, such as depot level or intermediate level, divided by the total number of failures within an item repaired at the level during a particular interval under stated conditions. This measure is directly related to the number (and cost) of spares needed for the pipeline to support MC date of weapon systems. Drills down to each type of spare universal needs statement (UNS).

$$\frac{\text{Sum of Corrective Maintenance Times at an Echelon Location}}{\text{Number of Maintenance Actions at an Echelon Location}} \qquad (8.13)$$

10. *Mean active maintenance downtime (MAMDT)*: MAMDT is the statistical mean of the individual elapsed times for all maintenance tasks during a specified period of time (clock hours). The MAMDT is the weighted average of the mean time to repair (MTTR) and mean preventive maintenance action time (MTPM). When the number of corrective maintenance actions (NC) and the number of preventive maintenance actions (NP) have been determined for a common reference item, the following formula may be used:

$$\text{MAMDT} = \frac{(\text{MTTR} \times \text{NC}) + (\text{MTPM} \times \text{NP})}{\text{NC} + \text{NP}} \qquad (8.14)$$

11. *Mean restoration time*: A mean of the elapsed times from the occurrence of a system failure or degradation requiring maintenance until the time the system is restored to its operational state. It is derived by dividing the sum of the elapsed times for all events when the system required maintenance by the total number of maintenance events. This metric includes more than just direct maintenance time. It embeds some logistics response times or an indication of the availability of supportability resources, such as mechanics, support equipment, and facilities.

$$\frac{\text{Sum of Times to Restore System to Operation}}{\text{Number of Restoration Events}} \qquad (8.15)$$

12. *Mean time to restore (with spares)*: The average amount of time, including maintainability to restore the system, when spares are available in the prescribed load list (PLL). It is calculated by adding a government responsible repair delay time, due to integrated logistics support factors not being perfect, to the equipment mean time to repair. Repair delay time factors account for the nonavailability of personnel and the noncollocation of spares with equipment.

$$\frac{\text{Sum of Times to Restore System to Operation When Spares Are Available}}{\text{Number of Restoration Events}} \qquad (8.16)$$

13. *Maintenance ratio (MR)*: MR is the cumulative number of man-hours of maintenance expended in direct labor during a given period of time, divided by the cumulative number of end item operating hours, miles, or rounds during that same time period. The MR is expressed at each maintenance level and summarized for all levels of maintenance. Both corrective and preventive maintenance are included. The MR is a useful measure of the relative maintenance burden associated with a system. It provides a means of comparing systems and is useful in determining the compatibility of a system with the size of the maintenance organization.

$$\frac{\text{Sum of the Direct Maintenance Man-hours}}{\text{Sum of the System Operating Units}} \qquad (8.17)$$

14. *Maximum time to repair*: The maximum corrective maintenance downtime within a specified percent (normally 90 or 95%) of all corrective maintenance actions that can be accomplished.

15. *Repair cycle time*: Repair cycle time is the elapsed time (days or hours) from the receipt of a failed item at a repair facility until the item is ready for reissue. It is the average elapsed amount of time from an item failure to the time the item failure is repaired and placed in stock or reissued. The retrograde ship time to the maintenance echelon added to the turnaround time at the maintenance echelon constitutes the repair cycle time associated with that maintenance echelon. Retrograde ship time is the average elapsed

time from an item failure to the receipt of the item by the maintenance echelon specified to repair it.

$$\text{Retrograde Ship Time (RST)} = \frac{\text{Sum of the Elapsed Times from Failure to Echelon}}{\text{Number of Retrograde Incidents}}$$

$$\text{Turnaround Time (TAT)} = \frac{\text{Sum of the Elapsed Times to Make Repairs}}{\text{Number of Repair Jobs}} \qquad (8.18)$$

$$\text{Repair Cycle Time} = \text{RST} + \text{TAT}$$

16. *Direct annual maintenance man-hours*: The sum of the working time of each skill specialty code required for the performance of a unit of work on the system accumulated for a period of 1 year.

17. *Direct maintenance man-hour per flying hour (DMMH/FH)*: The labor hours logged against each maintenance job, scheduled and unscheduled, performed in support of the flying hour program. DMMH/FH at the organizational level is directly related to built-in test effectiveness, interactive electronic technical manuals (IETMs) effectiveness, and training effectiveness. Improvements in any of these areas can lower DMMH/FH.

18. *Operations and support (O&S) cost per operating hour*: The sum of all (selected/relevant) costs required to operate and support a system divided by the number of system operating hours. If more applicable, miles, cycles, or rounds can be substituted for hours. This metric may be used to compare the supportability cost rate for a planned system with a predecessor or similar system based on system usage. It may also be used to monitor the supportability cost rate for a given fleet of systems at different points during its operational life. Key O&S costs, such as maintenance labor and material costs at the operational, intermediate, and depot levels, aviation fuel petroleum oil and lubricant (AVPOL) costs, along with other direct support costs, are divided by flight hours to derive a baseline cost. This baseline cost will be a point of reference for measuring logistics-related improvements, such as reliability, maintainability, and obsolescence.

19. *Maintenance task elimination*: This metric provides an indication of the relative reduction in maintenance burden in terms of quantity of maintenance tasks when compared to the number of tasks required for the baseline comparative system (BCS). The metric is derived by dividing the number of maintenance tasks that are not required for the planned system by the total number of tasks required in the BCS. Goals for maintenance task elimination can be built into requirements and contract documentation. This metric must be used with caution, since elimination of many minor tasks may not reduce maintenance burden as much as a single major task. But generally, less maintenance is considered better.

20. *Maintenance downtime (MDT)*: Total time during which a system/equipment is not in a condition to perform its intended function. MDT includes active maintenance time, logistics delay time, and administrative delay time.

21. *Repairs requiring evacuation*: The number of repair tasks that can be accomplished without evacuation vs. the total number of repair tasks applicable to the system. This metric would be used to get an indication of the maintenance burden. Evacuation adds time to the repair process and consumes limited manpower and equipment resources.

22. *Beyond capability of maintenance (BCM) and "D-coded"*: BCM is the Maintenance Data Collection (MDC) system code for an item shipped to the next higher level (D-level) of maintenance because of nonavailability of local resources, such as skilled people, tools, spares, etc. D-code is used when the shipment of the repairable item is to another I-level for the same reasons. These evacuation codes often relate to lack of the repair material and "bits and pieces" needed to repair the end items within allowable repair times.

23. *Percent organic support*: A measure of the proportion of the system support, usually maintenance, which is being provided organically and conversely, the proportion of the support being provided through agreements with contractors. This metric may be used as a means of comparison of the strategy used for supporting the predecessor or a baseline system. The proportion of support being provided organically vs. contractor support may also need to be tracked over the life of the system after fielding. One specific means of measurement may be used by dividing the number of work orders organically supported by the total number of work orders.

24. *Maintenance test flight hours*: One means of determining if maintenance requirements are increasing in a fleet of aircraft is to track the number of test flight hours due to maintenance being flown per aircraft per month. This number may be used as a means of comparison over a series of previous reporting periods to identify any trends within a fleet of aircraft.

8.5.3 Supply Chain Measures

1. *Issue effectiveness rate*: This measure is the percentage of customer requests that were filled by items in the inventory. Issue effectiveness is based on filling any request, not just requests for items supply is authorized to stock. It is used to measure how well the logistics customer is supported by supply. Issue effectiveness is usually lower than stockage effectiveness, but it is more representative of a customer's view of supply support.

$$\frac{Issues}{Issues + All\ Back\ Orders}(100) \tag{8.19}$$

2. *Stockage effectiveness rate*: This metric is the percentage of customer requests filled by items supply is authorized to stock. The significant difference between issue and stockage effectiveness is that stockage effectiveness uses only those back orders for items supply is authorized to stock. It measures how well the logistics customer is supported by base supply and depot replenishment. This is especially important since supply cannot possibly stock every possible part. It is funded to stock only the most used or critical parts. A high stockage effectiveness rate means success in anticipation of customer needs.

$$\frac{Issues}{Issues + All\ Back\ Orders - 4W\ Back\ Orders}(100) \tag{8.20}$$

3. *Total repair cycle time*: This is the average time, in days, an unserviceable asset spends in the repair cycle at a unit. This indicator is for aircraft only. It does not include engines or support equipment. The clock begins when maintenance orders a repair cycle asset from supply and ends when a like asset (serviceable or unserviceable) is turned in to supply. The time the

item is awaiting parts (AWP) in the repair shop is not included. This indicator is primarily a local management tool. To improve the process of repairing parts, the different steps in that process must be measured. This indicator and its components provide this capability.

4. *Not mission-capable supply (NMCS), also called average customer wait time*: The time (days or hours) the system is inoperable due to delays in maintenance that are attributable to delays in obtaining parts.

5. *Issue response time/average customer wait time*: This response time metric is derived from average customer wait time (ACWT). As used in this instance, it means the time the customer has to wait for the requisition. Since the vendor normally cannot deliver directly to the requisitioner, because it may be a deployed ship with the material often routed to the defense distribution depot for storage, the metric used to measure the vendor needs to be defined in each contract. Normally, average contract response time (ACRT) can be used to define the time between when the contractor gets the requisition to fill and when it is delivered to the continental U.S. (CONUS) point as defined by the ship's cargo routing message or the CONUS port of embarkation (POE) for OCONUS (overseas portal to the U.S.) shipments. ACRT should not be used for contracts citing delivery terms as "FOB Origin" (SMART Transportation Solution). An alternate metric could be used, such as issue response time, which measures the time between when the contractor receives the requisition and when material is made available for shipment.

6. *Requisition fill rate*: A measure of the effectiveness of supply support. This metric can be calculated by dividing the number of high-priority requisitions filled within a specified time limit by the total number of high-priority requisitions submitted. Any high-priority requisition must be met within the specified time limit to be considered a fill. This metric should concentrate on critical item stock availability (i.e., maintenance and readiness drivers). As an example, Naval Inventory Control Point (NAVICP) is funded by Naval Supply Systems Command (NAVSUP) to meet a requisition fill rate of 85%, but some systems may have a requirement for a higher fill rate. The fill rate is a measure of the volume of requisitions satisfied within the initial response time. PBL contracts should require the contractor to report any requisition that will not be satisfied within the initial response time and to provide an estimated shipping date. These are examples of requisition fill rate metrics:

   a. For issue priority group (IPG) I and casualty reports (CASREPs), the delivery goal is to fill all requirements within the specified delivery days 100% of the time.

   b. The IPG II and III delivery goal is to fill all requirements within the specified delivery days at whatever rate is applicable to reach a combined 85% fill rate for all requirements.

   c. Average fill rate (AFR) for stock numbered items is a measure (%) of the number of times a part is shipped to the CONUS customer, or POE for OCONUS customers, within the timeframes identified in system-specific addendum(s). AFR is calculated as a rolling average, updated monthly. Once 12 months of history is achieved, AFR calculations will be based on a 12-month rolling average.

7. *Issue response time*: Average issue response time (AIRT) is a measurement of time taken to ship parts in response to requisitions received. Both immediate shipments and delayed shipments are included. Measurement time begins when the requisition is received and ends when a positive supply action is posted. AIRT is calculated by dividing the sum of the number of days required to deliver parts for all requisitions received in a given period of time by the number of requisitions received. AIRT is calculated as a rolling average, updated monthly. Once 12 months of history is achieved, AIRT calculations will be based

on a 12-month rolling average. AIRRT includes supply response times for spares delivery from both the retail level and wholesale level. Aircraft downtime is directly related to time awaiting spare parts to complete repairs and scheduled maintenance actions. Retail-level spares directly support on-aircraft or plane-side maintenance, while wholesale-level spares replenish retail ready-for-issue spares. Wholesale-level spares also supply the parts needed for I-level (local plane-side) maintenance on selected I-level repairable components. Both operational availability (Ao) and retail supply responsiveness are lagging measures directly tied to the ability of the product support integrator (PSI) to get wholesale-level material to the required locations with minimum response time.

8. *Average CASREP response time*: Average CASREP response time (ACasRT) for stock numbered items is a measurement of the time taken to ship parts for all CASREP requisitions. Measurement time begins when the requisition is received and ends when a positive supply action is posted. ACasRT is calculated by dividing the sum of the number of days required to deliver parts for all CASREP requisitions received in a given period of time by the number of CASREP requisitions received. ACasRT is calculated as a rolling average, updated monthly. Once 12 months of history is achieved, ACasRT calculations will be based on a 12-month rolling average. This is an example:
   - Casualty report (CASREP) and priority 1 requisitions: 24 h
   - Priority 2 and 3 requisitions: 48 h
   - Priority 4 through 8 requisitions: 72 h
   - Priority 9 through 15 requisitions: 8 days

   CASREP requisitions are to be processed 7 days a week (or as negotiated). All other requisitions shall be processed as negotiated. Delayed requisitions, outside the 85% fill rate that could not be filled immediately, should not exceed the following timeframes:
   - Casualty report (CASREP) and priority 1 requisitions: 7 days
   - Priority 2 and 3 requisitions: 30 days
   - Priority 4 through 15 requisitions: 90 days

9. *Stock availability*: A measure of the percentage of time that demands are satisfied from items in stock. The metric can be calculated by dividing the number of incidents when parts sought from the stock point were on hand by the number of total incidents when parts were requested from the stock point. This metric is similar to the old percent stock availability (PSA), where 85% of all National Stock Number (NSN) items were required to be on hand.

10. *Readiness spares kit availability*: Measures the percent of the spares kits that are filled at any given time. A measure of the supply expediting activities of the contractor product support integrator (PSI). This assumes that the contractor PSI and the fleet support team detachment representative at the local (garrison and sea) base are members of the kit replenishment and parts replenishment team. Kits returned from deployments are normally excluded from performance measurement for 90 days to allow for stock replenishment.

11. *Authorized stockage list (ASL) percentage fill*: ASL is the percentage of time that demands are satisfied on the first pass from items on hand within the authorized stockage list stocks. It is calculated by dividing the demands successfully filled from ASL by the total ASL demands times 100. ASL percent fill can also be the percentage of parts in stock at the ASL location vs. the required stockage level. An example:
ASL stockage level = 10 main rotor blades
ASL actual stock on hand = 9
ASL percentage fill = 90%

12. *Back order rate*: A measure of effectiveness of supply support. The number of repair parts or spares for a given weapon system/end item that are not in stock at the time they are requisitioned divided by the total demand for parts. This metric may be calculated by dividing the number of work orders awaiting parts by the total number of work orders that required parts. Back orders cause delays in maintenance awaiting the arrival of repair parts and spares with which to complete maintenance.

13. *Unfilled customer orders (UCOs)*: If the contractor does not fill 100% of the requisitions off the shelf, it will have unfilled customer orders. A maximum age or maximum average age is used. If the UCO for any given National Item Identification Number (NIIN) reaches a certain level, the contractor should provide a "get well" plan and provide a report at a mutually agreed upon interval.

14. *Back order duration time*: The average amount of time elapsed between a requisition placed for a spare not in stock to receipt of the spare part to fill the order. The back-order duration time accounts for the time to receive a procurement that was previously ordered, and the administrative and production lead times are contributing factors to this wait time.

15. *Controlled substitution rate*: An additional means of identifying possible problems in supply is by tracking the total number of controlled substitutions per month for a fleet of vehicles. This number may be used as a means of comparison over a series of previous reporting periods to identify any trends in supply within the fleet.

16. *PMR failure factor accuracy*: The number of changed failure factors during a 2-year period after provisioning master record (PMR) load compared to total number of PMR failure factors. This metric measures the accuracy of part usage predictions based upon failure factor data incorporated during the initial PMR build. The number of updates or changes of a given magnitude to PMR failures factors reflect the degree of accuracy of the provisioning process regarding determining the range and quantity of required spare and repair parts. This metric may be used as an incentive for a contractor to create an accurate PMR.

17. *Inventory accuracy*: Percent accurate inventory data are the number of NSNs having accurate inventory data to the total number NSNs managed. A Web-based commercial asset visibility (WEBCAV) statement of work requires that an activity shall be responsible for maintaining an inventory accuracy of 98%.

18. *Order/ship time*: The time elapsed between the initiation of stock replenishment action for a specific activity and the receipt by the activity of the material resulting from such action. OST is applicable only to material within the supply system and is composed of the distinct elements, order time, and shipping time. It includes many segments, including order processing, shipping from depot to the consolidation point, consolidation point to the port of debarkation, in transit, arrival at destination port, distribution to a supply point, and finally delivery to the requiring unit.

19. *Spares cost-to-LCC ratio*: The total estimated cost of spares and repair parts divided by the total estimated life cycle cost for the system. This metric may be used to compare the supply support cost for a planned system with a predecessor or similar system. It may also be used to monitor the supply support cost for a given system at different points during its operational life to identify any changes or potential problems. A high proportion of spares costs may signal the need for reengineering or change to the support concept.

20. *Unit load—supply*: The total weight, cube, or quantity of repair parts and spares required to support the system in a given type unit. This metric may be used to compare the supply

support burden on a unit of a planned system with a predecessor or similar system in terms of extra materiel that a unit must manage, upload, and haul. It may also be used to monitor the supply support burden on a unit of a given system at different points during its operational life to identify any changes.

21. *Parts standardization*: This metric is a measure of how well standardization criteria for use of standard parts/components have been met. One way of calculating this metric is to divide the number of standard new NSNs by the total number of NSNs for the system. Another way of calculating this metric is to divide the number of standard NSNs in the bill of materials (BOM) by the total number of NSNs in the BOM for the system. The fielding of new weapon systems or major modifications requires added new NSNs to the inventory. It would be desirable to have a method for determining the adequacy of the standardization process for parts and components used in the engineering design. A comparison could be accomplished using the average number of new lines of supply (new NSNs) added for large, medium, and small systems, which could serve as an indicator of the adequacy of engineering and the maintenance planning. Compare the percent of new lines to the historical average, minus an improvement factor (i.e., 5%), as a standard for judging its improvement/accomplishment.

22. *Float utilization rate*: A means of optimizing the number of systems reserved as floats by tracking the percentage of time that the float systems are on loan to customer units. The utilization ratio can be calculated by dividing calendar time during which the float items are on loan by the total amount of calendar time during which the float items are available. A low ratio may indicate that fewer float items are needed. A high ratio may indicate the need for more float items.

23. *Recycle-ability*: This type of metric may be used as a means of determining how well environmental design goals are being met. Project managers are being encouraged to set recycling goals for their acquisition systems. Recycling helps reduce disposal problems for systems and components. Recycle-ability can be quantified by simply counting the number of parts or components that can be recycled. Comparison with similar or predecessor systems can also be made by noting the difference in the number of recyclable parts between two or more systems. If it is necessary to take into account the difference in total number of parts for the comparison systems, then the percentage of recyclable parts can be used.

24. *Percentage parts reduction*: This metric may be used as a means of determining if goals have been achieved in the area of reduction in the number of different part numbers applied to a given system. It is derived by comparing the number of part numbers required for supporting the objective system against the number of part numbers required to support a similar or predecessor system. This metric may also be evaluated by comparing the number of system part numbers with a specific threshold or a goal that represents a specific percentage reduction from the total parts count on a predecessor system.

25. *Asset/inventory turns rate*: This metric is an indication that spares inventory is being used enough to justify the investment in it. Excess inventory is considered a waste of resources, including the warehousing, transportation, and asset tracking of the asset. If the items are not contributing to weapon system readiness through usage, inventory turns rate is computed by dividing the total sales (issues) at the last acquisition price by the total value of the inventory excluding war reserves. The objective is to optimize inventory levels, in conjunction with maintenance repair turnaround time (TAT), and

thereby increase inventory turns. Wholesale inventory turns can be used as a measure of wholesale efficiency in cost terms.

8.5.4 Support Equipment Measures

In the following metrics, built-in test equipment (BITE) is being treated as operational-level test equipment. This treatment is independent of assignment of responsibility for controlling the level of performance of BITE. Each program should assign this responsibility to a designated agency of the supportability integrated product team.

1. *Built-in-test (BIT) detectability level percentage*: BIT consists of an integral capability of the mission equipment, which provides an on-board automated test capability to detect, diagnose, or isolate system failures. The fault detection/isolation capability is used for momentary or continuous monitoring of a system's operational health, and for observation/diagnosis as a prelude to maintenance action. BIT subsystems may be designed as an analysis tool for the overall system, integrated with several subsystems, or may be designed as an integral part of each removable component. Detectability level percentage is the probability that the malfunction or failure of the system will be detected by BIT.

2. *Percent BIT fault detection*: This metric is a measure of the percentage of total system fault diagnostic capability, which is performed via built-in test equipment/software embedded within the system itself. Such diagnostic capability is typically computer based and is often incorporated within the system along with other system software. This metric can be used to set threshold and objective goals for the percentage of embedded diagnostics that should be incorporated into the system. A requirement may also be established for an increase in embedded diagnostics over that contained within a similar or predecessor system. It is important to specify the level of ambiguity or the level of detail to which the BIT must diagnose faults.

3. *Percent prognostic aids*: This metric is a measure of the percentage of total system prognostic capability that is performed via equipment/software embedded within the system itself. Such prognostic capability is typically computer based and is often incorporated within the system along with other system software. This metric can be used to set threshold and objective goals for the percentage of embedded prognostics that should be incorporated into the system. A requirement may also be established for an increase in embedded prognostics over that contained within a similar or predecessor system.

4. *Unit load-support equipment*: The total cube or weight of support equipment required to maintain the system in a given type unit. This metric may be used to compare the maintenance burden on a unit of a planned system with a predecessor or similar system in terms of extra material that the unit must deal with. It may also be used to monitor the maintenance burden on a unit of a given system at different points during its operational life to identify any changes.

5. *Test accuracy ratio*: A measure of the accuracy of the test, measurement, and diagnostic equipment (TMDE) by dividing the number of system faults accurately diagnosed by the system TMDE by the total number of system faults tested by the TMDE. This metric is typically used in a requirements or contract document to set an objective or threshold level of performance for accurate fault diagnosis/isolation. The diagnostic performance is usually

verified during development, operational, production verification, and follow-on test and evaluation. It may be used as a means of comparison with a predecessor or baseline system.

6. *No evidence of failure (NEOF) rate*: The no evidence of failure rate is a measure of the effectiveness of fault diagnostics and fault isolation. It is also called cannot duplicate (CND). It is the number of components that were falsely diagnosed as faulty divided by the total number of components diagnosed. Another way of measuring this metric would be to divide the number of false removals by the total number of removals. Excessive rates of NEOF cause unnecessary delays in maintenance and extraordinarily high demands for spares and repair parts. High NEOF can be a symptom of such shortcomings as poorly designed support equipment or ineffective training. This metric is typically used in a requirements or contract document to set an objective or threshold level of performance for accurate fault diagnosis/isolation. It may be used as a means of comparison with a predecessor or baseline system. It can also be used to identify changes in the NEOF rate for a given system at different points in its life cycle. A comparison could be accomplished using the average number of NEOFs added for large, medium, and small systems that could serve as an indicator of the adequacy of engineering and maintenance planning. Compare the percent of NEOFs to the historical average, minus an improvement factor (i.e., 5%), as a standard for judging adequacy of engineering and maintenance procedure designs.

7. *Tools effectiveness*: The total number of tasks performed successfully using the specified tools divided by the total number of tasks performed. This metric provides an indication of how well the tools contribute to the optimization of the maintenance task by reducing time and effort to accomplish the task. This metric can be used in a requirements or contract document to set an objective or threshold level of effectiveness for tools. Typically, the requirement should always be 100% effective. It may be used as a means of comparison with a predecessor or baseline system.

8. *Minimize special tools and test, measurement, and diagnostic equipment (TMDE)*: The number of items eliminated during a given life cycle phase divided by the total number of items at the start of the life cycle phase. The support equipment recommendation data (SERD) list may be used as the source document to collect the data for this metric. Support equipment can be reduced in terms of number of different types of support equipment and in terms of the ratio of number of a given item of support equipment required per end item supported.

9. *Support equipment reduction*: The number of items eliminated during a given life cycle phase divided by the total number of items at the start of the life cycle phase. The support equipment recommendation data (SERD) list may be used as the source document to collect the data for this metric. Support equipment can be reduced in terms of number of different types of support equipment and in terms of the ratio of number of a given item of support equipment required per end item supported.

10. *TMDE operational test program sets (OTPS) available*: The total number of items of test, measurement, and diagnostic equipment (TMDE) (OTPS) required vs. the total number of items of TMDE/OTPS available. This metric would typically be used to set goals or requirements for percentage of range of quantity of TMDE/OTPS available at the time of system fielding.

11. *Support equipment available—range*: The total number of items of support equipment (SE) required vs. the total number of SE available. This metric would typically be used to set goals or requirements for percentage of range of quantity of SE available at the time of system

fielding. The top-level measure is the percent of SE available. This drills down to lists of SE that are not yet available at a location. The lists can be prioritized to show potential impact on weapon system readiness.

12. *Support equipment available—depth*: The total number of items of support equipment (SE) end item full quantities required vs. the total number of SE end item full quantities available. This metric would typically be used to set goals or requirements for percentage of range of quantity of SE available at the time of system fielding.

13. *Support equipment logistics available*: The percentage of the repairable end items of support equipment (SE) that have all of their logistics products delivered (technical data, publications, spares, provisioning) vs. the total number of repairable end items of SE. This metric would typically be used to set goals or requirements for percentage of range of quantity of SE available at the time of system fielding.

14. *Back-order duration time for support equipment*: The average amount of time elapsed between a requisition that is placed for a support equipment item not in stock to the receipt of the support equipment item to fill the order. The back-order duration time accounts for the time to receive a procured item previously ordered and the production and administrative lead times, which are contributing factors to this customer wait time.

15. *Repair cycle time for support equipment*: This is the elapsed time (days or hours) for a failed item of SE to be shipped to the SE repair organization and for the designated repair organization to make the item ready for issue (RFI). The average elapsed time from an SE end item failure to the time the item is back in stock as a ready for re-issue SE item. The SE repair cycle time (SE RST) is equal to the retrograde ship time (RST) plus the SE turnaround time (TAT). RST is the average time to ship the SE item to the SE maintenance organization. The SE TAT is the sum of the elapsed time to make repairs divided by the number of repair jobs.

8.5.5 Manpower and Personnel Measures

1. *Crew size*: The number of personnel required to operate a given system and perform all required mission functions. From a cost and supportability view, it is typically better to minimize crew size. This metric is typically used in a requirements or contract document to set an objective or threshold crew size required to operate and maintain a system. The quantitative goal is typically derived by comparing the crew size requirements for predecessor or similar systems.

2. *Maintenance cost per operating hour*: Same as direct maintenance man-hours per flight hour (DMMH/FH). The metric is used to obtain an indication of the cost of maintenance personnel for a given system. It is the total cost of maintainer personnel, charged as direct labor, divided by the total number of operating hours. This metric may be used to compare the labor cost maintainers for a planned system with a predecessor or similar system. It may also be used to monitor the maintenance labor cost for a given system at different points during its operational life to identify any changes or revise budget requirements.

3. *Skill level limit*: A measure of the level of expertise required for system operators to competently operate the system or for maintainers to competently repair or service the system. This metric is typically used in a requirements or contract document to set an objective or threshold reduction in the skills required to operate and maintain a system. The

quantitative goal is typically derived by comparing skill-level requirements for predecessor or similar systems.

4. *Maintenance man-hour requirements*: The number of man-hours required to support the system for a given military occupational specialty (MOS). This metric gives an indication of the maintenance workload for a system by MOS. It would typically be used to compare the support of a planned system with that of a predecessor or baseline system.

5. *Ratio of personnel cost to O&S cost*: An estimate of total cost for personnel (pay, benefits, and overhead) to operate and support the system divided by the total estimated operating and support costs of the system. The metric can be used to compare the relative cost of personnel between planned and current systems. It can also be used to identify changes in the relative cost of personnel for a given system at different points in its life cycle.

6. *Number of personnel on hand vs. number personnel authorized*: The number of personnel of a given military occupational specialty (MOS) on hand divided by the number of personnel of that MOS type that are required at the site of fielding to operate or support the system. This metric provides an indication of how well the system will be supported. Requirements for the same MOS horizontally across several different types of weapons systems/end items in the same unit must often be considered.

7. *Number of personnel required vs. authorized*: A comparison of personnel required to operate and support a weapon system to the number of personnel authorized for that weapon system. This metric provides an indication of the capability of the system to be properly operated and supported.

8. *Mechanic utilization*: A measure of the workload for a specified maintainer or group of maintainers. This metric can be derived by dividing actual hours worked by the total hours that the mechanic was available for work. This metric can be used to monitor changes in the utilization rates of maintenance personnel over time or as means of comparison with predecessor systems.

8.5.6 Training Measures

1. *Time to achieve proficiency*: The average time required for operator or support personnel to become proficient in effectively, efficiently, and correctly performing the required tasks associated with operation or maintenance of the system. This metric would typically be used to compare the time to train operators and maintainers to perform tasks within a new system vs. the time required on a predecessor or baseline system. Care must be taken in using this metric. The goal is to provide effective training in all required tasks in the least amount of time.

2. *Student failure rate or student pass rate*: The percentage of students who are not able to achieve or, conversely, who do achieve the training objectives after completion of the training course. This metric provides an indication of the effectiveness of the training in helping the target audience to learn the training objectives. This metric would typically be used to set threshold and objective goals for failure or pass rates. The content and length of programs of instruction (POIs) should be determined based on the training required to prepare soldiers to successfully perform their MOS-related tasks with minimal on-the-job training in the field.

3. *Percentage embedded training*: A measure of the percentage of total operator or support personnel training that is available within the system itself. Such training is typically computer

based and is simply incorporated within the system along with other system software. This metric can be used to set threshold and objective goals for the percentage of embedded training that should be incorporated into the system. A requirement may also be established for an increase in embedded training over that contained within a similar or predecessor system. The advantage of embedded training is that it allows frequent review and is available to the user upon demand.

4. *Ratio of training costs to LCC costs*: A simple measure of the relative cost of training to the total system life cycle cost. The total training costs divided by the total life cycle costs. This metric may be used to compare the relative cost of training between planned and current systems. It can also be used to identify changes in the relative cost of training for a given system at different points in its life cycle.

5. *Number of personnel trained vs. number required*: Provides a measure of the amount of training that has been accomplished for a given military occupational specialty (MOS) at the site where the system is being fielded currently. Number of trained personnel of a given MOS divided by the total number of personnel of that type of MOS at the site of fielding.

6. *Training systems available*: The number of training systems available at a given training facility vs. the number of training systems required. This metric would provide an indication of how well training requirements can be met.

8.5.7 Technical Data Measures

1. *Technical manual (TM) accuracy*: A rate can be obtained for accuracy of technical manuals (TMs) and equipment publications derived by tracking the number of change pages to correct errors over a given span of time divided by the total number of TM pages or the total number of change pages for all reasons. For electronic TMs it is necessary to track individual changes instead of change pages. The rate can be incorporated into a requirements document.

2. *TM Accuracy Department of the Army (DA) Form 2028*: A measure of accuracy of technical manuals (TMs) and equipment derived by tracking the quantity of DA Form 2028s submitted from the field that are actually approved and incorporated into TMs vs. the total number of DA Forms 2028 submitted. This metric can be used in a requirements or contract document to set an objective or threshold level of accuracy.

3. *Documentation rewrite requirement*: A measure of the accuracy of the technical manuals (TMs) and equipment publications derived by tracking the number of hours spent rewriting documentation to correct errors as a percentage of original document preparation time. A high rate of rewrite would indicate poor quality.

4. *Percentage of TMs embedded*: A measure of the percentage of the technical manuals (TMs) and equipment publications that are available within the system itself. Such technical documentation is typically computer based and is simply incorporated within the system along with other system software. This metric can be used to set threshold and objective goals for the percentage of embedded technical documentation that should be incorporated into the system. A requirement may also be established for an increase in embedded technical documentation over that contained within a similar or predecessor system. The advantage of embedded technical documentation is that it allows frequent review and is available to the user upon demand.

5. *TM effectiveness rate*: The total number of tasks performed successfully, where *successfully* means "first-time fix" within standard time limits, using the specified technical manuals (TMs), divided by the total number of tasks performed. This metric provides an indication of how well the TMs contribute to the optimization of the maintenance task by reducing time and effort to accomplish the task. This metric can be used in a requirements or contract document to set an objective or threshold level of effectiveness for TMs. Typically, the requirement should always be 100% effectiveness. It may be used as a means of comparison with a predecessor or baseline system. It can also be used to identify changes in the TMs' effectiveness for a given system at different points in its life cycle.

6. *TMs available*: The total number of technical manuals (TMs) available vs. the total number of TMs required. This metric would typically be used to set goals or requirements for percentage of range of quantity of TMs available at the time of system fielding.

7. *TMs produced vs. required*: The total number of technical manuals (TMs) produced vs. the total number of TMs required. This metric would typically be used to set goals or requirements for percentage of range of quantity of TMs actually published and distributed at the time of system fielding.

8.5.8 Facilities Measures

1. *Facilities limitation*: An objective and threshold percentage or specified reduction in facilities requirements may be incorporated into requirements documents and contracts. This metric is typically used in a requirements or contract document to set a goal for facilities required to support the system. Some project managers have set a requirement for no new facilities. The quantitative goal is typically derived by analyzing the facilities requirements for predecessor or similar systems.

2. *Facilities funded/available*: The total amount of facility space required vs. the amount of facilities space available. A metric used to determine if sufficient funding is programmed to support facility addition/upgrade. It is necessary to compare programmed funding to estimated funding requirements on a fiscal year basis. The formula is expressed as military construction programmed funding divided by facilities funding requirements.

3. *Facilities utilization rate*: A measure of the workload for a specific type of facility. This metric can be derived by dividing actual capacity of the facility used by the total capacity available during a given time period. This metric can be used to monitor changes in the utilization rates of facilities over time or as means of comparing facilities' utilization rates with those of predecessor systems. The type of units to be used for capacity will depend upon the type of facility being tracked. For a storage facility, square feet may be the best measure of capacity. A maintenance facility may require capacity to be measured in terms of the number of hours a day that the maintenance bays are filled with systems under repair. A more production-oriented facility may have capacity measured in units output per unit of time.

8.5.9 Computer Resources Support Measures

1. *Fault density*: This metric is a measure of the number of errors found in newly developed software. The fault density is derived by dividing the number of software faults that are identified by the number of lines of code in the software program. A specific fault density goal

may be included in the software specification to provide a quantitative measure by which to determine whether the government will accept delivery of the software.

2. *Software mean time between failures*: A basic measure of the reliability of software. The total functional life (time, rounds, hours, cycles, events, etc.) of a population or fleet of end items divided by the total number of software failures within the population during the measurement interval, given the end items are operated within normal mission profiles and under specified operating conditions and environments.

3. *Software modification rate*: A measure of the quality of the software development effort. The rate is derived by counting the frequency with which the system software must be modified over a specified interval of time. This metric may have some value when compared to a predecessor or baseline system. Caution must be used in using this metric. Software enhancements must be differentiated from software fixes and those driven by hardware modifications, etc.

4. *Ratio of software modification costs to LCC cost*: A simple measure of the relative cost of software modifications compared to the total system life cycle cost (LCC). The total software modification costs divided by the total life cycle costs. This metric may be used to compare the relative cost of software modification between planned and current systems. It can also be used to identify changes in the relative cost of software modification for a given system at different points in its life cycle. Caution must be used in using this metric. Software enhancements must be differentiated from software fixes.

5. *Computer resources available*: The total range and quantity of computer resources (hardware, software, firmware, documentation, support items) available vs. the total range and number of computer resources required. This metric would typically be used to set goals or requirements for percentage of range of quantity of computer resources available at the time of system fielding.

6. *Minimize postdeployment software support requirements (PDSS)*: An objective and threshold percentage or specified reduction in the number of different types of support equipment, software, and firmware required to support the software of an acquisition end item after fielding. This metric may be incorporated into requirements documents and contracts. It can be used to set a goal for the PDSS burden required to support the software of a materiel system. The quantitative goal can be derived by using the support requirements for predecessor or similar systems as a baseline.

8.5.10 Packaging, Handling, Storage, and Transportation Measures

1. *Percentage of packaging data*: This metric is a measure of the percentage of repair parts (that will be used to support the end item in a forward-deployed scenario) that have the packaging engineering data developed. It is the relationship between the number of repair parts provisioned to the number of repair parts with military packaging data. The quantitative goal is 100%.

2. *Percentage long-life reusable container (LLRC)*: This is a direct measure of the impact of the packaging methodology on the soldier. The higher the percentage, the less packaging training and equipment required by the soldier. It is the relationship between the number of repair parts that require evacuation for overhaul to the number of these parts provided with an LLRC. A high number is also a direct indicator of a lower life cycle cost for packaging and a lower environmental impact. The quantitative goal is 100%.

3. *Reduced weight and cube*: An objective and threshold percentage or specified reduction in system weight and cube as well as the weight and cube of the system support package may be incorporated into requirements documents and contracts. This metric (or set of metrics) may be used to set a requirement for minimizing the transport burden of the system. The actual quantitative requirements are derived by analyzing the weight and cube of predecessor or baseline systems.

4. *Reduced special storage requirements*: An objective and threshold percentage or specified reduction in special storage requirements may be incorporated into requirements documents and contracts. This metric is typically used to set a requirement or goal for conditions under which the system can be efficiently and effectively stored. Some project managers have set a requirement for no special storage requirements. The goal is typically derived by analyzing the special storage requirements for predecessor or baseline systems.

5. *Minimize preparation for shipment*: An objective or specified reduction in time (man-hours and total elapsed time) required to prepare a weapon system for shipment. The quantitative goal is typically derived by analyzing the time required for preparation for shipment for predecessor or similar systems.

6. *No special handling*: An objective and threshold percentage or specified reduction in special handling requirements may be incorporated into requirements documents and contracts. This metric is typically used to set a requirement or goal for the ease of handling for the system when being prepared for shipment. Some project managers have set a requirement for no special handling requirements. The goal is typically derived by analyzing the special handling requirements for predecessor or baseline systems.

7. *Hazardous material limits*: Objective and threshold percentages set to represent reduction in types or quantity of hazardous materials associated with the operation, sustainment, or disposal of an acquisition system. The baseline may be a predecessor system. Total elimination of hazardous materials may be the goal.

8. *Time to load/unload from transport vehicle*: A metric that compares the load and unload times for a proposed system to the load and unload times of a predecessor or baseline system.

9. *Time to configure system for transport*: A requirement of a time limit (such as 1 h) within which the system must be able to be configured for transport by a given mode of transport (e.g., air, ocean, or rail).

10. *Minimize transportability equipment*: An objective and threshold percentage or specified reduction in transportability peculiar equipment required to prepare a weapon system for shipment. The quantitative goal is typically derived by analyzing the transportability peculiar equipment requirements for predecessor or similar systems

11. *Military Traffic Management Command (MTMC) rating*: Transportability quantifiers are numerical determinations of the relative transportability of systems, based on predetermined values. These quantifiers measure the transportability of one system vs. another to give a better idea to decision makers just how good or poor is the transportability of various systems. The quantifiers are based upon a rating of 0 to 100% transportable for each of the methods of transport: fixed-wing air, rotary-wing air, ocean, logistics over the shore, highway, and rail, as well as lifting and tie-down provisions. Each of the methods has predetermined values based upon varying levels of transportability within each of the methods. These levels are based upon numbers of restrictions the item would face during transport as well as the number of transportation assets available to transport the item. The fewer the restrictions and the greater the number of available transportation assets, the higher the score. Transportability quantifiers only measure the ability of a single item to move through

the Defense Transportation System. They do not measure the impact that an item will have on the deployability of the force. It is possible that an item can be as transportable as another item, yet have a completely different impact on the deployability of the force. Therefore, transportability quantifier values must not be used in a vacuum. They need to be used in conjunction with a deployability analysis.

8.5.11 Design Interface Measures

1. *Mean time between failures (MTBF)*: A basic measure of reliability for weapon systems and end items. This metric measures the total functional life (e.g., time, rounds, hours, cycles, events, etc.) of a population or fleet of end items divided by the total number of failures within the population during the measurement interval. Typically there is a requirement for the end items to be operated within normal mission profiles and under specified operating conditions and environments.
2. *Mean flight hours between failures (MFHBF)*: Also called logistics reliability. The total flight hours of the population of aircraft divided by the total number of failures, requiring logistics support, within the population, during the measurement interval.
3. *Mean time between critical failures*: A basic measure of reliability that provides an indication of the probability that the system will perform essential mission functions. The total functional life (time, rounds, hours, cycles, events, etc.) of a population or fleet of end items divided by the total number of critical failures within the population during the measurement interval. Typically there is a requirement for the end items to be operated within normal mission profiles and under specified operating conditions and environments.
4. *Mean time between maintenance actions (MTBMA)*: The mean of the distribution of the time intervals between actions or groups of actions required to restore an item to, or maintain it in, a specified condition. This entry will be composed of the MTBF, mean time between maintenance induced (MTBM induced), mean time between maintenance no defect (MTBM no defect), and mean time between preventive maintenance (MTBPM) values. MTBMA may be calculated by the following formula:

$$MTBMA = \left(\frac{1}{MTBF} + \frac{1}{MTBM\ Induced} + \frac{1}{MTBM\ No\ Defect} + \frac{1}{MTBPM} \right)^{-1} \quad (8.21)$$

5. *Mean time between removal*: A measure of the system reliability parameter related to demand for logistics support. The total number of operational units (e.g., miles, rounds, hours) divided by the total number of items removed from that system during a stated period of time. This term is defined to exclude removals performed to facilitate other maintenance and removals for product improvement. *Note*: For a particular task to be applicable, it must meet *all* of these criteria:
   a. It must be either a remove or a remove-and-replace task.
   b. It must be categorized as either an emergency or an unscheduled task.
   c. The task must be performed by operator, crew, unit–crew, or organizational, on equipment, unit–organizational, or by a maintenance contact team.

    d. The task cannot be performed to facilitate other maintenance or for product improvement.

6. *Mean time between preventive maintenance*: The mean of the distribution of intervals, measured in hours, rounds, etc., between preventive maintenance actions. This is one of the four categories of maintenance events contributing to the mean time between maintenance actions value.

7. *Mean time between mission abort*: The mean of the distribution of intervals, measured in hours, rounds, etc., between events that render a system incapable of performing its mission. The emphasis for this metric is on system failures that directly impact the mission functions rather than non-mission-critical failures or preventive maintenance actions.

8. *Mean calendar time between mission failures*: The mean of the distribution of calendar hours between events causing a system to be less capable in performing its mission. The emphasis of this metric is on system failures that cause aborts or directly reduce mission effectiveness. In addition to mission aborts, this measure accounts for the loss of interoperability or loss of equipment use that improves the system capability to perform a mission without causing a mission abort.

9. *Mission completion success probability (MCSP)*: The probability that an end item will perform all essential mission functions and complete its mission successfully. This probability can be derived by dividing the number of missions successfully completed by the total number of missions attempted by the population of end items.

10. *Combat rate*: Combat rate is the average number of consecutive scheduled missions completed before an end item experiences critical failures. It is calculated by dividing the number of successful missions by the number of successful missions minus the number of aborts.

11. *Operational readiness*: Measure of a system's ability to perform all of its combat missions without endangering the lives of crew or operators. The metric is best used when comparing the readiness rates of a new system to rates of the predecessor (baseline) system.

12. *Operational availability (Ao)*: The probability that, when used under stated conditions, a system will operate satisfactorily at anytime. This differs from achieved availability in that Ao includes standby time and admin and log delay time.

13. *Achieved availability (Aa)*: The probability that, when used under stated conditions in an ideal support environment, a system will operate satisfactorily at any time. This differs from inherent availability only in its inclusion of consideration for preventive action. Aa excludes supply downtime and administrative downtime. Aa may be expressed by the following formula:

$$A_a = \frac{MTBM}{MTBM + MTTR_{(active)}} \qquad (8.22)$$

where:

$$MTBM = \left(\frac{1}{MTBF} + \frac{1}{MTBM - ND} + \frac{1}{MTBPM} \right)^{-1}$$

$MTTR_{active}$ = Mean time to repair for scheduled and preventive maintenance

Note: The measurement bases for MTBF, MTBM-ND, and MTBPM must be consistent when calculating the MTBM parameter.

14. *Inherent availability (Ai)*: The probability that, when used under stated conditions in an ideal support environment without consideration for preventive action, a system will operate satisfactorily at any time. The ideal support environment referred to exists when the stipulated tools, parts, skilled manpower, manuals, SE, and other support items required are available. Ai excludes whatever ready time, preventive maintenance downtime, supply downtime, and administrative downtime may require. Ai may be expressed by the following formula:

$$A_i = \frac{MTBF}{MTBF + MTTR} \tag{8.23}$$

where MTBF = mean time between failures and MTTR = mean time to repair.

15. *Training system operational availability*: A measure of the reliability and maintainability of the training system(s) associated with a given acquisition system. This metric is a measure of how many mission hours that a training system is available. Ao = (mission available time)/[(mission available time) + (mission nonavailable time)].

16. *LORA progress*: A measure of the rate of progress toward completion of all the level of repair analysis (LORA) computer runs required for determining optimum allocation of repair candidate components and maintenance policies.

17. *Interoperability*: Interoperability is the ability of systems to provide services to and accept services from other systems to enable them to operate effectively together. The goal of this metric is to provide a level of certainty that a given acquisition end item is able to support or operate with other predefined systems in specified functional areas. Interoperability is a difficult metric to measure quantitatively. Interoperability with other systems is verified through testing or simulation. Often, interoperability is measured simply by identifying whether or not the system is interoperable. It may be possible to derive a ratio of interoperability by dividing the number of systems with which the acquisition system is interoperable by the total number of systems with which the acquisition system should be interoperable. It may also be useful to compare the number of systems with which the acquisition system is interoperable with the number of systems with which the predecessor system was interoperable.

18. *Quality deficiency report (QDR) rate*: One means of identifying possible problems in the fielding process is to track the number of QDRs during a specified time interval (e.g., per month). This number may be used as a means of comparison over a series of previous reporting periods to identify any trends in submission of customer/user complaints. This metric helps to confirm the effectiveness of the design effort. Number of QDRs per interval of time.

19. *Engineering response time*: The number of hours required to provide an engineering solution to a problem or request for engineering assistance. The sum of the hours required to provide an engineering solution to a problem, divided by the number of calls for engineering assistance.

8.5.12 Logistics Footprint Measures

Reducing the size of the logistics footprint has several dimensions: (1) reducing the amount of logistics support resources in the warfighter theater of operations; (2) reducing logistics resources in the garrison and other CONUS locations, such as depots; and (3) reducing the logistics infrastructure in general. Major emphasis is to be placed on the number one dimension in order to achieve greater agility for the warfighting unit. Key measures for the first dimension are:

a. Amount and size of pack-up kit spares
b. Amount and size of support equipment
c. Number and size of vehicles and other facilities
d. Numbers and special skills of maintenance and other support personnel
e. Transportability of support material

The warfighting and sustainment doctrine is constantly changing, and the supportability analyses must focus on identifying and measuring opportunities for reducing the logistics footprint. Major emphasis should be placed on any items not currently self-deployable.

1. *Logistics footprint*: This measure reflects the presence of logistics support resources required to deploy, sustain, and move a weapon system capability. Elements such as spares, support equipment, facilities, people, transportation assets, and real estate are part of the logistics footprint. Both weight and cubic volume are important elements that impact the agility (movement ability) of logistics resources. The footprint baseline is established as the sum total of weight and cubic volume of selected logistics resources at each operating location. Footprint reduction initiatives are aimed at reducing logistics footprint resources while maintaining the readiness of the warfighting capability.

2. *Logistics footprint index*: A subjective measure of the contractor product support integrator (PSI) involvement in analyzing, identifying, and supporting initiatives that can reduce the logistics footprint. Logistics footprint elements include spares, support equipment, facilities, and people. A subjective evaluation measure is used because the contractor does not normally control all of the factors affecting approval and funding of many footprint reduction drivers.

3. *Operating and support (O&S) cost measures*: Historically, the two most important measures used in sustainment-related analysis have been weapon system readiness and life cycle cost (LCC). These two measures are always used in conjunction with each other. Readiness targets are set within LCC constraints, and LCC is calculated with respect to a set readiness level. LCC is the sum of research development test and evaluation (RDT&E), procurement, and operating and support costs. LCC analysis, which is the topic Chapter 9, is a decision support tool. Selected elements of LCC are considered in analysis related to supportability-related decisions. LCC and total ownership cost (TOC) are used interchangeably. While some sources use slightly different definitions for these terms, the analysis process is essentially the same in the context of PBL.

4. *LCC differential*: A measure of the LCC of a system compared with the LCC of its predecessor or baseline system. This metric is the projected LCC of the new system divided by the LCC of the current system or baseline system. Goals can be established for incorporation into requirements and contract documentation to reduce LCC for a new system.

5. *Total ownership cost reduction (TOC-R)*: The sum of selected cost elements applicable to program TOC-R management efforts. Selected cost elements are used to set the program

baseline, and improvement initiatives are analyzed based on resulting changes in LCC and TOC.

6. *Operating and support (O&S) cost comparison 1*: The goal in fielding a new system should be that the O&S costs for the new system, generally, should be no more than the costs of the displaced system. Knowledge of the costs of the displaced system will provide a benchmark early on in the development of the new system that the developer can aim for in planning the new system. Granted, the O&S costs for the new system will be based on engineering estimates, but having a benchmark will help the material developer to consider supportability more nearly equally with cost, performance, and schedule. Historical data for the system to be displaced must be available.

7. *Operating and support (O&S) cost comparison 2:* Many sustainment decisions compare alternatives using applicable cost elements of LCC as decision support information. Examples include:
   - O&S cost per operating hour
   - Spares cost-to-LCC ratio
   - Personnel cost to O&S cost
   - Training cost to O&S cost
   - Software modification cost to LCC
   - Performance improvement opportunities
   - Cost trade-off decisions

8. *Total operating cost reduction (TOC-R) index*: A subjective measure of the contractor PSI involvement in analyzing, identifying, and supporting initiatives that can reduce the operating and support cost portion of the enterprise metric cost per flight hour. This metric is a subjective measure, because the contractor does not normally control all of the factors affecting approval and funding of many O&S cost drivers.

9. *Customer satisfaction index*: A subjective measure based on satisfaction surveys of a broad range of supportability-related stakeholders. The contractor PSI participates in the survey creation and maintenance. The objective is to identify opportunities for sustainment-related process improvement and customer relationship management.

8.6 Case Study: Rockwell Collins San Jose (RCSJ), California

Since its founding as Collins Radio in 1933, Rockwell Collins and its products have been recognized for distinctive quality and state-of-the-art technology. Rockwell Collins aircraft electronics are installed in the cockpits of nearly every airline in the world, and its airborne and ground-based communication systems transmit nearly 70% of all U.S. and allied military airborne communication. The Rockwell Collins Avionics and Communication Division is a world leader in electronic information distribution, processing, control, communication, and navigation. Rockwell Collins Advanced Technology Center collaborates with commercial and government systems to bring new advancements to aviation electronics and communications markets. Rockwell Scientific Company, LLC, which is jointly owned by Rockwell Collins and Rockwell Automation, provides additional technological research.

8.6.1 The RCSJ Performance-Based Logistics Concept

The Rockwell Collins San Jose (RCSJ) performance-based logistics (PBL) program is designed to manage the Navy RCSJ-built F/A-18A/B/C/D and F-14D assets to meet a 91% availability rate in support of the intermediate-level maintenance activities at sea and on land. PBL activities also involve engineering support and field service. Asset management involves providing an RFI (ready for issue) asset upon demand by an intermediate-level maintenance activity, managing the repair of failed returned assets, and stocking of RFI assets to meet the Navy demands. Depending on the priority of the Navy demand, an RFI asset must be shipped to the site of a demand within 2 to 5 days of when the demand comes from a CONUS site, and 7 to 10 days of when the demand is from a non-CONUS site. Failed assets returned from the Navy will be processed through the repair cycle. Parts for repairs will be predicted, procured, stocked, and issued to repairs to support a 30-day-or-less repair cycle. RFI stock requirements will be determined based on the predicted demand and stocked by the Navy initially, then maintained by Rockwell Collins San Jose through the repair process. RFI stock requirements must consider the Navy's return time of 40 days minimum, 30-day repair turnaround for normal repairs, 90-day turnaround time for supplier-repaired items, and a 30-day buffer period for handling demand surges. Repair sites are at RCSJ and the two Navy organic depots at Jacksonville, Florida, and San Diego, California.

Engineering support involves parts obsolescence management, reliability recording and tracking and possible reliability improvements, support of Navy engineering investigations, and support of the Navy depots as necessary or required. Managing part obsolescence involves the identification of parts that will not be available to support repairs for the 15-year period. A plan concerning these parts will be created and executed depending on the expected life and risk associated with each part. A Failure Reporting and Corrective Action System (FRACAS) will provide the reliability information that will be used to see if any reliability improvements can be made to the fielded equipment.

RCSJ will perform four design activities in support of the performance-based logistic contract. Upgrading the F/A-18A/B MDI interconnect to newer technology will increase the reliability and dramatically decrease the time for the interconnect repair. The current repair cost is higher than that for a new interconnect. SJRC representatives will be selected, trained, and positioned at Naval Air Station (NAS) Oceana, NAS Jacksonville, NAS Lemoore, NAS North Island, MCAS Beaufort, and MCAS Miramar. The representatives at NAS Jacksonville and North Island will perform repair parts, repairables, and packing functions. The representatives at NAS Oceana, NAS Lemoore, MCAS Beaufort, and MCAS Miramar will perform technical assistance to the Avionics Intermediate Division maintenance shop and to the packing shop to reduce the number of weapons replaceable assemblies (WRAs) being returned for repair and reduce the handling damage to combiner glasses and optics. Customer training and publications management are not included.

8.6.2 Organization of the PBL Program

The RCSJ performance-based logistic program is organized as follows. A program manager from the production program product line has been assigned to the PBL program. However, a core group, including the manager of product support, the planning and administration manager, and the program manager are responsible for the establishment and execution of the PBL program. Product support is responsible for generating personnel requisition, interviewing, selecting, training, and locating all but the program administrator positions.

8.6.3 Program Phases

The base period consists of two phases of the program. Phase 1 is the transitional year where the U.S. Navy is responsible for providing RFI units that are required to meet the turnaround time (TAT), and RCSJ is responsible to establish the PBL infrastructure to receive and fill RFI repairable demands, track the on-time delivery performance, report on failures and trends, etc. Phase 2 is a full PBL 91% on-time delivery against demands in the delivery timeframe.

8.6.4 Maintenance Support

Repairs will be conducted on the F/A-18A/B/C/D and E/F Common equipment at three main locations: Rockwell Collins San Jose, the Navy depot at Jacksonville, Florida (NADEPJAX), and the Navy depot at San Diego, California (NADEPNI). The original supplier will perform the repairs of optics, control panels, and LCDs. All repairs will be routed to and from San Jose to the various repair sites. Figure 8.1 illustrates the flow of the repairables and repair parts.

Rockwell Collins San Jose will perform F-14D equipment repairs at the Orchard Parkway, San Jose, California, facility. RCSJ, Orchard Parkway, NADEPNI, and NADEPJAX will be facilities that perform troubleshooting and failed part replacement, including initial testing and retest. RCSJ will use test equipment that was built for F/A-18A/B/C/D and E/F heads-up display (HUD) and F-14D production. Most of this equipment is owned by the government. All facilities will adhere to good practices to prevent premature failures of prime equipment. Each repair facility is responsible for training and certifying the technicians and operators that perform PBL repairs. Design engineering, product engineering, and manufacturing will provide RCSJ repair support as requested by the PBL product support group.

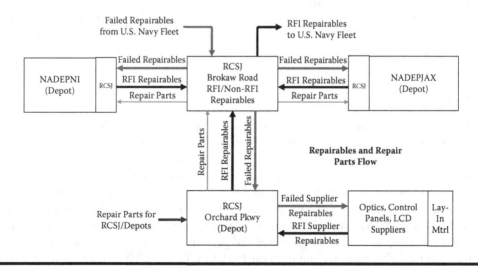

Figure 8.1   Repairables and repair parts flow. (Source: Rockwell Collins San Jose.)

8.6.5 Service Parts Provisioning

The types and quantities of repair parts will be determined from the repair and repair part prediction models used in the preparation of the PBL business case analysis. Initially, optics repair material and combiner glasses will be purchased to support the first 2 years of repairs, with yearly options for the additional 3 years. Other low-cost parts will be purchased at the predicted 5-year quantities to achieve economies of scale. A material tracking system will be implemented by the product support material analyst function that compares the actual parts used for repair to the predicted usage. The predictive model will be updated with actual data so piece-parts predictions become more accurate over time. Future parts orders will use the updated parts model to determine quantities to order. Part usage will rely on parts requisitions from Rockwell Collins San Jose (RCSJ) and from the representatives at the Navy depots.

Repair piece parts will be housed in carousels at the RCSJ plant, where the RCSJ repairs will be performed. The RCSJ repair line will order repair parts from the PBL portion of the RCSJ stockroom as needed. The PBL planning function will ensure these parts get issued to the appropriate repair technician or operator for installation into the repairable. Lay-in material for supplier repairs will be required to support the first 2 years of the PBL demand, with yearly options for the third through fifth years. Based on quarterly repair projections for the Navy depots (NADEPs), associated repair parts will be positioned at the NADEP prior to the start of a quarter to support those projected repairs. The RCSJ on-site representative will perform repair part storage and issuing.

A repair part obsolescence plan was developed for the repair parts identified for the PBL. This plan will initially run the parts list through a program that will analyze the life cycle of the parts. Once the life cycle profile of the parts is known, a plan for that part will be generated to resolve that part's obsolescence profile. Identifying an alternate part, lifetime buys, and redesign of the part might be possible solutions for parts obsolescence. Included in the repair parts procurement plan will be parts for subassemblies to support repairs and spare assemblies identified in the models used for the PBL proposal. Those parts orders and build plans will be generated and monitored by product support planning. Subassembly modules, when built, will be put into the Orchard Parkway PBL stockroom carousels to be requisitioned as needed. The planning of these builds should take into account the setback associated with the demand for the part, where the subassembly is used according to the repair demand prediction model.

8.6.6 Reliability

A Failure Analysis and Corrective Action System is incorporated into the PBL program. A unique identifier is created for repairables that return from the Navy under the PBL contract. That unique identifier will be selected during the generation of trouble failure reports (TFRs) for Navy returned repairables. TFRs will be generated when the product support planner schedules the returned Navy asset to go into repair. Repair parts removed from repairs will be retained for possible failure analysis except for those items that have natural wear-out, for example, cathode ray tubes (CRTs). PBL TFRs will be entered into the existing Failure Reporting and Corrective Action System (FRACAS) database. TFRs must be generated and parts retained for possible failure analysis from failed parts at the RCSJ depot site and from the NADEPs. Figure 8.2 illustrates the trouble failure reports (TFRs) flow.

Reliability engineering is responsible for analyzing the failures and detecting any trends. Reports will be generated to access the top ten reliability problem units, and root cause analysis

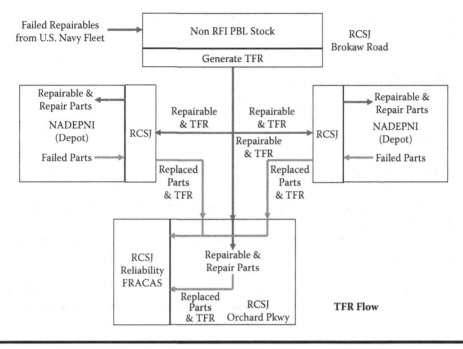

Figure 8.2   Trouble and failure report flow.

will be performed to evaluate potential improvements that would significantly reduce the number of failures.

8.6.7 Navy Depot Site Support

Rockwell Collins representatives will be located at the two Navy depots (NADEPs) and at four Navy and Marine Corp air bases. Both depots will strive to provide a stockroom and office area for the RCSJ on-site representatives. At the NADEPs, RCSJ representatives will provide administrative, stockroom, and shipping support. Repair parts and repairables will be shipped to the RCSJ representative at each depot based on the projected repairs. Repairables and parts will be issued to the NADEPs to meet the 30-day turnaround time for each repair. A first-in, first-out system for repair of repairables will be employed as much as practical. There may be times where priorities may change the first-in, first-out system. Tracking of the repairs through the NADEP systems on a noninterference basis will be performed by the RCSJ representative. A repair part usage reporting system will be developed and employed for use by the RCSJ representatives at the NADEPs. RCSJ representatives will receive failed parts that are candidates for failure analysis and return those parts to RCSJ upon request from the reliability engineer point of contact responsible for PBL. The original trouble failure report (TFR) will be generated in the PBL stockroom, and the repair information will be completed by the NADEP on-site RCSJ representatives.

Product support will train the NADEP on-site RCSJ representatives. The intent of this training is to provide the NADEP on-site RCSJ representatives the knowledge necessary to operate independently. The training shall include the handling, packaging, and shipping of repairables and piece parts, completing the accompanying documentation required for repairables and piece parts, stockroom operations, handling and documenting replaced parts on TFRs, time card operations, and tracking systems for repairables.

8.6.8 Navy/Marine Corp Base

At the four Navy and Marine air bases, RCSJ representatives perform technical management of the Avionics Intermediate Maintenance Department and shipping support of the shipping department. The intent of the field support is:

- Reduce, if not eliminate, return of repairables to the repair depot that do not have a fault, could not duplicate.
- Reduce, if not eliminate, handling and shipping damage to heads-up display combiner glasses and optics.
- Promote returning interconnects in chassis to the depot for repair and not removing interconnects from chassis at the intermediate level.

Product support will train the field engineers in the theory of operation of the units, assembly and disassembly of these units, display packaging and handling techniques, time card entry, query for repair status, and other database operations at RCSJ.

8.6.9 Engineering Design Activities

Two design activities are performed under this performance-based logistics (PBL) program.

- Technology updates
- Replacing obsolete technology

For these design activities, the plan below is:

- Perform a trade study and cost out option selected.
- Perform a cost-benefit analysis for the option selected (cost of redesign and qualification vs. cost of continued repair).
- If the cost-benefit analysis is positive, a return on investment of greater than 15%, then plan the design and qualification activity, which will include:
  - First-article test
- Qualification

Microsoft Project is used to plan the activities, and the costs will be tracked against the plan. Each planned activity will be added to the PBL master schedule.

8.6.10 Configuration Management

The configuration of the performance-based logistics products is maintained according to Rockwell Collins configuration management manual. First-article testing, including testing at the appropriate Navy depot and qualification, will be performed prior to the generation and submittal of the engineering change proposal (ECP). Qualification can be by similarity or by testing, whichever is appropriate. The original procurement specification qualification requirements will be used as the source for qualification requirements.

8.6.11 PBL Program Metrics

Rockwell Collins established these metrics for the PBL program.

- Availability rate
- Repair average turnaround time (TAT)
- Navy return time of failed assets
- Cash flow
- Cost (labor, material, other direct costs (ODC) against the base plan
- Sales per PBL headcount
- Profitability
- Top ten failure repairables and ten most replaced parts

The availability rate is determined by dividing the number of requisitions delivered on time by the number of requisitions for that given period. Both a cumulative rate and a monthly rate are plotted. An Excel spreadsheet is used for the rate calculations and plots. Availability rate is the key metric for PBL and will be reported during in-house and NAVICP program reviews. Figure 8.3 is an illustration of a proposed availability rate comparison tracking chart.

Average repair turnaround time (TAT) is calculated by dividing the cumulative repair time by the number of repairs. Average repair TAT is tracked by repair site. A repair TAT of 30 days is necessary to ensure the RFI shelf is stocked to meet demands. Figure 8.4 illustrates the average repair TAT tracking chart.

Navy return time of failed assets in 40 days is a requirement of the contract and is a dependent variable in the calculation for RFI shelf quantities to meet Navy asset demands. This time is measured from the time a demand is made for an asset until the failed asset reaches the PBL receiving dock. The tracking of this time is not serial number dependent, but is NIIN, National Stock Number, dependent. Since this is an important element of PBL, this measurement is calculated monthly and reported during in-house and NAVICP program reviews.

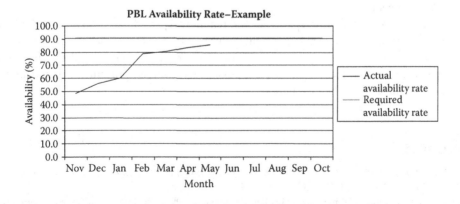

Figure 8.3   PBL availability rate chart.

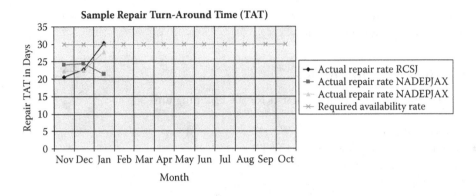

Figure 8.4   Sample PBL repair turnaround time (TAT).

Cash flow is tracked and reported to ensure the costs do not exceed the revenues. Revenues come from scheduled billings. Cash flow is determined on a cumulative basis and is charted as cumulative revenues less cumulative costs. Costs include the labor, material, and costs through all burdens. Cost against the base plan are also measured and reported. The base plan is based on the labor rates, material cost, and associated overhead rates, general and administrative overhead (G&A), and cost of money burdens, but modified by the PBL staffing and material procurement profiles. Actual costs are based on actual labor rates, actual material costs, actual overhead, actual G&A, and cost of money burdens. Both the base plan and the actual costs are charted in such a manner that each contribution to cost can be clearly tracked. These costs are reported on a cumulative basis. Annually, a year-end adjustment is made when the past year rates are determined.

Sales per PBL headcount are measured as a means for determining the efficiency of the PBL operations. From the base sales plan, the sales per PBL headcount target are determined and then the actual sales per headcount are compared. PBL sales are not recognized in a traditional manner because of the uniqueness and variability of the repair labor and repair material aspect of PBL vs. cost. Therefore, the sales per PBL headcount may not be totally known until the base period for PBL is completed. However, the target and actual sales per PBL headcount can be factored for a valid measurement. The gross profit margin and the percentage return on sales for the PBL program are also calculated. Profitability is calculated monthly and reported at a frequency to be determined by executive management.

In terms of the top ten failure repairables and ten most replaced parts metrics, reliability engineering reports on the PBL-related failures and failure parts. The report includes charts that detail the top ten part numbers that return for repair and the top ten parts that are replaced during repair actions. The intent of these reports is to explore possible reliability improvements that could reduce the number of failures over the PBL period.

References

Akao, Yoji. 1990. *Quality function deployment: Integrating customer requirements into product design*, trans. Glenn Mazur. Portland, OR: Productivity Press.
Basili, Victor R., Gianluigi Caldiera, and H. Dieter Rombach. 1994. The goal question metric approach. In *Encyclopedia of software engineering*. New York: Wiley.

Defense Acquisition University (DAU). 2008. Supportability. In *Defense acquisition guidebook*, chap. 4.4.9. Retrieved from https://akss.dau.mil/dag/ on October 25, 2008.

Mahidhar, Vikram. 2005, September. Designing the Lean enterprise performance measurement system. Masters thesis, Massachusetts Institute of Technology.

Massachusetts Institute of Technology. 1998, August 5. *Lean sustainment research, executive summary, goals, objectives and metrics*. Cambridge, MA: Center for Technology, Policy and Indaustrial Development.

Rome Laboratory. 1985. *Rome Laboratory Software Quality Framework*. RADC-TR-85-37. 3 vols. AD-A153-988, AD-A153-989, AD-A153-990. Rome, NY: U.S. Air Force.

Chapter 9

Affordability

For which of you, intending to build a tower, sitteth not down first, and counteth the cost, whether he hath sufficient to finish it? (Luke 14:28) (Figure 9.1)

Preface

It used to be that procurement cost was the primary, and sometimes only, criteria for system selection or new technology upgrades. But, this single purpose criterion often resulted in bad long-run financial decisions. Why? Because procurement costs tell only one part of the story. The complete story is told in the life cycle cost of a system from cradle to grave. Thus, *affordability* is really defined by the extent to which the life cycle cost is consonant with the long-range investment plans of the Department of Defense (DoD) or its military departments or defense agencies. Affordability considers not only development and investment costs, but also operating, support, and disposal costs.

Every recent issuance of the DoD 5000 series directives keeps emphasizing this life cycle fiscal responsibility theme, and every system sustainment program today must dictate that the control of life cycle costs receive an unprecedented level of management attention. In 1995, Dr. Paul G. Kaminski, the undersecretary of defense for acquisition and technology, underscored this message by issuing the memorandum "Reducing Life-Cycle Costs for New and Fielded Systems" (Kaminsky 2005) that stated: "Reducing the cost to acquire and operate the department's equipment while maintaining a high level of performance for the user is my highest priority." The latest revisions to the DoD 5000 series directives mandates that the sustainment process consider both performance requirements and fiscal constraints. Thus, the "knowledgeable use of life-cycle costing can be the catalyst in assuring affordability of systems when fielded for operations by the user" (Defense Systems Management College 1997, p. 12–2).

Defense policy, as stated in DoD Directive 5000.1 (DoD 2003a), includes the requirement to obtain quality products "at a fair and reasonable price." This directive, which governs the defense

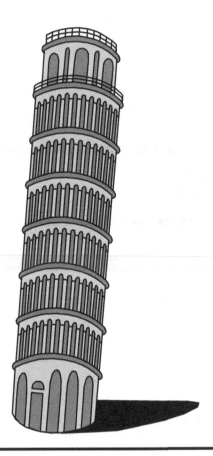

Figure 9.1   Building a tower.

sustainment system, goes on to address cost and life cycle costs in each of the three major policy areas. Requirements include the need to:

■ Minimize the cost of ownership in the context of a total system approach
■ View cost in the context of cost as an independent variable (CAIV), recognizing that the majority of costs are determined early in a program
■ Work closely with the user to achieve a proper balance among cost, schedule, and performance while ensuring that systems are both affordable and cost-effective

The program manager (PM), together with the user, proposes cost objectives and thresholds for milestone decision authority (MDA) approval, which will then be controlled through the acquisition program baseline (APB) process. Further, the PM is asked to search continually for innovative practices to reduce costs, including prudent investments in pollution prevention in an effort to reduce life cycle environmental costs and liability. Finally, the sustainment community was directed to recognize that competition was to provide major incentives for industry to enhance the application of advanced technology and life cycle cost advantages to defense programs as well as a mechanism to obtain an advantageous price. The emphasis on competition has decreased.

This chapter is aimed at a life cycle cost (LCC) approach to affordability. The chapter was prepared to help program sponsors, sustainment program managers, and other stakeholders understand LCC analysis. This understanding needs to be based on a common definition of terms and a common approach to the LCC analysis process. The chapter begins with an understanding of the life cycle of a system, then discusses the concepts of life cycle costing, the process of LCC, the requirements, capabilities, methods, and tools that one needs in order to guide the actions of the LCC analysis teams, and contains a real case study of an LCC analysis.

9.1 The Life Cycle

Military systems and the military enterprise follow a life cycle. Understanding this life cycle is important to understanding the life cycle costs. An excellent reference for the life cycle of a generic entity (system or enterprise) is the generalized enterprise reference architecture (GERA) framework developed by the International Federation for Information Processing/International Federation of Automatic Control (IFIP/IFAC) task force on information processing (Bernus 1998). The GERA structure is generic, so it would pertain to any system or enterprise. Figure 9.2 shows this generic structure. A good military reference is the U.S. DoD guidebook (2003a). Figure 9.3 is the DoD instantiation of this life cycle structure. The cycle begins with the determination of a mission requirement and initial concept, and then proceeds with design, production, deployment, operation and maintenance, support, refurbishment or obsolescence, and final disposal of the system. Following this life cycle structure ensures that the system would be designed with a cradle-to-grave concept in mind. It is not sufficient to simply apply a process improvement initiative or new technology insertion to an entity without thinking about the preservation of those important improvement concepts for the entire life of the enterprise or system.

9.1.1 Presystem Identification Phase

The presystem identification phase identifies the contents of the particular entity under consideration in terms of its boundaries and its relation to its internal and external environments. The concept phase includes the definition of the mission, vision, values, strategies, objectives, operational concepts, policies, and business plans of the system. The requirement phase is the set of activities that are needed to develop descriptions of operational requirements of the entity, its relevant processes, and the collection of all their functional, behavioral, informational, and capability needs. The design phases include all human tasks (those of individuals and organizational entities), all machine tasks concerned with the entity's customer services and products and related management and control functions, and all necessary information and resources (including manufacturing, information, communication, and control, or any other technology). Dividing the design phase into preliminary design (or specification) and detailed design permits the separation of overall system specifications. A concept decision is made by senior DoD staff members, called the Functional Capabilities Board (FCB), after a review of various analysis reports and an analysis of alternatives (AoA) plan. The FCB refines the concept, which is described in an initial capabilities document (ICD), and approves the AoA plan. The final refinement is conducted through the AoA. Upon selection of an initial concept, the project enters the technology development phase. It ends with a milestone A review, where the MDA assesses the results and evaluates the affordability of the proposed new program. This type of early analysis of all relevant factors would likely have prevented the situation depicted in Figure 9.1. A favorable decision establishes a new sustainment program, which is authorized to enter the next phase, as shown in Figure 9.4. A concept baseline is established that identifies the initial cost, schedule, and performance objectives. The purpose of these tasks is to reduce

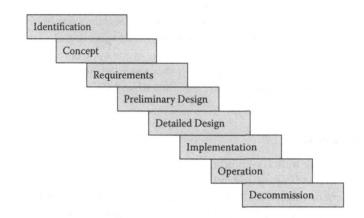

Figure 9.2 Generic life cycle phases for a system.

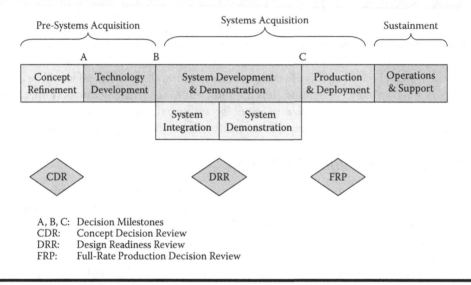

A, B, C: Decision Milestones
CDR: Concept Decision Review
DRR: Design Readiness Review
FRP: Full-Rate Production Decision Review

Figure 9.3 DoD life cycle phases for a system.

technology risk and to determine the appropriate set of technologies to be integrated into the full system. The important point here is that this major decision is supported by an AoA, and an AoA includes an LCC and a benefits analysis, which are described in detail in Section 9.4.

9.1.2 System Acquisition Phase

The systems acquisition or implementation phase covers commissioning, purchasing, and (re) configuring or developing all service, manufacturing, and control software as well as hardware resources; hiring and training personnel, and developing or changing the human organization; and component testing and validation, systems integration, validation and testing, and releasing into operation. The system formally enters the acquisition process at milestone B, when the MDA permits the system to enter the system development and demonstration phase. The purpose of this MDA review is to determine if the results of the first phase warrant a program's continuation.

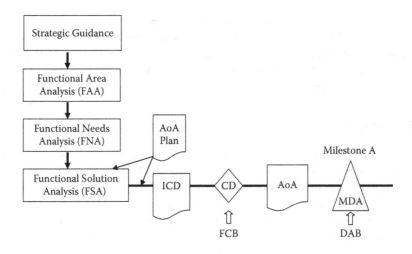

Figure 9.4 Presystem identification phase steps.

The MDA must assess the program's affordability and establish a development baseline containing the refined cost, schedule, and performance objectives. The life cycle logistics (LCL) emphasis during system development and demonstration is to ensure operational sustainment while minimizing the logistics footprint. The support concept and strategy are further refined, and potential performance-based logistics product support integrators and providers are identified. This phase is the most critical time point in which to optimize system sustainment through the design criteria. LCL documents and analyses are refined as a result of the developmental and operational tests and systems engineering analyses. LCL is also a component of the technical reviews, such as the critical design review (CDR), which is conducted during system development and demonstration.

The production and deployment/operation phase includes the set of activities for producing the customer's product or service along with all those tasks needed for monitoring, controlling, and evaluating the operation. The purpose is to achieve an operational capability that satisfies mission needs. Milestone C authorizes entry into a low-rate initial production mode, at which time the system design should be sufficient enough to initiate production, and the technical requirements have been demonstrated to be adequate for acceptable operational capability. At this point, the product support strategy is fully defined, a product support integrator has been selected, and performance-based logistics agreements that reflect performance, support, and funding expectations should be documented and signed. Also, funding should be identified and available for testing and implementation of the selected strategy with a selected product support integrator.

9.1.3 Sustainment Phase

The sustainment phase includes the activities for support, maintenance, remissioning, retraining, redesign, recycling, preservation, transfer, disbanding, disassembly, or disposal of all or part of the system at the end of its useful life in operation (Bernus 1998). Sustainment includes supply, maintenance, transportation, sustaining engineering, data management, configuration management, manpower, personnel, training, habitability, survivability, environment, safety, occupational health, protection of critical program information, antitamper provisions, and information technology (IT) functions. While the acquisition phase is critical to designing and implementing a successful and affordable sustainment strategy, the ultimate measure of success is the application of that strategy after the system has been deployed for operational use. Life cycle systems management and performance-based logistics enable that objective. Warfighters require operational availability (Ao) and operational effectiveness. However, regardless of how well one designs for sustainability, systems do suffer stresses during actual operational deployment and use that were not necessarily included in the design.

9.1.4 Final Disposal

The final phase involves the demilitarization, recycling, and disposal of the system. The demilitarization process must be carried out in a way that minimizes DoD's liability due to environmental, safety, security, and health issues. The environmental issues associated with disposal can be more significant than those created during all previous life cycle phases. Recycling is the preferred process. Reprocessing involves the use of the material in a different manner than originally intended. The least preferred approach is disposal.

9.2 Life Cycle Cost (LCC)

The life cycle cost (LCC) of a system is the sum total of the direct and indirect, recurring and nonrecurring, costs that are estimated to be incurred over the system's life cycle. It includes the cost of development, procurement, operation, maintenance, support, and disposal. All relevant costs should be included. Life cycle costing is the process of collecting and analyzing the life cycle cost in the various decisions associated with acquiring or sustaining the system. Another view of LCC is to think of life cycle cost as a noun that defines the total cost of ownership of any system, whereas life cycle costing can be viewed as a verb to describe the use of selected, relevant portions of LCC data to support decisions.

Three points are important:

1. The LCC analysis itself costs resources. The amount expended should be directly proportional to the cost of a bad decision.
2. There is a diminishing return on the amount of data collected or used to support a good decision. Only include enough cost information to ensure that the correct alternative is selected.
3. Some costs are purposely not included if they are the same for all alternatives or they otherwise cloud the issue.

Some readers may ask if LCC is the same concept as:

■ Life cycle cost procurement (LCCP) and life cycle cost management (LCCM)
■ Design to cost (DTC), with its variations, such as design-to-unit production cost (DTUPC) and design to life cycle cost (DTLCC)
■ Total ownership cost (TOC)
■ Cost as an independent variable (CAIV)

LCCP is the process of a system or program procurement in which LCC is considered in the source selection and awarding of the contract. LCCM is the management of a program with LCC as a primary decision criterion. DTC and its variations, DTUPC and DTLCC, are a costing concept that was used in the early 1980s. The basic idea of DTC was something like:

"Contractor: we want you to design and build three sizes of a surface ship electronic warfare system: a system that costs about $200,000 for small ships; a system that costs about $500,000 for medium size ships; and a more capable system costing about $1 million for large ships. This price should include the logistics support." In DTC, a system is designed to unit cost targets. The concept was generally not successful for two reasons. First, most of the systems designed under this concept ran short of funding and were fielded with little or no logistics support. Second, the sustainment strategy was to design and field the most technologically advanced systems possible. So, requirements creep made cost goals moving numbers. Cost and schedule were dependent variables, dependent on performance.

TOC is a variation of LCC where the scope for the bounds of costs, which go beyond those associated with the item or system, are included in the analysis. The idea here is for the program manager to consider the effect of his decisions on the operating and support infrastructure beyond those within his direct program control. TOC was coined to expand the bounds of traditional LCC analysis. The idea was for program or project decision makers to consider the bigger picture. The decision maker was to consider the impact of his or her decisions on the next higher portion of the enterprise. Implicit in this concept is for decision makers to coordinate with the enterprise entities that their decisions influence. For example, if enough individual program managers decide on contracting out depot support, eventually, organic depot facilities are no longer justified. Also note that TOC is not to be confused with total cost of ownership, which has historically been used as interchangeable with LCC.

The term *cost as an independent variable* (CAIV) was coined in the mid-1990s as a major rewrite of the DoD directive was being formulated. Many people thought CIAV was essentially the same as the concept of design to cost or design to LCC, which were invented in the early 1980s. DTLCC was doomed to failure because of conflicting strategy. Fifty years of system acquisitions during the Cold War years were marked with universal requirements creep, program stretch-outs, and the resulting cost growth. The taxpayer was constantly barraged with reports of weapons being finally delivered at a much higher price than predicted as the programs started. System performance and schedule were independent variables and cost was the dependent variable. What many people could not seem to understand was that there was a change in national tactical strategy to move acquisitions along that, in turn, required changes to performance requirements, schedules, and cost. The change was due to a Soviet strategy to freeze technology early in the weapons system life cycle and buy large numbers of weapons systems. The idea was to overwhelm enemies with numbers. The U.S. strategy was to field fewer systems that were technologically superior and to use advanced tactics and advanced technology to defeat the superior Soviet numbers. With a research and development and production cycle that usually exceeded 10 years, new technology opportunities were constantly emerging during the cycle. To take advantage of this new technology, schedules had to slip and cost had to increase. The Cold War was a weapons-system-buying race. Fortunately, it broke the Soviet bank first. When the Soviet threat collapsed, there was a demand for a peace dividend. As a result, CAIV emerged as a verb. LCC, the noun, is the same as before. The analysis process has not changed. What has changed is the imperative to hold cost down. When technology insertion was traded off against schedule and cost, technology nearly always won out in the past. Now, changing a design to incorporate any change must be analyzed and fully justified. Historically, requirements have been determined by early analysis, and requirements have been added as the program moved through the long sustainment process. Requirements were the independent variable, while both schedule and cost were the dependent variables. Cost is to be much less of a dependent variable if not totally independent—thus the name CAIV. Accordingly, program managers must establish aggressive but realistic objectives and follow through by trading off performance, schedule, and cost to achieve a balanced set of goals. CAIV is aimed at managing to a life cycle cost objective (Criscimagna 1998). On the other hand, there are some, for example, Rice (2000), that argue cost is not an independent variable. The relationship of designs and capabilities to increasing and decreasing costs actually demonstrates that cost is (mathematically) a constraint, not a variable.

Whatever term that becomes the flavor of the year for LCC, according to the *Acquisition Logistics Guide* (Defense Systems Management College 1997) the objectives for life cycle costing are clear:

1. Setting realistic but aggressive cost objectives early in each acquisition program.
2. Devising and employing a process for accomplishing cost-schedule-performance trade-offs during each acquisition phase and at each milestone decision point.
3. Managing risk to achieve cost, schedule, and performance objectives.
4. Devising appropriate metrics for tracking progress in setting and achieving cost objectives.
5. Motivating government and industry managers to achieve program objectives.
6. Establishing in-place additional incentives to reduce operating and support costs for fielded systems.

9.2.1 DoD Policy on LCC

Policy, as stated in DoD Directive 5000.1 (DoD 2003a), states that all participants in the sustainment system are expected to recognize the reality of fiscal constraints and to view cost as an independent variable (CAIV). The life cycle cost should be treated as equally important to performance and schedule in program decisions. DoD Directive 5000.2-R (DoD 2002) states that a life cycle cost estimate shall be prepared by the program office in support of program initiation, usually at milestone A, and all subsequent milestone reviews. The milestone decision authority (MDA) may not approve entry into engineering and manufacturing development or production and deployment unless an independent estimate of the full life cycle cost of the program has been completed and considered by the MDA. The life cycle cost estimates shall be:

- Explicitly based on the program objectives, operational requirements, contract specifications for the system, and a life cycle cost and benefit element structure agreed upon by the integrated product team (IPT).
- Comprehensive in character, identifying all elements of cost that would be entailed by a decision to proceed with the development, production, and operation of the system regardless of funding source or management control.
- Consistent with the cost estimates used in the analysis of alternatives and consistent with the staffing estimate.
- Neither optimistic nor pessimistic, but based on a careful assessment of the risks and reflecting a realistic appraisal of the level of cost most likely to be realized.

Policy also states that the DoD sponsor of the program should establish a description of the features of the program, referred to as a Cost Analysis Requirements Description (CARD), as a basis for the life cycle cost estimates. The description should be prepared in advance of a planned overarching integrated product team (OIPT) review. For programs with significant cost risk or high visibility, the component acquisition executive (CAE) may request that a component cost analysis estimate also be prepared in addition to the program office life cycle cost estimate. The Office of Secretary of Defense (OSD) principal staff assistant (PSA) or DoD sponsor should ensure that the component cost analysis is created for milestone A and updated for milestone B. The MDA may direct an updated analysis for subsequent decision points if conditions warrant. At milestone A, the sponsor may conduct a sufficiency review of the life cycle cost estimate in lieu of a full analysis. The integrated product team (IPT) would establish the content of the sufficiency review.

9.2.2 LCC Patterns

Figure 9.5 illustrates the typical life cycle cost pattern for a weapon system. The amplitude of the costs grows with each successive phase, and the LCC is at its greatest for the operation and support phases in the life cycle of the system.

What Figure 9.5 demonstrates is that the life cycle costing process should begin as early in the cycle as possible. It has been estimated that about 66% of a system's cost are already established, and the funds already committed, by the decisions that are made in the conceptual design stage (Followell 1995), as illustrated in Figure 9.6.

However, the opportunity to minimize these costs diminishes rapidly as the design and development of a weapon system proceeds through the cycle (Blanchard 1998), since the percentage of funds that have been committed levels off by the time the system reaches the sustainability phase (Figure 9.7).

9.2.3 LCC Categories

There are several ways costs associated with a program must be defined and estimated. They include funding appropriation, work breakdown structure (WBS), and life cycle cost (LCC) components.

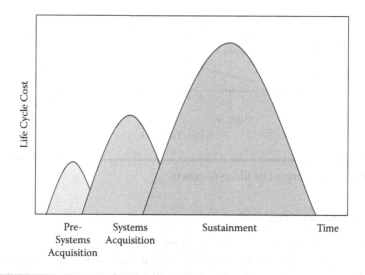

Figure 9.5 Weapon system life cycle cost pattern.

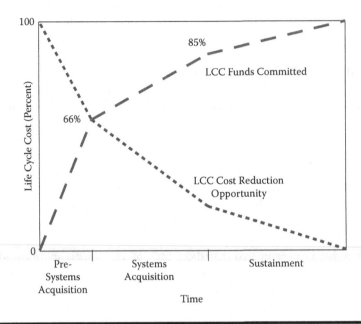

Figure 9.6   Funding trends by opportunity and commitment.

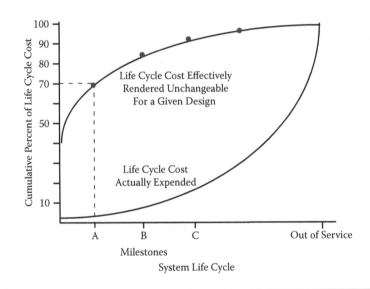

Figure 9.7   Cumulative percent of life cycle costs.

9.2.3.1 Funding Appropriation

Funding appropriation includes research, development, test and evaluation (RDT&E), procurement, operations and maintenance (O&M), military construction, and military personnel. These breakouts are necessary to develop internal budgets and for budget requests to Congress.

9.2.3.2 Work Breakdown Structure (WBS)

The work breakdown structure (WBS) is a tool used to specify work to be done and the associated costs to perform the work. U.S. DoD military handbook MIL-HDBK-881 (DoD 1998) provides a recommended WBS for various program categories, including aircraft, ships, armored vehicles, etc. It accommodates prime mission equipment, systems engineering, program management, systems test and evaluation, training, peculiar support equipment, data, operational site activation, initial spares, initial repair parts, and industrial facilities. Each of these categories is further broken down into indentured levels of detail. This method provides an organized, structured system of compartmentalizing work and its associated costs. It facilitates detailed visibility into those parts of the work that are expected to be the major consumers of resources. Further, the method tracks the contractors' actual work performance against their initial cost estimate by specific task, i.e., work packages. The progress of the contractor's work can be reported within the WBS structure. The historical files from the various projects and programs in service organizations form a wealth of data from which to estimate similar future projects.

9.2.3.3 Life Cycle Cost Elements

Life cycle cost components include acquisition, operations and support (O&S), and disposal. LCC includes all WBS elements, all appropriations, all contract and in-house costs, and all recurring and nonrecurring cost categories.

9.2.3.3.1 Acquisition Cost

Acquisition cost is the sum of all contract and in-house research and development (R&D) costs and recurring and nonrecurring investment costs that are required to transform the results of the R&D into a fully deployed operational system. R&D consists of those contract and in-house costs incurred from program initiation at the conceptual phase through the end of engineering and manufacturing development (Figure 9.8). R&D costs include the cost for feasibility studies, modeling, trade-off analyses, engineering design, development, fabrication, assembly and test of prototype hardware and software, system test and evaluation, associated peculiar support equipment, and documentation (Defense Systems Management College 1997).

Nonrecurring and recurring investment costs (Figures 9.9 and 9.10) are incurred during the production and deployment phases, although some investment expenditures can occur during the latter part of the full-scale development phase and the early part of the operations and support phases. Residual value benefits should not be included with investment costs, since the benefit might distort the LCC analysis. Investment costs include those associated with producing and deploying the primary hardware; system engineering and program management; support equipment, training equipment, and initial training, technical publications/data, and initial spares and repair parts associated with production; interim contractor support; and construction, operations, and maintenance associated with system site activation.

9.2.3.3.2 Operating and Support (O&S) Costs

O&S costs consist of the sustainment costs incurred from the initial system deployment through to the end of system operations (Figure 9.11). The category may include interim contractor support when it is outside the scope of the production program and the sustainment program baseline.

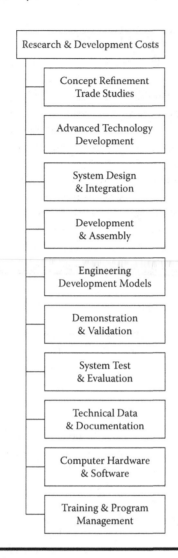

Figure 9.8   Research and development costs.

O&S costs include costs directly and indirectly attributable to the existence of the system regardless of funding source or management control. Direct costs refer to the resources directly associated with the system, whereas indirect costs refer to the resources that provide indirect support to the system. For example, compensation for a maintenance technician would be treated as a direct cost, but the cost of benefits (e.g., medical and dental) for the same technician would be an indirect cost.

Although product-specific estimates of O&S costs are required as part of the life cycle costing process, such estimates are just orders of magnitude at early milestones rather than accurate estimates. Early operating and support costs are highly sensitive to assumptions on the number and delivery sequence of the units that will become operational, and the operational scenarios planned for these units. Operational policies affect maintenance and manpower costs. Manpower and fuel consumption estimates can vary significantly throughout the phases of an acquisition. Sensitivity analyses should be performed to assess the effect of such long-term variable factors.

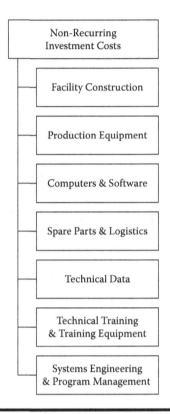

Figure 9.9   Nonrecurring investment costs.

Furthermore, there are two basic considerations for dealing with personnel costs. The first is whether to use man-hours or manning levels. The second is whether to use billet costs or pay and allowance.

9.2.3.3.3 Disposal Costs

Disposal costs are associated with the demilitarization and disposal of a military system at the end of its useful life (Figure 9.12). While these costs may represent an insignificant fraction of a system's life cycle cost relative to the other categories, it is important to consider them early in the planning process because of the environmental and safety characteristics of the system. Credit may be given in the cost estimate for resource recovery and recycling.

9.2.4 LCC Data Sources

The DoD (2007) cost estimating guide states that regardless of the source of the cost data, the validation of the data is a responsibility of the cost analyst. In many cases, the data will need to be adjusted or normalized. For example, in analogy estimates, the reference system cost should be adjusted to account for any differences in the system characteristics, support concepts, or operating environment between the reference system and the proposed system. For currently fielded major systems, historical cost data are available from the Visibility and Management of Operations and Support Costs (VAMOSC) data system managed by each military service.

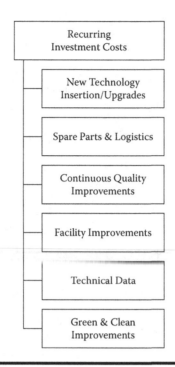

Figure 9.10   Recurring investment costs.

Data can be obtained for entire systems, or at lower levels of detail. VAMOSC provides not only cost data, but may contain related noncost data (such as operating tempo or maintenance man-hours) as well. This type of data is useful for analogy estimates (between proposed systems and appropriate predecessor or reference systems) and for bottom-up engineering estimates (for fielded systems or components, possibly adjusted for projected reliability and maintainability growth). VAMOSC data should always be carefully examined before use. It should be displayed over a period of a few years, and stratified by different sources (such as major command or base) so that abnormal outliers in the data can be identified, investigated, and resolved as necessary. VAMOSC data are sometimes supplemented with more specialized reliability and maintainability data, which can be obtained from the military service maintenance data collection systems. The importance of data validation is equally important when this type of data is used in a cost estimate. In addition, VAMOSC data for unit-level manpower are often supplemented with information from more detailed unit manning documents (such as tables of organization and equipment) (DoD 2007).

Data that can be used for detailed bottom-up engineering estimates can often come from contractor databases. Appropriate government personnel should validate this data source before use, possibly on a sampling basis. Validation is important in cases when the hardware is not yet tested or deployed. The validation should address the completeness of the component population, the realism of component reliability and maintainability estimates, and the legitimacy of the component unit prices (DoD 2007).

Described below are the individual cost elements and potential sources of the cost data. Each element should be based on an appropriate method of cost estimating. Four estimating methods are described in Section 9.3.1.5.

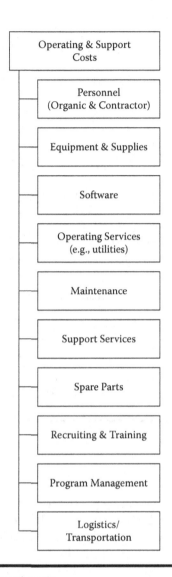

Figure 9.11 Operating and support costs.

9.2.4.1 Maintenance Data

This data element is for actual repair-type maintenance as established by the system's maintenance plan. The various subelements of maintenance include requirements for depot and intermediate investment costs, test-bed facilities investment, repair costs, including depot and intermediate repair, and support/training-related repair. Particular emphasis is now required in the area of contractor maintenance services. Some special analysis studies and plans may sometimes be included. Investment costs for maintenance should not duplicate requirements identified in other areas, such as support equipment and computer resources support. Primary plant equipment that is unique to depot or intermediate repair facilities should be included as investment costs. Past experience from contracting for maintenance and from the Visibility and Management of Operations and Support Costs (VAMOSC) database may be applicable as source information on maintenance.

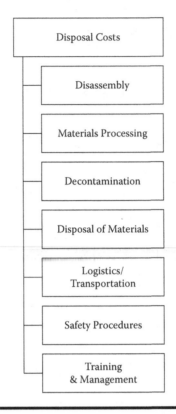

Figure 9.12 Disposal costs.

9.2.4.2 Technical Data

This data element normally refers to costs associated with purchasing operator and maintainer technical manuals and depot repair standards. Additionally, this element includes requirements for the development, in-process review, production, validation, verification, distribution, and updating of technical data and the associated data records. It also includes management, review, and source data. Specific subelements to be considered are technical orders/manuals and associated changes, technical orders/manuals management, drawings/reprocurement data, planned maintenance system requirements, analysis, studies, plans, and other. Sources of information upon which to base the estimate are analysis, past contract, and field activity tasking orders. It is not unusual to see backup data, which differentiate between the cost of technical data pages in categories such as pure text, text, and graphics, lists of information such as parts lists, and paper copy as compared to electronic methods. Further breakout details are also common, including operation manuals vs. maintenance manuals; manuals for organizational, intermediate, and depot; and breakouts for structural, electronics, and propulsion.

9.2.4.3 Supply Support Data

This data element summarizes funding requirements for spares and repair parts. Requirements for spares for training hardware and peculiar support equipment and outfitting buy-outs for aviation programs should also be considered. Specific subelements to be considered are development/test spares and repair parts; interim/initial spares and repair parts, including depot and intermediate maintenance support stocks; on-board repair parts; contractor support spares and repair parts; site outfitting; replenishment spares and repair parts; supply plans and analysis; and other. These cost requirements should be consistent with supply support planning data and provisioning requirements. Sources of this information include both the program office analysis in view of acquisition reform initiatives, past contracts, and the many contracts awarded and managed at the supply centers.

9.2.4.4 Support Equipment Data

Support equipment (SE) cost requirements should be projected for all planned levels of maintenance, test sites, training sites, etc. Specific subelements to be considered are common support equipment; automated test equipment, including test program sets, tools, jigs, and fixtures; calibration standards; analysis, plans; and data. The primary source of data is past program contracts. But SE is provisioned in the supply system, and inventory control point contracts are also regularly used sources.

9.2.4.5 Computer Support Data

This element summarizes the requirements for computer resources for the postproduction software support of materiel systems. Data, compilers, hardware, and sometimes unique training required to set up the Software Support Activity (SSA) are covered here. Other specific subelements are software support, software support-associated hardware, computer development, software documentation, independent testing, and simulation support. These should coincide with the computer resources planning documentation. Sources for this estimating data are past contracts for software support, which may include both prime contractors and other related contracts and field activity tasking orders.

9.2.4.6 Facility Data

This data element includes military construction, operations and maintenance minor construction appropriation costs, public works/facilities engineers, and utility requirements. Specific subelements include military construction planning and design, military construction, operation and maintenance minor construction, unspecified minor construction, facilities engineering/public works support, utilities, facilities analysis and plans, and other elements. Past contracts with weapons systems original equipment manufacturers rarely include lines for military construction. Contract information from separate agencies, such as the claimant civil engineering departments or, in the case of the services such as the Navy, the Naval Facilities Command, will be the sources of planning and cost estimating data.

9.2.4.7 Training and Training Support Data

All training course requirements from development to instructor services are part of this data element, including training equipment, aids, and training simulators. Specific subelements are training courses that include development, initial or contractor training services, technical training equipment, training devices/aids, analysis and studies, training equipment installation, engineering technical services, etc. These requirements must coincide with the applicable tasking in the training master plan. Past contracts often include lists of individual training devices and their costs.

9.2.4.8 Management Data

This data element covers all management activities for the entire program, which includes supportability analyses costs not covered under deliverables for other elements shown above. Subelements could include level of repair analysis (LORA) and reliability-centered maintenance (RCM) studies and plans. Thus, all of the performance needs generally defined as maintenance planning or management could be addressed in this section.

9.2.4.9 Related Programs Data

Related programs include requirements for all other support estimates under the PM's purview. Specific subelements include configuration management, installation, handling equipment, containers, packaging, handling, storage, transportation, and hazardous materiel control and management. Identification should be made of any other support-related activities, such as contractor or government laboratories and field activities that require DoD resources in any acquisition phase. Additionally, events such as special maintainability demonstrations, logistics demonstrations, and maintenance engineering conferences that the program is sponsoring (or otherwise wants budget visibility for) should be included in this portion of the funding profile. Sources of estimating data are generally historical contracts and program office analyses.

9.2.5 LCC Drivers

A cost driver is a program, system characteristic, or parameter that has a direct or indirect effect on life cycle cost. A cost driver may even be another cost element. Examples include the number of systems, number of operating sites, number of systems failures, and time to fix broken systems. The cost of operations and support is driven by the cost of individual spare parts and by the labor hour costs of operators and maintainers. Thus, costs sometimes drive other costs. In some instances, the term *cost driver* means all parameters and characteristics that drive costs. But, in some cases, the cost driver is intended to differentiate the parameters or characteristic with the most impact on costs.

9.2.6 Uses of LCC

The LCC estimate plays a key role in the management of a program. Its primary functions include providing:

- Major input to decisions among competing major system alternatives
- Input into the requirements determination
- Identification of cost drivers for a selected system alternative
- Trade-off evaluations in design, logistics, and manufacturing for a selected system
- Overall cost control for a selected system

9.3 The Life Cycle Costing Process

Life cycle costing is the process of collecting and analyzing the life cycle cost (LCC) in the various decisions associated with acquiring or sustaining a system. This section will outline the process.

The LCC estimates are normally prepared by a multidisciplinary team with functional skills in cost analysis, financial management, logistics, and engineering (e.g., skills in reliability and maintainability). The team also should include participants or reviewers from stakeholders and major affected organizations, such as the system's operating command, product support center, maintenance depot, and training center. The estimating team may best be organized as a formal integrated product team (DoD 2007).

The process of estimating the life cycle costs contains eleven steps (DoD 2007):

1. Identify the purpose of the analysis
2. Identify the baseline (reference system) and alternatives
3. Develop the ground rules and assumptions
4. Select the relevant cost structure and elements
5. Determine the cost estimating technique
6. Select or construct a cost model
7. Identify the input data sources and obtain the data
8. Estimate and evaluate the relevant costs—run the model
9. Assess the risk and uncertainty—rerun(s) of the model
10. Perform sensitivity analysis—rerun(s) of the model
11. Develop the recommendations and document the results

9.3.1 Identify the Purpose of the Analysis

The first step is to formulate the objectives of the LCC analysis. Suppose, as an example, a battery power supply for a handheld radio is no longer available from the original equipment manufacturer. The statement of the objectives must identify the decisions (e.g., whether to use new-technology batteries or replace the radio), which are based on the LCC analysis and the factors involved that affect the decision (e.g., weight of the batteries vs. functionality of the new radio). Properly formulated objectives limit the scope of the cost analysis effort to the alternatives at hand. The objectives may be limited by availability, scheduling, modeling, data, or personnel constraints. The objectives would include the cost goals for the unit production cost and operating and support (O&S) costs. The unit production cost goal typically would be established for a specified quantity of systems and peak production rate. The O&S cost goal would be the cost per deployable unit (e.g., battalion or squadron) or for the individual system (e.g., ship or missile). The goals should be realistically achievable and perhaps more conservative for programs with a greater degree of risk to provide for some margin for error.

9.3.2 Identify the Baseline (Reference System) and Alternatives

The baseline/reference system is an actual operating system with actual/known LCC information. The LCC for the baseline system is calculated using the actual data for model inputs. The LCCs for system design alternatives are then compared to this known reference point. Often the system being replaced by a new acquisition program is used as the baseline/reference. The system/program definition should include a technical description of the current reference system (and perhaps major subsystems) and the alternatives. Consider the obvious alternatives, such as do nothing, upgrade the components/subsystems, or replace the system with totally new technology. For each alternative, a full life cycle technical description is needed.

9.3.3 Develop the Ground Rules and Assumptions

The identification of the assumptions that influence the LCC analysis is critical if the exercise is to yield useful results. Some data elements critical to the LCC analysis may not be available to the cost analyst. In these cases the analysis team must use its best judgment and make assumptions concerning these data elements in order to meet the schedule for providing decision-support LCC estimates. The assumptions should have (DoD 1984):

- Validity: Consider the operational, engineering, organizational, and political environment.
- Boundaries:
  - Procurement quantity
  - Schedule and rate of production
  - Learning curve (training, investment, problem solving) for the new technology
  - Concept of operation (the way the system is to be operated)
  - Logistics support (maintenance requirements)
  - Operating life (physical life, technological life, economic life)
- Residual value, disposal issues and costs

9.3.4 Select the Relevant Cost Structure and Elements

Section 9.2.3 described three cost element structures (CESs): funding appropriation, work breakdown structure (WBS), and life cycle cost (LCC) components. The CES is a good, and most frequently used, tool for organizing the analysis. The structure should be chosen to integrate all of the DoD applicable cost regulations, directives, policies, and guidance. The CES is organized sequentially into the major phases of the system's life cycle. The cost elements that were listed by phase in Section 9.2.3.2 are a good starting point. The importance of completely defining the elements stems from historical cost overruns that can be traced to the use of incomplete cost structures for initial estimates. In addition, comparable independent cost estimates cannot be made if the estimates are not based on the same CES (DoD 1984).

9.3.5 Determine the Cost Estimating Technique

There are four major cost estimating techniques (DoD 1984):

1. Parametric: Parametric costing uses regression analysis to establish statistically significant functional relationships between the independent variables in the regression (e.g., performance, physical characteristics or system end item unit cost) and the dependent variable (cost). With this technique, the analyst strives to identify a cause-and-effect relationship between the independent and dependent variables. This approach is sometimes called the top-down approach.
2. Industrial engineering: The industrial engineering approach relies on a detailed accounting of all of the operations required to develop and produce the system. The approach is sometimes called the bottom-up approach.
3. Analogy: Analogy cost estimating relationships try to predict the costs of a new system/program from data on similar past efforts. The technique frequently involves an estimation of the incremental or marginal cost associated with changes.
4. Expert opinion: Subjective or judgmental cost estimating relationships are based on the judgment of experts. The technique is useful when a major change in the system design is involved and there are insufficient data to use the other techniques. When time and resources allow, Delphi techniques (i.e., the iterative soliciting of expert opinions) should be used.

9.3.6 Select or Construct a Cost Model

There are a number of different cost models that can contribute to the estimation of LCC. This is a list of cost modeling approaches that was given in the DoD (1983) handbook for the Navy:

- *Economic analysis model*: Considers the time value of money, specific sustainment schedule, and trade-off analyses between cost and the timing of the investment.
- *Accounting model*: Aggregates the individual costs, including personnel and material costs, into the total system or equipment LCC.
- *Cost factors*: Determines the factors for key parameters based upon the cost experience of analogous systems, subsystems, or equipment and uses these factors to estimate the cost elements.
- *Cost estimating relationship (CER) model*: Statistically derives equations relating cost to a product's design, performance, operating, and logistics characteristics.
- *Logistics support cost simulation model*: Determines impact of operational maintenance, provisioning, and resource allocation options on support cost via computer simulation.
- *Level of repair analysis (LORA) model*: Determines the optimum maintenance process for a specific product based upon maintenance plan options.
- *Reliability improvement cost model*: Specifies the mathematical relationship between cost and product reliability trade-offs.
- *Inventory management model*: Determines the optimum provisioning levels for a specific system or equipment based upon cost and operational readiness constraints.
- *Maintenance personnel planning model*: Evaluates the effect on cost of various maintenance personnel options or the effect on maintenance personnel requirements of product design alternatives.
- *Warranty model*: Evaluates the cost comparability of organic (in-house) maintenance concepts vs. contractor warranty maintenance.

Although generalized cost models are excellent tools for evaluating a variety of system/program decisions, they can be difficult to tailor to a specific need. The analysis of specific systems may require a model that is narrower in scope. However, the cost of developing and validating special purpose models precipitates the adaptation of existing general purpose models (DoD 1983). Five general purpose models dominate life cycle cost estimating. Some are commercial off-the-shelf (COTS):

1. Cost Analysis and Strategy Assessment (CASA)—DoD owned
2. Cost-Oriented Resources Estimating (CORE)—DoD owned, Air Force
3. Logistics Support Cost (LSC) model—DoD owned
4. Automated Cost Estimating Integrated Tools (ACEIT)—COTS
5. Programmed Review of Information for Costing and Evaluation (PRICE)—COTS
6. Equipment Designer's Cost Analysis System (EDCAS)—COTS
7. System Evaluation and Estimation of Resources (SEER)—COTS

CASA is the most widely used model for systems engineering cost estimating purposes. Since it is government owned, CASA has evolved into a powerful integrated data environment tool. It was designed as an engineering estimate or accounting model. The model conforms to the requirements of the Office of the Secretary of Defense (OSD) Cost Analysis Improvement Group (CAIG) guidelines for cost elements. It uses a number of algorithms and variables to capture all of the relevant costs, and it is flexible, which means most of the inputs are optional, so the model's capability can be tailored to the needs of the LCC analyst. Also, the model uses fixed formulas, so the analysis is completely repeatable. It is general purpose and has been used in all of the services to support an LCC analysis on a wide variety of systems and equipment (DoD 1997).

CORE is designed to provide a cost estimating technique to be used to develop aircraft operating and support (O&S) cost estimates. CORE uses data that are available from standard USAF data systems. It allows the estimating techniques to vary as the program progresses through the phases of acquisition (flexibility), and it estimates all common O&S cost elements (completeness). It uses the format, cost element structure, and procedures generally required for milestone briefings (usefulness) (DoD 1997).

LSC uses consistent data for comparable systems available from standard USAF data sources (consistency), and it also contains built-in factors, allowing the model to be used when few item-specific data are available. As item-specific data evolve, the factors are replaced, which results in an improved cost estimate (flexibility). The LSC model addresses spares, depot maintenance, and transportation in detail. Manpower, support equipment, and training are addressed only superficially; fuel and other costs of operation are not included in the model (DoD 1997).

ACEIT is a COTS spreadsheet-based tool set used predominantly in program-level estimates using one of the four cost estimating techniques described above. The other three COTS models are accounting or bottom-up models used for engineering decision support.

For a model to provide useful information in analyzing life cycle costs, there are certain characteristics that should be incorporated in the model's design. The following list was provided in the 1983 DoD handbook, and it is still applicable today:

1. The application of the model to day-to-day decision making is important. Consequently, the model should be responsive to management control factors, design changes, and various operational scenarios (e.g., reliability, maintainability, manpower, operating tempo, funding types, funding claimants, and sponsors).
2. All of the significant cost drivers that are relevant to the issue under consideration should be incorporated into the model as clearly as possible.
3. The development, alteration, updating, and operation of a model should be as inexpensive as possible. Documentation should be readily available and clearly written and understandable.
4. The model should be easy to operate by other designers or sustainment office personnel; i.e., it should be user oriented and not require programmer support.
5. The model should be sensitive to design parameters or sustainment characteristics that affect the cost of investment alternatives.
6. Valid, relevant input data should be readily available.
7. The model should be flexible, capable of accommodating the growing complexity of a system, and it should allow for the adjustment of inflation, discounting, and learning curve factors.
8. The model should be separated into interactive modules for easier modification.
9. Inputs and outputs should be expressed in terms that are familiar to users and that can be verified to ensure credibility.
10. Outputs should be reliable; i.e., results should be repeatable.
11. The model should compare and evaluate alternative investment options or strategies.
12. The model should identify areas and degrees of uncertainty.

13. The model should conduct sensitivity analysis.
14. The model should analyze and track the effort on a total life cycle basis.

9.3.7 Identify the Input Data Sources and Obtain the Data

The information needed to develop the LCC comes from many functional elements. Section 9.2.4 discussed these sources. Effective costing comes from the program manager's (PM) understanding of the information needed, who will provide it, and how to document it as usable input to the PM. LCC data are generally displayed in a document called a logistics funding profile. The amount of detail shown in the profile depends on the level of management attention required to keep the program funding risk to a minimum. The profile should provide a summary by funding appropriation, a summary of program description, and the assumptions upon which the budget is based.

There are usually three types and sources of data needed to run a LCC model. They are:

■ Program data, including procurement and deployment schedules
■ System data, including subassembly reliability and maintainability values and predicted unit costs
■ Support scenario data, including numbers of org/intermed/dep—sites and labor rates at these support sites along with the cost of support elements at the sites

9.3.8 Estimate and Evaluate the Relevant Costs: Run the Model

Using the techniques from Section 9.3.5 and the model from Section 9.3.6, the LCC cost analysis creates an estimate for each of the cost elements identified as described in Section 9.3.4. The estimates of RDT&E, production and disposal costs may only require a once-through set of calculations. However, summing up the O&S cost for a system that is in operation for 30 or 40 years will require scores of calculations. The O&S portion of costs nearly always involves the use of a cost model such as the case model. (Note: CASA is currently available on the U.S. Army "LOGSA" website.) The LCC analyst prepares a LCC cost spreadsheet showing all elements of cost for each year of the system life cycle and then sums this information into a single LCC number for use in decision support.

9.3.9 Assess the Risk and Uncertainty: Rerun the Model

Risk as discussed in this instance addresses the risk that the LCC estimate, as modeled, does not reflect reality. The decision maker is to make a current decision based on future operating and support (O&S) costs. These future O&S costs are being calculated based on the cost analyst's current knowledge of the cost drivers and other model input data. There is risk that these inputs may change or otherwise be incorrect. Risk is associated with variation. The greater the variation or uncertainty, the greater the risk. Each data element in the LCC computation contains variation. As an example, consider that two of the main drivers of LCC are parts reliability and manpower costs. Reliability, expressed as mean time between failures (MTBF), drives numerous O&S costs associated with returning failed parts to operational condition. Manpower cost for operators and maintainers is the largest component of LCC. Two manpower-related elements of LCC model input data are (1) mean time to repair (MTTR) a failed item, and labor rates for operators and maintainers. These data elements, and others, are used repeatedly in numerous LCC model algorithms. LCC model inputs are fixed, while in reality the data will contain variation.

Performing risk and uncertainty analysis of the LCC estimate is used to answer four main questions:

■ How much confidence can the decision maker place in the estimate?
■ What is the range between the upper and lower confidence limits?
■ Should the decision be based on an LCC point estimate or the range?
■ Should LCC targets and associated results be documented as point estimates or as ranges between the confidence limits?

To find the answers to these questions, it is usually necessary to rerun the LCC model computations many times while varying selected model input data, with each affected model input being varied using applicable distributions.

Variation, and therefore risk, is expressed statistically through confidence intervals or alternative scenarios, such as pessimistic, most likely, and optimistic estimates. Standard practice is to use normal (Gaussian) statistical distributions, characterized by a mean μ and standard deviation σ, to describe the uncertainty. Weibull distributions, characterized by a shape β and a characteristic life η, may be more representative of the life and repair times for equipment and systems (Figure 9.13) and are frequently used in reliability analyses. In risk analysis, selected factors (technical, programmatic, and cost) are described by the probability distributions. Where estimates are based on cost models derived from historical data, the effects of cost estimation error may be included in the range of considerations included in the cost risk assessment. Monte Carlo simulation models, which use random numbers, are used to associate the probability distributions with the cost data to analyze uncertainty and risk. Such models are often built using common spreadsheet programs, such as Excel™, or add-in programs, such as Crystal Ball™ or @Risk™. Variation in the results is obtained by repeating the Monte Carlo trials with different random numbers and then statistically analyzing the risk. It is then possible to derive an estimated empirical probability distribution for the overall cost estimate. This allows the analyst to describe the nature and degree of variability in the estimate (DoD 2007).

There are times when data for model input parameters are not readily available to LCC analysts. So they need a practical alternative. Many LCC analysts construct a triangular distribution using information from a subject matter expert of a Delphi group, as illustrated by Figure 9.14. They create a triangle using three values: the center value (a) is the expected or most likely value; the second value (b) is the "it could be as low as" value; and the third value (c) is the "it could be as high as" value. The distance between (b) and (c) forms the distribution space. They then use a random number generator to identify an appropriate number of instances of numbers within the space considering space density. These numbers, created for all of the selected inputs, are then run through the LCC model. The result is a range of LCC totals that are then subjected to a statistical analysis of confidence interval estimates. The entire process is automated as a risk analysis feature of the CASA model.

9.3.10 Perform Sensitivity Analysis: Rerun the Model

Sensitivity analysis allows the study of the LCC parameters to identify those element outputs that are particularly vulnerable to relatively small changes in LCC driver input values. Sensitivity analysis is performed by varying the data inputs of the cost drivers in the model with alternative

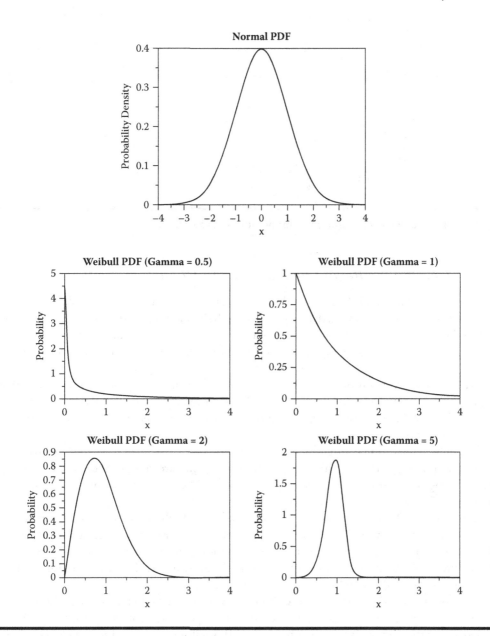

Figure 9.13   Standardized Gaussian distribution vs. Weibull distribution.

(pessimistic, most likely, and optimistic) scenarios. The analyst identifies the relevant cost drivers and then examines how costs vary with changes in those values. In good sensitivity analyses, the drivers are not changed by arbitrary plus/minus percentages, but rather by a careful assessment of the underlying risks. The purpose is to identify the magnitude of the uncertainty in the LCC estimate and to identify areas of high risk. Sensitivity analysis can also determine the effects of data uncertainties and changes in the ground rules and assumptions (DoD 1997). The sensitivity analysis is also an automated feature of the CASA model.

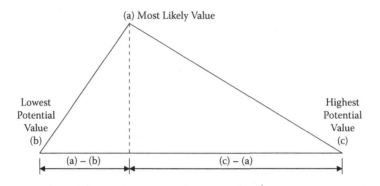

Figure 9.14 Triangular distribution of model input parameters.

9.3.11 Develop the Recommendations and Document the Results

Detailed documentation of the LCC analysis serves as an audit trail of the ground rules, assumptions, cost estimating techniques, data, sensitivity analysis, and results. The documentation should explain the methods used to establish the bounds and the data elements included in the sensitivity analysis, and it should provide sufficient information for the replication and confirmation of the estimate by an experienced analyst (DoD 1997). The Cost Analysis Requirements Description (CARD) is used to formally define the program and the system for purposes of preparing both the program office cost estimate and the Cost Analysis Improvement Group (CAIG) independent cost estimate. The CARD is prepared by the program office and approved by the appropriate program executive officer (PEO).

The LCC report format often requires presentation of costs in both current (or base-year) dollars and then-year dollars. This allows reviewers to compare costs to their reference materials, including program budget estimates. This topic will be discussed further in Sections 9.5.2 through 9.5.5.

Individual DoD organizations may impose locally standardized documentation formats. The Army has required submittal of cost information in a spreadsheet format called the ACET model. ACET is more of a spreadsheet reporting format than it is a model, since each organization develops and programs algorithms into the spreadsheet. The Navy has used the Logistics Requirements and Funding Plan (LRFP) and its variations for over 10 years.

The most useful cost profiles are those that the cost analyst has developed to satisfy the requirements for managing the program. Complex programs require cost element projections with milestone detail to the fifth or sixth level of indenture. This reflects the level of management attention intended by the analyst. Every milestone and activity described in the acquisition or sustainment plan will require funding resources for execution of that plan. For example, under the facilities cost element, there may be a milestone for a site survey at the training location in a given month and another milestone for a site survey for each of the stakeholder organizations during succeeding quarters of that phase. One would expect that each of the activities would be described in the acquisition or sustainment plan, and that the funding requirements for each of the site visits would be evident in the logistics funding profile. The funding profile is provided to the program budget or financial manager for consolidation into the overall program budget submission.

LCC backup documentation is also important. This backup documents the justification, rationale, estimation methodology, ground rules and assumptions, formulas, and cost estimating relationships (CERs) that were used to come up with the dollar values for each cost element. Because there are numerous people who participate in the budget formulation exercise, and because there are frequent and regular turnovers for the budget formulation team, the backup is a necessity. The almost constant drills associated with defending, adjusting, and resubmitting the budget, and the ease with which this is accomplished, will be directly proportional to the completeness of the budget backup documentation.

9.4 LCC Trade-Off Analysis Tools

The best time to reduce life cycle costs is early in the acquisition process. Cost reductions are accomplished by performing a cost vs. performance trade-off analysis, which is conducted before an approach is finalized. This section presents a summary of the tools that are available to conduct such an analysis.

Maximizing the program manager's and contractors' flexibility to make cost vs. performance trade-offs is essential to achieving cost reduction objectives. Therefore, the number of threshold requirements and baselines should be limited, the threshold values should represent true minimums, and requirements should be stated in terms of performance rather than technical solutions and specifications. The systems engineering process, the systems analysis process, and the control process are established to serve as a basis for evaluating and selecting alternatives, measuring progress, and documenting the design decisions. These processes include the conduct of trade-off analyses among requirements (operational, functional, and performance), design alternatives and their related manufacturing, testing and support processes, program schedule, and life cycle cost. Such trade-off studies should be performed at the appropriate level of detail to support decision making and lead to a proper balance between performance and cost. The studies would include a number of key performance parameters (KPPs) that will allow the maximum flexibility to meet overall program objectives at the lowest cost. The source selection criteria should reflect the importance of developing a system that can achieve the production and life cycle cost thresholds. To facilitate this process, the life cycle costing integrated product team (IPT) might wish to establish a cost vs. performance IPT (CPIPT). The user community and industry representation, consistent with statute and at the appropriate time, should be represented on the CPIPT.

For all of the tools discussed below, once a baseline cost estimate is complete, the impact of program performance and schedule changes on costs can be evaluated. One example of a design trade-off is an engineering change proposal (ECP). The ECP analysis is used to assess the cost implications of a proposed design change. The decision to accept or reject an ECP is made after considering the effect of the performance or schedule on system/program costs. Comparing the cost of the baseline configuration with the cost of the proposed configuration provides the cost-related assessment of the ECP. Areas of uncertainty are identified and appropriate sensitivity analyses can then be performed.

9.4.1 System Effectiveness vs. LCC Analysis

Blanchard and Fabrycky (1998) define system effectiveness as the probability that a system may successfully meet an overall operational demand within a given time and when operated under specified conditions. One tool for performing trade-off analyses on the LCC calculations is the system effectiveness equation. The equation provides the probability of producing the intended results that

Blanchard and Fabrycky discuss in their book. Each element in the equation is itself a probability that would be associated with a factor that would influence life cycle cost (Equation 9.1):

$$\text{Effectiveness} = P_i\, P_j\, P_k\, P_l\, \ldots \tag{9.1}$$

where i, j, k, and l are the factors influencing LCC, and P_i is the probability associated with the factor i. For example, effectiveness can be the product of the probabilities of operational availability (Ao), reliability, maintainability, and supportability. Thus, the equation is the product of the chance the system will be available to perform its duty (Ao), it will operate for a given time without failure (reliability—MTBF), it can be repaired without excessive maintenance time (maintainability—MTTR), and it can be logistically supported (MLDT). These are some of the "abilities" that were discussed in the earlier chapters of this book. The objective is to find a system effectiveness value that yields the lowest life cycle cost. The systems effectiveness value can be plotted against life cycle cost in a form similar to the Boston Consulting Group (BCG) growth-share matrix (Figure 9.15). The BCG matrix is based on the product life cycle, so the technique is an appropriate way of analyzing the trade-off between effectiveness and cost. The lower-right-side alternative in Figure 9.15 is the star, providing high system effectiveness (as a probability) at the lowest LCC. The upper left alternative is what is referred to as a dog, since it yields low effectiveness at high LCC. The other two alternatives (cash cow and problem child) raise questions about effectiveness or value.

9.4.2 Independent Cost Estimate (ICE)

Life cycle cost analysis and decision support are used by at least two levels of decision makers. Design-related trade-off analysis made within the project staff needs to use a methodology and cost model that the project trusts. When LCC estimates are used to support decisions by the MDA for major program decisions, confidence in the estimate requires the ability to replicate the LCC estimate by an independent agency, the DoD Cost Analysis Improvement Group (CAIG), which performs an independent cost estimate (ICE).

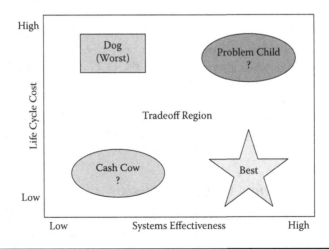

Figure 9.15 System effectiveness vs. life cycle cost.

The ICE serves as a basis for determining the reasonableness of costs and for comparing costs among competing alternatives. The costs include direct and indirect costs. A properly developed ICE provides acquisition managers with an essential part of their structured management process. ICE documentation is used to justify, defend, make trade-off decisions, and manage acquisitions throughout the life cycle of the system. An example ICE spreadsheet is provided on the CD that accompanies this volume (see "Independent Cost Estimate" on the CD).

9.4.3 Business Case Analysis (BCA)

Jacques S. Gansler, the former undersecretary of defense for acquisition, technology, and logistics for the DoD, said this about a business case analysis:

> BCA is an extended form of cost/benefit analysis where the alternatives' total costs for satisfying a business need are weighed against the alternatives' total benefits to determine an optimum solution. BCA goes one step further than cost/benefit analysis and links each alternative to fulfilling the strategic objectives of the organization, compliance with performance measures and impact on stakeholders. BCA identifies which alternative allows an organization to optimize mission performance given cost and other constraints. It not only includes analysis of cost, but also addresses qualitative and subjective factors directly impacting the decision-making process, along with risk and sensitivity analysis. The output of a BCA is an analysis of all viable alternative business strategies, along with recommendations for proceeding with the best value alternative.*

A business case analysis (BCA) is a tool that provides financial justification for an investment decision by analyzing the trade-off between the quantitative benefits and the costs under alternative solutions. The BCA should provide convincing evidence that justifies the investment decision. To be convincing, the benefits and costs should be unbiased, credible, and presented in a format that follows financial and statistical standards. Creating an effective BCA requires adequate knowledge of existing operational processes and metrics, an understanding of the goals, objectives, metrics, and strategy, and the costs. For each potential alternative, the BCA would identify the benefits and costs, and analyze the financial metrics (net present value, internal rate of return, etc.) to create the case. Approaches include project comparison estimates, parametric estimation models (for example, system utilization), and bottom-up assembly estimates.

The U.S DoD provides a good business case development guide (DoD 2003b). The guide proposes a seven-step process for building the BCA:

1. Stand the business case project team.
   1.1. Form business case development team.
   1.2. Confirm understanding of problem/opportunity statement.
   1.3. Develop detailed schedule for business case development.

---

* Jacques Gansler, as quoted in Defense Acquisition University's "LOG 304: Executive Acquisition Logistics Management Course, Business Case Analysis (BCA) Module," Defense Acquisition University, August 2003, https://acc.dau.mil/CommunityBrowser.aspx?id=46516&lang=en-US (accessed July 30, 2008).

2. Identify potential solution scenarios.
    2.1. Identify comparable solutions.
    2.2. Benchmark key benefits and costs from comparable solutions.
3. Develop primary and alternative solution scenarios.
    3.1. Analyze each alternative to detail benefits and costs.
    3.2. Capture key assumptions in spreadsheet and validate financial model.
4. Assess overall business case and key alternatives.
    4.1. Package analysis results for review by team.
    4.2. Critically assess model.
    4.3. Determine whether further analysis is warranted.
5. Address uncertainty in model for selected scenario(s).
    5.1. Perform sensitivity analysis.
    5.2. Simulate potential outcomes.
    5.3. Determine whether further analysis is warranted.
6. Package and present results.
    6.1. Capture results into standard business case template.
    6.2. Develop additional slide decks if required for sponsor review and buy-in.
    6.3. Present results.
    6.4. Revise based on feedback.
7. Business case closeout
    7.1. Secure business case approval.
    7.2. Prepare results for future project use.
    7.3. Add any captured metrics into organizational metrics repository.

The BCA is a spreadsheet tool that, once populated with the necessary information and financial data, projects the likely financial results of the investment and generates all of the required financial documentation to support the system development (see Figure 9.16). An example BCA is provided on the CD that accompanies this volume (see "Business Case Analysis" on the CD).

9.4.4 Analysis of Alternatives (AoA)

Analysis of alternatives (AoA) is another LCC trade-off analysis tool to aid decision makers in judging whether or not any of the proposed system alternatives offer sufficient operational and economic benefit to be worthy. An AoA is a comparison of the operational effectiveness and life cycle cost of alternative programs. The process follows the life cycle stages and program milestones. It starts in the presystem identification phase of the cycle by exploring the conceptual solutions with the goal of identifying the most promising options. This step guides the system concept refinement phase. At milestone B, which represents the first major funding commitment to the system/ program, the AoA is used to justify the operational and economic rationale for the program. In later phases, the operational and support cost estimates become an important part of the AoA. The system/program alternative that serves as the analysis baseline in the AoA normally becomes the continuation (or service life extension) of the existing system that the proposed program is intended to replace (DoD 2007).

The Defense acquisition guidebook (DoD 2003a) provides a good overview of the creation of an AoA. The first major step is the creation of a well-considered analysis plan. The plan should

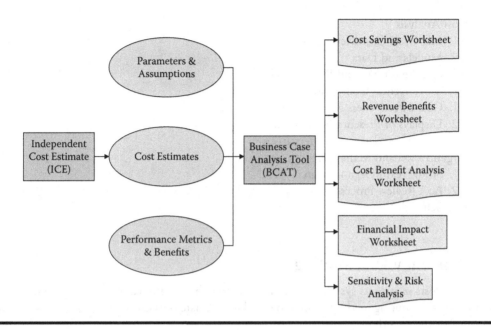

Figure 9.16   Business case analysis flow diagram.

establish a road map of how the analysis will proceed, and who is responsible for each of the tasks. A recommended outline for the plan is:

1. Introduction
    1.1. Background
    1.2. Purpose
    1.3. Scope
2. Ground Rules
    2.1. Scenarios
    2.2. Threats
    2.3. Environment
    2.4. Constraints and Assumptions
3. Alternatives
    3.1. Description of Alternatives
    3.2. Nonviable Alternatives
    3.3. Operations Concepts
    3.4. Support Concepts
4. Determination of Effectiveness Measures
    4.1. Mission Tasks
    4.2. Measures of Effectiveness
    4.3. Measures of Performance
5. Effectiveness Analysis
    5.1. Effectiveness Methodology
    5.2. Models, Simulations, and Data
    5.3. Effectiveness Sensitivity Analysis

6. Cost Analysis
   6.1. Life Cycle Cost Methodology
   6.2. Models and Data
   6.3. Cost Sensitivity and Risk Analysis
7. Cost-Effectiveness Comparisons
   7.1. Cost-Effectiveness Methodology
   7.2. Displays or Presentation Formats
   7.3. Criteria for Screening Alternatives
8. Organization and Management
   8.1. Study Team/Organization
   8.2. AoA Review Process
   8.3. Schedule

9.5 Currency Discounting

When the costs of various system/program alternatives have significantly different time periods, appropriate discounting methods should be used to calculate the cost of each alternative. This section reviews these methods.

9.5.1 Analysis Period

The analysis time period is the time over which the life cycle costs are to be evaluated. The analysis period usually spans many years, depending on the intended overall life of the system/program. The analysis period should follow the DoD recommended phases and milestones that were discussed in Section 9.1. The fiscal year in which there would first be a difference in expenditures among system/program alternatives is often referred to as the base year, program year, or project year.

Funds are typically disbursed for a program throughout a given fiscal year rather than at its beginning or end. Thus, mid-year, rather than end-of-year, discount rates may be used to approximate such actual disbursement patterns. When the precise timing of outlays is critical to program evaluation, monthly (or quarterly) rather than annual flows of funds may be considered for early program years.

9.5.2 Discount Rate

The discount rate is the rate of interest on the money that reflects the investor's time value of money. It is the interest rate that would make an investor indifferent as to whether the investor received a payment now (base year) or a (greater) payment at some time in the future. There can be two types of discount rates: nominal discount rates and real discount rates. The difference between the two is that the real discount rate excludes inflation. The nominal discount rate includes the rate of inflation. It is not that real discount rates ignore inflation. Their use simply eliminates the complexity of accounting for inflation within the discounting equations. The use of either discount rate in its corresponding present value calculation would derive the same result.

Do not confuse discounting with inflation. Discounting involves the concept of the time value of money, such as the interest that can be earned on financial instruments. Inflation involves changes in price levels. While expectations of inflation influence interest rates, the concepts of inflation and the time value of money are separate ideas.

Discount rates represent the government's cost of borrowing, as provided annually in the budget. Rates used for analysis are interest rates on Treasury notes and bonds with maturities of 3, 5, 7, 10, and 30 years. The rate to be used corresponds to the period of analysis. For periods of analysis between these specific maturities, interpolate between the rates. Though the yield curve is curvilinear, linear interpolation is acceptable for estimating purposes. Interest rates on Treasury securities are cited on both a real and a nominal basis.

9.5.3 Constant Currency vs. Current Currency

Just as discount rates can be defined as either real or nominal, so too can costs. Constant currency (e.g., constant dollars) is defined as currency of uniform purchasing power over the analysis period tied to a reference year (usually the base year) and exclusive of general price inflation or deflation. When using the real discount rate in present value calculations, the costs must be expressed in constant currency.

Current currency is currency of nonuniform purchasing power over the analysis period and includes general price inflation or deflation in which actual prices are stated. When using the nominal discount rate in present value calculations, costs must be expressed in current currency. Current (or then-year) currency contains an implicit adjustment for variation in the purchasing power of the currency over time. Current currency represent amounts that will be paid for resources in the actual years in which payments will be made (therefore sometimes referred to as budget currency). Do the cost analysis in current currency when cost information is obtained in inflated currency. If the inflation rate is zero, constant currency is equal to current currency, and the real discount rate is equal to the nominal discount rate.

The question is which currency to use. In practice, the use of constant currency simplifies the LCC analysis. By using constant currency, the guesswork of estimating the escalation or inflation of costs is eliminated. The future constant cost is the same as the initial cost. Any change in the value of money over time will be accounted for by the real discount rate. Constant currency reflects the value or purchasing power of that currency in a specific year, e.g., constant FY2010 dollars. Generally, use constant currency of the base year. But, do not mix constant and current currency in the same analysis.

Ordinarily LCC analyses use a real rate, consistent with a constant currency analysis. When inflated dollars are used, then the nominal rate is used. Conduct sensitivity analysis on the discount rate at ±5 or 10% of the rate used. Should the sensitivity analysis result in a change in the ranking of life cycle costs, report the rate at which the reversal occurs.

9.5.4 Differential Cost Changes

Even in a constant currency analysis, the analyst may need to adjust the costs of some elements of the system or project if economists project price changes significantly above or below general inflation. The core rate of inflation, for example, excludes energy costs, which is one of the most volatile sectors of the economy. If a project contains energy costs, or other costs not included in inflation estimates, adjustments to these costs in the out years may be advisable. Energy indices are net of general inflation; i.e., energy indices only represent how energy costs are projected to vary above or below general inflation. Any other significant costs that represent a volatile sector of the economy in terms of sector-specific inflation may require application of a sector-specific index.

9.5.5 Present Value of Money

To accurately combine expenses during all years of the analysis period, the net present value (NPV) of all of the expenses must be determined. The present value calculation uses the discount rate and the time a cost will be incurred to establish the equivalent present value of the costs in the base year of the analysis period. Thus, the determination of the present value of future costs is time dependent, and it is the equalizer that allows the summation of initial and future costs. The time period is the difference between the time of initial costs and the time of future costs.

Present value analysis takes into account the fact that a resource gain or outlay in the future is less valuable than the same sum today because organizations can borrow at a positive interest rate. For example, a debt of $1,000 due 1 year in the future at a simple interest rate of 10% would need only $909.09 today to meet the obligation. The present value of a future cost is determined using Equation 9.2:

$$PV = \frac{FV_t}{(1+r)^t} \tag{9.2}$$

where PV = present value, FVt = future value of a cost at a time t, r = real discount rate (which excludes inflation), and t = time (in years).

Net present value (NPV) or net present worth (NPW) is the total present value of the time series of costs incurred during the analysis period. It is a standard method for using the time value of money to appraise long-term projects. Each cost is discounted back to its present value. Then all of the costs in the base year are summed (Equation 9.3).

$$NPV = \sum_t \frac{FV_t}{(1+r)^t} \tag{9.3}$$

9.6 Case Study: Precision Approach Radar Modernization Project

The following life cycle cost (LCC) analysis was performed for a precision approach radar (PAR) modernization project for the U.S Navy and Marines. The AN/FPN-63 radar set (Figure 9.17) is installed in a mobile shelter used to provide radar guidance to aircraft for final approach landings. The radar set is normally used in conjunction with an airport surveillance radar system to provide a complete ground-controlled approach (GCA) facility. Azimuth (AZ), elevation (EL), and range information are displayed on the operator's console and are used to direct the aircraft commander, by radio communications, to a precision landing.

The AN/FPN-63 is an early 1960s' technology radar with a magnetron transmitter and large power transistors of the 2N222 variety. Typical of that era, there is literally no built-in test. Readiness is achieved by near total redundancy. Troubleshooting of system failures requires many hours of manual fault isolation using an extensive array of organizational-level support

Figure 9.17   AN/FPN-63 precision approach radar.

equipment. Also typical of this technology is high power consumption, high power output for acceptable performance, and the directly proportional high component failure rates.

The system has been in constant use for 30 years at over forty Navy and Marine air stations. Parts and technology obsolescence along with diminishing manufacturing sources have been problems for nearly 10 years. Costs of support are increasing because of systems wear-out, physics of failure, and a dramatic rise in replenishment spares costs. Vendors have no interest in continuing support to the obsolete technology. They will only tool up to produce spares if the quantity buy and unit price is cost effective for them.

The life cycle cost spreadsheet that was used for the analysis is provided on the CD that accompanies this volume (see "AN FPN 63 PAR LCC Case Study.xls" on the CD).

9.6.1 Purpose and Scope

The purpose of the analysis was to support preliminary baseline decision(s) concerning the PAR system modernization. There are to be two closely coupled parts and purposes of the analysis. The first purpose is to support a decision on whether to (1) incrementally upgrade the existing AN/FPN-63 PAR with various engineering change proposals (ECPs) to keep it operating until the year 2020, or (2) to completely replace the AN/FPN-63 PAR with a new next-generation PAR system. The second purpose is to support decisions on a multitude of issues, specifications, requirements, threats, options, and alternatives. This second part of the analysis, commonly referred to as the "what if" analysis, could address selection of specific replacement systems being offered by at least three companies. Developing the model capability to quickly address these "what if" issues is a prime justification for expending the resources necessary to completely address the first issue. The analysis purpose drove several decisions concerning the analysis methodology, as discussed below.

9.6.2 Alternatives

Three alternatives that were considered in the analysis are:

1. The null alternative, which is to document the LCC of the current (baseline) system.
2. Perform periodic major modifications to extend the life of the current system.
3. Replace the current system with an available commercial and nondevelopmental items (CANDI) system.

9.6.3 Methodology

The LCC analysis methodology that was used is a tailored version of the process that is recommended by the OSD Cost Analysis Improvement Group (CAIG) (DoD 2007).

9.6.3.1 Define the Purpose of the Analysis

The analysis approach must be able to accommodate the unique aspects of the program being assessed. Since the PAR modernization program will address a wide range of trade-off issues, and because the alternatives involve commercial and nondevelopmental items (CANDI), a detailed LCC model approach was recommended.

9.6.3.2 Identify the Baseline and Alternatives

A reference system is an existing operational system with a mission similar to that of a proposed system. The baseline reference system is the AN/FPN-65 PAR, which has been in operation in the fleet for over 30 years, and with data captured by the Visibility and Maintenance of Operating and Support Cost (VAMOSC) program to provide historical data when available. The alternatives were described in Section 9.6.2. PAR operating and support data are not captured by Navy VAMOSC. Other data collected by the in-service engineering agent (ISEA) were obtained from a variety of sources and used in this analysis.

9.6.3.3 Develop Ground Rules and Assumptions

The CAIG methodology requires a detailed definition of all analysis ground rules and assumptions in order to ensure that the analysis can be replicated by a third-party analysis organization if desired or directed. The basic ground rules and assumptions are usually derived from a detailed definition of how a system will be operated, maintained, and supported during peacetime operations. The ground rules and assumptions are:

■ The study period will be 25 years—5 years of production/deployment, plus 20 years of operations.
■ The base year of the study will be 2001.
■ Average system operation is 18 hours per day, 360 days per year.
■ The support concept for analysis purposes will be government organizational maintenance level to government depot-level maintenance.
■ Operator labor cost will be included even though it does not differentiate between alternatives. This cost is included as a perspective related to overall personnel costs. Other nonalternative differentiating costs were omitted from the study.

- The LCC estimate will include initial and recurring logistics costs for spares, support equipment, transportation, and maintenance labor.
- The LCC estimate will exclude recurring operator and maintainer training, operational-level maintenance facilities, and technical data. The estimate does not differentiate between alternatives.
- Depot-level facilities will be based on 20,000 square feet at $105.50 square feet per year.
- Site surveys for new installations cost is $25,000 per site survey (six people at 5 days labor, travel, and per diem).
- Tear-out and installation for a site is $250,000 per site (five people at 40 days labor plus materials other than the system).
- There will be no new military construction (MILCON) in the analysis.

9.6.3.4 Select Relevant Cost Elements and Structure

The cost element structure (CES) maps to the structure in the OSD CAIG guide (DoD 2007). Initial and recurring logistics element costs are reported by year and by integrated logistics system (ILS) element.

9.6.3.5 Determine Cost Estimating Technique

A detailed bottom-up accounting model, or engineering estimate technique, was employed. This approach was feasible and appropriate because of the availability of relevant model input data and the expectation for recurring detailed engineering trade-off decision support for specific reparable candidate levels of the system work breakdown structure (WBS) for this program.

9.6.3.6 Select or Construct a Cost Model

The new version of the Cost Analysis and Strategy Assessment (CASA) model was used for this analysis. CASA is a classic bottom-up, engineering-level cost accounting model. CASA is one of the most widely used and accepted LCC models in use today. CASA is actually a set of analysis tools formulated into one functioning unit. It collects, manipulates, and presents as much of the total ownership cost (TOC) as the user requires to perform a good solid decision support analysis. It contains a number of programs and models that allow the analyst to generate data files, perform life cycle costing, perform sensitivity analysis, and perform an LCC risk analysis along with LCC summations and LCC comparisons. Much of the routine time-consuming parameter-changing work of sensitivity and risk analysis is automated to minimize resources expended to obtain complete analysis. CASA contains 82 algorithms and 190 variables. The model can be comprehensive, but most data inputs are optional, allowing the analyst complete freedom in tailoring model use. CASA is the only LCC model that has the algorithms fully described in the program help screens. The model can capture enough of ownership costs to facilitate well-informed decisions. The model can capture the majority of ownership costs while minimizing the requirement for mandatory model input data.

9.6.3.7 Identify Input Data, Sources, and Collect the Data

Three types of analysis input data were included:

- Program data, including operating sites, schedules, and costs, were obtained from the program office.

- Operating scenario data, including labor rates and logistics element costs, were obtained from the in-service engineering agent (ISEA) and the Naval Inventory Control Point (NAVICP).
- Hardware system costs, including reliability, maintainability, and unit costs, were estimated from market research sources.

Some model input data were, of necessity, estimated using the Delphi technique. The rationale for these data is fully documented in the analysis records maintained by the ISEA. An important basic ground rule for the analysis was consistent use of input data across all alternatives, and the ability of the data to withstand a test of rationality and consistency with existing similar systems will be observed. The results of the model are intended for decision support. The estimates may or may not be used as source data for budget estimates for certain cost elements, but this is not a stated purpose of the estimates. Budget estimators may use same or similar input data, but may use different calculation algorithms.

9.6.3.8 Estimate and Evaluate Relevant Costs

Model runs used during the analysis will be maintained on file at the analysis activity. Selected output runs are included in the report.

9.6.3.9 Perform Sensitivity Analysis and Identify/ Verify Major Cost Drivers

Sensitivity analysis was performed on a variety of cost driving factors to identify and verify major cost drivers. Sensitivity to MTBF, MTTR, spares turnaround time, labor rates, and up to a dozen other factors were analyzed.

9.6.3.10 Perform Risk and Uncertainty Analysis

Risk and uncertainty analysis was performed to identify the range of costs that may be expected vs. point estimates during follow-on analysis concerning selection among the alternative commercial off-the-shelf (COTS) systems. The risk analysis focused on the areas of MTBF, MTTR, and unit costs.

9.6.3.11 Develop Recommendations

The recommendation is to replace the AN/FPN-63 PAR. The results include a detailed cost-based decision support analysis with a thoroughly documented audit trail of backup information. Additionally, the analysis provides all of the information required to replicate any part of the analysis by another experienced analyst.

9.6.4 Summary of the LCC Analysis

The center line in Figure 9.18 (indicated by the diamonds) is the total operating and support (O&S) cost for the present AN/FPN-63 configuration (the baseline discussed in the study plan). The work breakdown structure (WBS) for the system is shown in Figure 9.19. This

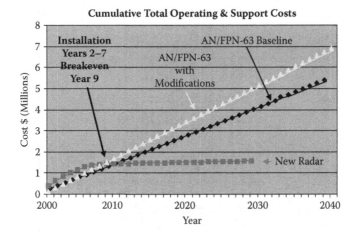

Figure 9.18 Life cycle costs for the AN/FPN-63 radar.

radar is basically a 1,000 h mean time between failures (MTBF) system. It does not employ built-in test (BIT). All failures are repaired at the organizational level. The mean time to repair (MTTR) is 7 h. MTTR is often defined to be the remove and replace time for faulty components of a system. A more useful definition is more inclusive. This is especially true for a system without BIT. The mean time to fault detect, fault isolate, remove, and replace the faulty component, and then retest the system, is the MTTR for the purposes of this study. Seven hours to fully repair each failure makes organizational maintenance man-hours a major cost driver.

The upper line in Figure 9.18 (indicated by the triangles) is the total O&S cost for the AN/FPN-63 with a modification program that has a primary objective of coping with parts obsolescence and diminishing manufacturing sources. This line reflects a slight improvement in equipment reliability (1% per year), since the major issue of the modifications is obsolescence, not reliability improvement. The targets of the modifications may not necessarily be the higher failure rate items. The cost includes blocks of modifications being installed over a 5-year time period. Each 5-year period, a block of modifications is to be approved, and then the modification kits are installed over the 5-year period. This results in a constant annual cost of $4 million. The modification program essentially does nothing to improve the MTTR, which is the major cost driver.

The lower line in Figure 9.18 (indicated by squares) is the O&S cost for a notional new replacement COTS radar. This line includes the cost of continuing to operate the AN/FPN-63 during the transition period of equipment replacements. This system is a composite of features currently available and being offered by industry. The WBS for this new system is shown in Figure 9.20. It is a 4,000 h MTBF system with an MTTR of 1 h. Current vendors are advertising an MTTR of 18 to 20 min, although the assumption is that this only includes the repair and replacement time for the components. The new systems feature state-of-the-practice BIT. Systems today can be monitored across the Internet. The ISEA can monitor the condition of any system in the fleet from his or her remote location. These systems can utilize a conventional contractor depot maintenance concept with considerable maintenance performed on a scheduled rather than on a condition of failure basis. The lower line in Figure 9.18 includes a $25,000 cost per system per year for

334 ■ *Enterprise Sustainability*

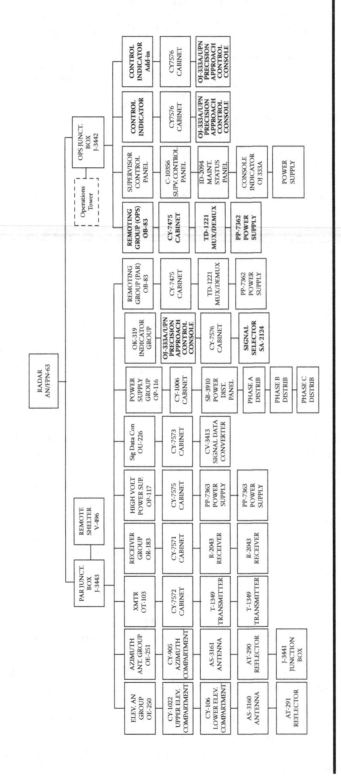

Figure 9.19   Work breakdown structure (WBS) for the AN/FPN-63 radar.

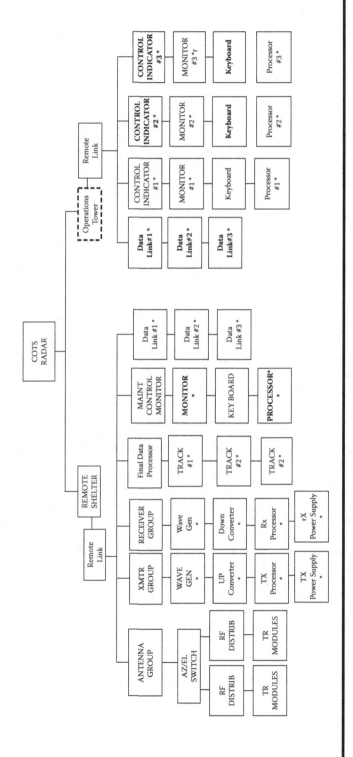

Figure 9.20 WBS for the new replacement COTS radar.

technology insertion to mitigate parts obsolescence. The reliability of this system is four times that of the AN/FPN-65 system, and the MTTR is seven times lower.

Conclusion: The analysis shows that by year 15, the new system would have paid for itself twice. *Recommendation*: Replace the FPN-63 as soon as possible.

References

Bernus, Peter. 1998, November19–20. Position statement—GERAM and its possible implications to system and software engineering applications. Paper presented to the International Federation for Information Processing–International Federation of Automatic Control Task Force on Enterprise Integration Strategic Workshop on Enterprise Integration and Enterprise Computing (Systems and Software Engineering Standards in the Context of Enterprise Integration), Enterprise Integration Group, School of Computing and Information Technology, Griffith University, Brisbane, Queensland, Australia.

Blanchard, Benjamin S. 1998. *Logistics engineering and management*. 5th ed. Upper Saddle River, NJ: Prentice Hall.

Blanchard, Benjamin S., and Wolter J. Fabrycky. 1998. *Systems engineering and analysis*. Upper Saddle River, NJ: Prentice Hall.

Criscimagna, Ned H. 1998. Cost as an independent variable. In *Selected topics in assurance related technologies (START) 98-2*. Vol. 5, no. 2. Reliability Analysis Center (RAC), Alion Science and Technology.

Defense Systems Management College. 1997, December. *Acquisition logistics guide*. 3rd ed. Fort Belvoir, VA: U.S. Department of Defense.

Kaminski, Dr. Paul G. 2005, December. Reducing life-cycle costs for new and fielded systems [Memorandum]. U.S. Office of the Secretary of Defense, Acquisition and Technology.

U.S. Department of Defense (DoD). 1983, April. *Life cycle cost model in Navy acquisitions*. MIL-HDBK-259. U.S. Navy.

U.S. Department of Defense (DoD). 1984, February. *Life cycle cost model for defense materiel systems. Data collection workbook*. MIL-HDBK-276-1, AMSC N3246. U.S. Marine Corps.

U.S. Department of Defense (DoD). 1998. *Department of Defense handbook. Work breakdown structure*. MIL-HDBK-881. (Superseding MIL-STD-881B25.)

U.S. Department of Defense (DoD). 2002, April 5. *Mandatory procedures for major defense acquisition programs (MDAPS) and major automated information system (MAIS) acquisition programs*. Dod 5000.2-R. Office of Under Secretary of Defense (Acquisition, Technology, and Logistics), Office of Assistant Secretary of Defense (Command, Control, Communications, and Intelligence), and Office of Director, Operational Test and Evaluation.

U.S. Department of Defense (DoD). 2003a, May. *Defense acquisition system*. DoD Directive 5000.1.

U.S. Department of Defense (DoD). 2003b, November. *Business case development guide*. EI Toolkit Guide. Submitted: Version 2.0. Available through the Defense Acquisition University at http://www.eitoolkit.com/tools/initiation/business_case/business_case_dev_guide.doc.

U.S. Department of Defense (DoD). 2007, October. *Operating and support cost-estimating guide*. Cost Analysis Improvement Group (CAIG), Office of the Secretary of Defense.

Chapter 10

Marketability

Preface

Enterprise administration is the art and science of deploying all of the resources of the enterprise—its people, technology, money, and management—to achieve established objectives in the context of a continually changing environment. Marketability is the ability of the enterprise to define what enterprise administration implies for specific operations, and it is the ability to market or sell its suggestions for change or improvement to its stakeholders. Marketing is more than advertising, more than selling. It involves all activities that relate the organization to the stakeholder it efficiently must serve in order to survive. It necessarily follows that marketing decisions are the riskiest and potentially the most profitable decisions that a program manager is ever called upon to make. Hence, marketing and managing change are essential for the success of the enterprise.

The focus of this chapter is marketing communications, because the most difficult part of implementing change is communicating the change to stakeholders who are naturally resistant to change. The most common questions asked by those to whom the change is directed are: Why change the way we do business? What does the change imply to me, specifically? Does change alter my work, lifestyle, or function? What is the motivation for me to change?

This chapter was prepared to help program sponsors, sustainment program managers, and other stakeholders understand marketing in their enterprise. This understanding needs to be based on a common definition of terms and a common approach to marketing communications. The chapter begins with a description of the marketing process, then discusses the concepts of target marketing and communications. The remainder of the chapter is devoted to the topic of change management because it is essential for the effective marketing of an enterprise. Finally, a case study of the Tobyhanna Army Depot in Pennsylvania is presented to illustrate a best practice for a plan in communications strategy.

10.1 The Role of Marketing

In 2008, the American Marketing Association's Board of Directors specifically defined marketing as "the activity, set of institutions, and processes for creating, communicating, delivering and exchanging offerings that have value for customers, clients, partners and society at large."*Marketing plays a very important role in military sustainability by controlling the traditional marketing mix, which consists of product/service/ideas, price, place, and promotion. In addition, when dealing with the marketing of services, there are three more controllable variables (people, process, and physical evidence), which in total make seven P's. The variables that the marketer cannot control are the environmental ones. These include the economy, technology, competition, political/legal, and social environments. In order to accomplish its mission, the military must meet the needs of its customers (target market) with the right product or service at the right price and place with effective promotion (communication) in a timely process by informed personnel in a comfortable physical setting.

10.1.1 Product

In the context of this volume, the product/service is *transformation*. To effectively respond to the increased, yet unpredictable, demand for mission-ready resources, the military must confront future challenges with a transformation plan for the entire enterprise: the military industrial complex and its processes. The focus should be on increasing throughput and customer support with the additional benefits of reducing flow time and increasing available capacity and labor productivity, so that the military can achieve more productive work. The transformation entails changes in repair processes, material support, financial accounting systems, and management mindset. The industrial space needs to be transformed to function with commercial efficiencies through the use of process improvement initiatives like Lean and cellular manufacturing. The goal is to achieve a quantum leap in sustainability throughput and efficiency by transforming workload and processes into those of a best-in-class enterprise using best practices, process improvement initiatives, and advanced manufacturing/sustainment processes and layouts.

10.1.2 Price

Price is *affordability* and opportunity costs, and affordability was defined in Chapter 9 by the extent to which the life cycle cost of a project is consonant with the long-range investment plans of the Department of Defense, its military departments, and defense agencies. Affordability considers not only development and investment costs of a program, but also the program's operating, support, and disposal costs. Opportunity costs consist of what other programs could be receiving support if the current one was not. In other words, where else would the money be used?

10.1.3 Place

A question arises as to whether to transform the entire military enterprise (e.g., an entire maintenance depot or a strategic business unit (SBU)) or to incrementally increase one maintenance cell at a time. Thus, the place is the *enterprise*, defined to be the facilities, technologies, operating systems, logistics systems, and other resources that are allocated to the organization to perform its function and meet its performance goals and objectives. In some cases, it may be better to

---

* American Marketing Association, Board of Directors, Chicago, IL (January 14, 2008).

transform the entire depot rather than each SBU to take advantage of economies of scale (e.g., change management, culture, leadership, and reporting), but resources are not always available to change an entire depot all at the same time. If the place is the entire enterprise, then viewing the implementation of the transformation across the entire enterprise minimizes the possibility of overlooking opportunities for further performance improvement. It eliminates the natural tendency to suboptimize functions and processes based on local metrics and organizational reporting. It also helps improve enterprise-wide quality, on-time delivery, and customer satisfaction by eliminating waste in the *entire* organization and supply chain, not just in one local repair/production cell. In turn, this helps reduce enterprise operating costs (taxpayer dollars) and minimize costs that affect the return on investment (ROI).

10.1.4 Promotion

Promotion is *communication*. A good communication plan provides the details on the flow of information about the enterprise transformation efforts to the stakeholders of that enterprise. The goal is to gain the visible unified support at every level within the enterprise by spreading the word about the transformation program, its approach to the transformation effort, and the progress on the program during its implementation. The military enterprise should create and maintain a global transformation information flow that will ensure the open flow of information between the enterprise and its stakeholders. By consistently promoting the processes, benefits, and successes of the transformation and establishing a free flow of information regarding the plan and its component projects, the enterprise should endeavor to gain momentum for the transformation through the support of a workforce that is fully knowledgeable and integrated into the transformation process. The enterprise should act as a clearinghouse for all information regarding the transformation plan and transformation projects to ensure a consistent message, adequate tracking, an educated workforce, and successful execution and implementation of the overall plan.

10.1.5 People

People are "all human actors who play a part in services delivery and thus influence the buyer's perceptions: namely, the firm's personnel, the customer, and other customers in the service environment."[*] In the military enterprise, this would include everyone from the base commander to those working on the shop floor. Table 10.1 lists the people that would be involved.

10.1.6 Process

Process is "the actual procedures, mechanisms, and flow of activities by which the service is delivered—the service delivery and operating systems."[†] In the military enterprise, it might be the planning, implementation, and control of a transformation project. Process also includes the transformation improvement initiatives, such as those given in Table 10.2.

---

[*] Zeithaml et al. (2006), 26.
[†] Ibid., p. 27.

Table 10.1 People Involved

Responsibility	Category
Maintenance—transformation office	Manager, staff
Major systems division	Managers, staff, shop floor
Subsystems division	Managers, staff, union steward, shop floor
Maintenance division	Managers, staff, shop floor
Process improvement and quality division	Managers, staff
Commodities division	Managers, staff, union steward, shop floor
Material division	Manager
Finance division	Staff
Software division	Staff
New work	Staff
Industry participants	Managers, union steward
Public affairs	Manager, staff
Transformation office	Managers, staff
Product support transformation office	Managers, staff

10.1.7 Physical Evidence

Physical evidence is "the environment in which the service is delivered and where the firm and customer interact, and any tangible components that facilitate performance or communication of the service."* This would include office, cafeteria, and any military base facility.

10.2 The Target Market

To sustain itself more effectively, the military enterprise undergoing the change or transformation needs to decide what particular group of stakeholders to target with its marketing efforts. Who are the stakeholders? Target marketing requires that marketers "identify and profile distinct groups of buyers [stakeholders] who differ in their needs and preferences (market segmentation); select one or more segments to enter (market targeting); and establish and communicate the offering's distinctive benefit(s) to the target segment (market positioning)."† In terms of market segmentation, an enterprise may decide to divide a group of stakeholders based on geographic variables, like location or region. For example, where do you start to implement a transformation or change project? What group or engineering cell? What military base? Other factors would include demographic variables, like the age of the weapon system. Behavioral variables, such as system benefits, user status, user rate, and readiness stage, would be particularly appropriate for the military.

---

* Ibid., p. 27.
† Kotler, Philip, and Kevin Keller, *A Framework for Marketing Management* (Englewood Cliffs, NJ: Pearson/Prentice Hall, 2007), p. 117.

Table 10.2   Transformation Improvement Processes

Process	Description
Lean	Lean manufacturing is a robust approach to operations that is responsive, flexible, predictable, and consistent. The operation is focused on continuous improvement through a self-directed workforce and driven by output-based measures aligned with customer performance criteria. The goal is to maximize value to the customer, and minimize waste and cost.
5S+1	Training about the Lean concept of 5S (sifting, sorting, sweeping, standardizing, and sustaining) + 1 for safety.
Six Sigma	Training black and green belts.
Kaizen events	Any action whose output is intended to be an improvement to an existing process. Such events rapidly implement work cells, improve setups, or streamline processes.
ISO	A set of International Standards Organization quality management standards and an ongoing certification process against those standards.
Benchmarking	An approach for gathering best practices from other organizations to use to improve one's processes.
Divestiture	An initiative to eliminate work that is redundant or unnecessary. People submit ideas (anonymously if they wish).
Affordable readiness	Because of efficiencies generated by a Lean, cellular workplace, additional capacity will be freed up and work that had been given to contractors can be brought back to the enterprise.

Not all markets are good target markets. A market must be large enough to be served profitably. It is also essential that this market can be easily measured and reached through effective communication strategies. These communication strategies can utilize external and internal strategies. Traditional external communications tools include personal selling, advertising, publicity/public relations, sales promotion, sponsorship marketing, and word-of-mouth marketing. Internal communication involves the working together of everyone within the enterprise to help each other as well as its customers. More recently, Internet marketing in the form of text messaging can be used for both external and internal communications. Internal marketing communications can also be both vertical and horizontal (Zeithaml et al. 2006). Particularly, for project teams, downward internal communication from management to employees is essential in the form of meetings, email, Web sites, and newsletters. Upward internal communication from front-line employees is essential so management knows what is happening at every level in the organization. Horizontal communication occurs between different departments within an organization. A great example of applying the critical skill of internal marketing occurs at Southwest Airlines, where the managers are good role models for learning.* Top management is involved in recruitment and training, internal communication, and workforce motivation. The CEO and president frequently goes to its facilities, gets to know its workers, and shares customer comments

---

* Gimble, Barney, "Southwest's New Flight Plan," *Fortune* (May 16, 2005), p. 93.

with its workers. Consequently, Southwest has very dedicated employees, who deliver service that is perceived to be best in class in comparison to that of many of the legacy airline carriers in the United States.

10.2.1 Stakeholders

The key stakeholders should include, but are not limited to:

1. Transformation areas—the facility location for the project
2. Transformation team—the integrated project team designing the project
3. Partners
    a. Current and future production partners
    b. Logistics partners
    c. Item supply managers
4. Product customers—warfighters
5. Workers
6. Managers
7. Supervisors
    a. Each work area
    b. Each shift
8. Senior leadership—higher-level military commanders
9. Support agencies
    a. Defense Logistics Agency (DLA)
    b. Vendors
    c. Suppliers
10. Union
    a. Membership
    b. Management
11. Public
    a. Cities or towns
    b. Chamber of Commerce
    c. Personnel service agencies (e.g., local companies)

10.2.2 Management

The program manager (PM) is responsible for the transformation project and the communication of information between and among every level of the program's management structure. To ensure successful execution of the transformation plan, each link in the communications chain has to strongly fulfill its specific responsibility, including tracking and reporting on the progress of transformation projects, guiding other personnel in executing transformation projects, and ensuring that the projects are consistent with the overall transformation plan. Thus, clear internal communications is crucial in the transformation. To help manage the communication exchange, four tiers of responsibility are recommended, as illustrated in Figure 10.1.

Planning information is generated and organized at the lower levels of the four-tiered communications chain and transmitted up, while program direction should flow down from higher levels of the tier. The goals of such a tiered structure are to:

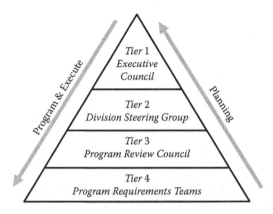

Figure 10.1 Communication management structure.

1. Clearly communicate the transformation vision across the enterprise.
2. Effectively coordinate the transformation process with every directorate, division, and shop in the enterprise.
3. Precisely execute the transformation plan as budgeted and scheduled.

10.2.2.1 Tier 1: Executive Council

The executive council (EC), tier 1, is chaired by the PM/director and is made up of division (business units in the enterprise) chiefs. The EC is responsible for setting the vision and the course for the transformation initiative and communicating that direction down through the tiers in the enterprise. The EC should meet quarterly to discuss and fine-tune the transformation vision and to review, approve, and advocate transformation programs as brought forth by the division steering group (DSG).

10.2.2.2 Tier 2: Division Steering Group

The division steering group (DSG), tier 2, is chaired by the PM/director and made up of all division chiefs. The DSG is responsible for reviewing and coordinating transformation efforts. The DSG should meet monthly to discuss transformation efforts and resolve any cross-division issues that could not be resolved in the program review council (PRC). In addition, the DSG will utilize the monthly meeting as an opportunity to agree on a unified plan to present to the director during the EC's quarterly meeting. Thus, the DSG will ensure the unified direction of transformation efforts throughout by communicating a unified plan to the EC and a vision and direction to the PRC.

10.2.2.3 Tier 3: Program Review Council

The program review council (PRC), tier 3, is chaired by the PM. Each division is represented on the PRC by a single point of contact (POC) designated by the division chief. The PRC should meet frequently to share information about transformation efforts among the divisions. This information exchange includes direction from the higher levels of the structure and the status of ongoing transformation efforts. The PRC is responsible for providing current transformation projects' status updates and coordinated plans to the DSG, as well as informing the DSG of any issues that the

PRC cannot resolve. The PRC also coordinates transformation projects with the program requirements teams (PRTs), informing them of the directives handed down by the DSG.

10.2.2.4 Tier 4: Program Requirements Teams

A program requirements team (PRT), tier 4, is established for each of the divisions: major systems, subsystems, and commodities. The PM, who is responsible for transformation efforts within that division, chairs each PRT, and each team includes the division POC assigned to the PRC. Additional membership in each PRT is determined by the PM and the division POC, and may include other division personnel, contract resources, or personnel from external organizations. The PRTs are responsible for executing the transformation efforts within their respective divisions. Each PRT will meet weekly to provide project updates, share information, and review and execute division transformation projects as directed by the higher tiers in the communications chain.

10.3 Communication Vehicles

To spread the word on a transformation program to a project team, a variety of communication vehicles should be used. Promotion and sales expertise will be instrumental in the successful communication and buy-in of transformation. It is very important that the same message be diffused at all levels. Information on the expectations of each stakeholder needs to be available to the entire community. Every stakeholder will not take the time to review and know what is happening with other stakeholders. So, for complete buy-in, everyone needs to have the same information. Below is a list of these vehicles.

10.3.1 Project Team Meetings

The project teams should meet regularly. Agendas should be prepared and distributed to participants prior to each meeting. Minutes and action item updates, resulting from the meetings, should be distributed to participants following each meeting. Refer to Appendices A and B for examples of an agenda, minutes, and action item updates.

10.3.2 Staff Meetings

Project teams should discuss the status, coordination, and planning of transformation efforts at regularly scheduled staff meetings. A manual should provide additional information regarding staff meetings. This information would include accomplishments to date, the current status of the transformation, and expectations for the next month. In addition, there should be questions and answers during the meeting. For assessment purposes, minutes should be taken and then the action items should be monitored.

10.3.3 Transformation Area Team Meetings

As plans for the transformation are developed, communication between the project team, management, and the transformation contractors will be critical. Each transformation area should form a transformation team and hold regularly scheduled meetings to develop a list of the processes, flows, and unique requirements of each area being transformed. The group should have regular contact with teams, and results from meetings should be recorded and shared. A basic outline of each group's tasks should be developed by the teams in conjunction with the transformation office.

An example of focus areas for the project team meetings might include:

- Shop requirements:
  - Workbenches
  - Cranes
  - Test stands
- Internal shop flow recommendations:
  - How would the workers organize the shop if given the chance?
  - Are there special requirements for clearances or floor space?
  - What utilities are required, like water power and compressed air?
- Coordination:
  - Delivery
  - Logistics supply support
  - Engineers, logisticians, item managers
- Supply and warehousing

10.3.4 Town Hall Meeting

The town hall meeting is a presentation by senior staff to provide a single vision and definition of the transformation to all stakeholders. The first step is to ensure everyone knows what transformation means and what it does not mean (e.g., workforce reductions). Project teams and other transformation offices should prepare/organize a single set of briefings for all employees that defines transformation, explains why it is necessary, states the end goal, and provides a timeline for the transformation process. Also, the role of each stakeholder should be defined, and what is needed and expected from each stakeholder should be addressed. Follow-up pamphlets could be distributed. The pamphlets could provide a synopsis of the facts presented at the meeting, the points of contact, and Web site information.

The briefing set might include:

- Short overview of the transformation:
  - Why is it necessary?
  - What does it mean to the project team and the surrounding community?
  - Growth: workload, jobs, opportunities
- Impact on the stakeholders:
  - Any surges or possible short-term delays expected during swings?
- Before and after transformation pros and cons:
  - Pictures of before and after
  - Production numbers before and after
  - Testimony from workers
- Examples of future transformation of one or two shops:
  - Pictures of one or two shops, and locations shown on a building map
  - Conceptual new location and shop flow diagram
- What will be happening in the next few months?
  - Will potential bidders be in the area to begin determining the scope?

- What transformations will be happening?
- Facility information: Will doors or aisles be blocked?
- Changes to entrances, restrooms, break rooms
- Stakeholder roles and responsibilities:
  - List of what is expected of each stakeholder group
  - List of what stakeholders can expect from project teams during the transformation
- Questions and answers

10.3.5 Story Boards

Story boards are bulletin boards, banners, and posters that depict progress on a project.

10.3.6 Email

Email is generally the preferred daily communication method for accomplishment of basic tasks, because it provides documentation that can be readily tracked and forwarded for further action if necessary. The project team procedures manual would provide further discussion about the use of email for internal communications.

10.3.7 Web Site

The project team should create and maintain a Web site as a means of providing personnel with the most current and easily accessible information and updates regarding the transformation initiative. In addition, this Web site should serve as a tool for educating the entire team about the benefits of the transformation and gaining the active and enthusiastic participation of the workforce. The Web site should contain all known information and be the posting place for current briefings, questions and answers, and meeting minutes. It also could be used as a promotional tool to the stakeholders. Public relations and Web site design experts should be used to develop and maintain the site. The Web site should include interactive questions, and perhaps use a bulletin board forum, to capture all stakeholder ideas.

- *Public access Web site*: Many workers do not have access to a computer, or do not have time during their shift, to surf. A public access Web site would provide a good source for workers, cities, and communities to see what is happening.
- *Transformation Web terminals*: Terminals set in public areas would allow any user to access the transformation pages, read updates, and submit suggestions and comments. They also help reach those individuals who do not have access.
- *Plasma displays*: These should indicate what has been accomplished to date and the current status of the transformation. In addition, they should indicate what to expect next with points of contact.

10.3.8 Newsletter

The project team should create and disseminate a periodic newsletter that will serve as a forum to highlight significant achievements in the transformation process. The newsletter could be distributed around the enterprise, via email, and also on Web sites to reach the broadest audience possible. The newsletter could contain:

- What has been accomplished to date
- Current status of the transformation
- What to expect in the next month
- Points of contact

10.3.9 Gap Workshops

Some enterprises hold workshops where employees from various functions meet for a day or two to understand the problems in matching promises with delivery accomplished by operations personnel (Zeithaml et al. 1990). More about the concept of gap analysis will be discussed in Section 10.8.

10.4 Communication Information Protocol

The communication information protocol is a plan that provides details on the flow of information about the transformation effort. The goal is to gain visible unified support at every level in the chain of communication by maintaining a global transformation information flow that will ensure the open flow of information between the enterprise and its stakeholders. An example protocol is represented in Figure 10.2.

10.5 Communication Schedule

A recommended schedule for the respective communication vehicles is given in Table 10.3.

10.6 Managing the Change

Every communications plan should speak directly to change and its impacts. Change communication is effective only when the focus is in the context of an overall change management plan. A widely accepted view of change management (Kotter 1996) outlines eight stages of organizational

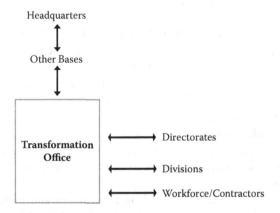

Figure 10.2   Global transformation information flow.

Table 10.3   Communication Schedule

Communication Vehicle	Frequency
Project team meetings	Monthly
Project team staff meetings	Monthly
Transformation area team meetings	Weekly
Town hall meeting	Annually
Email	Continuously
Web site	Continuously
Newsletter	Quarterly
Gap workshops	Quarterly

change. Research on best practices validates that organizations that follow this framework have the highest rate of success in their change efforts. The eight change stages are:

1. Establish the motivation for change and a sense of urgency.
2. Build a guiding coalition.
3. Develop a vision and strategy for change.
4. Communicate the vision, including key communication action steps.
5. Empower broad-based action, including key training action steps.
6. Generate short-term wins.
7. Sustain the momentum: consolidate gains and produce more change.
8. Anchor new approaches in the culture.

The intent of change management is to provide a tool to help focus transformation resources in the near term. As the transformation is implemented, changes will emerge that will need to be incorporated in longer-term plans. Therefore, more detail is provided for the near-term stages than for the longer term. The project team will develop future details as the plan is implemented.

Due to the complexities and challenges of the multiple organizations involved in a transformation effort, success is critically dependent on the relationships among the key leaders in each transformation office and key divisions, and the willingness of these individuals to work together and support each other. Thus, an effective communication plan identifies the key action steps needed to implement this change model. Details on each of the key action steps are provided in Section 10.7, while the gap analysis upon which these recommendations are based is described in Section 10.8. The key action steps from each of the eight change management stages are integrated into approximate timeframes for the change effort. Table 10.4 shows the timeframes for each of the key action steps. The myriad communications activities are incorporated in these stages as well. While there is a sequence to accomplishing these stages, it is not perfectly linear and often requires working stages simultaneously or going back to revise or repeat part of a stage. Therefore, the timeframes indicated are only approximations.

This plan for change management is based on government and industry best practices. It identifies specific actions that will ensure effective transformation. The most critical action for a project team is to direct a single office with full authority, talent, and financial resources to coordinate and integrate the transformation. Continuity of both leadership and vision are crucial in accomplishing this and the other key actions. Through demonstrated leadership and effective execution of this change management plan, people will know that this transformation effort is well supported and is moving along the path to success.

Table 10.4   Key Action Steps

Key Action Steps	Timeframe
To Establish a Sense of Urgency, You Need to:	
Direct a single office with full authority, talent, and financial resources to coordinate and integrate the transformation *C	Immediate!
Reconnect with customer needs	Near-term and periodic
Hold a transformation leadership off site	Within 30 days after stand-up single office
Closely coordinate all transformation approaches and integrate action steps	Continuous, after office stand-up
Hold all managers accountable for coordinated implementation of the transformation	Starting immediately after off site
To Build a Guiding Coalition, You Need to:	
Determine which internal and external stakeholders are part of the guiding coalition	Concurrent with each recurrence of "reconnect with customer needs"
Determine when and how you need these stakeholders to participate over time	Concurrent with each recurrence of "reconnect with customer needs"
Ensure customers' voices are represented in all transformation initiatives *C	Make first assessment prior to building management team; recurring
Build a change management team	After establish single office, prior to off-site
To Develop a Vision and Strategy for Change, You Need to:	
Refine and simplify the center's transformation vision and strategies	Off-site critical outcome
Define leadership's expectations of employees' role in transformational initiatives *C	Off-site critical outcome; reevaluate periodically
Tie vision, strategies, and objectives to planning and budgeting processes	Based on refined vision; reassess and redirect at least quarterly
Develop and use metrics that align behavior with strategy *C	Implement quickly after defining employees' roles; revisit with planning and budget
Align performance measurement, rewards, promotion and succession systems with vision and strategy *C	Establish initial incentives; work integrated long-term system

(Continued)

Table 10.4   (Continued)

Key Action Steps	Timeframe
To Communicate the Vision, You Need to:	
Create and implement a *Lean communications* plan for your Lean organization *C	Immediately after stand-up single office; continuous implementation
Communicate the center's visions and strategies at every opportunity *C	Immediately and continuously after refine vision *and* develop center-wide toolkit definitions
Develop center-wide definitions for the transformation *tool kit* *C	After off site and refine vision
Encourage, listen to, and use feedback on transformation initiatives *C	Continuously after stand-up single office
Ensure leadership is *walking the talk* and modeling new behaviors *C	After stand-up single office; use off site to instantiate
To Empower Broad-Based Action, You Need to:	
Create and implement a *Lean training* plan for your Lean enterprise	Initiate training planning off site; continuously
Use change agents to spread the word about the transformation *C	As soon as refine vision and clearly define what to communicate (in communications plan)
Ensure personnel, information, financial and management reporting systems provide appropriate support to empowered workforce	Start at off site; link to employees' roles, metrics, and performance system
To Generate Short-Term Wins, You Need to:	
Learn from and leverage existing short-term wins, such as the Lean cell teams *C	Inputs to off site; use lessons learned continuously in all aspects of transformation
To Sustain the Momentum and Produce More Change, You Need to:	
Address systemic issues to enable transformation success *C	Based on refined vision; continuously monitor, anticipate, and react
To Anchor New Approaches in the Culture, You Need to:	
Define and build the attributes of the new culture *C	Start off site; link to employees' roles, metrics, and performance system

Note: *C denotes a communications plan component or requires communications.

10.7 Key Action Steps

The following recommended tasks for change management break down the eight stages of Kotter's change management framework (1996) into key action steps (KASs). Each KAS provides a component of implementation, collectively achieving the transition from the current state to the desired future state. The detailed gap analysis supporting these KASs is provided in the Section 10.8.

Successful transformation depends on a closely coordinated and integrated approach, as described herein. Implicit in this model is a management structure that directs the change effort. The first key action step of Section 10.7.1 is the single most critical action.

10.7.1 Establish the Motivation for Change and a Sense of Urgency

1. Direct a single office with full authority, talent, and financial resources to coordinate and integrate the transformation.
2. Reconnect with the voice of the customer. What do the military, warfighters, and other key customers need to change in these transformation efforts? Take what you've done regarding the key customer needs and connect and incorporate this into all messages in the communications and change efforts. Align the message of "bring it to the enterprise" with your customers' needs. Stay connected with your customers and other key stakeholders throughout the transformation.
3. Hold a leadership off-site meeting for all transformation leaders to develop and agree upon:
   a. Clear charter and responsibilities for each transformation office and the coordinating transformation office. Senior leaders must provide role clarity between these offices and agree to coordinate the work of these individual efforts.
   b. Case for change, the urgency of the change, and a common view of the future state (the vision).
   c. Key messages to be used consistently and frequently by all transformation leaders (see details in Section 10.8.4).
4. Develop an elevator speech of four to six key points that describes the future state. These are points that everyone can easily understand and remember.
5. Develop the "burning platform"—a compelling communication idea that explains why things must change and overcomes organizational complacency. "Bring it to the enterprise" needs to be punched up to motivate people to buy-in. What are the consequences of not changing?
6. Develop a short, powerful linkage that explicitly describes how the future state will mitigate the burning platform.
7. Develop key messages and answers to anticipated questions, such as: What will happen to my job?
8. Closely coordinate all transformation approaches and integrate action steps. A toolbox approach can easily create confusion in employees' minds. Carefully explain only what workers need to know about these efforts just in time for them to use them. Keep detailed information and training about a particular tool set local and exclusive to the people who need to know, when they need to know.
9. Hold managers at all levels accountable for coordinated implementation of this transformation. Managers' performance goals need to outline not only their responsibility in implementing their own division's change efforts, but also their role in assisting with other change efforts, as appropriate.

10.7.2 Build a Guiding Coalition

1. Perform a stakeholder analysis to examine which internal and external stakeholders are currently part of the guiding coalition and who may be missing, for example, representatives from the community and political or regulatory stakeholders. Identify their "what's in it for me (WIIFM)?"

2. Determine when and how you need to have representation from each stakeholder group in the change process. Use an Office of Public Affairs to support you in developing a plan to appropriately bring in external stakeholders.

3. Bring those key stakeholders into the leadership off-site meeting, either during the off-site or after, via briefings or other communications as appropriate, to obtain their input, buy-in, and support for the changes that will be taking place. After the transformation effort engages a stakeholder or stakeholder group, maintain that engagement according to a plan based on time as well as accomplishment.

4. Ensure customers' voices are represented in all transformation initiatives, decisions, and actions of the guiding coalition.

5. Build a change management coalition, a team of representatives from each of the transformation initiatives, who include, for example, maintenance and product support people. Coordinate all transformation activities through this team (i.e., the transformation working group). Ensure they have direct support from, and are empowered by, center leadership. Clearly charter and delineate the team's roles and responsibilities, and identify the team's leadership and sponsors. Build trust among coalition members. Center leadership must publicly and frequently support the coalition by both words and action (see Section 10.8.4).

10.7.3 Develop a Vision and Strategy for Change

1. Refine and simplify the multiple layers of the transformation initiative vision and strategy. Focus on one single, compelling elevator speech of a vision that fits for the center and all transformation offices and initiatives. Paint a clear picture of the future and how you will get there.

2. Translate the current vision of world-class people and facilities in combination with synchronized and innovative business practices and systems—the warfighter's first choice for logistics—into a compelling vision for the transformation initiative, so that customers, employees, and other stakeholders are drawn into it.

3. Translate your strategy to continuously transform business practices, processes, and technologies to achieve world-class efficiency and effectiveness for all products and services into clearer language, describing how you plan to get there. For example, "bring it to the enterprise," the warfighter's first choice for logistics, speaks to the strategy, the vision, and the customer.

4. Begin to define the leadership's expectations of the employees' roles in the transformational initiatives.

5. Tie vision, strategies, and objectives to planning and budgeting processes. Develop and use metrics that align behavior with strategy.

6. Align performance measurement, rewards, promotion, and succession systems with vision and strategy. This will need to be addressed enterprise-wide. A performance system that rewards competitive individual performance undermines team-based goals.

7. Communicate the vision and strategy at every opportunity. Research shows that the brain must hear a message six times before it is implanted in memory. Goal clarity and alignment behavior are created when employees can cite the goal from memory.
8. Leadership must continue to publicly endorse the transformation in word and in action.
9. Leadership should use the same phrases and highlight the specific changes being addressed by the transformation team. This has to obviously support the actions of the team.
10. Develop enterprise-wide definitions for the transformation tool kit, including Lean, Six Sigma, cellular manufacturing, etc. Consistent definitions and messaging are essential to goal clarity and alignment. The definitions include the applications for each tool in the tool kit.

10.7.4 Communicate the Vision

1. Create and implement a Lean communications plan for your Lean organization. Lean communication is the ability to deliver the right message to the right people at the right time in the right way at the least cost.
2. Coordinate all transformation offices to develop a joint communication plan to address the information and education needs of all stakeholders, as defined in stakeholder analysis (stage 2).
3. Analyze the results of the various communication surveys that have been completed. Determine which communication vehicles are the most effective for each stakeholder.
4. Examine the number of newsletters, memos, and briefings being created. Streamline them into fewer vehicles, such as a single monthly transformation newsletter, a weekly plasma screen briefing, or a coordinated sign board usage.
5. Limit email and Web-based communication until the technology and access are more widely available. Have realistic expectations of shop floor employees' use of email, hand-held devices, and Web sites based on system realities and civil service computer usage policies. Managers who have complete access complain of receiving too much email. Most front-line employees don't yet have computer access or have restricted access to email.
6. Maximize the use of the preferred communication method: word of mouth. Have managers hold weekly stand-up staff briefings to convey the latest news regarding the transformation. Provide managers with talking points for those briefings. Talking points include carefully scripted, meaningful, catch phrases that are clearly understood and repeated often.
7. Coordinate all transformation messages. Agree on common language and definitions for transformational initiatives.
8. Conduct regular (e.g., weekly) meetings among divisions and transformation offices to keep each other informed regarding communication efforts and plans.
9. Actively solicit feedback on transformation initiatives: listen to it, use it. Create vehicles for ongoing feedback and timely response to issues/concerns. Devise ways to frequently receive information from employees, especially through informal conversations, such as weekly staff briefings with managers. Give recognition for feedback; using it while giving credit to sources provides greater endorsements.

10.7.5 Empower Broad-Based Action

1. Create Lean training for your Lean organization. Lean training is the ability to deliver the right level of training to the right people just in time to prepare them to be competent and effective in performing their work.
   a. Coordinate the transformation training within the enterprise. Develop a comprehensive and coordinated training plan, timed to address employees' needs just in time.
   b. Build a central database of training offerings in order to determine and track the appropriate training for a given individual or project team at a particular time. This database also helps identify your expert training cadre for sustainment.
   c. Provide Lean and cellular high-level awareness education to all employees prior to rolling out the Lean or cellular improvement process.
   d. Attend to middle managers' training needs first. They are key drivers of change and need to be well prepared and motivated to lead others.
   e. Design and deliver Lean or cellular concept and tool training as well as team development training for cell teams as they become involved in the process redesign for their cell. Others have established a best practice in this area. Follow their approach. It's excellent, and the evidence says it works.
2. Get out of your offices and talk with people. "Walk the talk" and model new behaviors:
   a. Listen to what people have to say. Actively solicit feedback and respond quickly to issues/concerns.
   b. Use the elevator speech to describe the future of the transformation, and get people excited about the change.
   c. Be prepared to talk about the consequences for people who don't get on board the transformation train.
   d. Look for people who see the WIIFM for themselves, because they will get on board the transformation train. Encourage them to participate as change agents. Support them in making a contribution and assure them that their ideas will be heard and respected.
3. Use change agents to spread the word about transformation.
4. Perform an assessment of personnel, information, financial, and management reporting systems to determine where there is alignment with the vision and provide appropriate support to empower the workforce.

10.7.6 Generate Short-Term Wins

1. Benchmark, learn from, and leverage existing short-term wins. Other Lean or cellular redesign teams have demonstrated great initial success. They are building morale and enthusiasm for a transformation. Their success factors need to be understood and replicated, and their stories need to be communicated more widely.
2. Develop a video that shows the Lean cells in action and show it to everyone associated with the transformation initiative.
3. Ensure the performance metrics are achieved by integrating the integrated master plan (IMP) and integrated master schedule (IMS) for the transformation project. Provide adequate resources to carry out this responsibility, and ensure all transformation offices coordinate their implementations.

4. Because a transformation takes time to complete, it is critical to manage stakeholders' expectations concerning the changes they will see over time. There will likely be a series of short-term wins that will build motivation across different stakeholder groups at different times.

10.7.7 Sustain the Momentum: Consolidate Gains and Produce More Change

Address systemic issues to enable the transformation's success:

1. The current performance system that measures process efficiency is inconsistent with a Lean approach. Measurement systems need to change and supervisors need to be trained in how to motivate others with this new performance measurement structure.
2. Government regulations constrain what can be done to compensate and motivate employees. Leaders need to explore what latitude they have with existing regulations and what needs to be changed.

10.7.8 Anchor New Approaches in the Culture

Employees believe the culture needs to change to support a Lean approach. These changes will have a significant impact on the psychological contract employees have established with the enterprise. Effective change management planning and implementation is essential to effectively implement these changes and retain key talent. This will be an ongoing effort as the transformation unfolds.

10.8 Gap Analysis

Gap analysis is the study of the differences between two different states, often for the purpose of determining how to get from one state to a new state. A gap is sometimes spoken of as the space between where we are and where we want to be. Gap analysis is undertaken as a means of bridging that space. As illustrated in Figure 10.3, the lower line is where you'll be if you do nothing: the current state. The upper line is where you want to be: the desired future state.

Current state (where you are): Comments on the current state of a transformation initiative would be based on observations from people representing a cross section of managers, staff, union representatives, and shop floor employees from most divisions. Also, base observations on an extensive review of documents, briefings, and change-related artifacts (such as newsletters, training manuals, and memos) related to the transformation strategy and initiatives need to be considered.

Desired future state (where you wish to be): Comments regarding the desired future state would be based on experience in communications/change management, as well as research on best practices in both the commercial and military sectors.

In the sections that follow, a gap analysis is performed between the current state and the desired state for each of the eight change management stages described above. The comments provided for each stage are hypothetical, but somewhat realistic, to illustrate the difference between the states. The gap is where the actions to achieve the future state are derived.

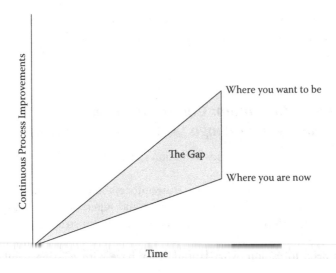

Figure 10.3   Gap analysis.

10.8.1 Stage 1: Establish the Motivation for Change and a Sense of Urgency

Current state:

1. Confusion and a lack of understanding stem from many uncoordinated transformation initiatives.
    a. There are many transformation initiatives under way being led by different change offices.
    b. Attempts to coordinate efforts have had limited success due to insufficient people and budget resources and an apparent lack of coordinating leadership.
    c. Employees' focus and allegiance are to their division's unique transformation efforts. Little information about initiatives flows across divisions, and few people understand how their division's transformation efforts link to others.
    d. Many believe that Lean and cellular are just for shop floor workers.
2. Employees have mixed reactions to transformation.
    a. Some employees in a few divisions may demonstrate significant excitement and enthusiasm for transformation.
    b. Most employees lack understanding, and many think they will lose jobs to contractors. Shop floor workers and some middle managers are concerned that transformation means they will streamline the work, and then contractors will be brought in to take over their jobs. For some employees, this view has its roots in an experience when the organization became "lean," the base was closed, and a commercial company took their jobs. Still others understand that Lean removes waste, and they fear that their jobs are waste and may be eliminated.
    c. Many employees need more details to trust the transformation, saying, "Show me the money!" This workforce has been through many changes in past years. They know the only way any change initiative will stick is if it is funded. They want to

know: Where is the money coming from? When will we see it? How long will it last? What is the backup plan if we run out of money? How do we know that this will still work if it's only partially complete? How are you going to track cost savings? You need to prove that this is not the "flavor of the month."

3. There is no sense of urgency; employees don't understand why this needs to be done now.
   a. Message is there is an opportunity to bring back previously outsourced work or bring new work.
   b. Leaders avoid the message everyone understands. In the future, a closing may occur if improvements are not made and the operation becomes more productive and cost-efficient.
4. People want to get on board. Early initiatives are building support.
   a. Employees are proud of their work and their role in supporting the warfighter. They want to be an integral part of this change initiative. They don't want it to be taken away from them.
   b. Many people want to help, but they lack resources, training, and information.
   c. The Lean cells are successful quick wins and are building enthusiasm for transformation.
   d. Shop floor employees like the idea of bringing the upstairs downstairs. They want more managers and technical people (schedulers, etc.) involved directly in their cells. But they are somewhat skeptical about this happening.

Desired future state:

1. All stakeholders understand the real or potential crisis or opportunity that is causing the change. Because crises are more compelling than opportunities, conversations about the urgency for change include the worst-case scenario, such as closings.
2. Employees thoroughly understand and can articulate the customers' needs when describing what needs to change/improve. The customer's point of view is articulated in the case for change.
3. Everyone has a common view of and is in agreement about the motivation for and urgency of change.
4. Common language and definitions are used to describe the future state. Everyone understands the transformation toolbox approach, and which tools will be used in their unit, and why.
5. Leaders are able to answer questions such as: Why should we do this now? What is at stake? What will happen if we don't do this?
6. All managers understand it is their responsibility to help implement change. Their future opportunities and compensation are commensurately affected by their performance.
7. There are consequences for employees who actively impede change.

10.8.2 Stage 2: Build a Guiding Coalition

Current state:

1. Little has been done to identify and bring in important stakeholders.
2. The voice of the customer is rarely mentioned.
3. A transformation office exists, and it has been charged with coordinating the integration plans for all transformation initiatives, as well as coordinating all change efforts, yet it is understaffed and underfunded. The transformation office has not coordinated their communication or training efforts.

4. Because multiple transformation initiatives are under way, using a variety of tools and approaches such as Lean, Six Sigma, and benchmarking, leaders believe they are speaking about a common transformation effort, but to employees it looks disjointed, confusing, and internally competitive.

Desired future state:

1. Center leadership provides resources and guidance to support the effective coordination of the various transformation initiatives.
2. Key managers and change agents have positional power, expertise, credibility, and leadership in change management as well as maintenance operations.
3. Key external stakeholders (including customers, suppliers, union, regulatory, military leadership, media, community, local and state political representatives, and groups) are represented in the guiding coalition.
4. Coalition members have validated the goals of the transformation initiative and shared their ideas in the vision.
5. The guiding coalition is a high-performing team.

10.8.3 Stage 3: Develop a Vision and Strategy for Change

Current state:

1. Multiple strategy statements exist for the center and for each transformation initiative. There are lots of words, but little understanding among employees about what it means to their work. What will change, and what will stay the same?
2. Vision, strategy, budgets, performance measurement, rewards, promotion and succession systems, and therefore behavior, are not systematically linked and aligned.
3. Town hall meetings and other communication efforts are under way to articulate the transformation vision and strategy.

Desired future state:

1. Center leaders regularly communicate a vision that is compelling enough to pull people through the status quo, that wins both their hearts and minds, and that motivates and helps coordinate people's actions.
2. Both the vision and the strategy have been simply defined so that all stakeholders see the logic and a first level of detail about how this future can be accomplished.
3. Employees understand their roles in creating this future: what will be expected of them, how they will be prepared or trained to participate in the change, how they will be rewarded for their contributions, and what the consequences will be if they impede the change.

10.8.4 Stage 4: Communicate the Vision

Current state:

1. Communication has not been coordinated across the transformation offices or elsewhere.
   a. There is a full spectrum of transformation-associated messaging and communication vehicles in place or in development.
   b. The center has the results of several independent communication surveys, and it is currently collecting data from a survey distributed at the recent town hall meetings. The results of these various surveys have not been pulled together, nor has any coordinated communication planning yet resulted from these surveys.

2. Word of mouth is the most frequently cited method of communication.
   a. The good news is that when messages are sent down the chain of command and passed along in staff meetings, they are heard.
   b. The bad news is that messaging is not occurring consistently, nor does it always reach all the way to the shop floor. In the absence of information, other messages are hypothesized. For example, some say that Lean means "less employees are needed."
3. Communication is predominantly top-down via briefings, signs, memos, newsletters, plasma screens, town hall meetings, etc.
4. There was no evidence of input from the shop floor employees except in the pilot Lean cells.

Desired future state:

1. All transformation communications are coordinated across the transformation offices and divisions and a plan is implemented to address the specific needs of key stakeholders.
2. The vision is articulated in a clear, simple message (focused and jargon-free). Everyone has a common understanding of the vision and their roles in accomplishing the change.
3. Consistent messages are delivered in timely manners to appropriate constituents using the best vehicles for that audience.
4. A variety of vehicles are used to communicate and inform constituents about the transformation efforts. Employees receive weekly updates.
5. The guiding coalition exhibits the behavior expected of all employees and "walks the talk."
6. Messages are conveyed using key elements of effective communication:
   a. Simplicity
   b. Metaphor, analogy, and example
   c. Multiple forums
   d. Repetition
   e. Leadership by example
   f. Explanation of seeming inconsistencies
   g. Give-and-take/two-way communication

10.8.5 Stage 5: Empower Broad-Based Action

Current state:

1. People want to get on board; early initiatives are building support; many people want to help, but they lack resources, training, and information.
2. Much training is taking place, but it has not been planned or coordinated across the transformation offices.
   a. There is a full spectrum of transformation-related training being implemented.
   b. Many people are attending Lean training programs and understand the concepts.
   c. Middle managers urgently need more training. From first-level supervisors to division managers, they are often caught in the middle. They need to support transformation and sometimes are managing people who have already been trained when they themselves have not been.
3. Lean management training is a best practice, and it was developed organically (in-house). Continue to expand the use of this training with a just-in-time approach.

Desired future state:

1. Leaders have identified and are supporting key change agents across the organization and are satisfied they have enough of the right people to implement the change.

2. The right people are receiving the right training, just in time.
3. Information and human systems (e.g., performance appraisal, compensation, hiring, promotions, succession planning) have been examined and are now aligned with the vision.
4. Financial and management reporting systems have been improved to provide information essential to empowered decision making.
5. Barriers to empowerment (e.g., troublesome supervisors) have been removed.

10.8.6 Stage 6: Generate Short-Term Wins

Current state:
1. The Lean cells are successful short-term wins.
2. Shop floor employees like the idea of bringing the upstairs downstairs. They want more managers and technical people (schedulers, etc.) involved directly in their cells.

Desired future state:
1. A series of short-term wins builds organizational momentum and motivation for continuing the change.
2. Leaders keep pressing for results and employees keep delivering.
3. Employees want to be change agents and rotate through that role to support and spread the word about transformation.
4. Early successes are communicated extensively and celebrated. Everyone feels part of a winning team.

10.8.7 Stage 7: Sustain the Momentum: Consolidate Gains and Produce More Change

Current state:
1. What is happening is important to the state and local community. In addition to providing a large number of jobs, families have worked at facilities for generations and are loyal and committed.
2. Systemic issues need to be addressed to enable the success of the transformation.
   a. The current performance system is inconsistent with Lean. Most supervisors are measured on efficiency metrics that conflict with Lean approaches. They aren't motivated to change until their performance measures are aligned with Lean goals. They don't know how to motivate their employees to make changes and still keep up production.
   b. Government regulations enforce an uneven playing field. People are ready to make changes but are constrained by government regulations.

Desired future state:
1. Family legacies, the local and state community, politicians and regulatory agencies, and military leadership feel like they have had a hand in success and are invested in continuing to support the transformation.
2. The cellular process improvement builds on the lessons learned and the successes of the early Lean cell efforts.
3. The Lean cellular redesign process is continually reinvigorated with new projects, themes, and change agents.

4. By using the increased credibility generated by these successful implementations, support has been given to make dramatic changes to systems, structures, and policies that previously didn't fit the transformation vision.
5. New performance measures have been implemented that reinforce the new strategy, performance behaviors, and personal responsibility.
6. People who were actively resisting or impeding the change have left. Leadership is hiring, promoting, and developing people who can implement the change vision.

10.8.8 Stage 8: Anchor New Approaches in the Culture

Current state:
1. People believe the culture needs to change to support a Lean approach. They don't have a common view of what the new culture would look like.
2. They want to be empowered and participate in making the changes, but don't know how this will happen.

Desired future state:
1. Culture change evolves from the changes in norms and shared values that emerge during the transformation process.
2. The new Lean and cellular processes are demonstrated to be more successful than the old way, which provides the foundation for a new culture.
3. There may be some turnover to replace active resistors with people who embody the new culture and behaviors.
4. A performance-focused mindset is in place demonstrated via customer and productivity-oriented behavior, more and better leadership, and more effective management.
5. People understand the connections between new behaviors and organizational success.

10.9 Best Practice Case Study: Tobyhanna Army Depot

The U.S. Navy's Best Manufacturing Practices Center of Excellence (BMPCOE)* has identified, researched, and promoted exceptional practices, methods, and procedures in the design, testing, production, facilities, logistics, maintainability, and management of products. BMPCOE exists to increase the quality, reliability, and maintainability of goods and services produced by American firms by providing benchmarking cases for applications.

Tobyhanna Army Depot (TYAD) is the largest, full-service electronics maintenance facility in the Department of Defense (DoD) with a total mission to "sustain and integrate command, control, communications, computers, intelligence, surveillance, and reconnaissance (C4ISR) systems for the joint warfighter." TYAD is the DoD's recognized leader in automated test equipment, systems integration, and the downsizing of electronics systems. TYAD is the DoD's only Joint C4ISR depot and its designated Center of Industrial and Technical Excellence for "C4ISR and electronics, avionics, and missile guidance and control." The following case study has been identified as an institution possessing best practices in communications by BMPCOE in a survey that was conducted at TYAD in Tobyhanna, Pennsylvania, the week of July 10, 2006.

---

* http://www.bmpcoe.org (accessed September 3, 2008).

10.9.1 Best Practice: Communications Strategy Plan

A 1996 employee survey identified communications as a major area for improvement at TYAD. The workforce pointed out that information flowed in "stovepipes" with little cross-communication between functional areas. The inconsistent transfer of information and data produced internal competition and conflict, adversely affecting morale and productivity. To improve communications, the leadership team developed a communications strategy and formal communications plan. The purpose of the plan was to formalize communications processes throughout the depot and standardize the methods of sending and receiving business and general information.

In developing the strategy, the leadership team reviewed existing tools, forums, and media, and identified business and general requirements. These were validated, consolidated, and deleted as necessary. New requirements were identified and added. The strategy was designed to ensure consistent, accurate, disciplined, and routine two-way communication at every level of the organization. Two categories were identified:

1. *Meetings*: The meetings category identifies more than twenty standard types of meetings and specifies the purpose, expectations, and outcomes for each. Four types of audit processes are identified to make sure that the communication processes are applied consistently and effectively. They are real-time audits, meeting questionnaires, meeting observation, and a review of meeting action registers and reviews. Audits are used to identify areas of improvement and to emphasize best practices.

2. *Communications support tools*: This category lists and defines sixteen other mechanisms besides meetings that can be used for disseminating business information. They are intended to augment but not replace face-to-face meetings or verbal communications. Examples include action registers, employee bulletins, and email. The communications plan is considered a living document, which is updated as necessary, and is available via the depot's intranet.

The Star Point Network is a related communications process that supports and enhances the overall communications strategy. It is such a key process that it is covered in its own dedicated plan and described separately in this report.

Key elements of the communications strategy that make it very effective are discipline and standardization. For each meeting, the sponsor of the meeting must specify and prepare the meeting type, proponent, purpose, frequency, duration, attendees, agenda, expected outcomes, special considerations, estimated start date, and the audit process to be used. All meetings are facilitated, and strict time keeping is used to ensure that the agenda is followed and accomplished on schedule. This keeps the process focused and enables information to be communicated efficiently without taking more of the participants' time than is necessary. Another standard tool is the use of cascading briefings to flow down information through the organization. In this process, the same briefing is given successively at the leadership, directorate, division, and team levels. By using this method, important information can be transmitted clearly to everyone in the depot within 2 days.

The communications strategy and plan represent the first time all communication methods have been identified, published, and standardized for all teams to use. It provides a very effective way to facilitate the application of proven best practices for communicating and to continuously improve. Now information is consistently and accurately passed through the organization up, down, and across all levels. Rumors have been reduced, and people are talking about issues with better understanding and more accurate information. The depot environment is more open for communication, and communication has improved at all levels. A survey of 260 employees conducted in October 1998 registered overall improvement in communications at 33% at the top management level, 26% at the middle management level, and 7% at the employee level. Improvement at the employee level was lower because the strategy had only been recently deployed at that level. All employees had completed training but had not had much time to experience its effect.

Appendix A: Example Meeting Agenda

Meeting Agenda

Meeting: Lean or cellular repair team	Requested Attendees:	
Date: Time: Location:	Information:	
Chairman:	Minutes:	

Meeting objectives:

1. Discuss progress and status of Lean or cellular repair effort.

2. Assign additional actions required to advance the Lean or cellular repair effort.

3.

4.

Proposed Agenda

	Start	*Finish*	*Topic*
1.	1:30	1:35	Opening remarks (Mr.)
2.	1:35	1:55	Review of open action items
3.	1:55	2:30	Open discussion
4.	2:30		End of meeting
5.			
6.			
7.			
8.			
9.			
10.			

Appendix B: Example Meeting Minutes and Action Item Update

Lean or Cellular Repair Team
Meeting Minutes

Date of Meeting: _____

Meeting Location: _____

Meeting Chair: _____

Purpose: Advance all actions necessary to implement the Lean or cellular repair on agreed schedule.

Discussion:

Ms. Dxxx Sxxxx opened the meeting by addressing the open action items from previous meetings; a number of action items were closed (see action items below for details).

Mr. Mxxx Wxxxx opened discussions about the installation of new steam coils in the chemical cleaning area. The coils are now physically located in the cleaning area awaiting installation. Mr. Wxxxx will initiate a work order to install the new steam coils (**Action Item 03.06.21.01**).

Mr. Mxxx Cxxxx suggested that, in consideration of the complexity of the nozzle repair process, a planner should be resident in _____. Mr. Jxxx Hxxxx will contact Mr. Bxxx Kxxxx to discuss placement of a planner, as well as a material planner (**Action Item 03.06.21.02**). At this meeting a workload transition plan will also be discussed.

Mr. Hxxxx discussed the necessity of _____ involvement in the start-up and maintenance of the chemical cleaning line as well as the Lean cell. Mr. Hxxxx will contact Ms. Axxx Txxxx and arrange a meeting to discuss support (**Action Item 03.06.21.03**).

The next meeting is scheduled for Monday, July 10, at 1:00 p.m. in Mr. Hxxxx's office. Direct questions and comments to _____.

Requested Attendees

	Organization	Name
*		
*		
*		
*		

*Denotes attendance at the meeting.

Additional (Information) Distribution of Minutes

Organization	Name

Action Item Update

Action Item Number yy.mm.dd.xx	Due Date dd-mm-yy	Task Description	Owner	Status	Comments
		Arrange for conference center for training.		Closed	Conference center has been reserved for _____.
		Document a schedule/plan for briefing appropriate offices/personnel at DMB.		Open	An initial draft has been put together, including brief to _____ week of _____.

Note: The user may wish to move closed action items to a separate table as the program progresses for better readability.

Appendix C: Communications Information Protocol

Communications Protocol				
What	To Whom	When	Control	How
Advocacy, plans, schedule, budget	CC	*Ad hoc*	Director	Briefings, memos, verbal
Mission/vision update by director and EC	DMB chief	During EC meetings, as required	Director	Verbal direction; recorded in EC meeting minutes
Mission/vision, plans/ direction, advocacy, progress, schedule, budget, contract status, success stories, lessons learned, history	EC, DSG, PRC, PRTs	During EC, DSG, PRC, PRT meetings	DMB chief for EC; chairs for DSG, PRC, PRTs	Briefing
Mission/vision, progress, advocacy, plans, history, success stories	Personnel	Periodically	DMB chief (approves content)	Newsletter, Web site

(Continued)

Appendix C: (Continued)

What	To Whom	When	Control	How
Agendas	EC, DSG, PRC, PRTs	Before meeting	DMB chief for EC; chairs for DSG, PRC, PRTs	Word document, sent out by email
Meeting minutes, action item updates	EC, DSG, PRC, PRTs	After meeting	DMB chief for EC; chairs for DSG, PRC, PRTs	Word document, sent out by email
Action item responses	DMB ops	As agreed	EC, DSG, PRC, and PRT members	Email
Policy/procedures, training	DMB personnel	Weekly staff meetings and *ad hoc*	DMB chief	Emails, manuals, briefings

CC = DMB commander; DMB = transformation office; EC = executive council (DMTB tier 1); DMB ops = DMB operations manager; DSG = division steering group (DMTB tier 2); DMTB = Depot Maintenance Transformation Board; PRC = program review council (DMTB tier 3); PRT = program requirements team (DMTB tier 4).

References

Kotter, John P. 1996. *Leading change.* Boston: Harvard Business School Press.

Zeithaml, Valarie A., Mary Jo Bitner, and Dwayne Gremler. 2006. *Services marketing.* 4th ed. New York: McGraw-Hill Irwin.

Zeithaml, Valarie A., A. Parasuraman, and L. L. Berry. 1990. *Delivering quality service: Balancing customer perceptions and expectations*, 120. New York: The Free Press.

Index

A

Acceptance testing, 104
Accounting cost model, 315
ACET model, 320
Achievability, estimation and costs, 90
Acquisition cost, 305
Acquisition Logistics Support Plan (ALSP)
    system development and demonstration phase, 102
    V-22 Osprey case study, PBL, 241
Acquisition process, 170, 172
Acquisition program baseline (APB)
    affordability, 296
    concept and technology development phase, 92
    preproject research and development phase, 91
ACRs, *see* Allowance change requests (ACRs)
Action items update, 364–365
Actions identification, 230
Active redundancy, 144
Activity Address Codes (DoDAACs), 7–8
Activity Address Directory, 7
Adaptive majority logic, 146
Adverse selection, 25
Aegis Ballistic Missile Defense AN/SPY-1 radar
    system, 143
Affordability
    acquisition cost, 305
    alternatives, 313, 324–326, 330
    analysis period, 326
    analysis purpose, 313, 330
    analysis summary, 332–333, 336
    assumptions, 314, 330
    baseline, 313, 330
    business case analysis, 323–324
    categories, 303–307
    computer support data, 311
    constant currency, 327
    cost drivers, major, 332
    cost elements, 305–307, 314, 331
    cost estimating techniques, 314, 331
    cost models, 315–317
    currency discounting, 326–328
    current currency, 327
    data collection, 317
    data input identification, sources, and
        collection, 331–332
    data sources, 307–312
    differential cost changes, 327
    discount rate, 326–327
    disposal costs, 307
    DoD policy, 302–303
    drivers, 312
    facility data, 311
    final disposal, 300
    fundamentals, *xxi*, 295–297
    funding appropriation, 304
    ground rules, 314, 330–331
    independent cost estimate, 322–323
    input data sources, 317
    life cycle, 297–300
    life cycle cost, 300–312
    life cycle costing process, 312–321
    maintenance data, 309
    management data, 312
    methodology, 330–332
    operating and support costs, 305–307
    patterns, 303
    precision approach radar modernization project case
        study, 328–336
    present value of money, 328
    presystem identification phase, 297–298
    purpose, 329
    recommendations development, 320–321, 332
    related programs data, 312
    relevant costs, 317, 332
    results documentation, 320–321
    risk and uncertainty, 317–318, 332
    scope, 329
    sensitivity analysis, 318–319, 332
    supply support data, 310–311
    support equipment data, 311
    sustainment phase, 299–300

system acquisition phase, 298–299
system effectiveness *vs.* analysis, 321–322
technical data, 310
trade-off analysis tools, 321–326
training and training support data, 311
uses, 312
work breakdown structure, 305
Age exploration program, 166
Agree technique, 137
Aircraft Sustainability Model (ASM), 68
Allocation, reliability by design, 133–137
Allowance change requests (ACRs), 115
ALSP, *see* Acquisition Logistics Support Plan (ALSP)
Alternatives
    analysis of, 324–326
    concept and technology development phase, 97
    life cycle costing process, 313
    mean logistics downtime determination, 183
    operational availability analysis, 83
    precision approach radar modernization project, 330
Analogy cost estimating technique, 314
Analysis
    of alternatives, 324–326
    concept and technology development phase, 94–97
    production and deployment phase, 110–117
    sustainment phase, 119–123
    system development and demonstration phase,
        101–106
Analysis guide, operational availability
    acceptance testing, 104
    achievability, estimation and costs, 90
    alternatives, 97
    alternatives checklist, 83
    analysis, 94–97, 101–106, 110–117, 119–123
    analysis phase, 86–90
    approval of analysis steps, 87
    assumptions, 76–78, 83
    calculations checklist, 84
    capability questions, 74–75
    changes impact assessment, 112–114, 120–121
    checklist, 83–84
    component quantification, 95
    concept and technology development phase, 91–97
    cost-benefit curves, 96–97
    cost-benefit trade-off analysis, 96, 106
    cost change evaluation form, 98
    cost effectiveness, 87–88
    cost elements checklist, 83
    data and data sources questions, 78–79
    data and models, 85–86, 92–94, 100–101,
        109–110, 119
    data checklist, 84
    demonstration testing, 104–105
    developmental testing, 100–101, 103–106
    deviation impact assessment, 112–114, 120–121
    documentation, 81–82, 91, 97, 106–108,
        110–112, 118, 123

effectiveness parameters checklist, 83
evaluation, 102–103
evaluation steps, 87
fleet reporting, 110, 120
fundamentals, 72–73, 83, 91–92, 99–100, 108,
    118–119
ground rules questions, 76–78
guiding questions, 74–82
life cycle cost, 79–81
logistics planning, 102
maintainability, 101–102, 104–105
methods and tools questions, 75–76
mission profile expansion, 94–95
models, 83–86, 92–94, 100–101, 109–110, 119
modifications impact assessment, 112–114, 120–121
monitoring, 102–105, 110, 120
objectives, 85, 92, 100, 108–109, 119
operational scenario, 88, 90
operational test and evaluation, 105
phase-related questions, 79–81
platform relationship, 89
postproduction support plan, 118
preproject research and development phase, 73, 82,
    85–91
production and deployment phase, 108–118
purpose checklist, 83
recommendations, 84
reliability, 101–104
reporting, 84
requirements questions, 74
risk checklist, 84
sensitivity checklist, 84
supportability, 100–102
sustainment phase, 118–123
sustainment plan execution, 121–123
sustainment plans, 114–117
system development and demonstration phase,
    99–108
techniques checklist, 83
technological opportunities identification, 95
transition plan, 118
Analysis of alternatives, 324–326
Analysis period, 326
Analysis phase, 86–90
Analysis purpose
    life cycle costing process, 313
    precision approach radar modernization project, 330
Analysis summary, 332–333, 336
AN/SPY-1 radar system, 143
AoA (Analysis of alternatives), *see* Analysis
APB, *see* Acquisition program baseline (APB)
APL data, 179
Applicability and effectiveness criteria, 162, 163–164
Applications
    failure mode, effects, and criticality analysis,
        139–140
    reliability by design, 139–140

Approval of analysis steps, 87
ARROWS, *see* Aviation Readiness Requirements
    Oriented to Weapon Replaceable Assemblies
    (ARROWS)
ASM, *see* Aircraft Sustainability Model (ASM)
ASO, *see* Aviation support office (ASO)
Assumptions
    life cycle costing process, 314
    operational availability analysis, 83
    precision approach radar modernization project, 330
    preproject research and development phase, 76–78
    sensitivity analysis, 319
    strategic directions, 199
Asymmetric investment, 25
ATE, *see* Automatic test equipment (ATE)
@Risk program, 318
Automated measurement data sharing, 217–218
Automatic test equipment (ATE)
    concept and technology development phase, 93
    corrective maintenance, 167
Availability, current status
    bullwhip effect, 16–17
    Defense Logistic Agency, 8–10
    echelon networks, 19–21
    fundamentals, *xix–xx*, 1, 58
    inventory management, 12–21
    kanban, 18
    military *vs.* commercial, 10–12
    push-pull supply chains, 17–18
    push *vs.* pull supply chains, 14–16
    risk pooling, 19
    supply chain and logistics system, 3–12
    to the warfighter, 1–3
Availability, enhancement
    best practice technologies, 30
    case studies, 40–49
    collaboration, 24–25
    commercial reliability-based RDF methods, 48–49
    communications, 36
    databases, 36–37
    disadvantage of current methods, 47–48
    goals, 35
    implementation, 28–31
    information technology enhancements, 35–39
    infrastructure, 36–38
    integrated product team establishment, 27–28
    integration, 23–24
    interface devices, 36
    logistics network redesign, 31–35
    performance measurement, 29
    principles, 23–27
    PRISM model, 45–49
    requirements definition and forecasting case study,
        45–49
    SCOR model, 40–45
    software enhancements, 39–40
    standardization, 38–39

systems architecture, 37–38
trust, 25, 27
U.S. Air Force process, 46–47
Availability, operational
    acceptance testing, 104
    achievability, estimation and costs, 90
    alternatives, 83, 97
    analysis guide, 72–123
    analysis phase, 86–90
    approval of analysis steps, 87
    assumptions, 76–78, 83
    calculations checklist, 84
    capability questions, 74–75
    changes impact assessment, 112–114, 120–121
    checklist, 83–84
    component quantification, 95
    concept and technology development phase, 91–97
    continuous-use systems, 64, 65
    cost-benefit curves, 96–97
    cost-benefit trade-off analysis, 96, 106
    cost change evaluation form, 98
    cost effectiveness, 87–88
    cost elements checklist, 83
    data and data sources questions, 78–79
    data and models, 85–86, 92–94, 100–101,
        109–110, 119
    data checklist, 84
    defined, 58
    demonstration testing, 104
    developmental testing, 100–101, 103–106
    deviation impact assessment, 112–114, 120–121
    documentation, 81–82, 91, 97, 106–108, 110–112,
        118, 123
    downtime equations, 60–62
    effectiveness parameters checklist, 83
    environmental profile, 70, 72
    evaluation, 87, 102–103
    fleet reporting, 110, 120
    fundamentals, 55–58, 124
    ground rules questions, 76–78
    guiding questions, 74–82
    historical perspectives, 58–59
    importance, 59–60
    impulse systems, 64, 65–66
    intermittent-use systems, 64, 65
    level of repair analysis, 66–67
    life cycle cost, 79–81
    logistic profile, 70, 71–72
    logistics planning, 102
    maintainability, 101–102, 104–105
    mathematical equations, 60–66
    mean time between failures, 62, 64
    methods and tools questions, 75–76
    mission profile, 68–72, 94–95
    models, 66–68, 83–86, 92–94, 100–101,
        109–110, 119
    modifications impact assessment, 112–114, 120–121

monitoring, 102–105, 110, 120
noncontinuous-use systems, 64, 65
objectives, 85, 92, 100, 108–109, 119
on-demand systems, 64, 65
operational profile, 70–71
operational scenario, 88, 90
operational test and evaluation, 105
phase-related questions, 79–81
platform relationship, 89
postproduction support plan, 118
preproject research and development phase, 73, 82,
    85–91
production and deployment phase, 108–118
purpose checklist, 83
recommendations, 84
reliability, 101–104
reporting, 84
requirements questions, 74
risk checklist, 84
sensitivity checklist, 84
single-shot systems, 64, 65–66
sparing to availability, 67–68
stakeholder objectives, 196
supportability, 100–102
sustainment, 114–123
system development and demonstration phase,
    99–108
techniques checklist, 83
technological opportunities identification, 95
trade-off threshold requirements form, 99
transition plan, 118
uptime equations, 60–62
Aviation Readiness Requirements Oriented to Weapon
    Replaceable Assemblies (ARROWS), 183
Aviation support office (ASO), 115

B

Balanced scorecard (BSC), *see also* Scorecard
    fundamentals, 212–213
    scorecard structure, 209–210
    tool features, 215–216
Baldrige National Quality Program, 214
Bar codes, 36
Baseline comparison system (BCS)
    concept and technology development phase, 92
    preliminary thresholds for alternatives, 97
    preproject research and development phase, 86
Baseline identification, 330
Baseline operational scenario (BOS), 134
Baseline performance metrics, 239–240
Baseline (reference system), 313
BCA, *see* Business case analysis (BCA)
BCS, *see* Baseline comparison system (BCS)
Best practices
    availability enhancement, 30
    marketability, 361–363

Bimodal parallel/series redundancy, 145
Bimodal series/parallel redundancy, 145
BIT, *see* Built-in test/built-in test equipment
    (BIT/BITE)
BITE, *see* Built-in test/built-in test equipment
    (BIT/BITE)
BOS, *see* Baseline operational scenario (BOS)
Boundaries, 314
Broad-based action
    gap analysis, 359–360
    key action steps, 354
Buffer stock, 12
Built-in test/built-in test equipment (BIT/BITE)
    concept and technology development phase, 93
    corrective maintenance, 167
    switching advantage, 148
    testability and diagnostics, 169
    trade-off threshold requirements form, 99
Bullwhip effect, 16–17
Business case analysis (BCA)
    program activities, PBL, 204–205
    trade-off analysis tools, 323–324
Business strategies, 199

C

CAE, *see* Component acquisition executive (CAE)
CAIG, *see* Cost Analysis Improvement Group (CAIG)
CAIV, *see* Cost as an independent variable (CAIV)
Calculations checklist, 84
Candidate identification, 201
CANDI system, 330
Capability
    fundamentals, *xx–xxi*, 60
    preproject research and development phase, 74–75
Capability, performance-based logistics
    actions identification, 230
    agreement formalization, 203
    baseline performance metrics, 239–240
    business case analysis, 204–205
    candidate identification, 201
    contractor logistics support, 239
    definitions, 191–192
    dispute resolution process, 225–226
    feedback, 245
    formal reviews, 230, 232, 245
    foundations, 193, 195
    fundamentals, 189–190
    implementation, 244–245
    improvement opportunities, 232, 236
    incentives, 244
    interim contractor support, 239
    interim support, 238–239
    key processes integration, 214
    lessons learned, 245–246
    maintenance support plan, 238–239
    management, 191

metrics and measures, 191
monitoring, 230, 245
opportunities identification, 201
performance baseline, 201–202
performance contracting and tasking, 227, 229–230
performance data and reporting schema, 215–225
performance metrics architecture, 206, 208–214
phased maintenance, 238
product support integrator, 205–206
product support provider, 203–204
program activities, 195–236
public/private support strategy IPT, 198
purpose, 190–191
requirements, 196
reviews, formal, 230, 232
roles defined, 197–198, 205
scope, 190–191
stakeholder objectives, 196–197
stovepipe organizational boundaries, 198
strategic planning, 198–200, 241–244
table, 195–196
team establishment, 197–198
third wave software, 192
V-22 Osprey case study, 236–246
win-win performance-based incentives, 225
workload allocation, 203–204
Capability, performance measures
capability maturity, 259
computer resources support, 278–279
configuration management, 290–291
control metrics, 254
customer focus, 259–260
data analysis, 253
data collection, 252–253
design interface, 281–283
engineering design activities, 290
enterprise measures, 257
enterprise stability, 260
facilities, 278
flow-related measures, 257–258
flying hours, 261–262
fundamentals, 249–250
general measures, 253–256
handling, 279–281
leadership-related measures, 258
lean measures, 256–258
learning environment, 260
logistics footprint, 284–285
maintenance, 262–268, 287
manpower, 275–276
metrics, 251–252, 254, 291–292
Navy depot site support, 289
Navy/Marine Corp base, 290
organizational design, 259
organization of program, 286
packaging, 279–281
PBL concept, 285–286

personnel, 275–276
planning metrics, 254
process development, 259
process improvement, 258–260
process metrics, 254
program organization, 286
program phases, 287
quality metrics, 254
readiness, 261–262
relationship development, 259
reliability, 288
reporting, 253
Rockwell Collins San Jose (RCSJ) case study, 285–292
Rome Laboratory Software Quality Framework, 252
selection, 250–251
service parts provisioning, 288
stability, 260
storage, 279–281
supply chain, 268–273
support equipment, 273–275
sustainability and supportability, 260–285
technical data, 277–278
technical performance metrics, 254
training, 276–277
transportation, 279–281
workforce capability, 260
Capability maturity, 259
CARD, *see* Cost Analysis Requirement Description (CARD)
CASA, *see* Cost Analysis and Strategy Assessment (CASA)
Case studies
availability enhancement, 40–49
PRISM model, 45–49
SCOR model, 40–45
V-22 Osprey, PBL, 236–246
CASREPs, *see* Casualty reports (CASREPs)
Casualty reports (CASREPs)
mean requisition response time, 179
production and deployment phase, 115, 116
sustainment phase, 119, 122
Categories, life cycle cost, 303–307
CBA, *see* Cost-benefit analysis (CBA)
CES, *see* Cost element structures (CES)
Change, producing more
gap analysis, 360–361
key action steps, 355
Change management, 347–349
Changes impact assessment
production and deployment phase, 112–114
sustainment phase, 120–121
Chrysler, 23
Cisco Systems, Inc., 28, 52
CLS, *see* Contractor logistics support (CLS)
CM, *see* Corrective maintenance (CM)
Coefficient of variation (COV), 14

Collaboration
    availability enhancement, 24–25
    software standards and packages, 39–40
Commanding officer narratives (CONARs), 115
Commercial and nondevelopmental items (CANDI)
        system, 330
Commercial off-the-shelf (COTS) products
    life cycle cost, 333
    maintainability and acquisition process, 172
Commercial reliability-based RDF methods, 48–49
Commercial supply chain and logistics system, 10–12
Communications
    information protocol, 347, 365–366
    information technology enhancements, 36
    Internet, 341
    promotion, 339
    schedule, 347
    Tobyhanna Army Depot case study, 362–363
Communication vehicles
    email, 346
    fundamentals, 344
    gap workshops, 347
    newsletters, 346–347
    project team meetings, 344
    staff meetings, 344
    storyboards, 346
    town hall meetings, 345–346
    transformation area team meetings, 344–345
    Web sites, 346
Compaq computers, 21
COMPASS (Computerized Optimization Model for
        Predicting and Analyzing Support and
        Structures), 66, 67
Complexity allocation method, 135–137
Component acquisition executive (CAE), 302
Component quantification, 95
Comprehensive software packages, 39
Computerized Optimization Model for Predicting
        and Analyzing Support and Structures
        (COMPASS), 66, 67
Computer resources support, 278–279
Computer support data, 311
CONARs, *see* Commanding officer narratives (CONARs)
Concept and technology development phase
    alternatives, 97
    analysis, 94–97
    component quantification, 95
    cost-benefit curves, 96–97
    cost-benefit trade-off analysis, 96
    cost change evaluation form, 98
    data and models, 92–94
    documentation, 97
    fundamentals, 91–92
    mission profile expansion, 94–95
    models, 92–94
    objectives, 92
    technological opportunities identification, 95

Configuration and component design, 142
Configuration management, 290–291
Constant currency, 327
Continental United States (CONUS)
    Activity Address Codes, 8
    lessons learned, 246
    PBL strategic planning, 200
    V-22 Osprey case study, PBL, 241
Continuous-use systems, 64, 65
Contracting and tasking, 227–230
Contract language, dispute-related, 226
Contractor logistics support (CLS)
    lessons learned, 246
    strategic planning, 200
    V-22 Osprey case study, PBL, 239, 241
Control
    performance measures, 254
    supply chain uncertainty, 12, 13
CONUS, *see* Continental United States (CONUS)
Cookbook approach, 124
Corrective maintenance (CM)
    objectives, 166–167
    preventive maintenance comparison, 156–157
    repair maintainability procedures, 167–169
    techniques, 167
Cost Analysis and Strategy Assessment (CASA)
    radar modernization project case study, 331
    relevant costs, 317
    risk and uncertainty, 318
    sparing to availability model, 67
Cost Analysis Improvement Group (CAIG), 315, 322,
        330–331
Cost Analysis Requirement Description (CARD)
    DoD policy on LLC, 302
    recommendations and documentation, 320
Cost as an independent variable (CAIV)
    affordability, 296
    DoD policy on LLC, 302
    life cycle cost comparison, 300–301
Cost-benefit analysis (CBA)
    design alternatives, 97
    system development and demonstration phase,
        106–107
Cost-benefit curves, 96–97
Cost-benefit trade-off analysis
    concept and technology development phase, 96
    system development and demonstration phase, 106
Cost change evaluation form, 98
Cost drivers
    defined, 312
    precision approach radar modernization
        project, 332
    sensitivity analysis, 318–319
Cost effectiveness, 87–88
Cost elements
    life cycle cost, 305–307
    operational availability analysis, 83

Cost element structures (CES)
  life cycle costing process, 314
  precision approach radar modernization project, 331
Cost estimating
  relationship model, 315
  techniques, 314, 331
Cost factors model, 315
Cost models, 315–317
Cost per piece, 258
Cost *vs.* performance IPT (CPIPT), 321
COTS, *see* Commercial off-the-shelf (COTS) products
COV, *see* Coefficient of variation (COV)
CPIPT, *see* Cost *vs.* performance IPT (CPIPT)
Critical few performance measures, 213
CRM, *see* Customer relationship management (CRM)
Crystal Ball program, 318
Culture, anchoring new approaches in
  gap analysis, 361
  key action steps, 355
Currency discounting, 326–328
Current currency, 327
Current state, *see* Gap analysis
Customer-driven organizations, 198–199
Customer focus, 259–260
Customer relationship management (CRM), 39
Cycle time, 258

D

Danaher Business System, 232
Dashboards, 215, 218–225
Data
  analysis, 253
  checklist, 84
  collection, 252–253, 317, 331–332
  computer support data, 311
  concept and technology development phase, 92–94
  data sources questions, 78–79
  facility data, 311
  input data sources, 317
  input identification, 331–332
  life cycle cost, 307–312
  life cycle costing process, 317
  maintenance data, 309
  management data, 312
  operational availability analysis, 84
  performance measures, 252–253
  precision approach radar modernization project, 331–332
  preproject research and development phase, 78–79, 85–86
  production and deployment phase, 109–110
  related programs data, 312
  sources, 307–312, 331–332
  supply support data, 310–311
  support equipment data, 311
  sustainment phase, 119

system development and demonstration phase, 100–101
  technical data, 277–278, 310
  training and training support data, 311
Databases, 36–37
DDC, *see* Defense distribution center (DDC)
Decision logic diagram, 159
Decision support systems (DSS), 34–35
Decision trees
  mean logistics downtime determination, 180–182
  reliability-centered maintenance, 152
Defect rate, 258
Defense Automatic Addressing System Center, 7
Defense distribution center (DDC), 8, 9, 10
Defense Logistic Agency (DLA), 5, 8–10
Defense National Stockpile Center, 10
Defense Reform Initiatives, 193
Defense Reutilization and Marketing Service, 10
Defense Supply Center Columbus (DSCC)
  Defense Logistic Agency, 8–9
  risk pooling, 19
Defense Supply Center Philadelphia (DSCP)
  Defense Logistic Agency, 9–10
  risk pooling, 19
Defense Supply Center Richmond (DSCR)
  Defense Logistic Agency, 9
  risk pooling, 19
Defense supply centers (DSCs), 8, 9
Dell Computers
  inventory turns, 21
  push-pull supply chains, 17
Demand
  supply chain uncertainty, 12, 13
  unstable, 11
Demonstration testing, 104
Department of Defense (DoD)
  Activity Address Codes, 7–8
  Activity Address Directory, 7
  life cycle cost, 302–303
  supplier locations, 6
  supply chain size, 2
Dependability, *xx*, 60
Design, reliability by
  agree technique, 137
  allocation, 133–137
  application, 139–140
  complexity allocation method, 135–137
  considerations, 134
  dynamic programming technique, 137
  equal allocation method, 135
  failure mode, effects, and criticality analysis, 139–142
  fundamentals, 131–133
  methods, 134–137
  minimization of effort technique, 137
  objectives, 133–134, 137, 139
  prediction, 137–139
  procedures, 137–139, 141–142

Design, supportability, 184
Design approaches, reliability
    active redundancy, 144
    configuration and component design, 142
    disadvantages of redundancy, 146–148
    fundamentals, 142
    graceful degradation, 142–143
    redundancy, 143–148
    standby redundancy, 144
    techniques, 144–146
Designated overhaul point (DOP), 115
Design interface, 281–283
Design-to-cost (DTC)
    design alternatives, 97
    life cycle cost comparison, 300–301
Desired future state, *see* Gap analysis
Detection, 11
Developmental test and evaluation (DT&E)
    concept and technology development phase, 94
    production and deployment phase, 112, 114
    system development and demonstration phase, 100,
        101–102, 105, 108
Developmental testing (DT)
    concept and technology development phase, 92
    production and deployment phase, 109
    system development and demonstration phase,
        100–101, 103–106
Deviation impact assessment
    production and deployment phase, 112–114
    sustainment phase, 120–121
Diagnostics, maintainability, 169
Differential cost changes, 327
Disadvantages
    RDF case study, 47–48
    redundancy, 146–148
Discount rate, 326–327
Disposal costs, 307, 314
Dispute-related contract language, 226
Dispute resolution process, 225–226
Distance moved, 258
Distribution depots, 7
Division steering group, 343
DLA, *see* Defense Logistic Agency (DLA)
Do, *see* Operational dependability (Do)
Documentation
    concept and technology development phase, 97
    preproject research and development phase,
        81–82, 91
    production and deployment phase, 110–112, 118
    sustainment phase, 123
    system development and demonstration phase,
        106–108
Document Automation and Production
        Service, 10
DoD, *see* Department of Defense (DoD)
DOP, *see* Designated overhaul point (DOP)
Downtime equations, 60–62, 63

Drivers
    affordability, 332
    inventory, 19–20
    life cycle cost, 312
    precision approach radar modernization
        project, 332
DSCC, *see* Defense Supply Center Columbus (DSCC)
DSCP, *see* Defense Supply Center Philadelphia (DSCP)
DSCR, *see* Defense Supply Center Richmond (DSCR)
DSCs, *see* Defense supply centers (DSCs)
DSS, *see* Decision support systems (DSS)
DT, *see* Developmental testing (DT)
DTC, *see* Design-to-cost (DTC)
DT&E, *see* Developmental test and evaluation (DT&E)
Duplex redundancy, 145
Dynamic programming technique, 137

E

Echelon networks, 19–21
Economic analysis cost model, 315
Economic life limits, 165
Economies of scale, 38
EDMs, *see* Engineering development models (EDMs)
Effectiveness parameters checklist, 83
EHC, *see* Explosive hazard classification (EHC)
Email, 346
Endpoints, moving, 11
Engineering change proposals, 329
Engineering design activities, 290
Engineering development models (EDMs), 104
Enterprise measures, 257
Enterprise resource planning (ERP)
    push *vs.* pull supply chains, 14
    standardization, 38–39
Enterprise stability, 260
Environmental profile, 68, 70, 72, 94–95
Equal allocation method, 135
Equipment reliability and maintenance, 11
ERP, *see* Enterprise resource planning (ERP)
Estimation, probabilities used in, 180–182
Evaluation
    preproject research and development phase, 87
    system development and demonstration phase,
        102–103
Excel software program, 318
Execution and Prioritization of Repair Support System
        (EXPRESS), 46–47
Executive council, 343
Expert opinion cost estimating technique, 314
Explosive hazard classification (EHC), 175

F

Facilities
    life cycle cost, 311
    sustainability and supportability, 278

Failure, categories of consequences, 152
Failure mode, effects, and criticality analysis (FMECA)
    redundancy disadvantages, 148
    reliability, 133
    reliability by design, 139–142
    repair maintainability procedures, 168–169
    system development and demonstration phase, 106, 108
False removal detection rates, 186
FCB, *see* Functional Capabilities Board (FCB)
Feedback, 245
Figures of merit (FOM), 58–59
Final disposal, 300
First removal rates, 186
First wave performance measurement, 192
Fleet reporting, 110, 120
Fleet support team detachments (FTS-Dets), 200, 241
Flow-related measures, 257–258
Flying hours, 261–262
FMECA, *see* Failure mode, effects, and criticality analysis (FMECA)
FNA, *see* Functional Needs Analysis (FNA)
Follow-on operational test and evaluation (FOT&E), 115
FOM, *see* Figures of merit (FOM)
Forecasting, 15–16
Formal reviews
    process, 235
    program activities, PBL, 230, 232
    V-22 Osprey case study, PBL, 245
FOT&E, *see* Follow-on operational test and evaluation (FOT&E)
FTS-Dets, *see* Fleet support team detachments (FTS-Dets)
Functional Capabilities Board (FCB), 297
Functional Needs Analysis (FNA), 92
Functional reliability prediction technique, 138
Function objectives, 12
Funding appropriation, 304

G

Gains, consolidating
    gap analysis, 360–361
    key action steps, 355
Gap analysis
    broad-based action, 359–360
    change, producing more, 360–361
    culture, anchoring new approaches in, 361
    fundamentals, 355
    gains, consolidating, 360–361
    guiding coalition, 357–358
    momentum, sustaining, 360–361
    motivation for change, 356–357
    short-term wins, 360
    urgency, 356–357
    vision development and communication, 358–359

Gap workshops, 347
Gate connector redundancy, 146
Generalized enterprise reference architecture (GERA) framework, 297
General measures, 253–256
Global Positioning Systems (GPS), 36
Goal, question, metric (GQM) approach, 251–252
Goals, IT enhancements, 35
Goldilocks syndrome, 212
Government Performance Results Act (GPRA), 193
Government Procurement Executives' Association, 254–255
GPRA, *see* Government Performance Results Act (GPRA)
GPS, *see* Global Positioning Systems (GPS)
Graceful degradation, 142–143
GRF, *see* Gross removal factor (GRF)
Gross removal factor (GRF), 185
Ground rules
    life cycle costing process, 314
    precision approach radar modernization project, 330–331
    preproject research and development phase, 76–78
    sensitivity analysis, 319
Guiding coalition
    gap analysis, 357–358
    key action steps, 352
Guiding questions, 74–82

H

Handling, 279–281
Hewlett-Packard, 23
Historical perspectives, 59–60
Honda of America Manufacturing, 23
Honeywell Electronics, 48

I

ICD, *see* Initial capabilities document (ICD)
ICE, *see* Independent cost estimate (ICE)
ICPs, *see* Inventory control points (ICPs)
IDEE, *see* Integrated definition (IDEE) modeling
ILS, *see* Integrated logistics support (ILS)
IMMs, *see* Integrated material managers (IMMs)
Implementation
    management, availability enhancement, 30–31
    plan development, availability enhancement, 28–29
    V-22 Osprey case study, PBL, 244–245
Improvement opportunities, identifying, 232, 236
Impulse systems, 64, 65–66
Incentives, 244
Independent cost estimate (ICE), 322–323
Industrial engineering cost estimating technique, 314
Information collaboration, 24
Information technology enhancements
    communications, 36

databases, 36–37
fundamentals, 35
goals, 35
infrastructure, 36–38
interface devices, 36
standardization, 38–39
systems architecture, 37–38
Infrastructure, 36–38
Inherent availability, 157
Initial capabilities document (ICD)
    preproject research and development phase, 73, 82,
        85, 88, 90–91
    presystem identification phase, 297
    production and deployment phase, 118
    theoretical scenario, 55
Initial operational capability (IOC) date, 111, 112
Input data sources, 317
In-service engineering agent (ISEA)
    life cycle cost, 333
    production and deployment phase, 109, 115
    radar modernization project case study, 332
    sustainment phase, 119
Integrated definition (IDEE) modeling, 29
Integrated logistics support (ILS)
    Logistics Management Information, 186
    operational availability, 59
    sustainability and supportability, 260
Integrated material managers (IMMs), 5
Integrated product and process
        development (IPPD), 127
Integrated product development (IPD)
    general performance measures, 253
    reliability, 127
Integrated product team (IPT), *see also* Overarching
        integrated product team (OIPT)
    availability enhancement, 27–28
    designing for supportability, 184
    DoD policy on LLC, 302
    identifying PBL opportunities, 201
    trade-off analysis, 321
    V-22 Osprey case study, PBL, 245
Integration, availability enhancement, 23–24
Interconnectivity, 38
Interface devices, 36
Interim contractor support, 239
Interim support, 238–239
Intermittent-use systems, 64, 65
International Council on Systems Engineering
        (INCOSE), 253
Internet, *see also* Web sites
    marketing, 341
    system architectures, 37–38
Inventory control points (ICPs)
    level of repair analysis, 186
    production and deployment phase, 115
    supply chain, 5, 6
Inventory levels/turns, 258

Inventory management
    bullwhip effect, 16–17
    cost model, 315
    echelon networks, 19–21
    fundamentals, 12–14
    kanban, 18
    push-pull supply chains, 17–18
    push *vs.* pull supply chains, 14–16
    risk pooling, 19
IOC, *see* Initial operational capability (IOC) date
IPD, *see* Integrated product development (IPD)
IPPD, *see* Integrated product and process development
        (IPPD)
IPT, *see* Integrated product team (IPT)
ISEA, *see* In-service engineering agent (ISEA)
Item variety, 11

J

Joint Sustainment Strategy Study (JSSS), 204

K

Kanban, 18, 34
Keiretsu approach, 23
Key action steps
    broad-based action, 354
    change, producing more, 355
    culture, anchoring new approaches in, 355
    fundamentals, 348, 351
    gains, consolidating, 355
    guiding coalition, 352
    momentum, sustaining, 355
    motivation for change, 351
    short-term wins, 354–355
    strategy for change, 352–353
    timeframes, 349–350
    urgency, 351
    vision development and communication, 352–353
Key performance parameters (KPP)
    operational availability, 56, 57
    trade-off analysis, 321
    V-22 Osprey case study, PBL, 239
Key processes integration, 214
Kmart, 21
KPP, *see* Key performance parameters (KPP)

L

LCC, *see* Life cycle cost (LCC)
LCCM, *see* Life cycle cost management (LCCM)
LCL, *see* Life cycle logistics (LCL)
Leadership-related measures, 258
Lead time, 258
Lean measures, 256–258
Lean supply chains, 12
Learning environment, 260

Lessons learned, 245–246
Level of repair analysis (LORA)
    cost model, 315
    management data, 312
    operational availability, 66–67
    supportability, 185–186
    system development and demonstration phase,
        102, 108
Life cycle
    affordability, 297–300
    final disposal, 300
    fundamentals, 297
    level of repair analysis, 185
    presystem identification phase, 297–298
    sustainment phase, 299–300
    system acquisition phase, 298–299
Life cycle cost (LCC), *see also* Affordability
    analysis of alternatives, 324–326
    business case analysis, 323–324
    concept and technology development phase, 91, 93
    estimation steps, 313
    fundamentals, 321
    independent cost estimate, 322–323
    model, 66
    objectives, 302
    operational availability, 59
    performance baseline, 201
    preproject research and development phase, 79–81
    production and deployment phase, 108, 109
    system development and demonstration phase,
        107, 108
    system effectiveness *vs.* analysis, 321–322
    trade-off analysis tools, 321–326
    training and training support data, 311
    uses, 312
    work breakdown structure, 305
Life cycle cost (LCC) process
    alternatives, 313
    analysis purpose, 313
    assumptions, 314
    baseline (reference system), 313
    cost element structures, 314
    cost estimation techniques, 314
    cost models, 315–317
    data collection, 317
    fundamentals, 312–313
    ground rules, 314
    input data sources, 317
    recommendations development, 320–321
    relevant costs, 317
    results documentation, 320–321
    risk and uncertainty assessment, 317–318
    sensitivity analysis, 318–319
Life cycle cost management (LCCM), 300
Life cycle logistics (LCL), 299
LMI, *see* Logistics Management Information (LMI)
Lockheed-Martin, 232

Logistic review group (LRG), 59
Logistics
    footprint, 197, 284–285
    fundamentals, 3
    network redesign, 31–35
    planning, 102
    profile, 70, 71–72, 94
    requirements, 170
    response time, 197
    support cost simulation model, 315
Logistics Management Information (LMI)
    performance measurement, 29
    production and deployment phase, 110, 118
    supportability, 186–187
    sustainment phase, 121
    system development and demonstration phase, 100,
        101, 107
Logistics readiness reviews (LRR), 118
Logistics Requirements and Funding Plan (LRFP), 320
LORA, *see* Level of repair analysis (LORA)
LRFP, *see* Logistics Requirements and Funding Plan
        (LRFP)
LRG, *see* Logistic review group (LRG)
LRR, *see* Logistics readiness reviews (LRR)

M

MAdmDT, *see* Mean administrative delay time
        (MAdmDT)
Maintainability, *see also* Mean time to repair (MTTR);
        Reliability and maintainability (R&M)
    acquisition process, 170, 172
    age exploration program, 166
    corrective maintenance, 156–157, 166–169
    demonstration testing, 104–105
    diagnostics, 169
    economic life limits, 165
    fundamentals, *xx*, 155–156
    inherent availability, 157
    logistics requirements, 170
    manufacturing process, 172–173
    objectives, 157–158
    preventive maintenance, 156–166
    production and deployment phase, 112
    reliability-centered maintenance analysis process,
        158–166
    repair maintainability procedures, 167–169
    safe life limits, 165
    safety, 173–175
    scheduled discard tasks, 165
    scheduled failure finding tasks, 165–166
    scheduled on-condition tasks, 162
    scheduled rework tasks, 162, 165
    techniques, 167
    testability, 169
    trade-off threshold requirements form, 99
    types, 159, 162

updating and verification, 101–102
uptime/downtime equations, 61
Maintenance
level of repair analysis, 185
reliability, 148–151, 153
sustainability and supportability, 262–268
Maintenance, repair, and overhaul (MRO) operations
depots, 7
fundamentals, 1
reliability, 127
supply chain, 5
Maintenance data, 309
Maintenance Data System (MDS/3M data)
mean requisition response time, 179
production and deployment phase, 109, 116
sustainment phase, 119, 122
Maintenance personnel planning cost model, 315
Maintenance support, 287
Maintenance support plan, 238–239
Major Commands (MAJCOMs), 91
Majority voting redundancy, 146
Malcolm Baldrige National Quality Award, 214
Management, target market, 342–344
Management data, 312
Manpower, 275–276
Manufacturing execution systems (MES), 40
Manufacturing process, 172–173
Marine Corp/Navy base, 290
Marketability
action items update, 364–365
best practice case study, 361–363
broad-based action, 354, 359–360
change, producing more, 355, 360–361
change management, 347–349
communication information protocol, 347, 365–366
communication schedule, 347
communications strategy plan, 362–363
communication vehicles, 344–347
culture, anchoring new approaches in, 355, 361
division steering group, 343
email, 346
executive council, 343
fundamentals, xxi, 337
gains, consolidating, 355, 360–361
gap analysis, 355–361
gap workshops, 347
guiding coalition, 352, 357–358
key action steps, 348–355
management, 342–344
meeting agenda example, 363
meeting minutes example, 364–365
momentum, sustaining, 355, 360–361
motivation for change, 351, 356–357
newsletters, 346–347
people, 339
physical evidence, 340
place, 338–339

price, 338
process, 339
product, 338
program review council, 343–344
project team meetings, 344
promotion, 339
role of marketing, 337–340
short-term wins, 354–355, 360
staff meetings, 344
stakeholders, 342
storyboards, 346
strategy for change, 352–353
target market, 340–344
tiers, 343–344
timeframes, 349–350
Tobyhanna Army Depot case study, 361–363
town hall meetings, 345–346
transformation area team meetings, 344–345
urgency, 351, 356–357
vision development and communication, 352–353, 358–359
Web sites, 346
Material readiness, 58–59
Material Readiness Database (MRDB), 115
Material resource planning (MRP) system
kanban, 18
push *vs.* pull supply chains, 14
Mathematics and equations
continuous-use systems, 64, 65
downtime equations, 60–62, 63
fundamentals, 60
impulse systems, 64, 65–66
intermittent-use systems, 64, 65
mean time between failures, 62, 64
noncontinuous-use systems, 64, 65
on-demand systems, 64, 65
reliability, 128–130
single-shot systems, 64, 65–66
uptime equations, 60–62, 63
MDA, *see* Milestone decision authority (MDA)
MDS, *see* Maintenance Data System (MDS/3M data)
MDT, *see* Mean downtime (MDT)
MDTD, *see* Mean downtime for documentation (MDTD)
MDTOR, *see* Mean requisition for other reasons (MDTOR)
MDTT, *see* Mean downtime for training (MDTT)
Mean administrative delay time (MAdmDT)
production and deployment phase, 116
system development and demonstration phase, 107
Mean administrative delay time (MAdmDT)
production and deployment phase, 116
sustainment phase, 121
Mean awaiting outside assistance delay time (MOADT)
production and deployment phase, 116
sustainment phase, 121
system development and demonstration phase, 107

Mean downtime (MDT), *see also* Supportability
    equations, 62–64
    preproject research and development phase, 73
Mean downtime for documentation (MDTD), 178
Mean downtime for outside assistance (MOADT),
    177–178
Mean downtime for training (MDTT), 179
Mean downtime supportability, 178–179
Mean logistics downtime (MLDT)
    alternatives, 183
    decision trees, 180–181
    equations, 62, 64
    fundamentals, 155, 179–180
    operational availability, 56
    preproject research and development phase, 90
    probabilities used in estimation, 180–182
    production and deployment phase, 109, 113,
        115, 116
    quantifying components of Ao, 95
    replacement rates, 182–183
    supportability metrics, 177
    sustainment phase, 121
    system development and demonstration phase, 107
    system effectiveness *vs.* LCC analysis, 322
Mean requisition for other reasons (MDTOR), 179
Mean requisition response time (MRRT), 179
Mean supply response time (MSRT), 177, 179
Mean time between failures (MTBF), *see also* Reliability
    continuous-use systems, 65
    corrective maintenance, 167
    default values for calculating, 183
    fundamentals, 155
    inherent availability, 157
    intermittent-use systems, 65
    level of repair analysis, 185
    life cycle cost, 333
    operating and support (O&S) costs, 317
    operational availability, 56, 62, 64
    preproject research and development phase, 73, 90
    preventive *vs.* corrective maintenance, 157
    production and deployment phase, 109, 112,
        113, 115
    quantifying components of Ao, 95
    redundancy disadvantages, 146
    reliability, 128, 132
    repair maintainability procedures, 168
    replacement rates, 182
    sustainment phase, 120
    system development and demonstration phase,
        104, 107
    system effectiveness *vs.* LCC analysis, 322
Mean time to repair (MTTR), *see also* Maintainability
    equations, 62, 64
    fundamentals, 155
    inherent availability, 157
    level of repair analysis, 185
    life cycle cost, 333

operating and support (O&S) costs, 317
operational availability, 56
preproject research and development phase, 73, 90
preventive *vs.* corrective maintenance, 157
production and deployment phase, 109, 113, 115
quantifying components of Ao, 95
repair maintainability procedures, 168
supportability metrics, 177
sustainment phase, 120–121
system development and demonstration phase, 107
system effectiveness *vs.* LCC analysis, 322
Measures, *see* Metrics
Measures of effectiveness (MOE), 59
Measures of performance (MOP), 60
MEC, *see* Military Essentiality Code (MEC)
Meetings
    agenda example, 363
    best practice, 362
    minutes example, 364–365
Memorandum of understanding (MOU), 203
MES, *see* Manufacturing execution systems (MES)
Methods
    allocation, 134–137
    preproject research and development phase, 75–76
Metrics
    frameworks, performance measures, 251–252
    performance-based logistics, 191
    Rockwell Collins San Jose case study, 291–292
    supportability, 177–179
Milestone decision authority (MDA)
    affordability, 296
    concept and technology development phase, 91
    DoD policy on LLC, 302–303
    independent cost estimate, 322
    preproject research and development phase, 73, 91
    presystem identification phase, 297
    system acquisition phase, 297–298
Military Essentiality Code (MEC), 183
Military supply chain and logistics system, 10–12
Minimization of effort technique, 137
Mission needs profile, *see* Initial capabilities document
    (ICD)
Mission profile
    environmental profile, 70, 72
    expansion, concept and technology development
        phase, 94–95
    fundamentals, 68–69
    logistic profile, 70, 71–72
    operational profile, 70–71
Mission statement, 199
Mitsubishi, 23
MLDT, *see* Mean logistics downtime (MLDT)
MOADT, *see* Mean awaiting outside assistance delay
        time (MOADT); Mean downtime for outside
        assistance (MOADT)
Models and modeling
    ACET model, 320

affordability, 315–317
concept and technology development phase, 92–94
cost models, LCC process, 315–317
integrated definition modeling, 29
level of repair analysis, 66–67
Monte Carlo simulation models, 318
operational availability, 66–68, 83–86, 92–94,
    100–101, 109–110, 119
preproject research and development phase, 83–86
PRISM, 45–49
production and deployment phase, 109–110
readiness-based sparing model, 107
reliability, 130–131
requirements definition and forecasting, 49
SCOR, 29, 40–45
sparing to availability, 67–68
sustainment phase, 119
system development and demonstration phase,
    100–101
Modifications impact assessment
production and deployment phase, 112–114
sustainment phase, 120–121
MOE, *see* Measures of effectiveness (MOE)
Momentum, sustaining
gap analysis, 360–361
key action steps, 355
Monitoring
production and deployment phase, 110
sustainment phase, 120
system development and demonstration phase,
    102–105
V-22 Osprey case study, PBL, 245
Monitoring performance, 230
Monte Carlo simulation models, 318
MOP, *see* Measures of performance (MOP)
Moral hazard, 25
Motivation for change
gap analysis, 356–357
key action steps, 351
MOU, *see* Memorandum of understanding (MOU)
Moving endpoints, 11
MRDB, *see* Material Readiness Database (MRDB)
MRP, *see* Material resource planning (MRP) system
MRRT, *see* Mean requisition response time (MRRT)
MSRT, *see* Mean supply response time (MSRT)
MTBF, *see* Mean time between failures (MTBF)
MTTR, *see* Mean time to repair (MTTR)

N

National Performance Review (NPR), 193
National Stock Number (NSN)
echelon networks, 19–20
production and deployment phase, 117
sustainment phase, 123
Naval Inventory Control Point (NAVICP), 332
Navy depot site support, 289

Navy/Marine Corp base, 290
Net present value (NPV), 238
Net present worth (NPW), 238
Newsletters, 346–347
Non-automated graphic presentations, 217
Noncontinuous-use systems, 64, 65
NORS, *see* Not operationally ready supply (NORS)
Not operationally ready supply (NORS), 115
NPR, *see* National Performance Review (NPR)
NPV (net present value), 238
NPW (net present worth), 238
NSN, *see* National Stock Number (NSN)

O

Oak Ridge Associated Universities (ORAU), 211
Objectives
allocation, 133–134
concept and technology development phase, 92
corrective maintenance, 166–167
failure mode, effects, and criticality analysis, 139
prediction, 137
preproject research and development phase, 85
preventive maintenance, 157–158
production and deployment phase, 108–109
reliability by design, 133–134, 137, 139
sustainment phase, 119
system development and demonstration phase, 100
OIPT, *see* Overarching integrated product team (OIPT)
OLSS, *see* Operational Logistics Support Summary
    (OLSS)
OMS, *see* Order management systems (OMS)
On-demand systems, 64, 65
Operating and support (O&S) costs
life cycle cost, 305–307, 332–333, 336
system development and demonstration phase, 107
Operating redundancy, 147
Operational availability
acceptance testing, 104
achievability, estimation and costs, 90
alternatives, 83, 97
analysis guide, 72–123
analysis phase, 86–90
approval of analysis steps, 87
assumptions, 76–78, 83
calculations checklist, 84
capability questions, 74–75
changes impact assessment, 112–114, 120–121
checklist, 83–84
component quantification, 95
concept and technology development phase, 91–97
continuous-use systems, 64, 65
cost-benefit curves, 96–97
cost-benefit trade-off analysis, 96, 106
cost change evaluation form, 98
cost effectiveness, 87–88
cost elements checklist, 83

data and data sources questions, 78–79
data and models, 85–86, 92–94, 100–101,
    109–110, 119
data checklist, 84
defined, 58
demonstration testing, 104
developmental testing, 100–101, 103–106
deviation impact assessment, 112–114, 120–121
documentation, 81–82, 91, 97, 106–108, 110–112,
    118, 123
downtime equations, 60–62
effectiveness parameters checklist, 83
environmental profile, 70, 72
evaluation, 87, 102–103
fleet reporting, 110, 120
fundamentals, 55–58, 124
ground rules questions, 76–78
guiding questions, 74–82
historical perspectives, 58–59
importance, 59–60
impulse systems, 64, 65–66
intermittent-use systems, 64, 65
level of repair analysis, 66–67
life cycle cost, 79–81
logistic profile, 70, 71–72
logistics planning, 102
maintainability, 101–102, 104–105
mathematical equations, 60–66
mean time between failures, 62, 64
methods and tools questions, 75–76
mission profile, 68–72, 94–95
models, 66–68, 83–86, 92–94, 100–101,
    109–110, 119
modifications impact assessment, 112–114, 120–121
monitoring, 102–105, 110, 120
noncontinuous-use systems, 64, 65
objectives, 85, 92, 100, 108–109, 119
on-demand systems, 64, 65
operational profile, 70–71
operational scenario, 88, 90
operational test and evaluation, 105
phase-related questions, 79–81
platform relationship, 89
postproduction support plan, 118
preproject research and development phase, 73, 82,
    85–91
production and deployment phase, 108–118
purpose checklist, 83
recommendations, 84
reliability, 101–104
reporting, 84
requirements questions, 74
risk checklist, 84
sensitivity checklist, 84
single-shot systems, 64, 65–66
sparing to availability, 67–68
stakeholder objectives, 196

supportability, 100–102
sustainment, 114–123
system development and demonstration phase,
    99–108
techniques checklist, 83
technological opportunities identification, 95
trade-off threshold requirements form, 99
transition plan, 118
uptime equations, 60–62
Operational capability (Co), 60
Operational dependability (Do), 60
Operational Logistics Support Summary (OLSS), 110
Operational profile, 70–71, 94
Operational reliability, 196
Operational requirements document (ORD), 134
Operational scenario, 88, 90
Operational Test and Evaluation Force (OPTEVFOR)
    goal, 105
    system development and demonstration phase, 100
Operational test and evaluation (OPEVAL)
    logistics planning, 102
    operational test and evaluation, 105
    system development and demonstration phase,
        107–108
    V-22 Osprey case study, PBL, 239
Operational test and evaluation (OT&E)
    concept and technology development phase, 94
    production and deployment phase, 112, 114–115
    system development and demonstration phase, 105
OPEVAL, *see* Operational test and evaluation
    (OPEVAL)
Opportunities identification, 201
Opportunity costs, 338
OPTEVFOR, *see* Operational Test and Evaluation
    Force (OPTEVFOR)
ORAU, *see* Oak Ridge Associated Universities (ORAU)
ORD, *see* Operational requirements document (ORD)
Order management systems (OMS)
    availability enhancements, 39
Organizational collaboration, 24
Organizational design, 259
O&S, *see* Operating and support (O&S) costs
OT&E, *see* Operational test and evaluation (OT&E)
Overarching integrated product team (OIPT), 302,
    see also Integrated product team (IPT)

P

Packaging, 279–281
Parametric cost estimating technique, 314
Part count reliability prediction technique, 138
Partnerships, *see* Collaboration
Patterns, 303
PBL, *see* Performance-based logistics (PBL)
People
    marketing, role of, 339
    supply chain management, 52

Performance-based agreement formalization, 203
Performance-based logistics (PBL)
    actions identification, 230
    agreement formalization, 203
    baseline performance metrics, 239–240
    business case analysis, 204–205
    candidate identification, 201
    contractor logistics support, 239
    definitions, 191–192
    dispute resolution process, 225–226
    feedback, 245
    formal reviews, 230, 232, 245
    foundations, 193, 195
    fundamentals, 189–190
    implementation, 244–245
    improvement opportunities, 232, 236
    incentives, 244
    interim contractor support, 239
    interim support, 238–239
    key processes integration, 214
    lessons learned, 245–246
    maintenance support plan, 238–239
    management, 191
    metrics and measures, 191
    monitoring, 230, 245
    opportunities identification, 201
    performance baseline, 201–202
    performance contracting and tasking, 227, 229–230
    performance data and reporting schema, 215–225
    performance metrics architecture, 206, 208–214
    phased maintenance, 238
    product support integrator, 205–206
    product support provider, 203–204
    program activities, 195–236
    public/private support strategy IPT, 198
    purpose, 190–191
    requirements, 196
    reviews, formal, 230, 232
    roles defined, 197–198, 205
    scope, 190–191
    stakeholder objectives, 196–197
    stovepipe organizational boundaries, 198
    strategic planning, 198–200, 241–244
    table, 195–196
    team establishment, 197–198
    third wave software, 192
    V-22 Osprey case study, 236–246
    win-win performance-based incentives, 225
    workload allocation, 203–204
Performance-based management, 191
Performance-based measurement, 191
Performance baseline, 201–202
Performance contracting and tasking, 227, 229–230
Performance dashboards, 213, 215
Performance data and reporting schema, 215–225
Performance measurement, 29
Performance Measurement Group (PMG), 14

Performance metrics architecture identification, 206, 208–214
Performance review process, 235
Personnel, sustainability and supportability, 275–276
Phased maintenance, 238
Phase-related questions, 79–81
Physical evidence, 340
Place, 338–339
Planning, programming, and budgeting system (PPBS), 91
Planning metrics, 254
Plasma displays, 346
Platform relationship, 89
PM, *see* Preventive maintenance (PM)
POM, *see* Program objectives memorandum (POM)
Postproduction support plan, 118
Power *vs.* trust, 25
PPBS, *see* Planning, programming, and budgeting system (PPBS)
Precision approach radar modernization project case study
    alternatives, 330
    analysis purpose, 330
    analysis summary, 332–333, 336
    assumptions, 330
    baseline identification, 330
    cost drivers, major, 332
    cost element structure, 331
    cost estimating technique, 331
    data input identification, sources, and collection, 331–332
    fundamentals, 328–329
    ground rules, 330–331
    methodology, 330–332
    purpose, 329
    recommendations development, 332
    relevant costs, 332
    risk and uncertainty analysis, 332
    scope, 329
    sensitivity analysis, 332
Prediction, reliability by design, 137–139
Preproject research and development phase
    achievability, estimation and costs, 90
    alternatives checklist, 83
    analysis phase, 86–90
    approval of analysis steps, 87
    assumptions checklist, 83
    assumptions questions, 76–78
    calculations checklist, 84
    capability questions, 74–75
    checklist, 83–84
    cost effectiveness, 87–88
    cost elements checklist, 83
    data and data sources questions, 78–79
    data and models, 85–86
    data checklist, 84
    documentation, 81–82, 91

effectiveness parameters checklist, 83
evaluation steps, 87
fundamentals, 73, 83
ground rules questions, 76–78
guiding questions, 74–82
life cycle cost, 79–81
methods and tools questions, 75–76
models, 83–86
objectives, 85
operational scenario, 88, 90
phase-related questions, 79–81
platform relationship, 89
purpose checklist, 83
recommendations, 84
reporting, 84
requirements questions, 74
risk checklist, 84
sensitivity checklist, 84
techniques checklist, 83
Present value of money, 328
Presystem identification phase, 297–298
Preventive maintenance (PM)
age exploration program, 166
corrective maintenance comparison, 156–157
economic life limits, 165
objectives, 157–158
reliability-centered maintenance analysis process, 158–166
safe life limits, 165
scheduled discard tasks, 165
scheduled failure finding tasks, 165–166
scheduled on-condition tasks, 162
scheduled rework tasks, 162, 165
trade-off threshold requirements form, 99
types, 159, 162
Price, 338
Principles, availability enhancement
collaboration, 24–25
integration, 23–24
trust, 25, 27
Priority, 11
PRISM model, 45–49
Probabilities used in estimation, 180–182
Procedures
failure mode, effects, and criticality analysis, 141–142
prediction, 137–139
reliability by design, 137–139, 141–142
Process
marketing, role of, 339
performance measures, 254, 258–260
supply chain management, 52
supply chain uncertainty, 12, 13
Product, 338
Production and deployment phase
analysis, 110–117
changes impact assessment, 112–114

data and models, 109–110
deviation impact assessment, 112–114
documentation, 110–112, 118
fleet reporting, 110
fundamentals, 108
models, 109–110
modifications impact assessment, 112–114
monitoring, 110
objectives, 108–109
postproduction support plan, 118
sustainment plans, 114–117
transition plan, 118
Product support integrator (PSI)
metrics mapping, 217
program activities, PBL, 205–206
Product support manager (PSM)
metrics mapping, 217
roles, defining, 205
Product support provider identification, 203–204
Program activities, PBL
actions identification, 230
business case analysis, 204–205
candidate identification, 201
dispute resolution process, 225–226
formal reviews, 230, 232
fundamentals, 195–196
improvement opportunities, identifying, 232, 236
key processes integration, 214
monitoring performance, 230
opportunities identification, 201
performance-based agreement formalization, 203
performance baseline, 201–202
performance contracting and tasking, 227, 229–230
performance data and reporting schema, 215–225
performance metrics architecture identification, 206, 208–214
product support integrator establishment, 205–206
product support provider identification, 203–204
public/private support strategy IPT establishment, 198
requirements, defining, 196
reviews, formal, 230, 232
roles defined, 197–198, 205
stakeholder objectives, defining, 196–197
stovepipe organizational boundaries, 198
strategic planning, 198–200
table, 195–196
team establishment, 197–198
win-win performance-based incentives, 225
workload allocation, 203–204
Program objectives memorandum (POM), 91
Program phases, 287
Program review council, 343–344
Program Support Inventory Control Point (PSICP)
cost-benefit trade-off analysis, 96
production and deployment phase, 112, 116

sustainment phase, 122
system development and demonstration phase, 102
Project road maps
   analysis of alternatives, 325–326
   SCOR implementation, 43, 45
Project team meetings, 344
Promotion, 339
PSICP, *see* Program Support Inventory Control Point
   (PSICP)
PSM, *see* Product support manager (PSM)
Public/private support strategy IPT establishment, 198
Pull *vs.* push supply chains, 14–16
Purpose
   operational availability analysis, 83
   precision approach radar modernization project, 329
Push-pull supply chains, 17–18
Push *vs.* pull supply chains, 14–16

Q

Quadrennial Defense Review, 193, 195
Quality function deployment (QFD), 251
Quality metrics and measures
   customer's satisfaction, 173
   performance measures, 254

R

Radar modernization project case study
   alternatives, 330
   analysis purpose, 330
   analysis summary, 332–333, 336
   assumptions, 330
   baseline identification, 330
   cost drivers, major, 332
   cost element structure, 331
   cost estimating technique, 331
   data input identification, sources, and collection,
      331–332
   fundamentals, 328–329
   ground rules, 330–331
   methodology, 330–332
   purpose, 329
   recommendations development, 332
   relevant costs, 332
   risk and uncertainty analysis, 332
   scope, 329
   sensitivity analysis, 332
Radio frequency identification (RFID) tags, 35, 36
RBD, *see* Reliability block diagram (RBD)
RBS, *see* Readiness-based sparing (RBS) model
RCM, *see* Reliability-centered maintenance (RCM)
Readiness
   supply chain comparisons, 10
   sustainability and supportability, 261–262
Readiness-based sparing (RBS) model, 107
Ready-for-issue (RFI), 4

Recommendations, 84
Recommendations development
   life cycle costing process, 320–321
   precision approach radar modernization project, 332
Redundancy
   active, 144
   design approaches, reliability, 143–148
   disadvantages, 146–148
   fundamentals, 143–144
   standby, 144
   techniques, 144–146
Related programs data, 312
Relationship development, 259
Relevant costs
   life cycle costing process, 317
   precision approach radar modernization project, 332
Reliability, *see also* Mean time between failures (MTBF)
   active, 144
   agree technique, 137
   allocation, 133–137
   application, 139–140
   complexity allocation method, 135–137
   configuration and component design, 142
   considerations, 134
   demonstration testing, 104
   by design, 131–142
   design approaches, 142–148
   disadvantages, 146–148
   dynamic programming technique, 137
   equal allocation method, 135
   failure mode, effects, and criticality analysis,
      139–142
   fundamentals, xx, 127–128, 131–133, 142–144
   graceful degradation, 142–143
   growth testing, 103
   maintenance, 148–151, 153.
   mathematics, 128–130
   methods, 134–137
   minimization of effort technique, 137
   modeling, 130–131
   objectives, 133–134, 137, 139
   prediction, 137–139
   procedures, 137–139, 141–142
   production and deployment phase, 112
   qualification testing, 103
   redundancy, 143–148
   Rockwell Collins San Jose case study, 288
   standby, 144
   techniques, 144–146
   trade-off threshold requirements form, 99
   updating and verification, 101–102
   uptime/downtime equations, 61
Reliability Analysis Center (RAC), 49
Reliability and maintainability (R&M)
   concept and technology development phase, 93
   continuous-use systems, 65
   importance, 59

operational availability, 56
system development and demonstration phase, 100, 102
Reliability block diagram (RBD), 87
Reliability-centered maintenance (RCM)
default decisions, 160–161
fundamentals, 148–153, 157
management data, 312
V-22 Osprey case study, PBL, 238
Reliability improvement cost model, 315
Repair cycle, 185
Repair maintainability procedures, 167–169
Replacement rates, 182–183
Reporting
operational availability analysis, 84
performance measures, 253
Request for Proposal (RFP), 172
Requirements
defining, 196
preproject research and development phase, 74
Requirements definition and forecasting (RDF) case study
commercial reliability-based RDF methods, 48–49
disadvantage of current methods, 47–48
fundamentals, 45–46
PRISM model, 49
U.S. Air Force process, 46–47
Residual value, 314
Resource collaboration, 24
Results documentation, 320–321
Reviews, formal
process, 235
program activities, PBL, 230, 232
RFI, *see* Ready-for-issue (RFI)
RFID, *see* Radio frequency identification (RFID) tags
RFP, *see* Request for Proposal (RFP)
Risk and uncertainty analysis
life cycle costing process, 317–318
operating and support (O&S) costs, 317
operational availability analysis, 84
precision approach radar modernization project, 332
Risk pooling, 19
@Risk program, 318
RLSQF, *see* Rome Laboratory Software Quality Framework (RLSQF)
Road maps
analysis of alternatives, 325–326
SCOR implementation, 43, 45
Rockford Consulting Group, 28
Rockwell Collins San Jose (RCSJ) case study
configuration management, 290–291
engineering design activities, 290
fundamentals, 285
maintenance support, 287
metrics, 291–292
Navy depot site support, 289
Navy/Marine Corp base, 290

organization of program, 286
PBL concept, 285–286
program phases, 287
reliability, 288
service parts provisioning, 288
Roles
fundamentals, 337–338
people, 339
physical evidence, 340
place, 338–339
price, 338
process, 339
product, 338
program activities, PBL, 197–198, 205
promotion, 339
Rome Laboratory Software Quality Framework (RLSQF)
metric frameworks, 251
performance measures, 252

S

SAAT, *see* Support Alternatives Analysis Team (SAAT); Sustainment Alternatives Analysis Team (SAAT)
Safe life limits, 165
Safety, 173–175
Scheduled discard tasks, 165
Scheduled failure finding tasks, 165–166
Scheduled on-condition tasks, 162
Scheduled rework tasks, 162, 165
SCM, *see* Supply chain management (SCM)
Scope, 329
Scorecard, *see also* Balanced scorecard (BSC)
metric linking, 217
performance metrics architecture, 206–207
reporting schema, 218–225
structure, 209, 211–212
SCOR model
availability enhancement, 40–45
supply chain design, 29
supply chain implementation, 31
Scrap rates, 186
SE, *see* Service centers (SE); Support equipment (SE); System effectiveness (SE)
Second wave performance measurement, 192
Security, 38
Selection, performance measures, 250–251
Sensitivity analysis
constant *vs.* current currency, 327
life cycle costing process, 318–319
operational availability analysis, 84
precision approach radar modernization project, 332
Series-parallel functional relationships, 128–130
Service, supply chain management, 52
Service centers (SE), 8
Service parts provisioning, 288

Setup times, 258
Short intermediate maintenance activities (SIMAs), 115
Short-term wins
    gap analysis, 360
    key action steps, 354–355
Signals, *see* Kanban
SIMAs, *see* Short intermediate maintenance activities (SIMAs)
Similar complexity reliability prediction technique, 138
Similar equipment reliability prediction technique, 138
Simple parallel redundancy, 145
Single-shot systems, 64, 65–66
SKUs, *see* Stock Keeping Units (SKUs)
SM&R, *see* Source, maintenance, and recoverability (SM&R) code
Software enhancements
    collaboration software standards and packages, 39–40
    comprehensive software packages, 39
    customer relationship management, 39
    manufacturing execution systems, 40
    order management systems, 39
    strategic planning software, 39
    transportation management systems, 40
    warehouse management systems, 40
SOO, *see* Statement of objectives (SOO)
Source, maintenance, and recoverability (SM&R) code
    level of repair analysis, 67
    replacement rates, 183
Space used, 258
Sparing to availability (STA) model
    fundamentals, 66
    operational availability, 67–68
Stability, performance measures, 260
Staff meetings, 344
Stakeholders
    objectives, defining, 196–197
    target market, 342
Standardization, 38–39
Standby redundancy, 144, 147
Star Point Network, 362
STARS (Strategic to Tactical Activity Reporting System), 232, 236
Statement of objectives (SOO), 227
Steps, 27–31
Stock Keeping Units (SKUs), 19–20
Storage, 279–281
Storyboards, 346
Stovepipe organizational boundaries, 198
Strategic planning
    program activities, PBL, 198–200
    V-22 Osprey case study, PBL, 241–244
Strategic planning software, 39
Strategic to Tactical Activity Reporting System (STARS), 232, 236

Strategy
    change, key action steps, 352–353
    supply chain management, 52
Stress analysis reliability prediction technique, 138
Successful *vs.* unsuccessful initiatives, 51–52
Suggestions, number of, 258
Supply
    fundamentals, 3
    supply chain uncertainty, 12, 13
Supply center (SC)
    echelon networks, 19
    inventory drivers, 19–20
Supply chain
    design, 29
    DoD Components, 5
    fundamentals, 3
    sustainability and supportability, 268–273
Supply chain and logistics system
    availability, 3–12
    Defense Logistic Agency, 8–10
    fundamentals, 3–8
    military *vs.* commercial, 10–12
Supply chain management (SCM)
    fundamentals, 3
    information technology enhancements, 35
    IPT establishment, 27
Supply Chain Operations Reference (SCOR), *see* SCOR model
Supply lines, 11
Supply support data, 310–311
Support
    infrastructure, 171
    supply chain management, 52
Supportability, *see also* Mean downtime (MDT)
    alternatives, 183
    analysis database, 100
    continuous-use systems, 65
    decision trees, 180–181
    design, 184
    fundamentals, *xx*, 177
    level of repair analysis, 185–186
    Logistics Management Information database, 186–187
    mean downtime for documentation, 178
    mean downtime for outside assistance, 178
    mean downtime for training, 179
    mean logistics downtime determination, 179–183
    mean requisition for other reasons, 179
    mean requisition response time, 179
    mean supply response time, 179
    metrics, 177–179
    probabilities used in estimation, 180–182
    production and deployment phase, 113
    replacement rates, 182–183
    system development and demonstration phase, 100
    trade-off analyses, 185–187

trade-off threshold requirements form, 99
updating and verification, 101–102
uptime/downtime equations, 61
Supportability and sustainability
 computer resources support, 278–279
 design interface, 281–283
 facilities, 278
 flying hours, 261–262
 fundamentals, 260
 handling, 279–281
 logistics footprint, 284–285
 maintenance, 262–268
 manpower, 275–276
 packaging, 279–281
 personnel, 275–276
 readiness, 261–262
 storage, 279–281
 supply chain, 268–273
 support equipment, 273–275
 technical data, 277–278
 training, 276–277
 transportation, 279–281
Support Alternatives Analysis Team (SAAT), 204
Support equipment (SE)
 life cycle cost, 311
 sustainability and supportability, 273–275
Sustainability and supportability
 computer resources support, 278–279
 design interface, 281–283
 facilities, 278
 flying hours, 261–262
 fundamentals, 260
 handling, 279–281
 logistics footprint, 284–285
 maintenance, 262–268
 manpower, 275–276
 packaging, 279–281
 personnel, 275–276
 readiness, 261–262
 storage, 279–281
 supply chain, 268–273
 support equipment, 273–275
 technical data, 277–278
 training, 276–277
 transportation, 279–281
Sustainment Alternatives Analysis Team
 (SAAT), 246
Sustainment phase
 analysis, 119–123
 changes impact assessment, 120–121
 data and models, 119
 deviation impact assessment, 120–121
 documentation, 123
 fleet reporting, 120
 fundamentals, *xxi*, 118–119
 life cycle, 299–300
 models, 119

modifications impact assessment, 120–121
 monitoring, 120
 objectives, 119
 sustainment plan execution, 121–123
Sustainment plans
 development, 114–117
 execution, 121–123
System acquisition phase, 298–299
System development and demonstration phase, 105
 acceptance testing, 104
 analysis, 101–106
 cost-benefit trade-off analysis, 106
 data and models, 100–101
 demonstration testing, 104
 developmental testing, 100–101, 103–106
 documentation, 106–108
 evaluation, 102–103
 fundamentals, 99–100
 logistics planning, 102
 maintainability, 101–102, 104–105
 models, 100–101
 monitoring, 102–105
 objectives, 100
 operational test and evaluation, 105
 reliability, 101–104
 supportability, 100–102
System effectiveness (SE)
 preproject research and development phase, 82
 vs. analysis, 321–322
System graceful degradation, 142–143
Systems architecture, 37–38
Systems Command (SYSCOM)
 cost-benefit trade-off analysis, 96
 system development and demonstration phase,
  105, 107
Systems operational reliability, 196

T

Table of program activities, 195–196
Target market
 division steering group, 343
 executive council, 343
 fundamentals, 340–342
 management, 342–344
 program review council, 343–344
 stakeholders, 342
 tiers, 343–344
Team establishment, 197–198, *see also* Integrated
  product team (IPT)
Technical data
 life cycle cost, 310
 sustainability and supportability, 277–278
Technical evaluation (TECHEVAL), 102, 105,
  106–107
Technical performance metrics, 254
Techniques

corrective maintenance, 167
design approaches, reliability, 144–146
operational availability analysis, 83
redundancy, 144–146
Technology, *see also* Concept and technology
  development phase
opportunities identification, 95
supply chain management, 52
TEMP, *see* Test and evaluation master plan (TEMP)
TEMPO, 232
Test, analyze, and fix (TAAF) program
production and deployment phase, 115
system development and demonstration phase, 103
Testability
fundamentals, *xx*
maintainability, 169
Test and evaluation master plan (TEMP)
preproject research and development phase, 91
production and deployment phase, 114
system development and demonstration phase,
  102, 108
Test and evaluation (T&E)
maintainability and safety, 175
system development and demonstration phase, 108
Third wave performance measurement, 192
3M data, *see* Maintenance Data System (MDS/3M data)
Tiers, 343–344
Timeframes, key action steps, 349–350
Time stress measurement device (TSMD), 153
Time to maintain (TTM), 240
TMS, *see* Transportation management systems (TMS)
Tobyhanna Army Depot case study, 362–363
TOC, *see* Total ownership cost (TOC)
Tools, preproject research and development phase,
  75–76
Total ownership cost reduction (TOC-R), 109
Total ownership cost (TOC)
life cycle cost comparison, 300–301
operational availability, 59
radar modernization project case study, 331
Town hall meetings, 345–346
Toyota, 23
Trade-off analysis
analysis of alternatives, 324–326
business case analysis, 323–324
fundamentals, 155–156, 321
independent cost estimate, 322–323
level of repair analysis, 185–186
Logistics Management Information database,
  186–187
system effectiveness *vs.* analysis, 321–322
Training
life cycle cost, 311
sustainability and supportability, 276–277
Transformation area team meetings, 344–345
Transformation Web terminals, 346
Transition plans, 118

Transportation, sustainability and supportability,
  279–281
Transportation management systems (TMS), 40
Trust, 25, 27
TSMD, *see* Time stress measurement device (TSMD)
TTM, *see* Time to maintain (TTM)

U

Uncertainty, 12, *see also* Risk and uncertainty analysis
Unit cost
level of repair analysis, 185
stakeholder objectives, 197
Unstable demand, 11
Unsuccessful *vs.* successful initiatives, 51–52
Uptime equations, 60–62, 63
Urgency
gap analysis, 356–357
key action steps, 351
U.S. Air Force process, 46–47

V

Validity, 314
Value-added time, 258
Values statement, 199
VAMOSC, *see* Visibility and Management of Operating
  and Support Costs (VAMOSC)
Variation
inventory management, 12
plan-based push systems, 15
risk pooling, 19
Variety of items, 11
Vertical approach, 23
Visibility and Management of Operating and Support
  Costs (VAMOSC)
LCC data sources, 307–308
maintenance data, 309
production and deployment phase, 109
radar modernization project case study, 330
sustainment phase, 119
Vision development and communication
gap analysis, 358–359
key action steps, 352–353
strategic directions, 199
V-22 Osprey case study, PBL
baseline performance metrics, 239–240
business case analysis, 204
coding to identify candidate, 201
contractor logistics support, 239
feedback, 245
formal reviews, 245
fundamentals, 236–238
implementation, 244–245
incentives, 244
interim contractor support, 239
interim support, 238–239

key processes integration, 214
lessons learned, 245–246
maintenance support plan, 238–239
metrics scorecard, 229, 233–234
monitoring, 245
performance-based logistics, 240–241
performance metrics architecture, 206–207
phased maintenance, 238
roles, defining, 205
strategic planning, 241–244

W

Wal-Mart, 21
Warehouse management systems (WMS), 40
Warranty cost model, 315
Web sites, 346, *see also* Internet
Win-win performance-based incentives, 225

WMS, *see* Warehouse management systems (WMS)
Work breakdown structure (WBS)
    AN/FPN-63 radar, 334
    concept and technology development
        phase, 92, 93
    level of repair analysis, 66
    life cycle cost, 305
    operational availability, 59
    preproject research and development phase, 86, 87
    replacement COTS radar, 335
    scorecard, 211
Workforce capability, 260
Workload allocation, 203–204
World Wide Web applications, 37–38

X

Xerox Corporation, 23

Printed in the United States
by Baker & Taylor Publisher Services